THE MANSIONS OF VIRGINIA
1706-1776

MONTICELLO, Albemarle County. Most highly personalized of Virginia's mansions, designed and built by Thomas Jefferson for himself. *Author, HABS.*

THE MANSIONS
OF
VIRGINIA

1706-1776

THOMAS TILESTON WATERMAN

CHAPEL HILL

THE UNIVERSITY OF NORTH CAROLINA PRESS

To My Aunt
JANE MAUD CAMPBELL
Of Lynchburg
and To the Memory of My Uncle
WILLIAM CAMPBELL
Of Charles Town
Who in Our Time Have Enriched
Virginia's Life With British Learning
as Did Other Virginians of British Birth
in the Colonial Period

CONTENTS

NOTE ON SCALE OF PLANS

A graphic scale, divided into one-foot and five-foot units, accompanies each plan at the lower left-hand corner. These scales are generally of a total of fifteen feet, except in cases of some larger buildings, in which it will be seen that scales are of a total of twenty-five feet.

THE MANSIONS OF VIRGINIA
1706-1776

LUDLOW, Shropshire. English architectural pageant, Gothic to Georgian. *Author*.

1. THE ENGLISH ANTECEDENTS
OF VIRGINIA ARCHITECTURE

I N ENGLAND the transition in architecture from Gothic to Renaissance was so long and gradual that it is difficult to fix a date for the actual beginning of the English Renaissance style. The first monument of the new style was the superb tomb of Henry VII, designed and executed by Torrigiano in 1512-18.[1] This monument stands in Westminster Abbey in the great Eastern Chapel, famous for its intricate fan vaulting. From this time on for thirty years Torrigiano and other Italian craftsmen, imported for the purpose, modeled such features as roundels, friezes, and orders for façades, tombs, or overmantels. These were grafted to native English structural forms, producing thereby the style that has come to be known as Tudor, one of the most romantic and beautiful of English architecture. After the break with Rome, these craftsmen returned to Italy, but natives and Flemings carried on the ideas they had implanted.

These new men were assisted by the first of English architectural publications, John Shute's treatise on the Classic Orders (1563). This, as well as translations of Italian and Dutch works, profoundly influenced contemporary architecture, which was increasingly discarding the garments of the Gothic period and taking on those of the Renaissance.

At this time John Thorpe (fl.1570-1610) and Robert Smithson (c.1567-1614) flourished as the first professional English architects. Many drawings by the two men and their sons are preserved in the Soane Museum in London. This remarkable group of documents shows the successive steps that were taken to bring the traditional mansion plan and elevation to meet the requirements of the new style.

In the older order of domestic planning [2] the primary element was the lofty great hall in which most of the activities of the household took place. This was entered at one side, near the end, through a screened passage, beyond which was the kitchen and buttery. At the opposite end of the building was a solar or family bedroom, sometimes over a withdrawing room, and reached by a gallery stair. When additional accommodations were needed, they were provided in wings enclosing courts or quadrangles.

Thorpe and Smithson attempted a twofold revision; first, to transform the old quadrangle plan into an open court of E or H shape, and at the same time to increase the depth of the house from one to two or more rooms; and second, to obtain symmetry about the center of the structure. Since all three of these moves were departures from the elemental ideas of traditional English architecture, they were of the greatest significance. The great hall of Medieval times became the ceremonial entrance hall; at one side was placed the dining room, pantries, and kitchen, and, on the other, withdrawing rooms and other living rooms. The great hall of the old days was retained, but was varied by centering the entrance into the hall instead of leaving it at the end behind the screens. The hall was no longer the scene of all household life, but was for the reception of guests, with separate rooms for dining, family uses, and sleeping. These rooms now began to be reached through halls and galleries instead of through each other, because of growing demands for privacy.[3]

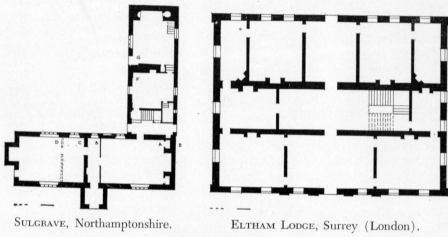

SULGRAVE, Northamptonshire.   ELTHAM LODGE, Surrey (London).

ENGLISH PLANS

On the exterior the tendency was to eliminate picturesqueness and informality. Windows were placed in long ranges of uniform openings; floor lines were kept level and emphasized by belt courses, and the roof lines by continuous cornices and parapets, though curvilinear and angle gables were often used as well. Turrets and towers, legacies of the preceding period, were used, but symmetrically placed either to give interest to the façade or to terminate it. Some of these turrets and towers contained the stair, as in Gothic times, but more often the stair was placed in the entrance hall, and the towers were merely decorative. The old enclosed entrance porch was seized upon as a feature for elaborate treatment, the doorway often being flanked by coupled columns or pedestals supporting rich entablatures, above which armorial bearings were carved in decorative panels framed by classic orders. Stone and brick were used separately or together, the combination of the two producing

SULGRAVE, Great Brington, Northamptonshire, England. The ancestral home of the Washington family, built by Lawrence Washington about 1540, enlarged about 1560, reduced in size 1700-1780. Restored, 1928-32. This is a typical minor manor house of the Tudor period.

PENSHURST PLACE, Kent, England, 1341. High perfection of English Mediaeval housebuilding.

BLICKLING HALL, Norfolk, England, 1619. One of the great Jacobean mansions of England.

clean-cut compositions such as Blickling Hall in Norfolk. The simpler designs of the great houses possessed a curious quality of militant repose, induced by the quiet rhythm of the fenestration, often marked by bays and oriels, and the daring vertical accents of the towers and turrets, from the parapets of which rose tall, pennoned weathervanes. In its overdecorated phases, where Teutonic influence prevailed, as at Wollaton Hall, by Smithson (1580 *et seq.*), the architecture lost its lithe freshness and became heavy and meaningless.

Into this picture of change and strivings for a new style came one of the great geniuses of English architecture, Inigo Jones (1573-1651). Although his parentage was obscure, he obtained recognition for his work as a delineator and went to Italy about 1603 to study the ancient buildings. On his return to England he became a designer of settings for the masks and pageants given at the Court, which work he continued in conjunction with Ben Jonson until the last of Charles I's masks in 1640. He was employed merely on minor architectural commissions before his second visit to Italy in 1613, but in 1617 he was appointed Surveyor of the Royal Works.

Jones had the ability to see that Italian architecture would have to be modified in plan and elevation to suit the English climate, but in his brief practice he did not contrive the full reconciliation of the two that Roger Pratt and the minor Palladian architects later did. In elevation, he enlarged the windows to admit the northern sun, and reduced the vast ceiling heights to a dimension suitable to the colder winters. In modifying the Italian design, however, he did not lose the essential Italianate character of the architecture. An instance of its retention is the exquisite Queen's House, the nucleus and central feature of Greenwich Palace. The design is perhaps a trifle loosely knit, but it has great charm and distinction, and its colonnaded second-story loggias forcibly recall Palladio's villas. Started in 1617 for Henrietta-Maria, the Queen's House was for many years under construction and was only completed in 1635. In the meantime, the burning of Whitehall Palace in London had presented Jones with a great opportunity for a building on the vast scale of the Italian architects. The Banqueting Hall, first unit of an enormous palace that was never completed, was constructed in 1619-22. The façade is one of the great works of English architecture and relies for its effect on the faultless proportions and skillful design of two superimposed orders which frame the window openings. By irony of fate, it was from the central upper window that Jones's beloved master, Charles I, stepped to the scaffold to his execution. This beautiful building is the first major work of the full Renaissance in England.

The inherent conservatism of the Englishman is well illustrated by the work of Jones's contemporaries, who housed the nobles in traditional palaces like Blickling (1619 *et seq.*) and Aston Hall, Birmingham (1618-35), budding examples of the Renaissance of which Jones's work was the full flower. One of Jones's contemporaries was Roger Pratt, who (perhaps under Jones's guidance) built Coleshill, Berkshire, for his uncle between 1650 and 1664.[4] This house has many of the attributes of the later Virginia house, though stone, the material of which it was built, gives it an appearance unfamiliar to the Virginia eye. Here was first wedded the Italian style with the northern climate. In Anglicising the design, all irrelevant ornament was eliminated from the exterior. Adequate windows were ranged in two equal tiers of openings, within which simple mullioned and transomed leaded sash (now altered) were arranged. The hipped roof, steeply pitched to shed snow and rain, was without the parapets so dear to the heart of the Italian. The roof was pierced with dormers bearing architrave trim and pediment roofs, the first of the type from which the Virginia dormer sprang. Tall, rectangular chimney shafts were paneled, with cornice caps, and the roof deck was surrounded by a balustrade and reached through a cupola. Coleshill is a strange, out-of-place example in the chronology of English architecture. It should succeed Wren's work, though it actually precedes it. In turn, Queen's House and the Banqueting Hall should follow it. At the crucial time when Palladian architecture should have developed in England under Jones and John Webb, his heir and disciple, the Civil War broke out, and artistic endeavor practically ceased.

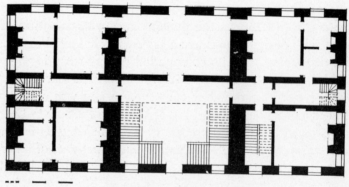

Coleshill, Berkshire, England.

After the restoration of the Stuarts in 1660, Christopher Wren (1632-1723) was appointed Assistant to the Surveyor of the Office of Works, which office controlled all government architecture. Through the influence of the Duke of Buckingham in 1669, on the death of Sir John Denham, Wren succeeded to the Surveyorship, which he retained for

Queen's House, Greenwich, 1617-35. English Palladian. Inigo Jones. *Belcher & Macartney.*

Coleshill, Berkshire, 1650. Virginia Georgian ancestor. Roger Pratt. *Belcher & Macartney.*

STOKE, near Ludlow, Shopshire, a Jacobean house in the Virginia manner. *Capt. Evans.*

THE MOOT, Downton, Wiltshire. Small mansion in style of Wren, parallel to Virginia work.

forty-eight years. Wren was the second of the great English Renaissance architects, and the one whose personality has colored English architecture, to some extent, ever since. What Wren's qualifications for the Surveyorship were is not certain. Though only thirty, he was already a distinguished mathematician and scientist. He early displayed an aptitude for architecture, probably fostered by his father, who is known to have prepared, while Dean of Windsor, a design for a house for the Queen.[5]

ASHBURNHAM HOUSE, London. The Stair. *Blomfield*.

Wren's two known buildings of the period between his appointment to the Assistantship in 1663 and the Great Fire of London in 1666 are Pembroke Chapel and the Sheldonian Theatre at Oxford. In both of these Palladian influence was paramount, and since both were built anew on ample lots, Wren's inventiveness in planning was not called into play. Like St. James, Piccadilly, which also is built on ample site, they are less characteristic than others of the great architect's work. A building hitherto attributed to Inigo Jones or John Webb, on little evidence, and very possibly by Wren, is Ashburnham House, in Westminster. Here the designer was restricted for space by existing walls (as Wren was in the city church sites), but in spite of these limitations produced a design of dignity, freshness, and practicability.

With the fire came the unprecedented opportunity that was to make Wren the most celebrated of all English architects. Before it was quenched, he had prepared a new plan for the rebuilding of London on formal and ample lines. This plan was finally rejected, to the lasting misfortune of London, on account of the readjustments necessary to real-estate holdings. However, the new designs for both St. Paul's Cathedral and the churches burned by the fire were awaiting Wren's hand, and from this time almost until his retirement from the Surveyorship he was constantly busy on a vast number of architectural projects, including such tremendous buildings as Hampton Court Palace, Chelsea Hospital, and Greenwich Palace. Of all the buildings he designed, only one dwelling can be ascribed to him with certainty, and that is Marlborough House (1709), now the Dower House of the Queens of England, and Wren's last important building.

In Marlborough House, Chelsea Hospital, and Hampton Court Palace Wren's style is seen at its best, and they exemplify his freedom from the domination of precedent, his skill and imagination in the design of form and ornament, and his amazing ability to arrange materials in harmonious combination. They illustrate, too, his flair for baroque and his superb mastery in subduing it to his uses.

Wren's greatness was based on his ability to work without selfconsciousness in the new style with an ease and familiarity that made it his own, and England's. His monumental works are almost uniformly successful, and on them his fame is based. It is, however, the minor architecture that he influenced, rather than designed, which is his glory and that of his period. Architects and craftsmen followed in the trail of Wren and his master craftsmen Grinling Gibbons,[6] carver and wood worker, and Tijou,[7] iron worker. Under this brilliant leadership they produced the Queen Anne style that in its Colonial phase became the Virginia style, which for felicity and livability has never been surpassed. In planning, the trend initiated by Thorpe and Smithson and established by Jones and Wren continued, the resulting structures marked with increasing compactness, formality, and privacy. Except in the great suites of state apartments in the palaces of the sovereign and the nobility, no room was usually entered from another. Even at Eltham Lodge built by Hugh May, 1668, where small rooms occur at the ends of the house beyond the major rooms, little subsidiary stairs were contrived to lead to them rather than entering them solely from the latter rooms. In general, on the ground floor the formal rooms flanked the central hall, but the kitchen, pantries, and offices were more often placed in wings which flanked the house and enclosed the forecourt. This was a scheme borrowed from Italy, where architects had found that the architectural pretensions of even a small villa could be immeasurably increased by flanking the villa with pavilions. This arrangement was utilized widely in the English Colonies, particularly in Virginia, South Carolina, and Maryland. In England, and frequently in the Colonies, the dependencies were connected to the house by arcades, colonnades, or passages. The milder climate of Virginia, and the problem of colored servants, however, worked for the omission of the passages and the use of free-standing dependencies. The first example of the villa-style dwelling in England was Stoke-Bruerne, in Northamptonshire, by Inigo Jones. In the Colonies the first example was probably the Governor's Palace in Williamsburg (perhaps by Wren) between 1705-20.

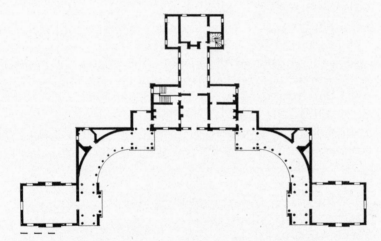

Stoke-Bruerne, Northamptonshire. *Inigo Jones.*

With the decline of Wren's star in the early years of the eighteenth century, champions of Jones, now long dead, hailed him as the leader of the new architecture, and called for the abandonment of the principles of Wren and the return to the pure Italian style of Palladio. Lord Burlington, the amateur, led the new movement with men like William Kent, Colin Campbell, and James Leoni in his entourage. Slavish copying of Italian buildings was looked upon by them as laudable, and huge and impossible structures in this style rose under their hands. The extravagant and impractical buildings of the Burlingtonians brought current architecture into ridicule at the pen of Pope:

> "............. 'Tis very fine,
> But where d'ye sleep, or where d'ye dine?
> I see by all you have been telling,
> That 'tis a house, but not a dwelling."

And:

> "Shall call the wind thro' long arcades to roar,
> Proud to catch cold at a Venetian Door;
> Conscious they act a true Palladian part,
> And if they starve, they starve by rules of art." [8]

Lord Hervey wrote of the English Palladian houses that they were "Possessed of one great hall of state, Without a room to sleep or eat." [9]

The vast number of great houses that fulfill these indictments is indeed staggering, some of the most extravagant and unlivable being Blenheim Palace (1706), built for the victorious Duke of Marlborough at the expense of the nation by Sir John Vanbrugh; Mereworth (1725), built for the Earl of Wiltshire by Colin Campbell; and Chiswick Villa, designed and built by Lord Burlington for himself. [10]

This was the type that was very properly satirized. Every feature that meant comfort was sacrificed to grandeur and symmetry. Light, air, and convenience were ignored in the pursuit of magnificence. Superb exteriors were created, but we find from occupants themselves that the external modishness often failed to compensate for the internal shortcomings. General Wade was enchanted with the façade of the house that Lord Burlington designed for him, but he found the interior impossible. It was Lord Chesterfield who advised him to take the house across the way so that he might admire the other's exterior but live in comfort. [11]

Chiswick Villa and Mereworth were built in the style of the Villa Rotunda, the design of Palladio, which was later adapted by Jefferson for his modest retreat at Poplar Forest in Bedford County, Virginia. The latter, by its small scale, attained livability; but the great marble halls of the English examples were impossible as a setting for home life, no matter how formal, or for comfortable living in the chill northern climate. The architects, such as James Gibbs (1682-1754), who accepted the Palladian precepts with reserve, or whose work was on a smaller scale, achieved no small success in creating from it an architecture that was sympathetic with the English scheme of living.

Gibbs and Sir William Chambers (1726-96), the Woods of Bath, and Carr of York were the most capable of the Georgian architects. They planned well and used classic features in domestic and public architecture with skill and discrimination. None of them were geniuses in the

NEWBY, Yorkshire. An eighteenth-century composition in English domestic architecture.

WIDCOMBE, Bath, England. Small English Palladian mansion, rich stone detail of the style.

sense that Jones and Wren were, but in their finest works they reached an extraordinarily high level.

The influence of the architect upon Provincial and Colonial builders was exerted for the first time to any great extent by means of published books of designs. Some scholars consider this one of the great achievements of the Georgian period. These publications gave rules of proportion, design of detail, and sample plans and elevations. The best of these were by Gibbs, Colin Campbell, William Adam, Batty Langley, William Pain, and Isaac Ware, though the number of such works was legion. The influence of the English books in American buildings from Portsmouth to Charleston is obvious, but the extent of such influence has never been fully appreciated.

When English Palladian was becoming dry and hackneyed, the third genius of the English Renaissance came into the scene and transformed current taste as much as Jones and Wren had. Robert Adam (1728-92, son of a distinguished Scotch Palladian architect, William Adam) as a student of architecture had measured, with his brother James, Diocletian's great Palace at Spalato. Though the exteriors of this building were monumental, Pompeian decorations had been adapted to the interior, and on this Adam based a "new" style of his own. This style has come to be known as Adamesque. On his return to England from Dalmatia Robert Adam became the vogue, and in London he and his brother embarked on a practice that reached tremendous proportions. They designed not only town houses, but great palaces for the nobility in the country and whole sections of cities such as London and Edinburgh. In their smaller work their exteriors attained grace and intimacy, but in their larger work the result was often cold and forbidding. Their interiors were characterized by intricate ornament—painted, or in relief, or both— with draperies, carpets, and furniture designed to harmonize. Their work in furniture inspired such designers as Hepplewhite and Sheraton.

The Adam brothers, or Adelphi as they were often called, used in planning such unusual forms as circles, ovals, octagons, or often projecting bays from rectangular apartments in these same shapes. The brothers were skillful designers, but their search for the novel sometimes led them into planning schemes that were unsound.

As can be seen from this brief outline, the architecture of the Renaissance in England was a series of progressions and reactions. The license of Jacobean inspired Jones's Palladian, just as Wren's Baroque later produced the Burlingtonian Palladian. From the cold austerities of this style came the intimate Adamesque, and from this latter the forbidding Classic Revival. The reaction from this latter produced the over-elaborate Victorian.

All of these periods and phases of English architecture are mirrored, to some extent, in Virginia house building. For the purpose of this book, the Adamesque is the latest real English influence, though the Classic Revival casts a shadow, first seen in the opening years of the Republic, in Jefferson and Clérisseau's great Capitol in Richmond, the forerunner of the many porticoed houses of the Piedmont.

REFERENCES

1. Sir Reginald Theodore Blomfield, *A History of Renaissance Architecture in England, 1500-1800,* I, 8-10.

2. Nathaniel Lloyd, *A History of the English House from Primitive Times to the Victorian Period,* p. 196.

3. *Ibid.,* p. 202.

4. *Ibid.,* p. 225.

5. *Dictionary of National Biography,* LXIII, 84.

6. Albert Edward Bullock, editor, *Grinling Gibbons and his Compeers.*

7. John Starkie Gardner, *English Ironwork of the XVIIth and XVIIIth Centuries,* pp. 37-58.

8. John Alfred Gotch, *The Growth of the English House from Early Feudal Times to the Close of the Eighteenth Century,* pp. 174-75.

9. Lloyd, *A History of the English House,* p. 127.

10. Henry Avray Tipping, *English Homes, Period V,* I, 39-66, 139-54.

11. Lloyd, *A History of the English House,* p. 248.

BACON'S CASTLE, Surry County. Unique survival of the seventeenth century.

2. THE SEVENTEENTH-CENTURY
VIRGINIA MANSION

THE POLITICAL troubles of the seventeenth century in England postponed the flowering of the Renaissance there for the two decades of the Commonwealth, a situation no less true in the English Colonies. The foothold which the new style had gained in the country by 1640 was very small, and traditional architecture was practically the universal building expression. In the Colonies this was even more the case, for the years before the execution of Charles I were the arduous ones of the first pioneer period. Virginia was hardly thirty years old; the settlements were sparse and clung to the shores of the lower reaches of the great tidal rivers. How the people housed themselves is not fully known, but it may be stated with certainty that simple cottages were the characteristic dwellings. As far as is known, no large house other than perhaps Greenspring, the home of Governor Berkeley, was built before the restoration in 1660. From about this time dates the one ambitious architectural essay of the seventeenth century still extant, and this, Bacon's Castle, is hardly larger than a modern farm house. However, this example is extremely significant in that it shows how completely lacking was Renaissance influence in Virginia at this time. St. Luke's Church, Isle of Wight County, is, with the exception of relatively small dwellings, the only other substantially unaltered survival of the century. This structure is essentially Gothic and has been called the last real example of the style.[1]

Greenspring, near Jamestown, was built by Berkeley after his arrival in Virginia in 1642 to take up his duties as Royal Governor. Whether the building was embarked upon immediately is not an established fact, but it certainly dates from about the middle of the seventeenth century. It was traditional in plan, having a long single file of rooms in the medieval arrangement with a wing at one end forming the shape of the letter L, with a front nearly one hundred feet long. The ell contained the kitchen only, but if other accommodations outside of the main block had been necessary, the plan would have been developed in a quadrangle, as was actually planned for the nearby College of William and Mary in Williamsburg (1695), or in a U, E, or H.

The house stood until about 1806, when it was destroyed under the architect Benjamin H. Latrobe, and a new mansion built near the site for

William Ludwell Lee. Latrobe regretted the destruction of the house, calling it the oldest inhabited dwelling in America, but he made a sketch of it and described it as having crude ornamental brickwork in the style of James the First. The sketch is said to show a building one story high beneath a high gabled roof pierced by dormer windows. In the center of the long façade was a projecting porch crowned with a curvilinear gable. The windows were shown filled with leaded casements divided by mullions. This type of glazing was universal up to the beginning of the eighteenth century in America, and pieces of the diamond-shaped panes, or quarries, were recovered at Greenspring when the site was excavated in 1929. The quarries with which the windows were glazed enter into the troubled history of the house. Records which remain show that Lady Berkeley watched the departure of the King's Commissioners in 1676 through a broken "quarrel" of glass. The Commissioners, come to investigate Sir William's conduct of office, had, by a contrivance of Lady Berkeley, been conveyed from Greenspring in a coach driven by the common hangman.

The setting of the house was upon rising land overlooking the low country towards Jamestown Island, and the drive, still remaining as a country road, described a straight line between the gate of the house and the island. Just what the original arrangement of the forecourt was is hard to say, but the excavations have shown the house to have been tied by long serpentine walls to several advance buildings.[2] From these structures an enclosing wall with pilasters completely surrounded a rectangular forecourt, except for a broad entrance gate. The forecourt treatment seems to date from the eighteenth century, in which case it would have been laid out by the Lees, to whom the place came by descent from Lady Berkeley, who married as her third husband Colonel Philip Ludwell.

Of the plan of the original house, however, there can be no doubt, for the foundation shows it clearly. It was in the L-shaped form described, with the three principal rooms across the front. In the center was the entrance hall, to the left the dining room, and to the right, beyond a stair hall, a sitting room.[3] The designation of these rooms was preserved in a drawing by Latrobe for a proposed remodeling, and showed a long section of the building looking toward the front wall.[4] Simple as it was, this plan was probably twice the length of that of any other contemporary house and one particularly distinguished as having a central entrance hall with flanking rooms. This arrangement was almost certainly unique in seventeenth-century Virginia, where the medieval plan of an entrance on the center of the building into one end of the hall, or living room of the house, persisted. Several buildings showing this feature, such as the

Wishart house in Princess Anne County, and the ruins of Malvern Hill in Henrico County, remain. Altered examples that now possess partitioned-off central halls are Bacon's Castle, the Thoroughgood house, and Criss-Cross in New Kent County. Even in England the use of an entrance door in the center of an axial hall was unusual at this period, Aston Hall near Birmingham being a rare example. Yet Greenspring, probably the greatest Virginia house of the century, was in a sense an overgrown cottage without the real attributes of a mansion. If Latrobe had spared the house to us it would have been an open sesame to the way an important personage housed himself in the first century of the Colony. Of the richness of the interior finish we can only conjecture, but it was probably paneled in oak in the style of Jacobean houses in England, though no example of such finish seems to remain in America.

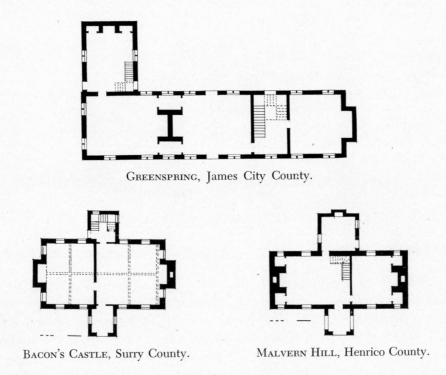

GREENSPRING, James City County.

BACON'S CASTLE, Surry County.   MALVERN HILL, Henrico County.

The usual conception of bare puritanical rooms in Virginia, examples of which still remain in New England, must be discarded in view of finds of remains of rich polychromed decorative plaster work in the foundations of an early house in Jamestown.[5] Parallel fragments from a destroyed house long forgotten were found in the bank of the Ware River on Robbin's Neck in Gloucester County. These pieces are large scale and beautifully modeled and probably once composed stucco-duro overmantels or perhaps ceilings. The Robbin's Neck fragments show leafy terminations of heraldic manteling and sculptured ornaments, including a horse's head, all with traces of polychrome work. The James-town fragments are more explicit, though still incomplete, and are not yet fully explained. They apparently once formed the arms of a Knight of the Garter, surrounded by the collar of the order, parts of the motto, *"Honi soit qui mal y pense,"* remaining. Pieces of the supporting figures are a beautifully modeled woman's head and a grotesque mask, as well as bits of mantling and heraldic charges. All of these pieces showed remains of blue, pink, and green coloring.

CRISS-CROSS (Poindexter house), Providence Forge, New Kent County.

The form of fine timbered ceilings of the period can be seen at Criss-Cross [6] and Bacon's Castle. In the former, the ceiling to the porch room has a transverse girder into which small floor joists are framed, all chamfered with low relief mouldings. At Bacon's Castle the lower part of the floor framing can be seen in a series of crossed and richly-moulded girders, [7] though the floor joists are plastered over. The girders, or summers, with their deep moulded chamfers recall the fine Tudor ceilings of England. Not only in detail is this ceiling unique in America but also in its system of double-crossed girders, forming a series of six panels in the upper room, a condition not equalled elsewhere in the country. An interesting detail is the chipped carved roundel at the intersection of the timbers on the first floor.

In size Bacon's Castle is not of mansion scale, but it was undoubtedly

BACON'S CASTLE, Surry County, c. 1650-76. Sole high-Jacobean house in America. *Brostrup*.

FAIRFIELD, Gloucester County, Virginia, 1692. The mansion was burned about 1897. *Cook*.

Malvern Hill, Henrico County. Seventeenth-century type; altered c. 1700; burned 1905. *Cook.*

Ringfield, York County. Built 1700-1710. Important early dwelling. Burned c. 1905. *Cook.*

one of the early distinguished houses of the colony, and if perhaps more elaborate than most, at least exemplifies them in size. It is two full stories high above a full basement, and it possesses a good attic story. Of brick, it has been well preserved and possesses unique curvilinear gables. Against these rise triple-stack chimneys, and in front and back are full-height porch and stair towers. Except for the loss of the original windows, and the nineteenth-century extension to the north, Bacon's Castle is a miraculous survival of a Jacobean Colonial dwelling. Across the flat fields of Surry County, beneath its great magnolias and hollies, it presents an incomparable picture of seventeenth-century America.

Other planters' houses of the seventeenth century, Sweet Hall, King William County, with its dramatic gables and chimneys, Foster's Castle,[8] New Kent County, and the diminutive Warburton house in James City County, remain. There are others as well, but none has the attributes of a mansion. Just what great houses existed before the turn of the century is hard to determine. Rosegill, the home of the Wormeleys, is said to be of seventeenth-century origin, but the present house is largely of the nineteenth century. Apparently, except for a derelict Corinthian stone capital in the yard, only a fine marble mantel of earlier finish survives. Whether this capital even belongs at Rosegill is a question. The estate was considered important enough in the seventeenth century, however, for Lord Howard of Effingham,[9] the Governor, to occupy, though it appears that it comprised a number of small structures grouped together rather than a mansion. The insurance policy of 1801 in the Virginia State Library shows the house to have been "a brick Dwelling house 87 feet long by 40 wide one story high with a Dutch Roof," of U plan with two brick wings "33 feet by 25 feet one story high." There was a brick kitchen ninety feet to the right twenty by forty feet, one story high, and a "washhouse" balancing it. A probably erroneous later description of the house enumerated a chapel, library, and twenty bed rooms.[10] Rippon Hall, near Williamsburg, on the York River, was an important early house of the Jennings family, but no trace of it remains. Its neighbor and near contemporary Ringfield is also gone, but its form is known from old pictures.

A curious transitional house, built about 1692, was destroyed by fire about 1897,[11] but photographs of it remain. This is Fairfield, the home of the Burwell family in Gloucester County, also sometimes called Carter's Creek House. Its exact original form has never been definitely established, claims being made that it was H-shaped. When it burned, it was L-shaped, but an old view from the northwest shows that it was planned or built as a T, and a corresponding wing at the other end would have completed the H. However, no evidence of this exists.[12]

England has a harbinger of the Renaissance in Cranborne Manor, which contains in a mid-seventeenth-century house many hints of things that were to come in the eighteenth century. Fairfield does the same for Virginia, and in a sense for the American Colonies, for it seems to be the first authentic hip-roofed house in the country. The hipped roof, often called in eighteenth-century publications the Italian roof, was a type devised not only to do away with the gable ends of the Medieval period but also to allow the classic cornice to carry around a building uninterruptedly. This gives repose and resemblance to classic buildings while still retaining a roof slope steep enough to shed the rains. In form the roof receded equally from the walls on all sides, like a pyramid, instead of only on two sides as in the gable form. Except where pediment roofs were used on mansions, the hipped roof was universal on mansions of academic design in eighteenth-century Virginia.

The wing of Fairfield possesses this "Italian" roof; and though this part of the structure was only one story high, it adjoined the full two-story gable-roofed house. Both buildings had chimneys in the style of Bacon's Castle, with the grouped stacks familiar to Tudor England. On the wing the triple-stack chimney rose from a plain rectangular base that pierced the hipped roof at the end wall. On the house, however, the two double-stack chimneys pierced the apex of the roof. Except for the diminutive chimneys at the quarters at Four Mile Tree in Surry County, no other examples of this latter type are known in this country. Aside from these features of past and future styles, Fairfield was a simple, unpretentious, and rather informal house. The wing, however, apparently contained a notable ball room, tantalizing references to which speak of carved paneling and a great marble mantel. One spoke particularly of the "reredos of the fireplace which was of wood wonderfully carved. Especially beautiful was a female head carved at the intersection of wooden curtains, which were drawn back with exquisite grace. All the paneling was gone but this, and this went too long before the house was burned." The writer also spoke of the great window seats in the room.[12]

Unfortunately, no representation of this extraordinary room remains, but of the mantel there are fragments at Shelly, the nineteenth-century Page home nearby. These show the facings to have been in the form of a wide architrave with double crossettes, or dog-ears, in the mitre of which were carved rosettes.[13] The general form of the mantel is therefore somewhat determined, but what extra ornament it possessed is hard to conjecture. At Timberneck Hall, the home of the Catlett family, not far away, is a derelict fragment from Fairfield of an urn, the back of which is flattened as though engaged. The bowl of the urn is carved with baroque bas-relief ornament of leafage and a grotesque monkey's head.

This may have been a central finial of the mantel, or one of a pair over the crossettes, or it may have had some other use entirely.

The question of house building in seventeenth-century Virginia is as yet unanswered by adequate research and excavation, but the economy of the period was not one to encourage mansion building; and the planters, even though they might have possessed the funds, had not the technical assistance to embark on building a pretentious house. Builders' guides, which were published so prolifically in the eighteenth century, were before 1700 confined to a small number, and these contained few appropriate designs.

REFERENCES

1. Martin Shaw Briggs, *The Homes of the Pilgrim Fathers in England and America* (1620-1685), pp. 195-96.

2. *William and Mary Quarterly and Historical Magazine*, 2nd Series, IX, 129-30.

3. *Ibid.*, XV, 117-22.

4. Thomas Tileston Waterman and John A. Barrows, *Domestic Colonial Architecture of Tidewater Virginia*, p. 13.

5. In Jamestown Museum.

6. *Virginia Magazine of History and Biography*, XLIII, 1-7.

7. Historic American Buildings Survey (Library of Congress).

8. *Ibid.*

9. *William and Mary Quarterly*, 1st Series, X, 174.

10. Katherine Prescott Wormeley, *Recollections of Rear Admiral Ralph Randolph Wormeley, R.N.*

11. A note by A. R. Reese reads: "B.B. Roane, clerk of the Court of Gloucester County says 'It appears from the records of this office that "Carters Creek" Farm was owned by the Estate of Elizabeth G. Boothe in the year 1897 at which time the estate was assessed on the land books with the buildings. In 1898 there were no buildings assessed in this estate, therefore it appears that the buildings were destroyed during the year 1897.'"

12. *Richmond Times Dispatch*, Nov. 12, 1911.

13. Waterman and Barrows, *Domestic Colonial Architecture*, pp. 31, 165.

GOVERNOR'S PALACE, Williamsburg. Virginia mansion in style of Wren. *Author.*

3. THE EARLY GEORGIAN PERIOD 1706-1750

The Style of Wren; Mansions With Related Detached Dependencies

WITH THE coming of the eighteenth century great changes in economics and style wrought a new order of architecture in Virginia, one that flourished beside the old for many years. Slavery had existed in the province since 1619, when twenty Negroes were sold from a Dutch privateer; but up to the close of the century it had not grown to any great proportion, mainly on account of the difficulty of obtaining Negroes for sale. The abrogation of the monopolies of the great companies engaged in the slave trade, the extension of the privilege to all British subjects, in 1697, and the encouragement given to the English slave trade by the Treaty of Utrecht in 1714 brought to Virginia almost numberless victims of this appalling commerce. The financial advantage of slavery was manifest, for the initial cost was soon defrayed by the slave's labor, and in addition his increase formed a source of future service and revenue. The planter who was able to afford slaves or indentured white laborers soon could stifle the competition of his farmer neighbor who, unless he resorted to the same expedient, usually gave up his holdings and moved away. The property thus vacated was absorbed into the contiguous estates, which accounts for the growth of large properties and the diminution of small holdings at this period.[1]

Few great houses, as has been seen, probably existed during the seventeenth century in Virginia. Those that did exist were probably themselves made possible by the possession of slaves or by means brought over from England to purchase them. The first of the eighteenth-century houses, which might be expected to have its origin on other grounds, the Governor's Palace in Williamsburg, itself owed, to some extent, its origin to a tax on slaves.[2] On June 10, 1700, Nicholson wrote to the Council of Trade and Plantations, "... I am in hopes that this year, please God (!) there will come in a good many negroes. So that there may be money enough in a year or two to build a house for his Majesty's Governor, as also the Capitol."[3] By the beginning of the second decade of the eighteenth century the new economic system was showing its effects, and the era of great houses in the new style had begun.

It has always been assumed that the eighteenth-century Virginia mansions were designed by their owners with the aid of design books, but this becomes increasingly unlikely, and it appears that the owners

29

heeded Price's warning: "First, let no Person, who intends to build a Structure that shall be either useful or ornamental, begin it without the Advice or Assistance of a Surveyor, or Master Workman, who understands the Theory of Building, and is capable of drawing a Draught or Model according to the Rules of Art. In a Draught (which may serve indifferently well in small Buildings) there ought to be an Ichonography of each Floor, and also the Orthography of each Face of the Building, viz, the Front, the Flanks and Rear." [4]

Unfortunately, no working drawings for any major Virginia house seem to exist before Jefferson's own drawings for Monticello, these dated about 1770. Those by John Hawks for Governor Tryon's Palace at New Bern, North Carolina, survive to show that precise drawings for mansions were actually made in the South at this period. [5] Hawks was an Englishman brought to this country for the express purpose of building the New Bern Palace.

That drawings existed for important Virginia buildings, such as the Governor's Palace and Capitol in Williamsburg, and for various churches, is patent. From the proceedings of the assembly and records of the vestries which specify exact sizes, heights, and arrangements, it can be deduced that drawings were placed before these bodies for their reference in preparing their orders. In the case of the Palace, the Governor was specifically asked by the assembly to provide a drawing for the building. [6]

In Virginia, government and parish records supply references to designers which private papers do not, even when they exist. For instance, during his building of Blandfield, William Beverley's letter books are silent concerning the designs or the architect. [7] A rare allusion to the designer as such is in the records of the vestry of Christ Church, Middlesex, which in July, 1707, provides "the rafters . . . for the body of the church to be according to architect." [8] Later records mention sums actually paid for the plans of the buildings. The vestry of Truro Parish paid John Ayres (Ariss) for plans of Paynes Church, [9] and the vestry of Fairfax Parish paid James Wren for drawings of Pohick, Christ, and Falls Churches. The plans and specifications for Cunningham's Chapel near Millwood were also by John Ariss. [10] Richard Taliaferro apparently was called in 1749 Virginia's "most skillful Architect." [10] William Buckland came to the colony as an indentured servant in 1755 to work on the construction of Gunston Hall, but he was classed as a joiner, and only after taking up his residence in Maryland does he seem to have become a recognized architect. [12]

These few references make it clear that architects did practice as such in Virginia, and although few written records remain of their activities, much can be learned from the buildings they designed. An inventory of the great eighteenth-century houses of Virginia brings certain design characteristics to light, and by this means it is possible to arrange the houses in groups and to attribute them to known or unknown architects.

The first of the Virginia houses to have real academic character was the Governor's Palace, and it initiated a period of mansion building unequalled in the history of England's Colonies. The ideal in the Virginia planter's mind was to have a house that would be as much in the current English style as possible, and almost any of the masonry buildings shown in this volume could stand as appropriately in Kingston-on-Thames as in Virginia. The Palace has many English compeers, like Eagle House in Mitcham, Surrey,[13] with which it could be transposed without inappropriateness. It is not inconceivable that these two particular buildings were by the same designer, though the architect of neither has been positively identified.

It seems certain, from the inferences of the records of its building, that the Palace was designed in London. On April 30, 1706, the House of Burgesses sent a committee to wait upon the Governor "with the proceeding of the House toward building a house for the Governor and desired His Excellency would be pleased to cause a draught of such a house as by him shall be thought most convenient to be laid before the House of Burgesses."[14] Certain requirements had to be met, as embodied in an Act of October, 1705. This provided "that the said house be built of brick, fifty four foot in length, and forty eight foot in breadth, from inside to inside, two stories high, with convenient cellars underneath, and one vault, sash windows, of sash, glass, and a covering of stone slate, and that in all other respects the said house be built and finished according to the discretion of the overseer, which shall be employed by virtue of this act to take care of the same, under the direction of the governor and councill."[15] The indefatigable Henry Cary, who had supervised the building of both the College and the Capitol, was appointed supervisor in the same year.[16]

The plans of the Palace (built, 1706 *et seq.*; destroyed, 1781; rebuilt, 1931) were probably prepared in London, but to the important fact of the authorship we have few clues. A fertile source of inspiration was, as has been observed, the published book of plans, but as far as can be determined by examination of available material, the Palace owes less to such plan books than to a definite remaining example, Ashburnham House,[17] in the precincts of Westminster Abbey in London. Unfortunately, the authorship of this building itself is doubtful. Its design has been attributed to Inigo Jones, but its construction is placed about ten years after his death in 1652. The striking resemblance between the plans of the two houses would make some relationship between them seem reasonable. This is especially true since each contains features unique to themselves. On comparing the plans one must remember that Ashburnham House contains several walls of earlier buildings around which it was built.[18] The Palace, however, was built entirely anew, so the architect was unfettered by such considerations.

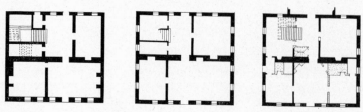

Left to right: ASHBURNHAM HOUSE; GOVERNOR'S PALACE, original plan (?), plan after c. 1770.

The two houses are almost square in plan, with two tiers of rooms in depth, a sure sign of the influence of the new ideas in planning. Both buildings are very nearly the same size, and have strikingly the same room arrangement. They are divided longitudinally in about the middle, with a central entrance hall in the front and a small room on either side. In the rear a large stair extends from the left side wall of the house to the right of the center line of the building. The stair does not ascend orthodoxly against one wall, with an open balustrade, but from the center of the hall between paneled walls enclosing small service rooms. In the right rear corner of each building is a rectangular room.

The resemblance of the rear halves of the buildings is more marked than the fronts, but this is not so if alterations to the original design are disregarded. In Ashburnham House the right-hand wall of the central hall is a modern partition, and the entrance hall was once a large room extending to the outside right-hand wall, as in a medieval great hall. The longitudinal wall was not used for the fireplace, as it was in the room above. This wall, however, was of ancient origin and was allowed to stand, and an existing fireplace in the side wall was used.

In the Governor's Palace the foundations showed no right-hand partition wall to the central hall and none would have been suspected to exist had it not been for a drawing, by Jefferson,[19] that indicated this partition in place. This drawing, which showed this wall in hatched lines, also similarly showed an angle fireplace in the hall, which excavations proved was an addition. The main chimneys were also indicated hatched, and a newel stair was drawn in the rear hall. It is the opinion of the writer that Jefferson's plan, instead of being a measured drawing, as has been thought, was a working drawing for an alteration actually carried out about 1773-76 in place of extensive rebuildings which he also planned. In support of this theory it can be shown that the angle fireplace was an addition and that no foundation existed for the right-hand wall of the hall, as there did for all other interior partitions. The chimneys perhaps were rebuilt of necessity, after sixty or more years of constant use. There are two pieces of evidence of importance in establishing the present entrance hall of the Palace as an alteration. One is in the letter of Lady Gooch saying that the hall of the Palace was as large as the first floor of her house in London,[20] a statement that could not be held true of the existing hall. Another is the extraordinary resemblance of the form of the demi-octagonal end of the present hall, with its corner fireplace and balancing closet, to Jefferson's work, including his own home at Monticello, where the salon also is treated as a demi-octagon.

The question of the source of the design of the Palace now comes to the fore. The design was obtained by the Governor, presumably from England, and presumably from the official source, His Majesty's Office of Works, of which Sir Christopher Wren was the Surveyor, or Chief. There is no assurance that all designs emanated from the Surveyor himself, but a man of Wren's capacity would certainly be identified with the work for which he was responsible. The attribution of the design of the Governor's Palace to him must, to some extent, be predicated on the story of Ashburnham House itself and of Wren's professional career.

Born in 1632 at East Knoyle, where his father was Rector, he lived in the country until he was sent to Westminster School, in London, in his tenth year. Before going to Oxford he lived for a year in the household of the great mathematician Sir George Scarborough, from whom he may have gained some interest in architecture.[21]

In spite of Wren's great celebrity and the vast numbers of written records that remain of his works, singularly little is known of his personal life or of the opening years of his professional career. Before 1665 Wren knew only the historic architecture of England, the Medieval, Tudor, and early Stuart, and the published works on architecture. Of English architecture none could have seemed worthy of emulation except the works of Inigo Jones and Sir Roger Pratt. Both of these men, under the limitations of the time of strife in which they lived, produced a pitifully small number of designs. The great monuments of Jones's career (the façade of St. Paul's, the Banqueting House at Whitehall, and the Queen's House of Greenwich Palace)—were all in London, readily available for Wren to study. The latter two still stand (if spared the present holocaust, as they were spared that of 1666, which devoured the great façade of St. Paul's). These two are extraordinary tributes to Jones's genius. Emerging in a period of transition and artistic turmoil, they are calm and finished examples of Palladian architecture, the like of which England was not to see for four-score years. Beautiful because they were simple and reasonable, revolutionary because they ignored all of English tradition, arresting because of their scholarly use of the ideas of Palladio's Italy, they could not have failed to impress Wren deeply.

Sir Roger Pratt's influence on Wren may have been extremely important, since he served with him on the commission for the restoration of St. Paul's Cathedral (1662-65) and later for the rebuilding of London after the Great Fire. Pratt, who had lived in Italy for several years prior to 1649 and had studied the monuments of the Classic and Renaissance epochs, had known and worked with Inigo Jones.[22] Surely Wren would have listened with respect to the opinions of this confrere and respected his taste.

Since there are, in this period, only two buildings of Wren's design to draw upon for study and analysis, and since both of these are radically altered on their interiors, no reliable conclusion can be reached concerning the authorship of Ashburnham House, unless other evidence of Wren's hand can be deduced. This, fortunately, is possible, and the conclusion, if reached only by circumstantial evidence, still provides perhaps a more reliable base for inquiry than any built before.

This evidence carries one into the history of the Court of James and Charles, the rise to power of Sir George Villiers, his accession to the Dukedom of Buckingham and his murder, the adoption of the heir and his brother into the Court of Charles I, the loyalty of the young Duke to the old and young kings during the Civil War and Commonwealth, and to his position of great power under Charles II. The nature of the relationship which Buckingham bore to Wren is obscure, but the fact that he was Wren's patron is made clear by a statement of Samuel Pepys in his diary. This fact seems never to have been observed by Wren's biographers, who have relied upon surmise for the reasons of Wren's progress and appointment to the Surveyorship of His Majesty's Works. On March 21, 1668-69, Pepys observes: "Met with Mr. May, who tells me the story of his being put by Sir John Denham's place, of Surveyor of the King's Works, who, it seems is lately dead, by the unkindness of the Duke of Buckingham, who hath brought in Dr. Wren." [23]

Here is proof of Buckingham's interest in Wren and his position as patron. How he came into this position is not hard to follow, if it be even by conjecture. His chaplain was John Sprat, later Bishop of Rochester and Dean of Westminster, friend and classmate of Wren at Wadham College in Oxford, and with Wren a founder of the Royal Society.

The period of Wren's life at Oxford may be responsible for his whole architectural career. To this period seems certainly due his first architectural commission, the Sheldonian Theatre. Wren was a member of a family distinguished for its churchmanship—his father, Rector of East Knoyle, was later Dean of Windsor and Keeper of the Insignia of the Order of the Garter; his uncle, Matthew Wren, was Bishop of Ely, noted for his devotion to the church and crown during fourteen years of imprisonment in the Tower of London under Cromwell. At Wadham, during the Commonwealth, Wren was in a position to hear the offices of the Church of England read in the secrecy of the rooms of Thomas Willis in Canterbury Quad and to associate with some of the great minds of the Church, many of whom had found a haven in Oxford. Imprisoned here by Cromwell was the great ecclesiastic Gilbert Sheldon, spiritual counsellor to Charles I and later Archbishop of Canterbury, to whom, John Evelyn says, "there was a great resort of people." It seems impossible to doubt that Wren, with his love of the church and inheritance of piety, and with the thought of his uncle in the Tower, should not have been among these attending Sheldon. Here he probably met Sheldon, who, on his accession to the See of Canterbury, was to commission him to design a theatre for the Acts formerly held in St. Mary's, Oxford. In Oxford, too, he was closely associated with Sprat, who was to commission him to restore Rochester Cathedral, and who indubitably recommended him to Buckingham. With friends such as these in court it is no wonder that for once the Surveyorship was to go to one so well prepared to fill it, and who did so with incomparable ability. In what way Wren manifested his architectural leanings to Sprat, Sheldon, and Matthew Wren must be conjectured, but that he did so is obvious.

This complicated picture has a profound bearing on Ashburnham House; for Ashburnham, the builder, was related through the Beaumonts to the Duke of Buckingham, and his mother was lady in waiting to the Duke's mother, Lady Barbara Villiers. If Buckingham should have taken the trouble to obtain the Surveyorship for Wren in 1669, why should he not have recommended him to Ashburnham as architect for his new house? Such a recommendation from a powerful noble and kinsman would have been compelling, and the more so since Ashburnham, unwittingly the co-betrayer with his brother John of the King at Carisbrooke, probably owed his restored position at Court to Buckingham, as his brother is known to have done. Here indeed is a roundabout path that leads from Wadham to Ashburnham House, which, curiously enough, was next door to Westminster School where Wren received his early education under Dr. Busby, the headmaster of the very school that now occupies the house itself.

Colin Campbell in his *Vitruvius Britannicus* assigns Ashburnham House to Jones, but on what basis is unknown. Extensive study of the records of Westminster Abbey, in the grounds of which it stands, and the archives of the period have never produced any evidence, express or implied, as to its designer.[24] Campbell's attribution to Jones should not be taken too seriously, as various misattributions are made in this work, including the extremely important mansion Coleshill (1650-62), in Berkshire. This, the first of full Renaissance English country houses, he assigns also to Jones, though in recent years the diary of Sir Roger Pratt, the nephew of the owner, has been brought to light and proves that the latter was the architect and builder.

The history of the site of Ashburnham House further undermines the Jones theory in that it seems improbable that the house in its present form was built, or at least rebuilt, before 1662. This is the year in which William Ashburnham acquired the lease of the Tudor house, built by Sir John Fortesque, Chancellor to Queen Elizabeth, around the ruins of the Priors House of the Abbey, about 1596. Up to that time no change of tenancy that would make likely a rebuilding seems to have occurred. The Keeper of the Muniments of the Abbey, Mr. Lawrence Tanner, who knows the house as no one else may, is of the opinion that the house dates from about 1662, the initiation of the Ashburnham lease. This would indeed seem most likely, for William Ashburnham's estates had recently been restored to him after sequestration during the Commonwealth, and his loyalty to the crown was rewarded by the position of Cofferer to the Household. The house must have been completed by 1666, since on June 10 of that year Pepys records having called upon Ashburnham in old Palace Yard.[25]

Some effort has been made to make valid the Jones authorship by claiming that the house was built from his designs after his death by John Webb, his kinsman and professional heir. In this case, the plans would have been made for Fortesque, and then built for Ashburnham, an unlikely sequence of events. It is even more unlikely that Webb was the builder, unless Jones detailed the building down to the last moulding, as it is characterized by extraordinary grace and beauty in its incomparable interiors. It bears no resemblance whatsoever to the crude and faltering interiors of Webb's known buildings, including Thorpe Hall, Northamptonshire, and probably Thorney Abbey nearby. The brilliant planning of Ashburnham House is paralleled in none of Webb's designs.

The preoccupation of writers and students with the theory of Inigo Jones's authorship has evidently prevented their examining the possibility that Ashburnham House is, with Pembroke Chapel, Cambridge (1663-66), and the Sheldonian Theatre, Oxford (1663-69), one of the early works of Wren's architectural career. A study of the other two buildings makes this supposition less untenable than does a study of his mature works. Not that there is immaturity in the design of any of the three, but there is rather a traditional Italian Renaissance flavor that is absent in Wren's works after the Great Fire of London in 1666. This full-blown style of Wren's was born of different influences, notably his trip to France in 1665, and the profound effect of his association with William of Orange. French influence gave Wren's work grace and freedom; Dutch, honesty and simplicity; and both freed it from the shackles of the Italian Renaissance.

Although the Palladianism of the interiors of Ashburnham House (the exterior having been extensively altered) is unfamiliar to students of Wren's work, the quality of the planning is not. Its outstanding characteristic is typical of Wren's genius, revealing his extraordinary facility in using the difficulties of the site to produce an ingenious, beautiful, and workable building. This quality he showed countless times in the creation of superb architectural schemes for churches on impossibly restricted and irregular locations in the city of London. Ashburnham House stands on a small site, hemmed in by buildings of the school and Abbey, and employing, in its construction, walls of the medieval and Tudor building that stood in the same position. Around the walls of the old house the architect produced a new dwelling of brilliance and nobility.

In a rectangle less than fifty by sixty feet, divided longitudinally by an old wall, he produced a large entrance hall at one side of the building facing Little Dean's Court. This and the adjoining room are now subdivided and have no distinguished finish. To the north, on the side facing the Abbey Church, he reversed the order so that the large room was to the west instead of to the east, but the two communicated in the center. The eastern part of this north hall he kept clear for entrance purposes, and placed the stair to the west, enclosing it in a paneled well. In spite of its small size the stair attains an effect of grandeur and mystery by clever changes in direction, changes which give a succession of impressions as one ascends. In the lower part, the walls of the stair well are treated simply with panels, but above the second-floor line they are enriched by tall paneled bays marked off by Ionic pilasters on pedestals. Where the ceiling beams cross the well, two fine Ionic columns, with engaged responds, support the intersection. The ceiling itself, richly ornamented above a bold cove, has an oval penetration in the center, and is open to the exquisite colonnaded lantern above.

Nothing in English architecture can approach this beautiful stair for ingenuity of planning, disposition of the architectural elements, and for extraordinary perfection of detail. It is a work of genius, and for all time sets this building apart as a milestone in English architecture. Although itself the cynosure of the house, the stairway leads to a superb suite of rooms, two of which possess their original trim. These are the lobby, over the small, front, first-floor room, and the great drawing room to the east. In the lobby the walls are clothed with woodwork of great elaboration, and the plaster ceiling is decorated with a broad border of leaves and medallions. This plasterwork acts as an introduction to the magnificent ceiling of the great drawing room with its central oval panel, once surmounted by a low dome, and flanking rectangular panels, the surrounds of all the panels being of richly modelled ribs of fruit and flowers.

One may choose, therefore, in deciding the authorship of this fine house, between Inigo Jones, who must surely have been dead many years before it was built and who has apparently no connection with its builder or site, and Sir Christopher Wren. Both to builder and site Wren had certainly had considerable relation, and the house in its warmth, beauty, and brilliant planning betrays the qualities of the man whose monument in St. Paul's reads: "Si monumentum requiris, circumspice."

It may seem a far cry between the Ashburnham House of 1662 in London and the Governor's Palace of 1706 in Virginia, but the most plausible source of both is in Wren. In the former the evidence has been canvassed, and for the Palace, the design would most logically have come from the official source, the Office of Works. Wren was still Surveyor, but a sad and disillusioned man who was finding his work disparaged by the Burlingtonians and was being superceded for both governmental and private commissions by less competent men who aped the current fashions. For the first time in his long career, since there was little else for him to do except carry forward the work on St. Paul's, now nearly complete, Wren found time to give his attention to small problems.

If a request from the governor of Virginia came to the Office of Works, Wren himself was likely to have taken it under advisement. A request for the design of a Colonial official residence, equivalent to a prosperous London merchant's house, would be refreshing in its simplicity after Hampton Court, Greenwich Hospital, St. Paul's, and the hundred other important buildings he had created. The scheme of Ashburnham, tantalizing because the conditions of the site prevented its full development, may have presented itself as an interesting and unusual solution to the problem. The difference between the two plans, shorn of their alterations, make this logical development the only substantial difference. The longitudinal wall instead of being the old reused medieval wall, became

GOVERNOR'S PALACE, Williamsburg. Gate as rebuilt on old foundation. *Author*.

GOVERNOR'S PALACE, Williamsburg, 1706-1720. Burned, 1781; rebuilt, 1931-33. *Brostrup.*

GOVERNOR'S PALACE, Williamsburg. Foundation walls, uncovered in 1930 excavations. *Barrows.*

a well planned structure which placed the chimney stacks exactly where they were needed to give the design emphasis and unity. The development of the façade became a simple matter of the grouping of the elements and the adding of the accent of the cupola.

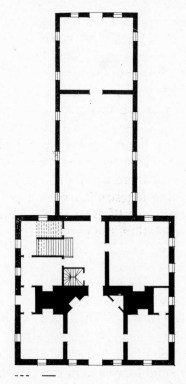

GOVERNOR'S PALACE (after 1770).

An English house that has something of both the Palace and Ashburnham House, though smaller in scale and higher in the elevations, is little Raynham Hall in Essex.[26] This house possesses the off-center hall with the mantle against the central partition-wall, and an arch to the stair hall. Here the resemblance ends, the stair being arranged in the conventional way against the side wall of a rear center hall. An interesting Colonial counterpart was in the remarkable Brick House[27] on Edisto Island, South Carolina, unfortunately destroyed by fire in 1929, except for the masonary walls, and in the extant frame house, Limerick, in Berkeley County[28] of the same state.

Turning to the Palace, one is confronted by the matter of its two phases, that from 1706 to 1781, and that of the rebuilding of 1931-33. The latter is naturally based on the former, but not more than the general elements can be shown to be exact parallels.

The superstructure was totally destroyed by fire and demolition in 1781. The foundation, excavated in 1930, the transcript of the act of building of 1705, the Bodleian Plate, and Jefferson's plan remained as major evidences for the restoration. The first gave exact information as to the size and internal arrangement of the building; the second gave the general characteristics and materials used; the third, the façade and cupola (as well as the garden); and the last, confirmation and explanation of the first together with story and window heights, as well as location of doors and stairs. There were numberless brief and vague references to the Palace, many of which gave minor clues, but the only other one of outstanding importance was the inventory of Lord Botetourt's estate, made in 1773.

This fund of information, the minor evidence, and the artifacts found at the site, combined to produce the present restoration. Of the exterior exactness of the main block there can be no doubt. The horizontal and vertical dimensions and the fenestration were established by the documents and the foundation. The artifacts gave the bond and glazed pattern of the brick wall and its jointing, the exact design of the lower window arches, the string-course, water-table, and steps. Of the rear wing, built in 1749-51, there was no evidence beyond the plan, shown in general by the foundation, and in particular by Jefferson's drawing. The elevations of the wing are purely assumptions.

Of all exterior trim of the Palace there was no evidence beyond the Bodleian Plate. This undated copper plate found in the Bodleian Library in 1930 showed an elevation of the Governor's Palace, as well as sketches of the College of William and Mary and of the Capitol. The plate showed the cupola in general form, the small size preventing inclusion of the detail. This was developed in the restoration so as to give architectural character without contradicting the engraving. The lines of the weather-vane and the roof balustrade are not based on the Bodleian Plate but on American examples of more familiar form.

This review of the evidence gives the basis of the present form of the exterior of the Palace. Of course, many of the details were obtained from contemporary practice, and are certainly characteristic. Examples of such details were the glass size and detail of the sash, the broadening of the second-floor central window (as at Rosewell), the paneling of the doors and detail of the transom, the design of the wrought-iron balcony, and the detail of the cornice, dormers, and chimney caps. Both of the side elevations and the rear were well established by the documents and artifacts. A part of the west wall fell; a large section of it was preserved, however, and thus established the detail of the masonry.

The forecourt of the Palace is one of the most appealing features of

Williamsburg. It is shielded from the street by its shoulder-high brick wall, and is pierced in the center with the tall gate piers surmounted by the Lion and the Unicorn. Behind the painted and gilded wrought-iron gates lie the stone walks and formal beds of greenery of the court-yard, which is enclosed on either side by the low, gabled dependencies. These are in dramatic contrast to the high brick façade of the mansion, with its tall sash windows, steep roof, and lofty cupola and chimneys. The composition remains as it was shown on the Bodleian Plate, and it has more English eighteenth-century quality than perhaps any other building in this country.

The entrance gate, with the piers and finials shown, was indicated roughly on the plate. The design of the gate was reconstructed from the engraving and from a wrought-iron guard bar from the lock rail found in the excavations. This design was in the form of a wavy flower stamen issuing from two unfolding leaves. In the overthrow is the royal crown also shown in the engraving. The present stone finials of the gate piers were designed after the drawing, were carved in England in Portland stone, and are models of heraldic sculpture.

The plan of the wall, shown in its entirety by the excavation, is curious. It commences from either dependency by convex curves, then after long, straight runs meets the gate piers in concave curves. The original specification of 1710 provided for a brick wall four feet high with a wood balustrade on top, somewhat like the wall at present at the Moot at Downton, Wiltshire. On the strength of the Bodleian Plate the balus-trade was omitted, but it may be questioned whether the small scale of the engraving would have allowed it to be shown.

The advance buildings, or guard house and office, are connected to the Palace by high battlemented walls, a romantic touch hard to relate to the period but as indicated by the engraver. The design of these two buildings was entirely authenticated by the records. They both have tall chimneys within the end walls, high-pitched gable roofs, and five hipped dormers above the openings in the wall below. The center of these dormers is the doorway, the exact form of which was evolved from the entrance of Four Mile Tree, in Surry County. The doors are double, with glazed transom above, and have three panels with the upper panel scrolled at the top.

The interiors of the dependencies are in the style of the period, but were done without any exact knowledge of the original form of the trim. The rooms have high paneled dados, and were all planned to have broad roll mouldings around the fireplace openings. However, antique mantels were used, those in the east building being from the Hancock Lee house, or Greenview, in Fauquier County, which was built about 1765, and are similar to one still in place in Salubria. The reredos in Little Fork Church, nearby, is evidently by the same craftsman, and exhibits the provincialisms that the others possess. All four pieces have Doric pilasters on low pedestals. Those at the Palace flank the mantel and paneled over-mantel and support a full entablature with triglyphs and carved metopes. Over the pilasters the entablature breaks out, the break occurring in the center of the metopes, so that the carved medallion is halved, part being on each plane.

In Greenview the cornice of the chimneypiece was a continuation of the cornice of the room, but in the office it is below the main cornice so that there are two parallel members.

The dependencies of the Palace possess central halls with a single room to the north and to the south. This arrangement was made clear by the foundations and by the elevations of the Bodleian Plate and photographs of the buildings during the Civil War, when they stood in ruins. Subsequently, the bricks are said to have been used to build Fort Magruder, nearby. Both buildings escaped the fire that swept the Palace in 1781, and after the abandonment of Williamsburg as the Capitol were sold to citizens for dwellings. The Saunders family occupied one of the buildings, and the repairs and alterations they made to the structures on the site are to some extent listed in the ledger of Humphrey Harwood, a builder of the town of the post-Revolutionary period.

Aside from the mantels, the buildings have a satisfying simplicity and robustness, in keeping with their eighteenth-century usage. In the basement of the east building were found the remains of what seems to have been a strong room for the governor's papers. It is very small and possesses the original undisturbed stone floor and brick sidewalls, though the brick vault and door are new. The latter was designed after an old one in the jail near the Capitol, and has a huge lock from the old Leesburg jail.

Accepting Ashburnham House as the prototype of the Governor's Palace, we find a town house built on a most restricted site, transformed by outlying buildings into a country place. We have seen that it was at Stoke-Bruerne Hall, Northamptonshire, by Jones, that the Palladian grouping of utility buildings with wings as connections to the mansion house in the center was first seen in England. Jones, with his superb common sense, refrained from attempting to combine elements that would not coalesce gracefully. Therefore, at Stoke-Bruerne [29] we find the library and chapel forming the outlying buildings of the forecourt scheme, perfectly agreeable adjuncts to the entrance court. These, however, were luxury apartments that the average household did not require, and later architects were forced to the expedient of using service buildings in this location. Where the forecourt was large enough, such a condition was no more than ordinarily unpleasant, but in cases where the forecourt was restricted, this must have been an insufferable arrangement. In summer, both odors and noise were objectionable, especially in the southern Colonies, where this disposition was probably first used at the Palace.

The Act for building the Palace definitely required "That a kitchen and stable, suitable for such an house be likewise built upon the land." The earliest representation of the Palace is on the Bodleian Plate, and in this no clue as to the use of the advance buildings is evident, but in English examples and at Tryon's Palace at New Bern, North Carolina, the forecourt sides of the flanking buildings are invariably inscrutable and betray no sign of their function. In view of the foregoing facts, and further in view of the absence of the authorization for any other building in the Act of 1710, it seems reasonable to assume that these advance buildings were actually built and used as kitchen and stable. Another point in favor of the theory that these two buildings were the service structures authorized in the Act of 1705 is the constricted forecourt that they enclose.

The growing tendency in the treatment of the forecourts in Virginia was to isolate the kitchen and stables. In general Virginia practice the latter was probably soon relegated to a location outside the formal plan, as at Mount Airy, but the former remained appendaged to the house by necessity even through the Classic Revival, as for instance at Bremo. The kitchen was balanced by buildings of various domestic uses, such as guest house, school house, etc. Thus the first authenticated enclosed court, that of the Governor's Palace, has a width between buildings of but one hundred feet. The manifest disadvantage here of the close proximity of the service buildings to the main house must have demonstrated the need for greater separation,[30] for Kingsmill, James City County, probably built in the second quarter of the eighteenth century, has the advance buildings spaced one hundred and sixty-six feet apart. These two mansions and later ones such as Blandfield, Mount Airy, Mount Vernon, Mannsfield, and Menokin, and probably many others no longer standing, had the service buildings widely spaced but enclosing the court. A superb example of such an enclosed court is at Shirley, where the dependencies are still standing and give a real sense of enclosure to the forecourt.

Undoubtedly the advance buildings of the Palace were converted to uses other than those first intended, for the foundations showed that the north fireplace of the west building had been narrowed from a great width to a normal one at some time subsequent to the original construction. In addition to this fact, the evidence of a water sluice under the rear window would tend to indicate that the kitchen was originally located in this situation, and later rebuilt elsewhere. The excavations of the east building showed a normal two-room-and-hall plan, to which the stable may have been converted.

The evidence for the reconstruction of the interior of the Governor's Palace was of a somewhat different nature from that of the exterior.[31] Concerning the former, the information regarding the finish was vague and indecisive, and only the fragments of the marble mantels, found calcined and broken in the excavation, supplied specific information. Even this evidence provided only enough data to establish decisively the designs of two of the mantels, and these were in the two front flanking rooms.

The entrance hall is paneled in walnut, a small worked fragment of which wood was found in the foundations, and the design is based on that of the entrance salon at Carter's Grove. The Ionic pilasters flanking the doorways and arch rest on a richly moulded dado and support a full entablature of architrave, pulvinated frieze, and modillioned cornice. The overmantel is simply paneled with the royal coat of arms hung against it. Below the overmantel is a white and grey-green marble mantel, the design of which is a conventional one of the period. The artifacts, however, gave little information except the color and type of marble and a few of the mouldings. The beautiful key block panel, carved with a garland of flowers and fruit, was much calcined and broken, so a new panel was carved to take its place. The stone underfire is the original one, found below, and the raised hearth is based on moulded fragments of stone found on the spot, but not conclusively those of the form rebuilt. This was a familiar type of hearth in fine English houses of the period.

One of the features of the hall is the black and white marble floor, the restoration of which was influenced by the floor of the entrance of the little Raynham Hall, referred to above.[32] The grouping of the black marble squares on the white background, instead of an all-over pattern, was an attempt to make the floor quieter and larger in scale. The fact that a marble floor existed is attested not only by the large number of broken squares of marble in the excavation, but also by the bases of two piers which supported the under-timbers of the floor and which would not have been required if the flooring had been of wood. English examples were often supported on timber, but perhaps the only surviving example in this country is that of the Miles Brewton house in Charleston, South Carolina. A number of marble floors must have existed in Virginia, but no old ones seem to survive in dwellings of the Colonial period. The use of masonry vaults under the halls of several important mansions indicate that they were arranged to support marble floors.

The hall paneling was ornamented originally with arms set in patterns, as described by Celia Fiennes at Hampton Court: [33] "Here you Enter the guard Chamber adorn'd with pikes, Halberts, Biounettes, Daggers and Pistolls and with Bandeleers or pouches for ammunition, all set in workes and figures about the Wanscote, over the Chimney Pistolls and Dagger sett like the starr in the garter." [34] On October 29, 1711, William Byrd wrote: "I went to wait on the Governor but he was not at home and I walked after him to the new house and found him there and saw several of the Governors contrivances, and particularly that for hanging the arms."

The present paneling of the two front rooms was designed to cover the walls in the simplest and most logical way, allowing the form of each room (a near cube) to provide the individuality of the interior. The only difference between the two is the use of sunk panels in the east room and raised ones in the west room. The difference in color of the two is marked, the cream color of the reception room (to the east) being established by records.[35] The marble mantels in both rooms are authentic, possession of the fragments allowing the reconstruction of the original design. The mantel in the family dining room (to the west) is a mere surround of Fleur-de-Pêche marble worked with a white marble, fluted keystone. The carved wood backband, outside the marble, and the acanthus frieze are conjectural, but they are in the style of the period.

The reception room mantel, with its carved panel and its inlaid white and pink structure, must have been one of the most elaborate in the Colonies. It was not, however, elaborate in the monumental style of that in the Banquet Room of Mount Vernon, or that, enriched with medallions of the king and queen, in the Governor's Palace at New Bern. When found, the reception room mantel was in a thousand fragments, and the design was established only by making charts of all mouldings with their mitres and returns. Thus the moulded frame of the fireplace opening, and the continuation of the same moulding as a cap for the flanking pilasters, was determined. The full profile of the cornice remained. At first the pieces of pink inlay and white bandings were not understood, for no other example is known in this country. When their use was determined and when the delicately carved central block showing flora and fauna was found broken and damaged in the basement, the full original design of the mantel was resolved.

After the reconstruction of the mantel was determined, an extraordinary parallel was observed by the writer in a photograph of an

GOVERNOR'S PALACE, Williamsburg. The supper room, in the ball room wing of 1748-51; rebuilt in 1933 on the old foundations. c. *Lincoln.*

GOVERNOR'S PALACE, Williamsburg. The great staircase. c. *Lincoln.*

GOVERNOR'S PALACE, Williamsburg. Family dining room. c. *Lincoln.*

interior of Eltham Lodge in Surrey, England.[36] This parallel repeats the elements of the Williamsburg mantel with only small deviations in detail. Later the writer compared the profiles of the latter with the English example and found that they deviated by only the width of a line. It is not unreasonable to presume the two mantels came from the same workshop in London. A further commentary on the period of the two is that the Eltham Lodge example was installed by Sir John Shaw on his redecoration of the house in 1752 on the occasion of his second marriage. This makes it clear that the Palace mantel was installed at the time of the alterations to the Palace in 1749-51 for Governor Dinwiddie who, in fact, may have brought the mantel with him when he came from London in 1751.

The reception room is a comparatively small room, being only sixteen feet square, but with its clean-cut, functional paneling and its warm color, fine mantel, and beautiful furnishings, it must be considered one of the most beautiful of the style in Virginia. Between this and the state dining room, in the inventory, is a very small room called a closet. This has the simplest possible trim and a diminutive fireplace, half round in plan, constructed, as all the Palace fireplaces and throats are, after the fine examples in the ruinous Rosewell in Gloucester County. No evidence for the woodwork of this room remained, the mantel being derived from a small one at Honington Hall in Oxfordshire, England.[37]

The largest paneled room in the Palace is the state dining room in the northeast corner of the building. Here again no record of the finish remained, and for the wall spaces the paneling was designed as logically and simply as possible, the emphasis being reserved for the marble mantel. This is framed by full-height Corinthian pilasters, which are planted on a chimney-breast of slight projection against which demi-pilasters of the same order are placed. This arrangement presents an unusually rich and important motive. It is based on a fine mantel at Dyrham Hall, Somersetshire, England, built during William and Mary's reign. The fragments of the marble mantel were very sparse, but the moulding of those available implied a design like that in the Randolph-Peachy house, on the Court House green, which was followed. Both mantels have a broad marble surround chamfered with mouldings around the fireplace. Above the surround, below a narrow moulded shelf, there is a broad panel. Both the shelf and the panel are in white marble, but the jambs of the fireplace are of gauged brick. A device of this nature is sometimes used to soften the contrast between the highly finished marble and rough fireplace brick. The east wall of the rear hall was designed with the front hall and was based on the beautiful paneling and door trim in little Raynham Hall. The feature of this wall is the richly carved frieze (or rinceau) of scrolled leaves of the overdoor. Into these leaves were worked the initials J. B. by the writer, in memory of the designer of the hall, John A. Barrows.

By fortunate chance the stairway was adapted from that of Ashburnham House before the parallel of the two plans was appreciated. As shown by Jefferson, the stair ascends in a straight flight, returning in another reverse flight after the ascent of a riser on the landing. The directness of this plan deprives the stair of the rich and complex architectural effect of that of Ashburnham House. Considering the many alterations the building underwent, it is very possible that the scheme of the latter stair was originally carried out, in full, at the Palace. A piece of evidence that the stair actually was changed is the racking in the brickwork of the cellar wall, east of the present partition containing the stair arch. If this partition were moved to the line of the racking, the whole scheme of the Ashburnham House stair could be accomplished. It is possible that Jefferson altered the stair so as to obtain space for the service stair.

The scheme of decoration of the Ashburnham House stair is employed in modified form in the Palace stair. The wall is divided horizontally at the line of the second floor by a simple cornice, below which the walls are paneled and above which they are divided into pilastered bays enclosing windows or wall panels. On the hall side there is a double arcade. The ceiling is coved and enriched with an oval panel enclosing George the First's cypher. The Italianate balustrade of Ashburnham House is modified here by the use of twisted balusters. The carved baskets of fruit, used as newel finials, are an anachronism, for these were in vogue only in houses of the Restoration period (1660-82).

The great stair terminates, as was customary both in England and Virginia, at the second floor. Westover and Shirley are among the few major stairs that ascend higher. Celia Fiennes, the diarist, remarks that the stairs in Coleshill "goe but to the first story,"[38] and again of Sir John St. Barbe's house near Rumsey, "a large back Stair that Leads to the Next Story, the Great stairs Ending here." [39] It was the inconvenience of having the servants use the main stair for cleaning the upper rooms that led to the use of secondary stairs. This was the practice at Rosewell, though examples are now rare in Virginia. Whether the minor stair at the Palace is original or an introduction of the period of the Jefferson drawing is not known. Its awkward projection indicates the latter, and the reference of 1720 to "white washing the passage and private Staires" [40] may refer to the stair to the attic, or one in another location.

The ball room, which is reached through the first-floor stair hall, must have been one of the great rooms of the Colonial period. Even the splendor-loving Governor Tryon, who received in regal style at his Palace in New Bern, North Carolina, seated with his wife on a dais in the great drawing room, could not match the magnificent setting of the functions of the Royal Governor of Virginia. The ball room, twenty-six by forty-seven feet, was richly furnished and in it hung Allan Ramsay's portraits of George III and Queen Charlotte, both attired in their royal robes. The original portraits were lost (presumably in the fire of 1781), but others, also by Ramsay, the gifted Scottish painter, hang in their places.

As to the architecture of the interiors of the ball room or supper room beyond, there is no clue; the plan only was preserved. The form of the rooms was modelled on those of the drawing room at the Miles Brewton house, in Charleston, and the salon at White Hall, Anne Arundel County, Maryland, both of which have lofty coved ceilings. The walls of the ball room are hung with blue paper, edged with a gold binder, such as William Beverley referred to when he wrote, "Ld. B. had hung a room with plain blue Paper & border'd it with a narrow stripe of gilt Leather."[41]

The supper room is purely an assumption as far as the decorative treatment is concerned. The use of the so-called Chinese Chippendale style was based on its vogue at this time in England, and its dissemination through architectural publications took it to the farthest parts of the English Colonies. The *Carolina Gazette* for April 1, 1757, notes for sale the Reid house "new-built . . . after the Chinese taste." As exemplified by the supper room, there was little actual Chinese ornament in the architectural decoration of rooms in this style. Rather richly carved trim with baroque touches was given an oriental cast by, perhaps, a single motive. In the Chinese Chippendale style the Oriental effect is achieved by the use of concave pediments above the doorways, recalling the curved roofs of pagodas. In Badminton, the vast house of the Duke of Beaufort, kinsman of Lord Botetourt, next to last and most beloved of Virginia's Colonial governors, concave pediments are used in the drawing room. The single Chinese note of the supper room is made dominant by the superb eighteenth-century wall paper, painted for an English house in China in the eighteenth century. This is in grisaille, against a soft blue ground, with birds and flowers in full color.

In form, the supper room is twenty-six feet square, with a coved ceiling eighteen feet high, similar to that in the ball room. Great walnut double doors of fine craftsmanship lead into the room in the south wall, and opposite matching doors lead to the magnificent garden. This relationship to the grounds makes especially happy the floral quality of the supper room.

GOVERNOR'S PALACE, Williamsburg. Southeast chamber, paneled in style of 1720. c. *Lincoln.*

GOVERNOR'S PALACE. Reception room mantel, designed from the original fragments. c. *Lincoln.*

The tall windows of the supper room are set in deep reveals, the jambs of which are paneled with true and elongated octagons, as in the Harwood house in Annapolis,[42] and Honington Hall.[43] The architraves of the windows, the chair rail, and cornice are all richly carved. A beautiful Waterford chandelier hanging in the center of the room is of the mid-eighteenth century, and replaces one itemized in Lord Botetourt's inventory. It was made in Ireland and later hung in one of the East India Company's houses in Canton, from whence it was brought to America about 1930. Its smoky crystals and baroque feature pieces fit it especially for this room. One was inventoried for the ball room; and another old example from the same source takes the place of the missing original, together with a reproduction, to make a pair.

The second floor contained the sleeping rooms and the sitting room of the governor's family. The latter is directly over the entrance hall and is finished in the style of William and Mary. The walls are paneled in walnut to the chair rail, above which they are hung with tooled and gilt Cordova leather. Such leather wall hangings were also inventoried in Lord Botetourt's estate, but there was no further description of them. Cordova leather was employed in fine English houses, especially in the later seventeenth century. At Honington Hall, one set of scenes, painted on leather (called Japan skreens), are said to be Chinese. In these, the skins are covered with silver leaf and partly glazed with transparent pigment, giving the effect of gold.[44] The present hangings in the Palace are enriched with conventional and floral ornament and seem to be covered with silver and gold leaf.

The doorways are framed with architraves, broken out at the head in crosettes, or dog-ears, above which are pediments resting on bellied friezes. Across the south wall are three windows, with walnut sash, the center one opening upon a balcony by means of hinged panels under the sash. This was the original arrangement which was recorded in a carpenter's bill for making them hinge out instead of in.[45] This same device was used in the reconstruction of the cupola on the roof. There are surviving early examples in the Hammond Harwood house in Annapolis and in English houses of the period. The question of the original form of the entrance hall concerns this room also. If the fireplace were built into the hall substantially later than the completion of the building, the restoration of the set-back corner fireplace, in the manner of Wren at Hampton Court and Kensington Palace, is earlier than the period of the feature itself. This now is of walnut with a carved marble surround incorporating an antique fragment, and with a wood panel over and above a mantel shelf. The flue is carried back within a concave pyramidal feature. Such overmantels, sometimes in several steps, were used for displaying porcelain ornaments.[46] The fragment of carved marble, now used in the surround, was found near the Carter-Saunders house at the southwest of the Palace. It has beautifully-carved fruit and foliage with a fish-scale textured background. It was assumed at the time that it came from the Palace, but there is no further information regarding it. A carved panel, identical in technique and ornament, has been seen by the writer in the churchyard of the Cathedral at Antigua, British West Indies, and brings up the question as to whether the Williamsburg fragment was not from Bruton churchyard, south on the Palace green.

The governor's bedroom, called "His Lordship's Chamber" in the inventory, to the west and with the east bedroom, is ensuite with the sitting room. Both of these rooms are paneled to fit the window and door openings, any enrichment centering on the mantels. In the former room the fireplace is framed with a roll moulding below a paneled overmantel. In the southeast bedroom a frontispiece mantel motive, a possible insertion of the 1751 alterations, is used. This is an accurate copy of an English example from a house in Stonegate in York.[47]

The state bedroom, in the northeast corner, was probably used for guests, and is the finest chamber in the house, corresponding to the state dining room below. No information concerning the finish of the room survived, the present scheme resolving itself from a study of the various wall areas and from the same room at Dyrham that inspired the mantel motive of the room below. The scheme is identical, with Doric pilasters taking the place of the Corinthian below, though on account of the lower ceiling they are not placed on pedestals.

The fireplace is the interesting feature of the room, the curved jambs and the facing being covered with blue Delft tile. Fragments of these tiles were found in the excavations, but there was no further evidence concerning their use. Although there is no extant tiled fireplace of the period in Virginia, there are many in England, including one in the Ranger's house in Greenwich Park. The example followed, however, was one uncovered in the demolition of the Province house (1679 *et seq.*) in Boston, Massachusetts. This usage is certainly a reflection of Dutch taste and is due to the influence of William of Orange. The room is painted off-white and is fully paneled, with an entablature at the ceiling line supported at the mantel by the pilasters.

The interest in the third floor centers in the hall, the rooms being simply trimmed, and lighted by dormer windows. The hall occupies the whole of the middle of the house, and in the center of it ascends the circular stair to the cupola. The hall, a long rectangle, is covered by an elliptical barrel vault, with a hexagonal penetration in the center. This relates to the cupola by a broad concave bell chamfer at the intersection

GOVERNOR'S PALACE, Williamsburg. Garden from the roof deck, looking northwest. *Author.*

GOVERNOR'S PALACE, Williamsburg. Ball room wing, built 1748-51; rebuilt 1931-33. *Johnston.*

of the two forms. The whole scheme of the hall was inspired by Thorpe Hall in Northamptonshire, England. This remarkable house was built during the Cromwellian period and is almost unique in a period practically devoid of mansion construction. It was probably built by John Webb, heir of Inigo Jones, and has distinguished but rather curious woodwork of the period.[48]

The part of the Palace that brings one closest to the early days is the basement, the floors of which are largely original and untouched squares of Purbeck stone. The walls, in part, are also original for several feet above the ground. In some of the great brick vaults the lower courses are original, and determined the height and center of the vault. These compartments were used for storage of vegetables and wines and were common to almost all Virginia mansions. Under the hall the inserted brickwork of the corner fireplace can be seen, and it is interesting to note how the floor near the east chimney was driven down when the chimney fell in the fire of 1781. In the basement is preserved the fragment of the west wall showing the brick bonding and the gauged window arch, string course, and the rubbed jambs.

The garden of the Palace was to the north and enclosed with brick walls. At the building of the ball room wing in 1749-51, the old walls were demolished and new ones built at a greater distance. The Bodleian Plate shows walks with lozenge-shaped beds of flowers or topiary, and two small garden buildings at the northwest and northeast corners with the adjacent walls. All of this is indicated in a very primitive way, the buildings designated only as being rectangular, with one door each, steep hipped roofs, and little cupolas or dove cotes.

The garden walls of about 1751 were found by excavation to have had square piers set at an angle in the wall and regularly spaced at intervals. The restored form of the walls and grilles is based on a group of garden walls measured by the writer in England. The moulded brick cap was reconstructed from brick found on the site after the design of the wall at Bruton Church, this design having half-round brick set on steep splays. Fragments of stone mouldings that were used for pier caps and bases were found. The only ball finial discovered was at the College, and the present ones were designed from that. The fact that ball finials were used is indicated by the ledger of Humphrey Harwood under the date of July 27, 1788, when he makes an entry referring "To Repairing Pillars to back Gate & Cutting the Stone & puting on Balls...." This was during the repairs made after the burning of the Palace and the division of the property.

The north wall of the garden with its great central gate is occupied, to a great extent, by a clairvoyée, or screen, above a low brick base, all the bays being set off with piers and finials. The clairvoyée is conjectural, but the fact that a "visto" was cut from the Palace through John Custis' woods made its existence almost certain. These features, which brought the fields, woods, and streams into the view of the walled garden, were popular in England. Celia Fiennes constantly referred to them in her journal. Of Mr. Hendley's house near Axminster she says, "the Gardens ... are ... Capable of being very handsome if made with open Grates to set one out to see the orchards and woods beyond." [49] Of the approach she says, "there is designed a visto to be Cut thro the wood to the water." This attention to a vista was a frequent Virginia device and both at Stratford and Mount Vernon it is observed, the first toward the river and the second toward the approach, where indeed it contained the drive.

In order to reduce the visibility of the screen itself, the design was made in an open and lacey pattern, almost universally of wrought iron, often painted a neutral color to further open the view. This may have been the reason for the "... Large Iron Barr-gate" at Sir Edward Blacket's house at Rippon being painted green with gold tops.[50] Other gates here and at Epsom were painted "blew wth Gilt tops." [51] The screen at the Palace is now of wood, perhaps after that existing at Westover in the nineteenth century, but the heavy wood grilles and white paint tend to block the view toward the York River.

The existence of this great clairvoyée (and of the little ones in the side walls at the cross walk gates) was predicated not only in the records of the vista through Custis' woods, but also by the finding of curious moulded slabs of stone sixteen inches across one face and about half that across the other, of different lengths, and moulded with a scotia and ovolo in the thickness of four inches. It finally occurred to the writer that instead of being originally placed with the mouldings projecting toward the top, the slabs were set with the mouldings receding, to form the base of iron screens. This theory allowed the emphasizing of features which, in the case of the side gates, were only four feet wide in the foundations. The use of stone urns on the piers of the three gates allowed the fulfilling of the inventory of Lord Botetourt's estate, which listed six stone vases and twelve lead ones. These latter, in the original restoration design, were placed on a range of twelve stone pedestals on the low retaining wall across the garden near the cross walk. Six, however, were actually constructed, these flanking each of the three flights of steps, though two extra ones were later placed near the steps to the supper room, and four on the side walks.

At the north end of the Palace garden, at the intersection of the east and west walls with the clairvoyée, are two small garden houses. These show in the Bodleian Plate view, in accordance with which they were rebuilt on the old foundations. The buildings are curious particularly because they are set diagonally, rather than square, with the garden walls and walks. This is an unusual position, but in Kip's engraving of Beaufort House in London, by Inigo Jones, two garden houses similarly placed may be seen.[52] Nothing beyond the size and general appearance of the Williamsburg buildings was known, but the exterior appearance now can be little different from the original. They are square in plan, each one story high, with a high hipped roof. At the apex this is lifted to form a little cupola, which originally was probably a dove cote. The entrance front, which has a single door in a brick opening, is set at an angle between the side walls and clairvoyée. On the three rear walls are single windows under flat arches. The designs are simple, but they form effective accents at the bounds of the great walled garden. Garden houses were usual adjuncts of English gardens, and a number of examples, remarkably like those at the Palace, survive in Shrewsbury in Shropshire. They were used for afternoon tea or tête-a-têtes, and would have been particularly useful at the Palace for private conversations.

Based on the fact that a gap occurred in the wall of one of the buildings, they were restored as privies, or necessary houses. However, it should be pointed out that the gap was probably made after the burning of the Palace and the division of the property. In 1785 Humphrey Harwood, the contractor, rendered a bill for, among other things, "4 arches at 10/ for necessary House in Garden at Palace." [53] There can be little doubt that these were the openings found in 1930.

The rebuilding of these structures brings up the question of sanitary facilities in the Virginia mansions. Before the Civil War there were few bathrooms in the modern sense, those at Camden, in Caroline County, and Mount Erin, in Petersburg, being among the earliest examples, and these date from just before 1860. A bagnio [54] was mentioned at the Palace, but nothing more is known about it. Water closets before the nineteenth century were almost unknown, though rare examples did occur here and in England. An instance is that described by Celia Fiennes at Windsor Castle in the Prince of Wales' dressing room. This was probably much like the medieval garderobe, but instead of being corbelled out over the moat was evidently over an inclosed shaft. It was described as "a seate of Easement of Marble wth sluices of water to wash all down." [55]

In the great houses both abroad and in Virginia the older and more important members of the family used commode chairs [56] in their rooms, or dressing rooms, and did not use outside privies. Such chairs were cleaned by the servants, and it is probably for this reason, more than any other, that service stairs, such as that in the Palace, were desired.

Examples of commode chairs still remain in Virginia, including a fine one at Sabine Hall which belonged to Landon Carter.[57] This is now upholstered as a regular chair, but its original purpose can be discerned by the deep carved apron. The receptacles for these chairs were relatively small and light, several examples being recovered from the English frigate *Charon*, sunk in the York River during the siege of Yorktown. These are all of grey-blue pottery.

There were, of course, privies adjacent to the mansion, but they were for the use of the younger members of the family or white members of the staff. Few examples of such buildings, contemporary with the houses such as that at Cleve, King George County, remain. This is built of brick, is octagonal in form, and has arrangements for a number of people. It was probably built for the younger white male members of the family and staff. At Westover the existing necessary house at the left of the forecourt is of a later date than the house by perhaps a hundred years. At Brandon there is such a building, also octagonal, at some distance from the main house. This is smaller in size than that at Cleve, and it is concealed in shrubbery.

Perhaps the best preserved and most architectural examples are at Poplar Forest, in Bedford County; and though these are post-Colonial in period, they are pre-Revolutionary in form and detail.[58] The main house of Poplar Forest is, of course, an octagon in plan, with the approach on one front and a vista toward the mountains on the other. Considerable grading was done, and the fill was used to make high crescent-shaped mounds on either side of the house and to the rear, behind which two small necessary houses were built. These are identical, being polygonal in plan, with high brick walls supporting domical roofs. The cornices, doors, and interior trim are all Georgian in detail, for these little buildings escaped the fire that destroyed the main house in 1845.

The present arrangement of the utility buildings to the east and west of the Palace is somewhat conjectural. They were rebuilt on old foundations, but since there were a great number of them it was impossible to determine which stood at the same time. An interesting study of this problem, made in the office of the architects of the restoration, showed the very strong possibility of a symmetrical layout to the west. This included a large, square courtyard with buildings facing it on three sides. Various documents referred to the kitchen gardens and orchard, but there was no evidence as to their location. The present kitchen garden, on the slope going down to the water garden, seems inadequate and the location doubtful, for it would be hard to work. It seems more probable that the kitchen garden was where the new geometric box and crape-myrtle garden is planted. The orchard may have been in the corresponding space to the east where the bowling green is now laid out. This is a possibility, especially since it is not known that there ever was a bowling green at the Palace. The terraces of the water garden were well defined before the restoration was embarked upon, as was the area of the lagoon, though its exact shape was not obvious. It was the building of the "falling gardens" that was mentioned when Spotswood was stigmatized for "lavishing" away the province's money on the Palace, and the elaborate grading for the terraces and the creation of the lagoon must have been extremely expensive. This seems to have been the only water garden in Virginia, though in South Carolina both Crowfield [59] and Middleton had them.[60] The former had an artificial lake with an island, and the latter a "long water", as in English formal gardens, and two half-crescent pools at the foot of the terraces. The Palace water garden was built on the side of a natural ravine through which a small stream flowed. As a whole, the gardens must have presented a stately and beautiful aspect, well worthy of the admiration they inspired in travelers of the period.

The Governor's Palace initiated the great period of Virginia building which produced a larger number of fine Georgian mansions than any of the other English Colonies. However, the Palace had no major contemporaries that are extant, nor do the records indicate the architectural importance of the larger houses that have disappeared. It is difficult, therefore, to tell whether it had any compeers, or to study mansion building up to 1720, except from fragments of less important buildings.

Possibly belonging to the early years of the century, Kingsmill, a Burwell plantation house, stood just east of Williamsburg. Little is known of the place beyond the fact that it was owned originally by the Kingsmill family and was advertised for sale by Lewis Burwell on January 31, 1781,[61] and again by Peyton Randolph somewhat later.

It was described as built of brick, with four rooms to a floor. The house itself was burned about 1900, but the foundations, as well as the two advance buildings, remain. The arrangement is exactly the same as that at the Palace, with the dependencies projecting from the plane of the front wall of the mansion, thus closing the forecourt at either side. Also like the Palace, there was no connection between the three buildings. The plan of the house is a moot question, as there were evidently no masonry partitions and the foundation provides only the overall size and the advertisement indicated no room arrangement. The forecourt is roughly one hundred and sixty-six feet wide, an improvement over the Palace, where it is only one hundred feet.

The advance buildings still stand, but they are in bad condition, and the western one has been re-roofed after a fire.[62] The exteriors are identical, being one story high below high gable roofs with inside end chimneys. The buildings are four bays long, with a door in each of the two center bays, and windows flanking them. A particularly fine feature of the buildings is the brickwork, which is laid in Flemish bond with glazed headers. For many years the walls were whitewashed, but the pigment clung only to the unglazed brick so that the green glaze of the headers was seen against the white stretchers, giving a curious effect, and showing well the color of the Virginia glazed brick. The interiors are divided into two equal rooms. The Kingsmill house site is on an eminence overlooking the James River, with terraces descending from the level of the house to the broad meadows and woods which border the river.

A house of the first quarter of the eighteenth century that stood, at least in part, until recently was Morattico, in Richmond County. It was built by Charles Grymes, probably before 1717.[63] Before the house was destroyed about 1927, through the erosion of the Rappahannock River bank, it was a story and a half high with one room and a hall on each floor. An old photograph shows the house to have had a simple exterior three bays long, with an inside chimney. This probably was a wing or dependency of a larger building.

Fortunately, when the house was destroyed the woodwork of the interior was preserved and now has been re-erected elsewhere. That of the great drawing room is the finest of its type in Virginia, if not in the country. It is in the Queen Anne style, of large scale and size, with a high paneled wainscot and paneled fireplace end. In the latter are set three fine, original, painted panels framed in bolection mouldings. These are noteworthy examples of early decorative painting. The smaller ones show exotic birds in full color, and the larger a scene with a mansion set in formal grounds, and a river and town in the background. From one of the garden gates are issuing huntsmen and hounds. This is an unusually important painting, and while the subject has not been identified, it seems probable that it is a Virginia house, perhaps Rippon Hall, Frances (Jennings) Grymes's birthplace.

Centered in the room is a very large fireplace, framed by a roll moulding. In the rebuilt room this replaces a large carved mantel reused in the present house at Morattico. This latter is unusual in having pilasters tapering toward the bottom and considerable rich but crude carving.[64] It was found that this replaced the original paneled mantel, of which small fragments remained. At either end of the long, painted overmantel panel are short, paneled pilasters of a type familiar in early South Carolina, Maryland, and New Jersey woodwork, but apparently unique in Virginia. Flanking the mantel motive is a small closet door on either side,

KINGSMILL, James City County. Site of mansion, showing dependencies. *Author, HABS.*

ROPER HOUSE, Williamsburg, c. 1725. Photo 1927; rebuilt 1939. *Metropolitan Engraving.*

Painted Overmantel Panel from MORATTICO, Richmond County. An unidentified mansion (probably Virginian) of the late Stuart period, situated on a river with a town beyond, a garden with its walls and gates, is portrayed. It is possibly Rippon Hall, York County.

MORATTICO, Richmond County. The Great Room, rebuilt elsewhere, with the original woodwork, saved from the house after its destruction by erosion of the river bank about 1928. The only important Virginia room remaining from the Queen Anne period. Walls are hung with Flock hangings. Original blue paint remains on the woodwork. *Reconstruction by author. Wallace.*

with the smaller painted panels centered above them. Decorated panels such as this were often employed in English work of the period. Celia Fiennes describes Sir Thomas Cooke's house at Epsom as having "Very good Pictures in all the roomes over Chimneys and doores, all fixed into the wanscoate." [65]

Each of the side walls of the rocm has two large windows set in paneled reveals, with window seats, and the hall wall has two doors, one close to either side wall. The doors are particularly interesting for their unusual paneling, which consists of two tiers of three vertical panels with a pair of horizontal panels above. The walls between the openings are plastered above a very high dado, which is treated with a single row of broad, tall panels. The woodwork throughout has its original grey-blue paint, but the moulded chair rail is of walnut, as are the sashes. At the ceiling line is a fully moulded cornice. The plastered walls are now hung with flock [66] hangings, one of the earliest types of English wall coverings. The fabric base is painted buff, and on it is a large floral pattern. This was made by painting it in adhesive and powdering it with plucked flock, dyed grey-green. Notes of terra-cotta orange are painted on.

From the hall, which had a lower dado of design similar to that of the drawing room, ascended the stair. This stair, re-erected in the new house at the site of the old, was thoroughly in character with the rest of the house. Of the closed string type, it has curious heavy square posts that above the handrail level are chamfered into octagonal finials. The balusters have broad shallow turnings, and the handrail unramped primitive balustrade mouldings. Parts of the stair have the original brown-red paint.

There was another Morattico, in Lancaster County across the Morattico River, that belonged to the Ball family. No sign of this house seems to remain, but the Downman-Ball letter book gives interesting facts concerning it. [67] One reference to the windows speaks of the sashes, and another to boarding up the windows to the transoms, indicating perhaps a transitional window type.

In spite of the fine interior of Morattico, it had a traditional plan based on the old one-room-deep house of English medieval origin. At the time it was destroyed it was probably only a fragment of a larger dwelling, but still of the same type. There are a number of other houses of the same style and period in the Chesapeake Bay region, but none of them possess interiors as important as that of the Morattico Room.

Perhaps the Virginia dwelling most nearly contemporary with the Governor's Palace, and possessing an academic plan, was the Chiswell house (demolished about 1941), [68] a neighbor in Williamsburg of the equally venerable but traditional Galt house. There is no record of the date of the building of the house, but the character of the interior trim suggests the first quarter of the eighteenth century. It was a simple frame story-and-a-half building, with a gable roof. Its plan, however, is significant, for it possessed a double depth of rooms, perhaps the oldest example of this arrangement in Virginia. The plan was not the central-hall type with two rooms on either side, but a curious variant seen in perhaps not more than two other houses. The chimney was in the approximate center of the building and around it were arranged four rooms, one of which was utilized as a stair hall.

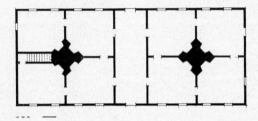 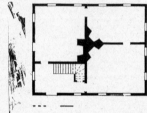

SCOTCHTOWN, Hanover County.　　　CHISWELL HOUSE, Williamsburg.

Although the house had suffered from many alterations, it still possessed important early trim, including a very unusual stair. The hall, in the northeast corner, had wall finish unique in form. It was of vertical sheathing, the boards alternately projected and recessed, the former being moulded on both edges. This parallels Tudor sheathing and may have been the earliest wood wall covering extant in Virginia. Against the central longitudinal wall the stair ascended in a long flight with winders reversing the direction toward the top. The great weight of all the members of the stair places it as exceptionally early, perhaps even earlier than that now in place in Bruton Church, which may date from shortly after 1715. Of the closed string type, the Chiswell house stair had a heavy cove moulded stringer which received broad, short, turned balusters, which in turn were received by a heavy and boldly-moulded handrail. The newel was a four and one-half inch square shaft over which the handrail mouldings carried. Particularly significant were the turnings of the balusters, which had lost any traces of Jacobean influence (seen in the only Virginia example remaining, in the Wishart house, in Princess Anne County),[69] and had shafts turned in imitation of the classic baluster. On account of their short length and great width of two and one-quarter inches (one and three-quarters is normal), they actually came nearer the classic type than any other in a Virginia staircase, though of course they did not accomplish the ideal, the medium of which was stone. Under the stair was a closet, to which a curious arched door with rich trim led.

MORATTICO, Richmond County. Detail of the fireplace wall showing the painted panels and marblized bolection mouldings. *Reconstruction by author. Wallace.*

RANDOLPH-PEACHY HOUSE, Williamsburg. Perhaps the oldest formal house in Virginia. It was originally square, covered by a double gable roof. *Author, HABS*.

The northwest room was the most important and retained more early finish than any other in the house. This finish took the form of full-height paneling of conventional design, except for the treatment of the panels, which were merely sunk. Apparently then unique in this country was the panel section. The only other example, known to the writer, of plain sunk paneling of the period (except the reverse side of doors) was in the Casey house, destroyed about 1930, which stood between the Blair house and North Henry Street, on the Duke of Gloucester Street, and had a plan similar to that of the Chiswell house. This type of paneling is the same as that referred to in William Salmon's *Palladio Londinensis,*[70] and is estimated as "Plain square Deal Wainscoting" @ two shillings and sixpence a square yard. It is not an uncommon form to see in English work. The Chiswell house room may have been the oldest paneled room then in Virginia, and the earliest with a corner fireplace. Unfortunately, the mantel was a replacement, but perhaps originally it followed the lines of that in the Casey house. This was of stone, simply moulded, with broad pilasters and a lintel, which Salmon listed as "Portland Stone Chimney-pieces, Inch and Half thick, in London, at 1s. 6d per Foot, superficial." A mantel from the Chiswell house, but the original location of which is not determined, is now in the middle room in the Carter-Bland house opposite the Raleigh Tavern. This has eight-inch piers, enriched with three wide flutes, which support a ten-inch plain lintel, broken in the middle by a fluted key. There is a narrow cyma-reversa shelf. The whole is in Purbeck marble and has an opening five feet long and thirty-nine inches high. Unfortunately, the other rooms in the Chiswell house had been retrimmed, and little other early work remained.

Another Williamsburg house possesses the same plan and is perhaps equally old. This is the Randolph-Peachy house directly behind the Court House on Nicholson Street. It is a frame building, two stories high, and was built in two units. The western section has a plan similar to that of the Chiswell house, also with a stair hall in one corner of the building. The plan of the east end, however, is of the traditional type with a hall at one end of a large room which occupies the full depth of the building. At the east end is a large inside chimney. The roofing of this building is particularly interesting, the western end now being covered by a hipped roof and the east by an asymmetric gable. However, under the hip could be seen (in 1930) two gable roofs, or perhaps hipped roofs, side by side, and between them, in a valley, a huge gutter hewn out of a solid timber. No other example of this center valley roof type seems to remain in this country, but it is often seen in England, where lack of extremely cold weather does not make it impracticable. This type is illustrated in Plate

O of *Palladio Londinensis,* and it is referred to as follows: ". . . a Roof
so formed, that if the foregoing Pitch . . . is judged to be too lofty, then
by this Method of having a gutter in the Middle, one third Part of the
Height of the Roof is taken off . . . and these are called M Roofs, from
their likeness of an M." This roof type (especially of a much lower pitch)
effectually prevented the use of the attic, as in the Chiswell house; so
the building was constructed two full stories high.

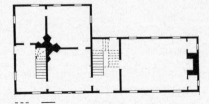

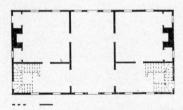

RANDOLPH-PEACHY HOUSE, Williamsburg.   RANDOLPH-TAZEWELL HOUSE,
                                          Williamsburg. Diagrammatic.

These two related buildings show the rapid advance of a designer,
working with traditional materials and background, from an entirely
informal exterior to a genuinely formal one. From the plan of the Randolph-Peachy house it can be seen that the present façade was accomplished by joining two structures, but it apparently was done almost
immediately and a symmetrical elevation was obtained. This façade
is seven bays long with a center door, three windows on either side,
and a range of seven windows in the second floor. The former are nine
over nine light sash, and the upper six over nine. The wall surface is
weather boarded, and at the eaves is a modillioned cornice. A significant
feature of the front is a wood string cornice at the second-floor line, a
feature of great rarity in frame buildings, but paralleled at Tuckahoe.
The only obvious asymmetry is in the hipped roof at the west end
and the gable at the east, but this is not readily apparent.

Unfortunately, the interior has suffered from changes, including the
removal of the old stairs and some other early woodwork. However, the
east drawing room, some of the hall, and the middle (south) room were
spared. The doors are of an extremely unusual type and are paneled
after the design of Plate XXVII in *Palladio Londinensis.* They are symmetrical about the lock rail, with a pair of long panels above and below,
and at top and bottom a pair of horizontal panels. Although actually an
eight-panel door, it is not of the usual type, also illustrated by Salmon,
in which the lower pair of horizontal panels comes immediately under
the lock rail. The widespread use of this latter door type makes it difficult
to identify the examples that may have been derived from Salmon's
design.

Plate XXVII, from the old style book *Palladio Londinensis, or the London Art of Building,* by William Salmon. This plate shows door paneling and door frames which are also exhibited in a few early examples of Virginia architecture.

MARMION, King George County. Perhaps the oldest of Virginia Georgian stairs. *Johnston.*

RANDOLPH-PEACHY HOUSE, Williamsburg. The paneled room in the east wing. *Metropolitan Eng.*

The Randolph-Peachy-type doors are found in few other Virginia houses, the entrance door of Mount Vernon (probably of the 1743 period) being an example. It is interesting to note that the beautiful eight foot, inch thick doors at Cound, in Shropshire, England, are of this same design, though it is seen more in England than in the Colonies. Another feature common to Cound (of which more is to be said later) and the Randolph-Peachy house is the roll mouldings framing the windows, though the profiles are not exactly similar. Those in the middle room in the latter house seem to be the only examples of such a use in Virginia, though others occur outside the state.

The drawing room, fully paneled in walnut (now painted), is a particularly distinguished room, and contains, undisturbed, all of its original finish. It is in a wing, with three windows in either side wall, all with paneled window seats and paneled piers between. The east wall has, centered, a fine marble mantel flanked by two doors, one on each side, to lighted closets. These doors follow those in the west end of the house, and are trimmed, as are these windows, with fully moulded architraves with an early type of backband formed of a cyma-reversa and bead. All of the paneling is simply moulded, with a bead and bevel panel section. Salmon calls this "Quarter-round, and Pannels raised square," and values it at three shillings nine pence a yard.[71]

The mantel is of white marble delicately veined in grey and consists of plain jamb pieces chamfered. It has a large marble panel in the slab above the fireplace and below a narrow moulded shelf. The profiles of the chamfers and panel mould are unusually delicate and refined. It is interesting to compare them with the vigorous profiles of the baroque overmantel slab of the Carter-Bland house in Williamsburg, said to have been altered to its present form by Councillor Carter. It can hardly be more than a coincidence, but the Bland house mantel is almost a counterpart of one in the Thomas Carter house at 9, Henrietta Street, in Dublin, Ireland.[72]

The completeness of the Randolph-Peachy room extends to the fireplace, which has jambs lined with finely-worked, gauged brick laid in Flemish bond. These gauged jambs, as has been observed, were used to form a transition between the highly finished marble of the facing and the rough brick of the back wall. Another detail of interest is the type of door hinges used. These are of a rare type seen at Westover, Mount Vernon, and Carter's Grove, and which are known to have been used at Nomini Hall. They were called mortised, dove-tailed hinges, and were used in the finest work to conceal the hardware, only the butt showing. This, like the rest of the hinge, was of brass (though some found at Mannsfield were of iron) with the butt ornamented with turned pin ends. Some of these hinges apparently were of the self-closing variety with beveled joints, which Salmon calls "rising Joints." [73] The flange of the hinge coming against the door jamb was rectangular and drilled for screws, and offset half an inch or so and applied under the finish trim. The other flange was dove-tailed in shape and undrilled. This was let into a mortise in the door and was wedged in place with wood wedges laid in glue. The almost complete concealment of the hinge is a commentary on the modern practice of painting old door hardware black instead of the door color. Salmon lists dove-tailed hinges in three, three and one-half, four, four and one-half, and five inch sizes.[74]

Chiswell's country house, Scotchtown (c.1725), Hanover County,[75] is a peculiar example of a semiformal frame house of large size. It is over eighty feet long and nearly forty deep, but is only one story high, though it has a full-height basement. The building is covered by an enormous jerkin-head roof, unbroken the full length of the house. During the nineteenth century most of the interior trim was removed and the chimneys rebuilt. Although there are four now, formerly there were only two, each set diagonally and serving four rooms on each side of the center hall. This hall retains its high paneled dado and the doors paneled like those in the Randolph-Peachy house. A closet door in one of the flanking rooms has the top panels arched. Fragments of a marble mantel-facing and a paneled overmantel remain elsewhere in the house.

The great height of the first floor above the ground recalls Stratford, the home of the Lee family. At Scotchtown there are three long flights of exterior stone steps notable for the unusual treatment of the risers, which are paneled. The panels are flat and extend the whole length of the step. They are framed by quarter-round mouldings at the sides, which at the nosing become half round. This latter detail varies from the usual nosing in that it lacks the filet and cove on which the half round normally rests. Other paneled stone steps are those at the Archibald Blair house, just west of the Randolph-Peachy house in Williamsburg (they are enclosed by the porch), and those formerly at Ampthill before its removal from Chesterfield County to Richmond.[76]

The occurrence of corner fireplaces in the Chiswell houses and in the Randolph-Peachy house may not seem as significant as it really is for the reason that such fireplaces are not uncommon in early Virginia houses. However, it should be made clear that theirs was a form rarely found in traditional English architecture, and rather an innovation of the period of William and Mary. In his diary John Evelyn remarks: "So, passing through Newmarket, we alighted to see his Majesty's house there, now new building. . . . Many of the rooms above had chimneys in

SCOTCHTOWN, Hanover County. Probably oldest of Virginia plantation houses. *Green. HABS*.

MARMION, King George County. Present mansion perhaps incorporates earlier house. *Johnston*.

MARMION, King George County. The drawing room, probably installed about 1735. The paneling was covered with painted decorations at a later period. This is the most elaborate scheme of paneling used in Virginia, all of the features of the room being framed with pilasters. The room, removed many years ago, is now installed in the Metropolitan Museum. The marble fireplace facing and the Chippendale mirror are original. *Metropolitan Museum.*

the angles and corners, a mode now introduc'd by his Majesty which I do not approve of. I predict it will spoil many noble houses and rooms if followed. It does only well in small and trifling rooms, but takes from the State of the greater." [77] Apparently, angle fireplaces were not used in seventeenth-century houses in Virginia, for plans were only one room deep. This was a condition that continued until after 1725, but from about this time until after 1750 they were often seen in the lesser mansions. Of these the most famous and important is undoubtedly Marmion, in King George County,[78] which in size is equal to houses of the first rank. Salmon refers to the building of angle fireplaces.

The almost symmetrical plan of Marmion shows an academic quality, but the dissimilar treatments of the two chimneys show that this was accomplished probably in a rebuilding rather than originating in the first design. A persistent tradition that the house built by William Fitz-hugh shortly after 1670 is incorporated in the present one would explain this fact. The appearance of the building would tend to confirm it, but nothing of the early house seems to be exposed, unless it be the south chimney. The rest of the exterior and all of the interior are in the style of the second quarter of the eighteenth century, and probably are due to John Fitzhugh, who married in 1719, or to his son, who inherited the property in 1735.

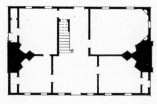

MARMION, King George County.

In plan Marmion belongs definitely to the group which includes Mount Vernon and Belvoir, not far from it in the upper reaches of the Potomac. It is the plan, later formalized at Cleve and Carter's Grove, having a broad entrance hall from which a narrower stair hall opens. On either side of the entrance hall are two nearly square rooms, and behind them are two larger, unequal, rectangular rooms flanking the stair hall. Besides this asymmetry, it can be seen that the stair hall is not exactly on axis with the entrance hall. Belvoir was of masonry unlike Marmion and Mount Vernon, which are of frame construction, and while considerably larger than its two fellows it was even less symmetrical, if the evidence of the foundation can be depended upon. The room sizes and arrangement of Mount Vernon and Marmion are nearly identical, but the former has a central hall without the broadened entrance hall. The chimneys, at present, do not show closet recesses as do those at Marmion, but they may have originally.

The woodwork of Marmion is generally simple, lacking all ornament, except in the superb parlor, which has now been removed for display elsewhere. The hall and other rooms have high paneled dados, with horizontal panels above vertical ones, in some cases separated by a moulded chair rail. Above the dado the walls are plastered, and wood cornices occur at the ceiling line. The angle chimney breasts are paneled the full height of the rooms, each overmantel having a rectangular center panel surrounded, as at Tuckahoe, by four square and four long panels. The chimney breasts are not balanced, however, for there are cupboards with paneled doors at one side.

The stair with its strong, closely-spaced balusters and heavy newel has an early quality. The newel supports a large volute which terminates the stair rail. An interesting feature of the rail is that at the first landing it does not ramp over the top of the post, as is usual in Georgian stairs, but is received against it; and the post, above, has a turned finial. Both balusters and newel are simply turned, and the step-brackets are scrolled but not carved. The stair has a broad tread and low rise, and ascends in an initial long flight and two short ones at the top.

The parlor, now removed, was one of the most distinguished and interesting rooms of the period in Virginia. It seems to be of a later date than the rest of the interior woodwork, in spite of certain features with an early quality, such as the capitals of the pilasters. In altering the room from its earlier form for the accommodation of the paneling the chimney closet was removed. This produced a room of curious shape, rectangular, with a corner fireplace and a broad recess against the south wall. The problem of the treatment of this plan was solved by placing corner cupboards at either end of the south recess and unifying the whole room by means of a full entablature at the ceiling line. This entablature is supported by Ionic pilasters flanking all features including the door, windows, mantel, and pairs of wall panels.

The center of interest is the mantel, with its marble facing and backband. This is surmounted by a baroque overmantel mirror, apparently made for the position, for there is blind paneling behind it. Above, however, the paneling is moulded, showing a square central panel with vertical side panels. Flanking this motive are a pair of the full-height pilasters, which are of particularly rich form. They stand on triple plinths with fully moulded Attic bases and have fluted and reeded shafts. The capitals have flat volutes which are enriched with archaic leafage; the two lower members are carved, also, the echinus with egg-and-dart ornament and the necking with bead and billet. The abacus moulding

MARMION, King George County. A detail of the drawing room paneling. *Metropolitan Museum.*

RANDOLPH-TAZEWELL HOUSE, Williamsburg. Pilastered side wall of the hall. *Metropolitan Eng.*

RANDOLPH-TAZEWELL HOUSE, Williamsburg. Drawing room chimneypiece and arches. *Met. Eng.*

RANDOLPH-TAZEWELL HOUSE, Williamsburg. Detail of drawing room paneling. *Metropolitan Eng.*

is carved with a water-leaf motive. Supported by the pilasters is a triple moulded architrave, a flat frieze, and a cornice with modillions and dentils.

On the north and west walls and between the windows are ranges of tall, broad panels running from a moulded chair rail to the cornice. In the long ranges of panels on the north and west walls, the central panels are grouped in pairs, with one long panel below, and this whole motive is framed by the pilasters. It is interesting to note that at least one of the sashes in this room is of walnut, and originally probably all were. This is a very unusual condition, and few sashes built of other than pine remain. The door, too, is of hardwood, but whether walnut or mahogany is open to question.

The wall treatment of the Marmion parlor is the richest scheme found in Virginia woodwork, and there are a number of fine examples of it. No other, however, has the sumptuous extra feature of marblized and painted decoration, probably an addition of about 1770-80, which this displays. This includes scenic panels as well as others decorated with urns, baroque scrolls, festoons and cornucopiae, with marblized background.

Marmion possesses a fine setting on an eminence overlooking the Potomac River, and has not only the advantage of superb old trees but of original dependencies. These are arranged at four corners of a large square bounding the lawn around the house, as at Stratford, and formerly at Nomini Hall, both not far away. The house itself is notable as one of the most important transitional mansions in Virginia. That it lacks real formality of plan has been pointed out, but certainly it is the inception of the most beautiful of the Virginia mansion plans, now to be seen only at Carter's Grove. In elevation, in the uneven arrangement of the windows, in the exposed chimney shafts, and in the use of a jerkin-head roof instead of a true hipped roof, Marmion lacks full formal quality. The weather-boarded exterior is also informal. Another house of this period with a much more highly-formalized plan is the Randolph-Tazewell house in Williamsburg (called Tazewell Hall for nearly the last hundred years). This was built for Sir John Randolph in the first half of the eighteenth century and is also weather-boarded. About 1900 it was moved from its original site at the south end of England Street to one facing the street. The architectural evidence indicates that the house was considerably altered by Senator Tazewell before the Civil War.

As it now stands, the house is tall and rather gaunt, two full stories high above a full basement. The roof is a flat hip which, in the center, breaks out in a pediment, covering a two-tiered, neoclassic porch. In plan there is a very large central hall or salon with a long, narrow room on either side at the front and two large, square rooms in the rear. At present a nineteenth-century stair ascends across the rear wall of the salon. The original arrangement seems to have been the same, except that the front rooms, which open into the salon by means of arches, were perhaps used for staircases. The salon was the same except for the absence of the stair, and the flanking rooms are apparently unchanged.

If the house had ever been any larger in extent, it would seem reasonable that it would have had further rooms at the end of the cross halls, like Elmwood, Essex County, built just before the Revolution. There seems to be no example, contemporary with the Randolph-Tazewell house, with cross halls, unless it be Pembroke, Nansemond County (early eighteenth century), which is U-shaped, with rooms on either side of the cross halls. Elsing Green, built in 1754, has a similar plan. Either of these arrangements is possible, and the house might have been one story above a high basement like Scotchtown or Stratford, or two full stories. Until the house is stripped of modern work an answer to these questions is not possible.

As far as the interior finish is concerned there are several features to relate it to *Palladio Londinensis*. These include the arch imposts, in the hall, with cyma-caps similar to those shown on Plate XIV. Doric pilasters are used at intervals around the salon to frame all of the door and window openings. They have fluted shafts with Attic bases, and between the two front pairs are the arched openings with moulded imposts and keystones and paneled piers. Strangely enough, a cornice at the ceiling line is lacking, a fact which recalls that tradition has it that this hall was once two stories high. While it seems questionable that such was true, it is entirely possible that there was once a "tray" ceiling extending into the roof space, as at Stratford, if the house were ever one story in height. This extension into the roof space would have been done away with in raising the house to two stories, and the entablature over the pilasters destroyed.

Both flanking rooms are fully paneled with chimney breasts projecting from the end walls. The recesses are arched over with moulded archivolts resting on moulded imposts, as at Wilton and Chelsea. Though the mantels themselves are nineteenth-century Classic Revival pieces in marble, the old paneled overmantels survive. The entablatures traverse the length of the breast where the architrave and cushion frieze are dropped. This cushion frieze occurs in almost all the houses showing the influence of *Palladio Londinensis*, but here is broader and less convex than most examples.

It is unfortunate that the Randolph-Tazewell house has been in obscurity for so long, for both historically and architecturally it deserves to be in the first rank of domestic architecture of the period. Its unhappy

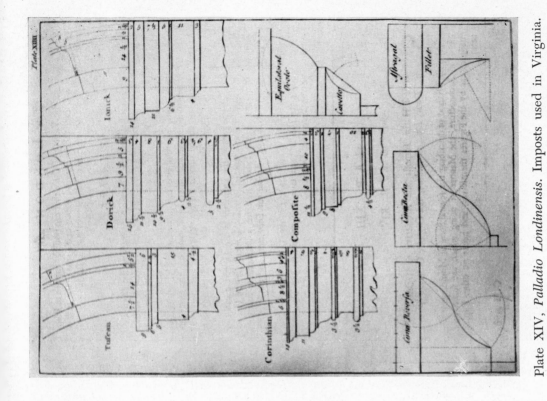

Plate XIV, *Palladio Londinensis*. Imposts used in Virginia.

RANDOLPH-TAZEWELL HOUSE. Hall arch. *Met. Engraving.*

TUCKAHOE, Goochland County. A general view, and the street of plantation buildings. Near-by is the schoolhouse where Thomas Jefferson received his early education. Tuckahoe was probably commenced shortly after 1712 and enlarged to its present form after 1730. The exterior is entirely original with its old weatherboarding and sashes. The south wing (left in the picture) is apparently earlier, and was modernized at time of extensions. *Johnston.*

site between a large hotel and a suburban development hardly permits a restoration of its one-time rural character, but in the environs of Williamsburg another site for it might be found.

These houses, although employing unusual plan arrangements, were still merely rectangular buildings, unless the form of the Randolph-Tazewell house was once more complex. As has been pointed out elsewhere, fanciful plans were much in style in England during the seventeenth century, and in provincial areas in the early eighteenth century as well. H, E, U, and T plans were frequently used, the first of which was used in the Capitol in Williamsburg (1699) and was illustrated in Stephen Primatt's *The City and Country Purchaser and Builder,* published in 1667. The virtues of such a plan were also extolled by Blome in his *The Gentleman's Recreation,* printed in London in 1709. He observes that "in building of houses long, the use of some rooms will be lost, in that more room must be allowed for Entries and Passages and it requires more doors; and if a Building consists of a geometrical square, if the house be large, the middle rooms will want light, and many therefore commend the form of the Capital Roman H, which, they say, makes it stand firm against the winds, and lets in both light and air and disposes every room nearer to one another."

Perhaps the builder's own enterprise caused the plan of Tuckahoe, in Goochland County, to take this shape. It seems that the house was actually built as a smaller rectangular structure, but that extensions, soon after the building, caused it to become H-shaped in plan. Unlike the great formal brick pile of Stratford, in Westmoreland County, also H-shaped in plan, Tuckahoe has an ingenuous charm. Of frame construction, weather-boarded, with a low gable roof, it is two full stories in height. The two end units, as well as the connecting one, are all one room in depth, and the narrow projecting gable-ends give the design a marked verticality which is accentuated by tall, slender, end chimneys. There are, however, horizontals in the high brick basement wall, in the wood belt-course at the second-floor line, and in the fine old modillioned cornice.

The two long fronts are five bays long with center doors, and the central arm has three bays. All of the gable ends are blind, and each two display different chimney treatments. Those in the north building project, but those in the south building have their outside faces flush with the wall, which is here of brick. The windows uniformly have nine over nine light sash with the original broad muntined sash.

All four doorways are original and interesting. Those of the north and south fronts have low porches with square posts covered with pediment roofs. On the south elevation the porch ceiling, as well as the

wall areas between the door and posts, is paneled with a pattern of
long and short units. It is approached by a long flight of stone steps,
splayed as at Stratford, but lacking the balustrade. The door of this
opening is unique in having two tiers of curious panels, as shown in
Plates XXIII and XXVI of *Palladio Londinensis.* The lower is in the
form of St. Andrew's Cross, and the upper a quadrant in each corner
of a square, with a lozenge center panel having indented sides. Above
are two square panels. The doors of the central unit are the usual eight-
panel type, with narrow paneled facings. They are covered by bracketed
pediment hoods with paneled soffits and have flights of stone steps.

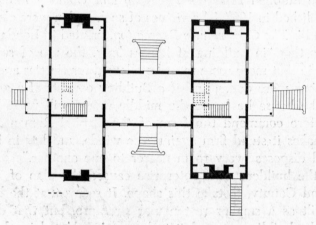

TUCKAHOE, Goochland County.

The plan of Tuckahoe follows, to an extraordinary degree, Primatt's
design, but actually it is so much a compound of the usual two-room-
and-central-hall plan that it is questionable whether Primatt's plan
really inspired it. This is especially true when it is remembered that
Thomas Randolph, the builder, brother of Sir John, frequented the
Capitol in Williamsburg and had been familiar with its form. The use
of an H-scheme with the normal Virginia floor plan would have resulted
in the Tuckahoe arrangement. This arrangement consists of two wings
with the central-hall-two-room plan, connected by a large single room,
or salon, like that at Stratford, but not oriented to present the court to
the approach. The first-floor rooms have fine wall paneling of an unusual
form, perhaps inspired by Moxon's *Mechanick Exercises,* published in
London in 1703.[79] The dado is paneled below the chair rail, and above
is a tall matching panel with a narrow horizontal panel between it and
the cornice. There are few examples of frieze panels, and the only
other Virginia example known to the writer was formerly in the Ritchie
house in Tappahannock. In the wing rooms at Tuckahoe these narrow

TUCKAHOE, Goochland County. West Court and doorway. *Johnston.*

TUCKAHOE, Goochland County. A detail of south door. *Johnston.*

TUCKAHOE, Goochland County. North stair and gallery, showing the carved fascia. *Johnston.*

TUCKAHOE, Goochland County. Entrance salon looking toward arch to north wing. *Johnston.*

Tuckahoe, Goochland County. Burnt Room with archaic pilasters and later mantel. *Johnston.*

Tuckahoe, Goochland County. White Parlor, paneled as in *Mechanick Exercises. Johnston.*

Tuckahoe, Goochland County. Carved fascia of the north stair landing. *Metropolitan Eng.*

Tuckahoe, Goochland County. North stair with carved newel, brackets, balusters. *Johnston.*

upper panels are worked into the overmantels with narrow, vertical, matching panels flanking a pair of wide center panels. At the corners are little square panels. In the drawing room the fireplace is framed by full-height Corinthian pilasters. The shafts are unfluted, with an entiasis, and have curiously carved caps and light moulded bands at pedestal height. At either side are arched paneled cupboard doors.

At either end of the salon are untrimmed arches with paneled reveals, leading into the cross halls. The stairways are fine examples of the period of the enlargement and show remarkably different degrees of elaboration, having much of the richness of the great stair at Rosewell, in Gloucester County. The north stair is, however, much smaller in scale, and the south is more in the style of that at Sabine Hall. Both stairs, due to their small scale, have only two balusters to a tread, a condition repeated only in major building in Virginia at Gunston Hall, in Fairfax County. Normally three balusters occur, and in a few cases even four, as at Woodstock, Matthews County, where, however, they are not turned. At Tuckahoe they are both turned and spiraled.

The north stair, which ascends in two flights with a broad landing between, has the newel in the form of a Corinthian colonette, carved with vines and flowers, and square fluted posts. Both forms are unusual, the newel being paralleled only by that at Rosewell, and the posts by the fluted wall posts at Westover. The beautiful brackets are almost identical with those at Carter's Grove and the Page house in Williamsburg. They are scrolled, feathered with acanthus, and carved with five-petaled blossoms. Perhaps the most spectacular features of the stair are the carved landing and gallery fascias. The former, being narrower, is simpler, but displays scrolled strap work, also feathered with acanthus interspersed with blossoms. This is a simplification of the superb Rosewell fascia, which has generally similar motives of greater elaboration. In the Tuckahoe gallery fascia a more flowing design is used, but this one lacks the strapwork frame. It has the same central motive as that at Rosewell, a basket of flowers from which issues convolutions of acanthus leaves extending the full width of the gallery. The moulded handrail carries over the posts in ramps and easings, the profile of which is followed on the opposite wall by a paneled dado.

The south stair lacks all carved trim but has the same flowing rail and newel and posts spiralled to match the balusters. These recall the Carter's Grove posts, but in this case there are no responds, the dado opposite having no enrichment. The brackets are simply cut to a profile, without other decoration, much like those at the Wythe house in Williamsburg.

Both lower and upper rooms at Tuckahoe have fine, simple paneling, and in the master's room is a marble fireplace facing with flat lintel and keystone. The two finest rooms are those already referred to, the east and west parlors of the north wing. In both of these, and in some of the other rooms, early nineteenth-century mantels replace the originals.

The remarkable survival of the house, and its out-buildings, almost unchanged in a setting of great trees and fine boxwood gardens, makes Tuckahoe pre-eminent among Virginia houses.

At Yorktown is the site of another H-shaped house, the elder Nelson house, across the main street from the present Nelson house. However, the site has not been investigated, and little or nothing is known of the house, though there seems some reason to believe that wings were added to an older house to produce the H form. Town records show that there were two structures, thirty by fifty-one feet, which were connected by a narrow passage. One of these was, perhaps, the house in which "Scotch Tom" Nelson died in 1745, and which he bequeathed to his son "President" Nelson. The addition is reputed to have been made by the latter about 1765, and the house seems to have burned in 1814.[80]

Stratford was conceived as an H-plan and took this form in a continuous building operation. The monumental qualities of the plan effectually deny any origin such as that of Tuckahoe, obviously an alteration. It is not unreasonable that in addition, perhaps, to literary sources the Stratford plan is due to the precedent of the Capitol in Williamsburg. The dimensions of the two buildings alone indicate it, but the plan of Thomas Lee's house is far more advanced in style than the Capitol in that both wings have a double depth of rooms. As will later be pointed out, there is good reason to believe that the architect of the great group of related Virginia mansions from Rosewell to Wilton, who also seems to have designed Stratford, was indebted to the building of Shropshire, in England, for much of his precedent. It is interesting, therefore, to note the remarkably large group of H-plan houses there, including Stoke Park, Langleys, Dullingham, and Condover.[81] None, however, have been examined by the writer, so any detailed parallels are unknown to him. The plan was frequently used in other parts of England, as well, Groomsbridge Place,[82] often attributed to Sir Christopher Wren, being perhaps the most beautiful example of them all.

To some extent a rebuilding of an early moated house in the late Stuart style, Groomsbridge is a brick house with hipped roof and large sash windows. It stands beyond its walled moat, with its arched bridge and high wrought-iron gates, as an ideal of architectural picturesqueness. In its appearance the house is not particularly akin to Stratford, due to the raising, in the latter house, of the first-floor line to almost ten feet above the grade. This is a Burlingtonian device, exemplified at Chiswick Villa[83] and borrowed from Italian examples such as the Villa Rotonda.

TUCKAHOE, Goochland County. Long run of south stair. *Johnston.*

TUCKAHOE, Goochland County. South door; stair newel. *Johnston.*

STRATFORD, Westmoreland County. Built about 1725 in the style of Sir John Vanbrugh. The oldest of the eighteenth-century brick mansions and the most monumental design. The house is remarkably little changed from the year of its completion, except for the steps, window sash, and interiors of the wings, which have recently been restored. Here were born Thomas Lee's sons Richard Henry and Francis Lightfoot, and their cousin Robert E. Lee. *Bagby. HABS.*

In mansions of this type the minor rooms are placed on the ground floor and major apartments on the upper, so the house in effect was one story high. Sir Henry Wotton, in his *Elements of Architecture,* had already propounded this idea.[84] He advised that the principal floor was to be raised fifteen feet "to add to the majesty of the Whole Aspect." Celia Fiennes observed a house "high built according to the Eastern building near London, also many steps up to the house from the Court." [85]

Undoubtedly the current Palladian style was the motive for designing Stratford in this form, and if it had not been that stone trim was abnormally expensive in Virginia and stucco unprecedented, the exterior, with its simple brick walling, might have been much less traditional than it is.

The great arched and clustered chimneys at Stratford are definitely not Palladian in character but are paralleled in the work of Sir John Vanbrugh in Blenheim Castle [86] and Kings-Weston Manor and in Hawksmoor's works.[87] Neither of these men were strict Palladians, but were more Classic Romanticists, and it is the influence of their baroque designs which is responsible for the general effect of Stratford.

The house was built about 1725 by Thomas Lee (1690-1750), of Mount Pleasant, nearby. During the construction of Stratford the older house was destroyed by fire set by malefactors that Lee, as magistrate, had sentenced. For this reason, the crown contributed £300 toward the new building. It has recently been restored on the exterior by the reconstruction of the steps and installation of new sashes, and on the interior by moving several partitions to their original positions and reinstating woodwork of an early style in place of nineteenth-century work in several rooms.

One courtyard elevation faces the approach and the other the vista to the river. These elevations, overall ninety feet in length, are divided into nine bays, three of which are recessed in the courts. The doorway, on either front, is centered in the court and is reached by a long flight of Portland stone steps, designed from fragments found in the grounds. The flights toward the doorway taper in without curved or scrolled steps (as also at Tuckahoe), producing a rather awkward effect. They have heavy stone balustrades with moulded copings, similar to some at 12, St. John's Hill, Shrewsbury. The balusters themselves have typical classic profiles, but they are rectangular in plan instead of circular.

The ground-floor walls are of large brick laid in Flemish bond with glazed headers. Above a heavy water table, however, the first-floor walls are laid in a smaller, even-colored, pink-red brick without glazed headers, producing a definite color contrast. In the lower wall the windows have segmental arches above almost square openings filled with eight over eight light sash. The windows in the upper walls have gauged flat arches over tall openings filled with sixteen over sixteen light sash.

In addition to the refinements of size and color of the brick walling, the windows and corners of the building are bordered by red rubbed brick. In the lower story these are one brick in breadth, but above they are a stretcher closer and a header broader. The upper arches are richly worked with fine splayed and horizontal joints. In the doorways plain piers and flat arches support simple pedimented overdoors. Both the horizontal and the raking moulds are formed by two simply-moulded courses approximating a cornice profile. These doorways are important as the first examples of a fairly large number, among which were several beautiful and elaborate specimens, such as those at Carter's Grove.

The side elevations of Stratford are five bays in breadth, with un-trimmed, central doorways. These are reached by enormous flights of brick steps, recently rebuilt, from the evidence of the old foundations and of profiles against the walls of the house. These steps are very much in the style of those at Chiswick Villa, designed by Lord Burlington, but simplified to only two ascents of two flights in each block of steps. Brick is the material of both steps and balustrades, except for oak nosing pieces.

At the eaves line of the house the original wood cornice, enriched with curious small modillions, remains. A recent replacement is the wood balustrading of the look-out platform within the great chimney arches.

These chimneys are unique, in America, in their general design, but it is important to notice the relationship of their detail to those of Nelson House in Yorktown and Carter's Grove. Those at Stratford are the earliest, but have the same plain shafts, laid in Flemish bond, and the same cornice type of capping of moulded and corbelled brick. The cornice-cap is deep and richly moulded, but falls far short of attaining a real cornice profile. At Nelson House a much more conventional profile is found, but not as fine as the correct and beautifully-worked caps of Carter's Grove.

Like Nomini Hall and Marmion, Stratford was built in the center of a square parterre, the corners of which were defined by four dependencies. Fortunately, all four buildings at Stratford remain and are in two pairs. Across the south forecourt, facing each other, are two long, story-and-a-half buildings. The library is to the west and the kitchen to the east. The two north buildings, the school and office, are set at right angles to their fellows, with their long fronts facing south. All four buildings are of brick, laid in Flemish bond, with glazed headers, but have different roof forms, the south dependencies having jerkin-head, and the north having hipped roofs. The former have center chimneys with single arched panels, and the latter have, each, a single end-chimney.

Stratford followed another of Sir Henry Wotton's recommendations which provided that in the center was to be a room "for Feasts and other Jollities." [88] Blome's *The Gentleman's Recreation,* published in London in 1709, advocated the H-plan, since it made the building "stand firmer against the winds" [89] and reduced the numbers of halls necessary to give private communications to all rooms.[90] Stratford embodies the ideas of both of these writers. In plan it has the great hall, or salon, in the center, at either end of which is a cross hall separating the four wing rooms. Both floors are substantially the same in plan, though in the basement the area under the central part is subdivided.

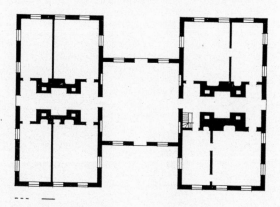

STRATFORD, Westmoreland County.

The great hall is the largest and most important early paneled room in Virginia, if not in the Colonies. In its scale, symmetry, and highly-organized architectural ornament, it is the most monumental design of the period. All of the window and door openings are flanked by Corinthian pilasters (with a diminution rather than an entiasis) set on pedestals. These support a full entablature which is continuous around the room and breaks out over each pilaster. The walls are paneled in large, simply-moulded units, with a moulded base and chair rail. In profile, the latter is apparently unique in Virginia, except that which is in reversed position in the Morattico Room. This type of chair rail is best described as an ogee bolection mould, with a bead at one edge and a small cyma at the other. The panels, which are above a paneled dado, are moulded with the bisection profile of *Palladio Londinensis*.[91] In this the edge of the styles and rails is run with a small-scale cyma in addition to a bead. The field of the panel is beveled and raised on a bead and

STRATFORD, Westmoreland County. South aspect of the mansion and dependencies. Raised first story is a Palladian device. *Johnston.*

STRATFORD, Westmoreland County. The Great Hall, finest American room of its period. "Tray" ceiling is unique in Virginia. *Demarest.*

STRATFORD, Westmoreland County. A detail of the Great Hall. Although this is the first fine paneled room of the style it displays the most elaborate scheme of paneling used during the Georgian period in Virginia, with pilasters carrying around the four walls of the room, framing the openings. The early period is shown by the unacademic proportions of the pilasters and entablature and by the design and execution of the pilaster caps, which resemble those in the Burnt Room at Tuckahoe. The panel mould is the "bisection" profile referred to in *Palladio Londinensis,* and found in all houses of this group. Paneling is entirely original and has been restored to its early grey-blue color. *Scott.*

filet. This is the most elaborate of all sunk panel moulds and is characteristic of this group of houses.

The windows all have paneled shutters in the reveals as well as window seats, but are untrimmed around the opening in the paneling. However, as has been observed, all are set off by pilasters which give them architectural importance. Centered on the north and south walls are double entrance doors (restored), paneled to match the doors to the east and west passageways. The latter are of the familiar eight-panel type with two long panels below two square panels in both upper and lower parts of the doors. Though it is a familiar type, these may be the prototypes of all other Virginia examples, and by referring to the Morattico doors it can be seen that at this early period the designs were not yet standardized. It was a type described in *Palladio Londinensis* and shown in several of its plates.[92] In Virginia, it is more usual to find it with a wide lock rail, as at Carter's Grove, instead of with equal rails and styles as found here. Both in English and Virginia work this is an indication of an early period. At either side of the east and west doors are wall closets with two panel doors. For many years the upper parts of these doors were glazed, but panels have now been reinstated. It is interesting to note that the H-hinges of these doors have brass plates such as formerly existed at Tuckahoe. These plates can be removed for polishing. This may have been an early effort to get rid of the crude effect of exposed, wrought-iron hinges, which in many of the other houses of the group, and elsewhere in Stratford, was achieved by the use of mortised, dove-tailed hinges.

The importance of this fine room was increased by recessing the ceiling into the roof space, thus creating a clear height of nearly eighteen feet. The slope of the roof is exposed and plastered to the underside of the tie beams. Such ceilings are often seen in the West Indies, where they are called tray ceilings. An early period is indicated by the whole character of the great hall woodwork, but the crudities of, for instance, the pilaster capitals, like those of Tuckahoe, may be as much due to unskilled craftsmen as to the period.

The two wings, or "legs," of the H were each originally planned with four nearly-equal rooms, two on either side of a central passageway. This produced eight rooms, nearly similar in size, on each floor. For general usage some proved too small and some too large. For this reason, from time to time, but mainly about 1800, all of the partitions on the first floor were moved, and at the beginning of the restoration almost all of the trim of these rooms dated from this period. The southeast room of the east wing, as the birthplace of Robert E. Lee and of his distinguished cousins, has been unchanged in the restoration and has good simple trim of the period. The northeast room of the west wing has been also left with its early nineteenth-century trim, but this is more elaborate, the chair rail, cornice, and mantel being enriched with fluting and reeding. The dining room, or northwest room, in the east wing was originally one of the larger rooms which lost its trim, but it is now restored to its early aspect. The library, or southeast room, in the west wing is similarly restored. It is interesting to note that the conditions encountered in the restoration work indicated a scheme of paneling such as that at Marmion, and it is more than possible that the same workmen were employed at the two houses.

Although Stratford was built before Jefferson was born, the same Palladian idea of subordinating the stair was employed here as he later advocated. An examination of the Stratford stair, a tiny one with steep risers and many winders, brings forcibly to mind the Monticello stairs. Unfortunately, the original Stratford stair was destroyed in one of the alterations, but the present one is built in the old location in the style of the period.

Among the most interesting features of Stratford are the fine original fireplaces, long concealed by later fireplaces. These are largely laid in English bond and have curved jambs and recessed fireback panels. The fireplace openings are spanned by segmental arches of considerable rise. The plaster, in the ground-floor rooms, is brought to the fireplace arch and finishes against it. It should be noted that in some of the fireplaces the jambs were plastered. This recalls the fine plastered fireplaces of the Province House in Boston [93] (1679—destroyed, 1922), this one having similar curved jambs and brick herringbone fireback panels. In several cases in this latter house the line of the jamb, floor, and fireback were accented by broad painted black bands, scalloped at the intersections. Perhaps the finest fireplace in Virginia is the great kitchen fireplace at Stratford, which is twelve feet long, four feet deep, and seven feet high at the crown of the arch. This is a wonderful example to show the manifold uses of kitchen fireplaces on Virginia plantations in their heyday.

Stratford stands in grounds carefully restored to their old appearance with a grassy forecourt to the south, a geometric boxwood garden to the east, and beyond the north lawn a broad vista cut through the woods to the Potomac River. In addition to the mansion and gardens, many other plantation buildings remain, or have been reconstructed. The whole gives a memorable picture of a great southern estate of the eighteenth century which was the home of an almost unparalleled number of great Americans of one family.

The Northern Neck of Virginia, the fertile peninsula between the Rappahannock and Potomac Rivers, on which Stratford stands, was an area of early settlement, and on it stand many fine eighteenth-century houses. The whole region extending from Chesapeake Bay to the Shenandoah River, containing over five million acres of land, was granted, as a refuge, to a group of his courtiers by Charles II in 1649. None of them ever used it as such, however, and later Lord Culpeper, one of the grantees, purchased the shares of the others. Through his heiress it passed to Thomas, Lord Fairfax, and only on his death, in 1781, was this great estate liquidated. Until Fairfax came to Virginia, in 1747, to administer the estates, various Virginians had acted as steward or factor for them. One of these men was Robert Carter of Corotoman (1663-1732), whose family became the dominant one of the region. Carter, whose father John emigrated from England and established himself first in Maryland and later in Virginia, was born on his father's place near the eastern end of the Northern Neck. On John Carter's death, during his son's childhood, the latter inherited a large estate, which through a long minority in skillful care, increased enormously. Robert Carter's natural acumen and his position in the colony enabled him to obtain distinguished official positions in the colony as well as the proprietary stewardship, and to increase his land holdings and capital to the point where he was, perhaps, the richest man in the Colony. To him is probably due a considerable part of the credit for developing the architecture of Virginia from its traditional to its academic phase.

Although the Governor's Palace must have inspired wealthy planters to new ideas in housing themselves, no other house is known to have been designed from it. Robert (King) Carter not only rebuilt his own house, Corotoman, in Lancaster County, but also built Christ Church, nearby, and was probably active in the construction of the dwellings of his children, all mansions of high architectural quality. Of these— Berkeley, Sabine Hall, Rosewell, Nomini Hall and Cleve—only the first two stand. However, the ruins of Rosewell remain, the walls of Cleve stood until recently, and a drawing and description of Nomini Hall survive.

In addition to the houses of Carter's children a number of other distinguished houses of the period are apparently not only by the same designers but also detailed from the same style book. This group includes Nelson House, Carter's Grove, Elsing Green, Westover, Wilton, Powhatan, and Wythe House. Of these the first three were built for Robert Carter's grandchildren and the last two for and by the architect, who probably designed all of the others as well as the Randolph houses and Stratford. This was Richard Taliaferro (1705-1779) of Williamsburg.

Little is known of Taliaferro, but it is clear that he was a person of distinction and reputation in the Colony. Thomas Lee, acting Governor,

STRATFORD, Westmoreland County. Library, newly paneled. *Scott.*

STRATFORD, Westmoreland County, West hall, new finish. *Scott.*

STRATFORD, Westmoreland County. The Birth Chamber, refinished about 1800. Here on January 19, 1807, Robert E. Lee was born. *Scott.*

ROSEWELL, Gloucester County. Bird's-eye view. *Perspective, author; rendering, Collins.*

COUND, Shropshire, England. Architect's drawing. Mansion with many parallels to Rosewell.

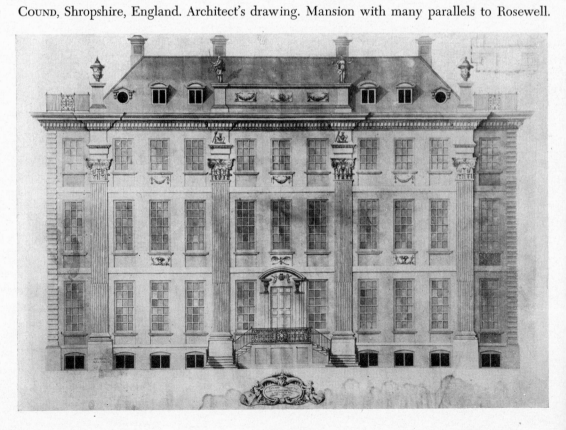

wrote in 1749 to the Board of Trade in London that the Palace has been viewed by "our most skillful architect." [94] and the records of the period show an estimate made for alterations. It is assumed that Taliaferro was referred to, for he was in charge of the additions to the building of 1749-51. In what capacity is not stated, but John Blair entered in his diary under date of August 30, 1751, that he had completed his contract with Taliaferro at the "Governors House" [95] (the Palace was so called until after these additions). It might be inferred that Taliaferro acted with full architect's authority and not only designed the building but awarded the contracts. Unfortunately, nothing is known of the addition except the plan, and this has no stylistic qualities. The only other building with which, at present, he is known to have been associated is the President's house at the College of William and Mary. This was built in 1732,[96] but it was not until 1756, when he made some repairs, that Taliaferro is known to have been connected with it.[97] In this case he acted as contractor and he seems to have done so in other cases.

It is a possibility that Taliaferro, like John Ariss, the architect, studied in Great Britain. If this is the case, the extremely English quality of Rosewell, Sabine Hall, and Christ Church would be explained. If he did not study there, it would seem that they were the work of an Englishman who came to this country to erect them (and perhaps Stratford, Rippon Hall, and Corotoman) and under whom Taliaferro served an apprenticeship. Such an apprenticeship would have equipped him to continue the work after the Englishman's return, or perhaps demise. In either case, the buildings have not only a definite English quality but also a definite county quality, which is Shropshire. It is necessary only to visit Shrewsbury, the shiretown, to observe the remarkable kinship of its building with that of Virginia. Both are primarily brick architectures, and not only employ the same, and usual, techniques of bricklaying but also of moulding, rubbing, gauging, and similar designs of window arches, doorways and external and internal woodwork. In certain cases there are extraordinary plan parallels.

Shropshire and neighboring Cheshire are counties rich in associations with Virginians, including the Carters, Hills, Byrds, Lees, and Pages, though the exact English ancestry of some of these families is in doubt. An emblazoned list of mayors in St. John's Church, Chester, includes a William Byrd (for 1557 and 1580) and John Page (after 1600).[98] These arms (with the marks of cadency) are those borne by the Virginia families.

Rosewell is the focal building of the entire group of Virginia mansions, and the first clue to its Shopshire antecedants was in a published plan and elevation of Cound,[99] a mansion just outside of Shrewsbury. Although this is a building larger than Rosewell, the planning is strikingly alike in both houses, and both are unique in their areas. The plans comprise large rectangular blocks, having off-center halls (occupying one corner of the building), three square rooms, one in each of the three other corners, with a central hall between the two rear rooms, and a service stair hall between the two side rooms. At Cound the rear hall becomes a salon by the greater length of the structure.

This plan is individualized by large end pavilions that contain the chimney stacks as well as large lighted closets, some of which have fireplaces. Both houses are three stories in height above high basements. The use of heroic stone pilasters on the façades at Cound prevents much exterior resemblance to Rosewell, but the fenestration and doorway treatments are somewhat similar. An interesting fact concerning Cound is that the interior doors and exterior doorways are derived from Plate XXVII in *Palladio Londinensis*. Here it is known by what hand the book was used, for the original drawing of the house is preserved, signed and dated by the architect, John Prince, in 1704. Little else is known of Prince, and there are few records of him in Shrewsbury after this date. A man of this name was a subscriber to James Gibbs's *Book of Architecture* in 1725. It is possible that Prince himself came to Virginia, but no mention of his name has been found in the early records.

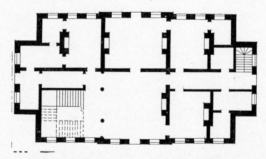

Cound Hall (shown transposed), Shropshire, England.

The development of the Cound plan seems to have resulted from earlier Shropshire houses such as Soulton.[100] This is a Jacobean house, square in plan, with the chimney stacks located in the same position as those at Cound, but it lacks the end pavilions. Soulton is three stories high, and although in a different style it has a definite resemblance to Cound. The doorway and entrance steps show the evolution of those at Stratford.

The local derivation of the Cound plan would explain the absence of similar plans in the great English houses of the period. Prince was evidently a local man who worked from precedent and style publications.

He, or another equally capable architect, practiced in Shrewsbury and produced many beautiful brick houses. Unfortunately, these are not generally appreciated locally because of the vogue of half-timbered black and white. Among the fine houses is one, the Judges' Lodging, that forms an amazing parallel to Sabine Hall. As far as the interior is concerned, the resemblance is so great that it is almost impossible to distinguish between the great paneled halls of the two houses with their arched and recessed stairs. The complete plans were once parallels except for the location of the chimneys, which at the Judges' Lodging are in the center wall and at Sabine Hall are in the end walls. John Prince probably designed Number 25, Claremont Hill, which possesses a beautiful stair. This has its initial flight between two fine scrolled rails (somewhat in the style of the Cound stair, which is now altered), and has turned and spiraled balusters.

Study by the writer of Shropshire houses other than Cound was limited to published sources, and such study did not reveal examples showing specific relationship to Virginia buildings. Some, such as Stoke, are definitely in the Virginia vernacular, but this example is of traditional design. Eaton Hall, in neighboring Cheshire, has much the style of Rosewell, but it had only a single cupola. Other English houses, such as Hampstead Marshall, had several.

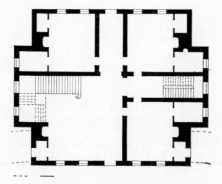

ROSEWELL, Gloucester County.

Not only the designer's individualities and those of a particular region are shown in the Virginia buildings, but those of an English architectural publication as well. This publication is *Palladio Londinensis, or the London Art of Building* by William Salmon, a builder of Essex, who compiled this book to give current practice and prices of London building. This is a valuable handbook of the period with drawings and text covering decorative and structural problems. After Salmon's death (c.1700-1725) the book was republished several times by his son. The original edition, which seems to have been published early in the century, has not been available for the present work.

The first of the Carter buildings was undoubtedly Corotoman, which, judging from King Carter's great wealth and the extant remains, was a major architectural work. Fine as it was, the mansion was destined for a short life. Built in the first quarter of the eighteenth century, it was burned in 1729 and never rebuilt. The *Maryland Gazette* for February fourth of that year noted: "... The fine large house of Col. Carter on Rappahannock was also burnt lately. [The other was Mount Pleasant, Thomas Lee's house.] The particulars of this loss we cannot give you but we are informed it is very great." [101] King Carter's will,[102] written on August 22, 1726, bequeathed his "mansion dwelling" to his son John, husband of Elizabeth Hill of Shirley, and further provided to "give unto my son John all my furniture in the New house and half of the rest of the Furniture in my kitchen other houses about my mansion Dwelling ..." This instrument was drawn before the destruction of the house by fire, and the inventory of 1732 lists only the items in a small dwelling. This may have been John Carter's house, built after the purchase of the land about 1659,[103] or a dependency of the new mansion. It was probably the old gabled house, standing in ruins, which finally disappeared about 1930. Sometimes called the Spinsters' House, it was of frame, a story and a half high, with large end chimneys. It had a curiously complex plan, complete records of which no longer remain. The site of the great house, on a broad headland looking down toward Chesapeake Bay, is strewn with pieces of cut stone and marble. Scrub undergrowth prevents a close examination of the area, but stone revetments in the river are said to bound the old formal shore line which, in turn, bounded the forecourt. In the yard of a small house nearby is the great well, superbly built of wedge-shaped, cut-stone blocks.

It is only conjecture that the Morattico panel represents Corotoman; it has also been conjectured that the panel might represent Warner Hall, Rippon Hall, or Turkey Island. However, the design of the house is certainly akin to that of Rosewell and was probably the work of the same architect. It can be seen that the building, while badly out of perspective, was four stories high, seven bays long, with a deck-on-hip roof. The deck was balustraded, and in the center of it rose an elaborate cupola. Although the end pavilions of Rosewell and Cound did not occur in the same positions, the chimneys were in the same location and had the same cornice caps. Superimposed orders framing the windows of the first and second floors gave the façade a highly architectural character. The ground floor was rusticated, and the third floor was plain. Above the entrance door was a window opening on a corbelled balcony.

The arrangement of the wings was unusual and rather unsatisfactory, and except for Ashdown House, Berkshire,[104] did not seem to occur elsewhere. The wings were parallel to the main house, and were attached to it by overlying the front enough for communication. The wings were two stories high, four bays long, with the first story arcaded. It is a curious circumstance that both sash and casement windows are shown in the openings. This arrangement would imply that the house was built with leaded glass casements and that some openings had been altered to sash. Although this might sometimes mean a long lapse of time between the building and the alteration at the period of 1700-1725, it does not necessarily imply a time lapse in this case because of the rapid coming into style of sash windows. The Capitol (1699-1703) was probably the first building to have sash windows in Virginia,[105] but by 1725 it is not unlikely that they were universal in important buildings.

Only by excavations at various sites can the identity of the building shown on the painted panel be determined. In the meantime, it may be surmised to be an early Virginia mansion, for scholars who are fully acquainted with the English buildings of this period do not recognize it as an English example.

Of the extant mansions of the Shropshire type in Virginia, Rosewell is the earliest. It is known to have been under construction in 1726 by King Carter's will of the same year (he provided £100 toward furnishing a brick house his son-in-law was building),[106] and from the records of the Virginia Assembly. The latter passed an act in 1744 to break the entail on some of the Page properties which act would enable Mann Page II to sell lands and to complete the house.[107] Rosewell, therefore, was begun before 1726 and stood incomplete on the death of Mann Page I in 1730.

The history of Rosewell has been one of financial difficulties due to the vast cost of construction and maintenance. The mansion itself stood complete from 1744 to about 1838, with a pair of dependencies toward the north, though it is not sure the connecting passageways were ever built. The west dependency remained in altered form until after 1900, but the east building was destroyed earlier. However, it is known that the latter was built, for it was described in the insurance policy of 1802 as being twenty-four feet by sixty,[108] and one story high. A brick stable was also insured, and noted as twenty-four by one hundred and twenty feet. Rosewell passed from the Page family in 1838 on the death of the widow of Governor Page, and was substantially altered and modernized by the purchaser. At this time the house was largely resashed, new entrance doors were hung, and the cupolas and parapets removed. The roof was also changed from a deck-on-hip to a low hip, and pediments were added to the end pavilions. The lead roofing referred to in the policy of 1802 was removed and tin substituted. The fine paneled interiors, said to have been of walnut (and also of mahogany), were removed, probably because they were old-fashioned. Some claims have been made that the fine old wood was sold for use in fabricating the doors for the old Treasury in Washington, but this cannot be confirmed. The latter building was burned in 1838. Finally Rosewell itself fell a prey to flames and was destroyed on March 24, 1916.[109] With it went the last of its superb interiors, the magnificent stair that survived in part the nineteenth-century alterations. Now only the walls of Rosewell, once the finest of all American houses, stand, and even in their ruined state they form the finest example of early brickwork that remains to us.

The plan of Rosewell has been discussed, but the elevations have just been touched upon. Five bays long on each façade, the building is three stories high above a high basement, and the centers of interest are the two fine brick doorways. These have pilasters and pediments in cut stone and gauged, moulded, and carved brick, and were originally reached by broad flights of Portland stone steps and platforms. The windows are of great height on the first floor, diminish on the second and third floors to normal height, and occur in the basement as square openings. An almost unique condition is seen in the broader windows in the center of each façade, the only other examples, except the rebuilt Governor's Palace, being in the Shirley advance buildings. An unparalleled feature of the design was the use of two cupolas on the roof. Although these were removed in the 1838 alterations, they are shown in an old engraving and referred to in a description of the house. They gave Rosewell something of the appearance of a public building, but unified the structure as one cupola could not. Their exact design has not been established.

The end elevations are formed largely by the great pavilions, the features of which are the tall arched staircase windows. These lighted the landing of the east stair and the hallways of the west stair. Windows of such pronounced height and in this location are rare, the only other Virginia examples being at the Randolph-Peachy house and Sabine Hall. The Rosewell windows had sashes four lights wide and nine lights high with geometric heads. They are flanked by single windows of normal size on the first and second floors, and there is a series of three on the third floor. In the basement of both pavilions are wide arched openings which were probably service entrances. The brickwork of the sidewalls of the house, just north of the pavilions, shows the location of the passageways to the wings in racking on either side of each of the door openings.

Rosewell's greatest distinction lies in its superb brickwork. The bricks, according to custom, were probably made near the site. Mann Page II seems to have provided the brick for Carter's Grove,[110] indicating that

ROSEWELL, Gloucester County. Before 1916 fire. The house was being built in 1726 but stood incomplete many years. The finest, largest American house of the Colonial period. *Wallace.*

ROSEWELL, Gloucester County. The east pavilion, showing the great staircase window and the east door, with the brickwork beside it racked for the connection. The upper sashes and window frames here seen are original, the former with the characteristic broad muntins and the latter with the narrow exposed face in the London style. The pediment dates from c. 1838. In the chimneys can be seen cap of parapet removed at this time. The walls still stand. *Wallace*.

he had good brick clay deposits competently worked. At Rosewell the walls are laid in Flemish bond with random glazed headers, and all the corners of the building and window jambs are of rubbed brick of selected vermilion color. Gauged brick of similar color occurs in the great doorways, belt courses, window arches, and sill panels. Portland stone trim forms the window sills, keystones, pilaster bases and caps for the doorways, the parapet, chimney caps, and formerly the great flights of steps.

The brick doorways, apparently both inspired by *Palladio Londinensis*,[111] are the finest and most elaborate of the period, with the possible exception of those of Christ Church. That on the north front has a richly moulded architrave frame, with crossettes, flanked by narrow paneled pilasters. The latter support scrolled brackets with carved reveals, upon which rest the elaborately moulded pediment. In profile the mouldings are excellent, and the moulding, cutting, and rubbing of the bricks is superbly done, as it is throughout the structure. Unfortunately, the center of the pedimented overdoor has fallen, but the sections of the cornice over the brackets show the rich moulding and the carefully cut dentils.

Although the north door employs stone only in the pilaster bases, the south door has elaborate stone caps as well. The design of this latter doorway is less successful, the pilasters and segmental pediment being awkwardly detailed. Partly covered by stucco, the pilasters are fluted and show an entiasis; they have full Attic bases and curiously moulded caps rather like the Tuscan cornice on Plate IV of Salmon's book. Although the original doors were already gone at the time of the fire, the frames remained, and a fragment of one survives. It was of solid oak, recessed from the face of the brickwork and run with a bolection moulding finishing against the brick with a small cyma backband.[112] The use of a roll moulding in this location is very unusual, the example at Fork Church in Hanover County being perhaps the only other in Virginia.

The masonry trim of the Rosewell windows possesses great refinement and distinction. It is composed of broad dressings of rubbed brick with moulded stone sills which receive the gauged brick "bibs," or panels, below. The arches are flat on top but are cut to a shallow segment on the soffits, as in the basement windows at Cound. This form reoccurs at Nelson House and in the Shirley dependencies, but on a more robust scale. The keystones of the Rosewell windows are unusually elaborate, with narrow fluted central segments, moulded at the top and set against plain wing pieces. Almost similar to the Christ Church keystones, those of the great arched windows are broader with extra fluting and curious scrolls carved on the wing pieces. The moulded caps in both are modified from one on Plate XIV of *Palladio Londinensis*. All of the windows at

Rosewell have the gauged brick bibs already referred to, but at the arched windows they hang free and in the normal windows form a panel between the sill and the belt course below. In form the water table is unlike any other in Virginia except that at Nelson House. It approximated the profile of a balustrade cap with a torus above a fascia, and below a cyma wash. The belt courses at the second- and third-floor lines are of gauged brick, laid in Flemish bond, five courses high with the lowest course moulded. Before the fire the original heavy muntined sash existed only in the third-floor windows. These had six over six light sashes. The later sash below, which followed the original, had on the second floor nine over six lights, and the first floor nine over nine, all three lights wide. In keeping with current London fashion [113] the windows had narrow frames, only about an inch and a half showing.

The parapet above the main cornice was removed when the roof was changed, but the cut stone cap remains where it crossed the chimney-stacks. These latter have rather top-heavy stone cornices which are exact copies of the Tuscan cornice in Plate IV of *Palladio Londinensis*. Of the stone steps to the two great doorways, some sections remain, one of which, cut in the form of a huge volute or scroll, was a terminal step and fashioned probably from Plate XXXII of Salmon's book. The present steps are concrete, but the line of the original can be seen in the brick-work.

A fine masonry detail of the interior is the great vaulted cellar under the entrance hall, which may have supported a marble floor. Marble is known to have been used for the original mantels, but no fragments seem to remain at the site, and it is probable that all were removed in the alterations. The recollections of the persons who knew the house before the fire do not provide information on this point, nor in any other important detail. A photograph of about 1915 shows the hall mantel, which was of nineteenth-century date. As far as can be determined, no early trim remained except the doors and stair. The former were of six and eight panel design with Classic Revival trim.

Unrivaled as the finest of all American examples, the stair at Rosewell ascended in an initial long, broad, straight run with a short one under the great arched window and another to the second-floor line. All of the finish except that of the stringer and balustrade was destroyed in the alterations, but some details are preserved at Shelly, a Page house nearby, where other fragments from Rosewell may be seen. The balustrade was formed of three turned and spiraled balusters to a step supporting a richly moulded handrail and resting on superb carved brackets. The form of the bracket was that of a scrolled console feathered with acanthus leaves. These were supported on a fine moulded architrave

ROSEWELL, Gloucester County. Great staircase showing terminal scroll, carved newel, and spandrel with "bisection" paneling. *Wallace.*

ROSEWELL, Gloucester County. The staircase showing the fascia, carved in the style of Daniel Marot, with scrolled leaves and fretwork. Each minor post matched the newel, with tendrils and vines carved on the shaft of a Corinthian colonette. Pilaster responds in the dado were removed after 1838. The walls of the entrance hall were originally hung with tapestry and were at least partly paneled, with full-height Ionic pilasters. *Wallace.*

paralleling the soffit of the stair. The triangular spandrel under the first run was fully paneled. The stair was initiated with an intricate volute like those in Salmon's Plate XXXII, terminating in a post carved with tendrils and vines. The newel within the scroll was so large and open that a person could stand by it. The minor posts of the stair were also carved, as were the beautiful pilaster wall responds, preserved at Shelly. The most elaborate motive of the staircase, however, was the fascia board around the well, and this was carved with scrolled leafage, flowers, and rosettes. This carved fascia, almost a repeat of that still remaining at Tuckahoe, was a fine example of the high craftsmanship of the period. The design consisted of scrolled strapwork, with leafage and blossoms, and as a center there was a basket of flowers. The full coverage of the design, the disposition of the accents, and the crispness of the carving were notable features of the fascia. Some of this carved finish may have been imported from England, inspired by designs of Daniel Marot.

How extensive the wall paneling of the hall was is uncertain, but the descriptions of the house written by Ann Page Saunders, who knew it as a child, say that the walls were entirely paneled. Even the vast expanse of paneling which this would have presented is possible when the fabulous amount at Sabine Hall and Shirley is considered. The wall areas were probably paneled in high ranges of vertical panels above a dado. The arches or mantel may have been flanked by pilasters. Mrs. Saunders, a daughter of Governor Page, refers to Corinthian pilasters as part of the wall treatment, though four Ionic capitals at Shelly make it seem she was mistaken in the order.[114] The walls in places were hung with tapestries which were used in colonial mansions, the copy of the order for a set for Bedford, by William Fitzhugh, still being extant.[115]

No knowledge of the rest of the interior of Rosewell remains, except from the rather general, but colorful description of Mrs. Saunders, which in full is as follows:

"There is now, in the State of Virginia, a venerable building, inhabited by a large and charming family; but it is so modernized, as scarcely to be recognized as the old mansion, where the events occurred, which are here recorded. It was called Rosewell, from an abundant spring, near which the house was built.

"A wall of bricks, surmounted by large flagstones, surrounded the top of the building. At each end was a turret, within which were small apartments, and on the roof of each large weather cocks whirled mournfully. Into one of these rooms, you ascended from the winding staircase, leading from the basement to the roof. From the other, called the summer-house, you beheld from its four fine windows beautiful views of the winding Carter's Creek, and the majestic York River, which expanded wider and wider as you gazed. Then looking over the battlements, upon cedars and holly and pines overhanging the high banks, and cultivated fields, and flocks and herds grazing, you would imagine it all encircled by the deep blue waters, and that you were upon an island more attractive than the James River Island, which attracted the footsteps of our forefathers.

"An immense floor of lead, with wide gutters to let off the melting snow, or falling rain, was much admired by visitors, and it was asserted in 'Howe's History of Virginia' that Governor P. and his friend Jefferson caught fish up there. It is true, however, that upon that house-top they often looked at the stars; and that old telescope is now kept in Washington City, as a relic of those by-gone days, when these wise men, with all their cares and toils as statesmen and patriots found time to contemplate the 'firmament and stars, which express their great Creator's skill.'

"The grand staircase was also an object of admiration to all who saw, or ascended it, and looked down upon the large hall, with its wainscoted walls of mahogany, and pillasters of Corinthian order, and the great hearth and marble mantelpiece.

"All the rooms were wainscoted with wood of different colors, and had marble mantels, the ceilings were also of great height."

The reference to rooms of different colors recalls Celia Fiennes' description of Hampton Court in which she says, "Prince George's dressing roome, hung, and window Curtains, Chaires and stooles, all wth yellow damaske, wth marble Chimney pieces as all the Roomes have Differing Coll^{rs} black, white, grey, rance, etc., etc." [116]

In addition to the great stair, the minor stair which was much simpler, but had an excellent balustrade, remained until the fire. It ascended in two reverse direction flights in a rather narrow hall, and had a tall staircase window on the landing. It was also an open string stair, but in place of the carved brackets had plain scrolled consoles, similar to those at Sabine Hall, set above a moulded architrave. There were three balusters to a tread supporting a moulded handrail. The turnings of the balusters were exceptionally crisp, and above a series of vase profiles were delicately spiraled. The relationship of these balusters to those of the gallery stair at Christ Church is marked.

The masonry of the fireplaces remains largely intact and was used as precedent for the chimneys of the Governor's Palace. The jambs, as was usual at this period, are curved, and in the back is a recessed smoke channel. The flues, which are very large, are divided into two equal areas by their brick partitions and are supported by parabolic arches. A diminutive fireplace, which is half round in plan, and which formed the precedent for the fireplace in the closet of the reception room at the

ROSEWELL, Gloucester County. Great stair balustrade. *Wallace.*

ROSEWELL, Gloucester County. Minor stair balustrade. *Wallace.*

CHRIST CHURCH, Lancaster County. Side door.

CHRIST CHURCH. West doorway. *Author, HABS.*

CHRIST CHURCH. The great arched windows.

Doorway, Plate XXII, *Palladio Londinensis.*

Palace in Williamsburg, is found in one of the chimney closets at Rosewell.

The original roof, which must have been a deck on hip, was covered with lead, according to the insurance policy of 1802. Writers have described it as having an aquarium, but this word apparently referred to the cupolas rather than to a fish pond. Tryon's Palace in New Bern, North Carolina, also possessed a cupola and was referred to as having an aquarium on the roof, so it seems that the two words may have been used synonymously in the eighteenth century.

Rosewell is on a promontory in the York River at Carter's Creek in Gloucester County. The water view is now to the east, but the south front may once have commanded a view across the river. On this axis is the remains of an allée of crape myrtle, terminated by two huge box-woods, once clipped to standard topiary forms. Just east of the house is the cemetery comprising a superb group of table tombs. The slabs are carved with Latin inscriptions and the family arms, and the sides and ends with conventional devices and funerary ornaments. This is certainly one of the finest groups of family tombs in America, in spite of neglect and decay. Its desolation epitomizes that of Rosewell, once the scene of Colonial life at its most luxurious development, and now a ruin in a pastoral wilderness.

In contrast, Christ Church, built in 1732, stands in a pleasant setting, complete and in good condition in spite of its two-hundred-odd years of existence. It is fortunate that the finest of Virginia's churches almost alone should have survived intact the vicissitudes of the period following the disestablishment of the church. This was perhaps due in part to its remote location, almost at the end of the Northern Neck, an area which did not figure in the Civil War campaigns. The fabulous tradition of King Carter, its builder and patron, who lies in the shadow of the chancel, was perhaps also responsible for the care and respect the church received before the revival of the parish.

The architectural style of Christ Church is almost entirely foreign to church building of the eighteenth century in the state. The floor plan, however, shows the traditional Virginia cruciform scheme with equilateral chancel and transepts and longer nave. This may mean that the plan-type, which of course was English in derivation, was also current in provincial work of the period in England, and so was naturally used by the architect, who obviously had an English background. On the other hand, an inclination on the part of the designer to use a more academic plan may have been thwarted by King Carter, as George Mason must have thwarted young William Buckland at Gunston Hall, where the form of the house was kept traditional even if the fine detail was in the current London style.

In the architectural design and detail of Christ Church, the influence of *Palladio Londinensis* is all-prevailing. It is especially obvious in the curious concave roof which covers the building. The figure on Plate P, entitled "Concave Roof," was certainly the source of the roof design, though the architect vastly increased the scale. Both the barrel vault of the interior of Christ Church and the steep hipped roof with sharply splayed eaves are fully shown in this plate. In it the exterior surface was actually curved, though the frame was not. The form of the roof is daring, and particularly when seen from a distance is unusually effective. Although there is no reference to a Chinese source for the roof type, it is definitely reminiscent of a pagoda, framed, as it is at Christ Church, by the venerable pines.

The great height of the side walls of the building produces a pronounced vertical effect, Virginia church buildings being normally horizontal in character. Here, however, the additional height was used to allow the creation of a great range of fine arched windows and three superb entrance doors. The walls are an excellent example of Virginia brickwork at its best. Probably made nearby, the bricks have unusually good color, shape, and texture, and are evenly laid in Flemish bond. The brick dressings and trim are richly moulded, gauged, and rubbed, the stonework elaborately worked, and all the woodwork of the great doors, though now painted, is of walnut. In the fields of the three materials and crafts, Christ Church is unrivaled in American architecture and is on a par with fine English work of the period.

The doorways are based on plates in *Palladio Londinensis*, both for the masonry trim and the doors themselves. The main entrance is derived from Plate XXII, which also has a Doric order on pedestals supporting a pediment and enclosing an arched opening. At Christ Church the design was modified by the use of pilasters instead of engaged columns, by the omission of triglyphs in the entablature, and by a segment for an angle pediment. For the detail of the pedestal cap and base the profile from Plate VI was used. The unusual feature here is the deep undercut ogee moulding that forms both the soffit of the upper member and the main moulding of the lower. This detail was used both for the pedestal cap of the reredos, within the church, and for the stone window sills of the church. Although no material was indicated in the plate, the executed doorway is all of gauged brick, with superbly cut and moulded entablature and pediment. The elliptical steps, pedestal, the pilaster caps and bases, the imposts, and keys are all of Portland stone. The moulding profiles are similar to those in the stair archways at Sabine Hall, and are inspired by *Palladio Londinensis*, the pilaster detail from Plates VI and XVIII, the pedestal from VI and E, and the impost from

XIV. In this doorway, the use of the materials, the intricate jointing, and the perfection of craftsmanship are all notable.

The transept doors are simpler and perhaps better in scale with full-height Doric pilasters and angle pediments framing square-headed openings. The pediments rest on entablatures, characteristic of Salmon's style, with cushion friezes and three-plane architraves. The latter forms the flat arch over the door so that each two voussoir were cut to a different center. Here, too, the elliptical steps and pilaster cap and base are of Portland stone.

Except for the part below the lunette in the front door all three openings possess all their original woodwork. The doors of the main entrance are replacements of the early nineteenth century, but apparently reproduce the original paneling. The design of the doors is unusual, all having lower panels in the form of St. Andrew's Cross, the rails being diagonal, with ranges of vertical and horizontal panels above. The design of the woodwork of the front door is based on Plate XXIII of *Palladio Londinensis*, though this latter is for a smaller opening. However, the architect merely doubled the doors in width, carried each leaf up another vertical panel in height, and added a paneled lunette. Salmon used a typical six-panel door for his design, replacing the vertical lower panels with his diagonal cross, and it is this exactly, with the superimposed panels, that occurs in the main doors of Christ Church. For the transept doors a different device was used to increase the height above the cross panels. This was to employ above them the full design for a paneled door shown in Plate XXVII. It is the same that was used at Cound and again in the Randolph-Peachy house in Williamsburg and in Scotchtown in Hanover County. The detail of the sunk panel moulding employed at Christ Church is also found at Stratford, Rosewell, Sabine Hall, and most of the other houses of the group. The panel mould consists of a cyma and bead, and the field of the panel is set out on a beading. This seems to be what Salmon referred to on page forty-nine as "Bisection Wainscoting," which he differentiates from quarter-round panel moulds.

Another feature drawn from the same publication is the great wood entablature at the eaves which is derived from Plate VI, as far as the architrave and frieze is concerned, and from Plate XXX for the cornice itself. This entablature, usually showing the triple plane architrave, cushion frieze, and fully moulded cornice, with a blocked dentil course, is to be found throughout the buildings referred to in this chapter.

A curious feature of the west front is the oval window over the doorway. This is not an entirely successful element, but it has a certain quaintness. No such design occurs in *Palladio Londinensis*, but there are numerous examples in other design books such as Gibbs's and Langley's publications. The great arched windows of the side walls are, as has been observed, remarkable parallels to the stair windows of Rosewell. The jambs have broad rubbed-brick dressings, and cut stone sills, imposts and keys. The brick arch is especially notable for its fine workmanship in gauging and jointing. The narrow staff bead of Rosewell is also seen here, and the original sixteen-light walnut sash remain, along with two-inch moulded muntins.

The interior of Christ Church, with its original furniture almost intact, is no less complete than the exterior. The furniture includes high box-pews, a lofty pulpit with its curved stair, its domed and inlaid sounding board, a paneled gallery, and chancel woodwork. Included in the latter are the reredos, altar table, communion rail, and marble font. All of the woodwork is original, but it has recently been reconditioned after being damaged by termites. In addition, the aisles have their original Purbeck stone paving of random blocks. The survival of so much early finish is remarkable and is approached in the state only by Aquia Church in Stafford County (1757), where, however, the pews have been cut down and the communion table replaced. The quality of the design, too, is not as high as that in the former building.

The Christ Church pews have paneled sides, with a horizontal panel above a vertical one, and a moulded cap. Within them are plank seats set on scrolled supports fixed to the paneling. All have paneled doors with early hardware. At the crossing, the paneling of the sides of the pews is curved to ease the angle. The pews are of pine, probably originally painted but now stripped, but the chancel paneling is of walnut. The latter is curious in form, covering, as it does, only the angles of the chancel and rear walls between the four windows. Therefore, it comprises only relatively small sections on the side walls. Each section is composed of a single panel flanked by Doric pilasters (with an ogee echinus) which supports an entablature and pediment. Occuring in the corner, one end of each of the two pediments is cut off by the rear wall.

The reredos, which is also of walnut, recalls the west doorway in design, for it has a segmental pediment supported by Doric pilasters (also with ogee echinus) on pedestals. The baptismal font at the right of the communion table was undoubtedly imported from England. It is of marble with a slender turned shaft supporting a graceful bowl carved with cherubs' heads and acanthus leaves. This was broken and profaned during the Civil War, but is now repaired and in use again. The communion rail, all of walnut, is rectangular in plan with curved corners. It is formed of a base receiving elaborately-turned balusters, which are capped by a moulded rail. In the style of the period, the gate is concealed. The pulpit is the tall type and is reached by a curved stair with scrolled

CHRIST CHURCH, Lancaster County. Built by Robert (King) Carter in 1732; the finest and least-changed Virginia church of Colonial period. Masonry detail parallels Rosewell. *Author*.

SABINE HALL, Richmond County. The south front. Built by King Carter for his son Landon about 1729. Except for lowering of the roof, the addition of porches and wings, and loss of dependencies, the house has been little changed from time of building. *Metropolitan Eng*.

SABINE HALL, Richmond County. The north front, showing the later portico, together with the original stone pavilion. *Johnston.*

Sabine Hall, Richmond County. Southeast room; mantel. *Johnston.*

Sabine Hall, Richmond County. Stair arch and order. *Johnston.*

brackets and turned balusters. As is the clerk's enclosure below, the pulpit front is paneled and is further enriched with pilasters. The hexagonal sounding board is bracketed out from a paneled pier fixed to the southeast angle of the crossing walls. The soffit of the sounding board is sheathed with walnut and inlaid with pine. Around the edge is a full entablature, and the top is formed of an ogee dome with a finial. The south transept gallery is supported on tall, slender, fluted posts, and is simply enclosed by a paneled front. It is reached by a fine stair with richly-turned balusters.

Presumably presenting today a picture not much different than it did when newly finished in 1732, Christ Church is a remarkable survival of the eighteenth century. There is probably no other building in the state which possesses not only its architectural form unchanged but also its original color and furnishings. The high, white, vaulted interior, with its dark furniture and tall, arched, walnut sashes, is an object lesson in Georgian design in Colonial Virginia. The church is a monument to Robert Carter, who built it from his private funds, and who lies beneath his superb marble tomb under the chancel wall. The tomb has recently been repaired after lying in fragments for many years, but even mutilated it is one of the finest of the period in Virginia, from which many sumptuous examples remain.

Of the three houses which King Carter is said to have provided for his sons, only Sabine Hall, the home of Landon Carter, still stands. This must have been the next building project after Christ Church, or it may have been erected at the same time, for it is said to have been under construction in 1729. Although it has escaped some of the catastrophes that overtook many of its neighbors, it suffered from alterations in the Classic Revival period.[117] In these, the high Georgian roof was flattened in pitch, the windows resashed, the entrance doors and transoms replaced, and the great north portico added. A low porch across the south front was also constructed, but, however, upon an old terrace, once paved. This was built on a continuous vault the whole length of the house. The limestone paving of the front walk, with diagonal dark Purbeck insets, may have originally paved the terrace. Fortunately, the superb interior woodwork was spared, and it remains almost unchanged from the time it was installed, and is among the finest examples of the period in America.

The exterior of Sabine Hall was originally a simple block with separate brick dependencies,[118] spaced one hundred and sixty-two feet apart as shown on the insurance policy of 1805. The present east wing was shown on the insurance policy as a "covered way, one story high, brick covered with wood 40 by 24 feet," and a kitchen beyond, which had been destroyed before 1929, when the west wing was added and the east one lengthened. This was described as "one story high the walls of brick covered with wood 44 x 22 feet." The foundations were removed in 1929. The two fronts are identical, except for the added porches, and are seven bays in length and two stories high above a low basement. The roof, now a low hip, was probably originally a higher hip similar to that formerly at Carter's Grove, the original mortises in the reused timbers indicating this. Built of brick with stone trim, the house has a narrow pavilion on each long front. These are built entirely of Portland stone with rusticated joints the entire height. At the first floor of each is the entrance door below a flat segmental arch with scrolled keystone. The line of the second floor is marked by a cornice (now replaced in wood) which supports a pedestal running beneath the upper window. In the case of the rear window, the pedestal has been cut through to allow the window to open on the porch roof. The upper windows have frames of moulded stone architraves, interrupted by rusticated blocks. Above the window arches are stone cornices, fully moulded, and enriched with a dentil band.

On either side of the pavilions are three windows on each floor. As at Rosewell, the height of the openings is reduced on the second floor and the glass lights from nine over nine to six over nine. This diminution gives the design vigor, increases the apparent height, and is characteristic of most of the Virginia mansions, though Carter's Grove lacks it.

The masonry trim of the windows, for work of the period in employing lintel heads, is perhaps unique in this country. An example, however, was seen in Shrewsbury. Here, as at Sabine Hall, the stone lintel carries over a foot into the wall at either side of the opening, as does the moulded stone sill, to terminate the rich rubbed-brick dressings of the jamb. The lintels are plain except for a beading around the edge and a raised keystone. The present shutters conceal the brick dressings and change the intent of the design. At the first-floor line is the water table, run in stone with a torus below a scotia. At the second-floor line there is a flat string course of gauged brick laid in Flemish bond. The chimneys, of which there are two in each end wall, have all been rebuilt except the southwest stack, and this still shows the original brick bond. The effect of the exterior, now so changed by the portico and painted walls, must originally have had interesting contrast with the strong vertical of the pavilions and the horizontals of the stone lintels and sills in the brick walls. In the end elevations, the tall void of the staircase windows introduced a different type of vertical accent. These tall windows were flanked with a single typical window on each floor. Under the east window the low door to the stair hall remains, but on the west the exact original condition is hard to establish on account of the abutting wing and alterations.

In plan, Sabine Hall has a vast central hall nearly eighteen feet wide and the whole depth of the building, or about thirty-eight feet long. At each end is a center door with a window on either side, giving the hall

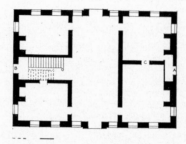

SABINE HALL, Richmond County.

ample light and through ventilation. To the east of the hall, the house is divided into two square rooms, one in either corner, and a cross hall, in which ascends the stair. To the west there are two unequal rooms, the large drawing room to the north connecting with the smaller library to the south. The second floor varies from this plan, for there a narrow hall separates two equal rooms on the west side of the house. The only changes from the original arrangement lie in the space between the western chimneys and the partition between the drawing room and library. This now has a wide double door, dating from the nineteenth-century alterations. The original paneling is somewhat disturbed at this point, but it may be due to superceding the original single door with the double one. A more perplexing problem is the space between the chimneys. This is now inaccessible for examination except from the attic and the second floor, where the walls are furred and plastered. It appears that there was a secondary stair here, reached perhaps from the exterior door. However, this is now gone, but in the attic can be seen a square brick shaft descending to the north of the southwest chimney, the use of which is unknown. It may be that this area was occupied by a small pantry on the first floor, from which ascended a narrow service stair. A pantry of about the same size and in the same location can be seen at Westover. At the very similar Judges' Lodging in Shrewsbury, a service-stair hall occurred in the same location as the little west hall on the second floor of Sabine Hall. The creation of a large drawing room in the first floor could have eliminated this feature except for the utilization of the space between the chimneys, where a "ship's stair" could have been contrived.

Most of the rooms of the first floor, in addition to the second-floor hall, have full paneling detailed with the rich "bisection" panel mould. The panel arrangement is typical throughout the house, the panels of the dado corresponding to those in the tall field above. Both the base and the chair rail are moulded, the latter being of the balustrade type common to the Wren period. There are variations in the cornice, which in the hall is after the style of many of Wren's, with a conventional crown mould and fascia being supported by a large cove springing from a necking, exactly as in the northeast room at Cound. This form of bed mould was often used in work of the Queen Anne period in England, but is very rare in America. Here it is used with a conventional crown mould, which, however, in the other rooms is combined with the usual double-bed mould. The paneling in the hall is very effective, the long west wall displaying a superb range of panels unbroken for its whole length, except at the ends where the doors to the rooms beyond occur. On the east side, the wall is broken in the center by a broad elliptical arch to the stair hall. This is framed by Doric pilasters on pedestals, and these carry a full entablature with the cushion frieze found characteristically in the buildings of this group. It is in the pedestals here that the cap with a cove wash is seen. This, the cap, and the base (now incomplete) all have the same profiles as those in the Christ Church doorway and reredos, the former in stone. A curious feature common to both wood mouldings is the projecting filet under the undercut cyma of the cap, and the bead run on the top edge of the fascia. The impost moulds are adapted from Plate XIV of *Palladio Londinensis* and have the same ogee fascia seen in the stonework of the arched windows at Christ Church. Another familiar motive is the fluted keystone with moulded cap that appears in wood on the stair arch at Sabine Hall, and over the windows in stone at Rosewell. Over the four interior doors in the hall are entablatures, but from the manner in which they are applied over the panels, it would seem they are not original, though old. It is difficult always to identify the design of the doors themselves, for in Salmon's book are several panel arrangements similar to those customarily used in Virginia. These include the ordinary six-panel arrangement, which is used in Sabine Hall. The interior treatment of the windows throughout the house includes paneled reveals and window seats.

The great drawing room has, in addition to the usual wall paneling, a fine mantel treatment with the fireplace flanked by full-height fluted Doric pilasters with entiasis. Over the mantel a cushion frieze and architrave are added to the cornice to form an entablature. The overmantel area is filled with a narrow panel below a broad one. Unfortunately, the place of the original mantel is taken by one of the period of the altera-

Sabine Hall. Stair arch, central hall. *HABS.*   Sabine Hall. Detail of the stairway. *HABS.*

Sabine Hall, Richmond County. West wall of west room showing later paneling at the left, and the original paneling, with Doric pilasters, in the drawing room beyond. *Johnston.*

tions when all the mantels were replaced. In the library as well, the paneling of the west end of the room is also of this period, but the reason for the replacement is unknown.

Probably at this time the southeast room lost its paneling, but recently the room has been refinished and an old stone mantel, original with the house, set in place. This and its mate (now disused) are particularly interesting as examples of baroque design of the period. They are of red-brown sandstone and consist of plain broad piers and paneled lintels cut on the soffit to scrolled arched forms. The keystones are carved with a grotesque mask. It may be noted that the pilasters of one mantel and the lintel of the other were used in the rebuilding because of fractures in each complete assembly of the old pieces. The only details to relate the pieces are the chamfers on the outside of the pilasters, and these continued up and across the end of the lintel. Toward the fireplace opening is another chamfer which continued around the scrolled soffit of the lintel. These varied on each mantel and the variation can be seen in the rebuilt pieces. This brown-stone, certainly imported, is infrequently found in early Virginia buildings and is very much like the Wallasey stone in current use in England.

The stair at Sabine Hall is one of the most refined and beautifully finished of its period in Virginia. It ascends against the south wall of the cross hall, and returns against the north wall in an equal flight. The walnut balusters are almost identical with those at Rosewell, spiraled above vase turnings, but are considerably lighter and are counterparts of those at Tuckahoe and Westover. They support a moulded handrail, which terminates in a shallow half-turn above a fluted newel. It should be noted that no minor posts were used. This was a step in the progress of eighteenth-century stair design which aimed at suppressing the intersecting angles of the posts and straight rails at the landings, and at the smoothing of the balustrade to a continuous flowing feature.

The step ends are simple scrolled consoles, but originally instead of being received against a string piece were carried back to the wall in an open scrolled soffit. This device was used in England in the late seventeenth and early eighteenth centuries. One at Sir John St. Barbe's house was noted by Celia Fiennes who wrote: "Then the great hall is divided in halfe by the Staircase, wch hangs on its own work...on the Side they are of oake, the rails and Banisters are varnished." [119] Examples are found in this country, that at Shirley being perhaps the only other example in Virginia. The construction of these stairs is puzzling: at Shirley the steps must be supported by iron straps, since they are freestanding, but at Sabine Hall they may be cantilevered or bracketed from the cross walls, as a stair of this type is at the Chase house (1775) in

Annapolis. In the latter case the steps seem to be hewn out of solid baulks of wood, one end of which was built in the wall. Warping of the members indicates this construction.

The lofty stair well at Sabine Hall is paneled its complete height, and in the east wall appears the great landing window. In the upper main hall the panels were removed in the nineteenth century, but the styles and rails were left and the fields plastered; so the effect is much the same. The attic still retains the original roof framing, even though the room pitch has been changed.

Sabine Hall is situated on the north ridge of the Rappahannock Valley facing toward the river some miles away to the southwest. The sloping ground south of the house has a broad terraced parterre which still possesses its old geometrical layout of walks and flower beds. An enormous boxwood hedge to the east was once dwarf edging of a cross walk. This well-tended garden and the great trees make an incomparable setting for the house, which has descended for over two hundred years in the family of the builder, many of whose possessions are still preserved within it.

In contrast to the completeness of Sabine Hall, Nomini Hall, in Westmoreland County, the home of Robert (Councillor) Carter is only a memory. All that remains at the site is a magnificent avenue of tulip poplars, broken and knarled after the storms of over one hundred and seventy years. Tumbled bricks in the hollow of the cellar show where the house stood. Fortunately, unlike other great houses that have disappeared without a trace, there are many references to Nomini Hall in Councillor Carter's papers as well as in the diary of Philip Fithian (1747-76), tutor to the Carter children. There is as well a sketch by E. Maund, perhaps drawn from memory after the fire of October, 1850. Although the evidence is far from definitive, it is still enough to allow a reconstruction of a general picture of the house, which was certainly one of the most important of its period.

The date of its construction has not been authenticated, but it is usually placed at 1730, which makes it contemporaneous with Christ Church and Sabine Hall. It was built for Robert Carter, son of the "King," and father of the Councillor.[120] The latter inherited the place while he was yet a child, and his minority was largely spent in his stepfather's house, Warner Hall, in Gloucester County. It was not until his marriage in 1754 that Nomini Hall finally became his residence. From then until 1761, when he closed the house and took up his residence in Williamsburg, Nomini Hall was his home and administrative center of his vast estate. During the ten years of his political activities, Westmoreland County saw little of the family, but in 1771 they returned, and the

NOMINI HALL, Westmoreland County. Built c. 1730; burned 1850; drawing by E. Maund. Except for glazing this agrees in general with description of Fithian, the diarist. *Louis Morton.*

NOMINI HALL, Westmoreland County. A perspective from the northwest, based upon Maund's view and corrected with Fithian's comprehensive description. The exact roof form and locations of the chimneys are doubtful. *Perspective, author; rendering, R. E. Collins.*

NOMINI HALL, Westmoreland County. A restored bird's-eye view from the southeast showing avenue, great house, and subsidiary buildings. *Perspective, author; rendering, Collins.*

WESTOVER, Charles City County. An aerial photograph of the mansion, its elipse of tulip poplars fronting the James River, and its garden where William Byrd II is buried. *Dementi.*

great days of the house began. It was probably at this time that Councillor Carter made the substantial alterations to the house which are referred to in his accounts and journal. The old sketch of Nomini Hall is preserved in the house now on the site. This shows a large rectangular building with a hipped roof and a number of chimneys. The inaccuracies of the drawing make it difficult to locate each stack precisely or to be entirely sure of the full roof form. The view shows the south, or garden front, with four openings on each floor. There are two doors in the center, flanked by a Palladian window on either side (which Carter called Venetian windows on April 22, 1791),[121] and above are four equal windows. On the east side is a center door with a single window on either side and three above. The window glazing is not accurately shown, but the three doors are indicated with glazed lights above diagonal crossed panels. A "handsome jutt" of three columns that Fithian spoke of must have been removed before the time of the sketch. To supplement Maund's drawing there is a sketch of the house on a survey, dated after the fire, which shows a hipped roof with two ridge chimneys.

Fithian's description is extraordinarily detailed and is as follows: [122]

"This House is built with Brick, but the bricks have been covered with strong lime Mortar; so that the building is now perfectly white; It is 76 Ft. long from East to West & 44 wide from North to South 2 Stories high; the Pitch of the lower story 17 Ft. & the upper Story 12— It has 5 Stacks of Chimneys tho' 2 of these serve only for ornaments.

"There is a beautiful Jutt on the South side, 18 ft. long & 8 Feet deep from the wall, which is supported by 3 tall pillars—On the South side or front in the upper story are 4 Windows, each having 24 Lights of Glass. In the lower story are 2 Windows each having 42 Lights of Glass & 2 Doors each having 16 Lights—At the East end the upper story has 3 Windows each with 18 Lights & below, 2 Windows both with 18 Lights & a Door with 9.

"The North side I think is the most beautiful of all; In the upper Story is a Row of 7 Windows with 18 Lights apiece; & below 6 windows with like number of lights; besides a large Portico in the middle...At the west end are no Windows—The Number of Lights in all is 549—. There are 4 Rooms on a Floor, disposed of in the following manner. Below is a dining Room where we usually sit; the second is a dining Room for the Children; the third is Mr. Carters study; & the fourth is a Ball-Room 30 Feet long—Above stairs, one Room is for Mr. & Mrs. Carter; the second for the young Ladies; & the other 2 for occasional Company. As this House is large & stands on a high piece of Land, I have seen it at distance of six miles.

"At equal Distances from each corner of this Building stand 4 other considerable Houses which I shall ... describe. First, at the North East & at 100 yards Distance stands the School House. At the North-West Corner & at the same Distance stands the stable; At the South-West Corner & at the same Distance stands the Coach-House; and lastly, at the South-East corner & at an equal distance stands the Wash-House. These 4 Houses are the corner of a Square of which the Great-House is the Center—First the School-House is 45 feet long, from East to West, & 27 feet from North to South; It has 5 well finished, convenient Rooms, 3 below stairs & 2 above; It is built with Brick a Story & a half high with Dormant Windows; In each Room is a fire; In the large Room below-Stairs we keep our School; the other 2 Rooms below which are smaller are allowed to Mr. Randolph the Clerk; The Room above the School-Room Ben and I live in; & the other Room above Stairs belongs to Harry & Bob. Five of us live in this House with great Neatness & convenience; each one has a Bed to himself—

"And we are call'd by the Bell to the Great-House to Breakfast etc— The Wash-House is built in the same form, and is of the same Size of the School-House—From the front yard of the Great-House, to the Wash-House is a curious Terrace, covered finely with Green turf, & about 5 foot high with a slope of 8 feet, which appears exceeding well to persons coming to the front of the house—This Terrace is produced along the Front of the House, and ends by the Kitchen; but before the Front Doors is a broad flight of steps of the same height, & slope of the Terrace.

"The Stable & Coach-House are of the same Length & Breadth as the School & Wash-House, only they are higher pitched to be convenient for holding Hay & Fodder.

"Due East of the Great-House are 2 Rows of tall, flourishing, beautiful Poplars, beginning on a Line drawn from the School to the Wash-House; these Rows are something wider than the House, & are about 300 yards Long, at the Eastermost end of which is the great Road leading through Westmoreland to Richmond. These Rows of Poplars form an extremely pleasant avenue, & at the Road, through them, the House appears most romantic, at the sametime that it does truly elegant—The Area of the Triangle made by the Wash-House, Stable & School-House is perfectly levil, & designed for a bowling-Green, laid out in rectangular Walks which are paved with Brick, & covered over with burnt Oyster-Shells—In the other Triangle, made by the Wash-House, Stable & Coach-House is the kitchen, a well built House, as large as the School-House; Bake-House; Dairy; Store-House & several other small Houses; all which stand due West, & at a small distance from the Great House, & form a little handsome Street. These Buildings stand about a quarter of a Mile from a Fork from the River Nomini, one Branch of which runs on the East of us, on which are two mills; one of them belongs to Mr. Tuberville the other to Mr. Washington, both within a mile—another branch of the River runs on the West of us, on which and at a small distance above the House stands Mr. Carters Merchants Mill, which I have in other places described; to go to the mill from the House, we descend I imagine along an 100 Feet; the Dam is so broad that 2 carriages may pass conveniently on it; & the Pond from 12 to 18 Feet water—at the fork Mr. Carter has a Granary where he lands his Wheat for the mill, Iron for the Works, etc—"

A comparison of Fithian's text with the Maund sketch bears out the latter in almost every way. It shows that the fenestration was unchanged from 1772 to 1850, and that there were two doors on the south front and one on the east, and that they were glazed. Fithian's counting of the lights of the windows shows the sketch was inaccurate as to the number in each sash. Instead of six over six light sash (unless they were changed in the meantime), the normal lower and upper windows had nine over nine sashes. This applied to the main, or north, front which Fithian describes as having seven openings in the length of the structure, with a portico in the center which would give an elevation strikingly like Sabine Hall, except for the stone trim.

A few notes on the house by Dr. Beale of Westmoreland County give additional information concerning the plan. He says that there were cellar vaults under the entire house, that the ball room was in the northwest corner, and that there was a secret stair to the attic. In the latter he says there was a large unfinished room and on the roof an observatory.

Incomplete as are both Fithian's and Beale's descriptions and Maund's drawing, they provide enough information to relate Nomini Hall to other Virginia houses that themselves can explain these documents. These are Westover (c.1730), Charles City County; and Nelson House (c.1740) at Yorktown; Wilton, Henrico County (1753); and Elsing Green, King William County (1758). The plans of these mansions, when related to the Nomini Hall evidence, show an extraordinary kinship between the five buildings. In the surviving houses the familiar four-room-and-central-hall plan is varied by the halls' being set considerably off-center. This produces two smaller rooms on one side of the hall and two larger on the other. One of the latter at Nomini Hall would be the thirty-foot ball room to which Fithian referred, comparable to the drawing room at Westover or the dining room at Nelson House. Except for these houses cited, this plan does not seem to occur in any other major Virginia dwelling of the period but it did in an English building, Queensferry House in London, illustrated in Leoni's *Designs for Buildings*, published in 1726. The off-center hall was wide enough to embrace, in addition to the entrance door, one of the three windows flanking it. The long rooms, therefore, were lighted by ranges of three windows, but the short ones had only a pair.

The main variations in plan between Westover and Nelson House are in the fenestration and location of the chimneys. In the case of the former building there are two matching façades of seven bays, and two pairs of end chimneys; in the latter house there is a river front of five bays, a land front of four, and a pair of chimneys on the ridge.

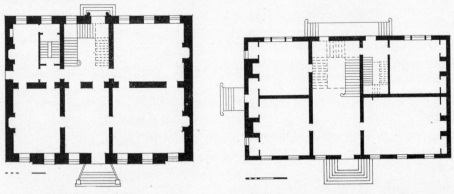

QUEENSFERRY HOUSE, London.   NOMINI HALL, Westmoreland County.
NOMINI Prototype.   Conjectural Restoration.

It was apparently a combination of the two that occurred at Nomini Hall. Both the drawing and Fithian's description specify four windows for the south front, and Fithian enumerates seven openings on the north, or river front. One main elevation would therefore have the fenestration of Nelson House and the other that of Westover. The plan, similar in its main elements to both, apparently had its hall off-center toward the east. This gave two smaller rooms toward the approach (the east end was on axis with the drive), with a service entrance, lobby, or pantry between and facing east, and two large rooms on the south side. Recalling the Nelson House plan, which has the inside end of one of the larger rooms partitioned off for a service stair, and Beale's reference to a stair from attic to cellar, such a stair might be located in the east end of the southwest room. This would explain why Fithian spoke of only one thirty-foot room, not two, which would have been the case if the present Westover arrangement of two, almost equal, large rooms prevailed. With this disposition of the plan, the ball room would have been in the northwest corner, as Beale recalled, perhaps Councillor Carter's study across the hall in the northeast corner, and the family dining room in the southeast, accessible to the front room and outside kitchen. The children's dining room probably was located in the southwest corner, accessible to the exterior through the service stair door, as well as to the second floor without using the main stair.

In this plan there could have been two ridge chimneys as at Nelson House or four end chimneys as at Westover, but there is no dependable evidence on this point. The Maund drawing shows several, but not clearly, and apparently after Councillor Carter had added a chimney or chimneys to produce the five which Fithian spoke of, an impossible number for the original design. Fithian described two as for ornament only, and it may be assumed that these were two originals which were abandoned because of their age and the resulting fire risk, after the family reoccupied the house in 1771.

The form of the roof is doubtful, for it is shown in an eccentric way on the Maund drawing, and there is no other documentary evidence except Beale's statement that it had an observatory. This in itself does not mean much, for it may have been merely a wood platform built on the apex of the roof, as seen in the Civil War painting of Westover,[123] or it might have been a real deck, as at Rosewell. The alterations to the Sabine Hall roof prevent that being cited as evidence, and it is only an assumption, based on the precedent of Westover, Wilton, and Elsing Green, that the original roof of Nomini Hall was hipped. It is clear that it had no dormers, as Westover did, for Maund showed none, and Beale referred to a large unfinished room in the attic.

The evidence, even if somewhat circumstantial, relates Nomini Hall definitely to two buildings in the group under discussion and also to *Palladio Londinensis*. This is in the glazed doors appearing on the north and east elevations. These not only relate to the doors in Plate XXV with the upper part glazed in twelve lights but also to Plate XXIII with the lower section paneled in diagonal crossed panels. Glazed exterior doors are practically unknown at this period either in England or the Colonies, so their use at Nomini Hall, and their portrayal in Salmon's book, are significant. The sketch does not show the number of lights, but this information is supplied by Fithian, who also gives those of the window sashes. It will be noted that he gave the typical lower windows, as well as the upper, eighteen lights. The lower south windows are described as having forty-two, and the four windows above, twenty-four lights. These latter were probably not taller than their mates of eighteen lights on the other elevations, but they were one row of lights wider. The windows were probably the characteristic type of the period with wide muntins and ten by twelve glass.

The large windows on the south elevation were features shown by Maund and referred to by both Councillor Carter himself and Fithian.

These were of the so-called Palladian (or Venetian) type with center arched windows flanked by narrow, square-headed openings. Whether they were original or part of the alterations of the early seventies is a question, but there is such a window shown on Plate XXVIII in *Palladio Londinensis*. If they can be authenticated as of about 1730, they might be the earliest example of this window type in American architecture. The rooms they lighted must have been very effective with the Palladian window framed in a paneled wall, at right angles, or opposite fine pilastered chimneypieces. Of the ·detail of the interior of the house no clue seems to remain, except that in 1775 Councillor Carter noted: "Mr. Collis, Joiner, began to make the Balusters & Rails of black Walnut Stair Case in my dwelling House," [124] but why the original balustrade was changed we are not informed. From the evidence of the other houses of the group we can assume that Nomini Hall was completely paneled, with some pilastered wall treatments and stone or marble mantels. A marble floor may have been used, for Beale noted that the whole cellar of the house was vaulted.

It would be interesting to know just what alterations Carter made in the house. That he added the "handsome jutt" with three columns on the south front which Fithian referred to is almost a certainty, and it must have been a curious feature with its column on axis with the center of the house. It may have been one or two stories high, but the inference is that it reached to the main cornice. The portico, on the north front, of which Fithian spoke, might actually have been a classic portico with columns and pediment, or this term, loosely used by a layman, might have referred to doorways like Rosewell's or to a narrow pavilion such as those at Sabine Hall, which were simply applied entrance motives. If it were the latter it might be original, but if it were a real portico it must have been an addition, since their first known use in this country dates from the years just after the Revolution. However enthusiastic Fithian may have been over the beauties of the house, the changes made, presumably after 1771, must have been detrimental to the architectural design. In its pristine state Nomini Hall must have been one of the finest mansions of its period in Virginia, as it was also one of the largest. It must have deteriorated rapidly after Councillor Carter left it to live in Baltimore in 1791. After his death the division of the estate left the home place too small to maintain properly. However, it never passed from the family, and the lands now remain with a descendant. The history of the great house came to an end in October, 1850, when it burned, and today only broken fragments of brick and stone in the depression of the basement show where the mansion stood.

Although the plan and elevations of Nomini Hall have to be deduced

WESTOVER, Charles City County. Range of stone piers and finials of clairvoyée. *Johnston.*

WESTOVER, Charles City County. Detailed view of the mansion from the northwest. *Johnston.*

from scanty documentary evidence, its superb contemporary, Westover, remains little changed from the date of its completion. In its setting of fine old trees and green lawns that reach to the James River, Westover can have no peer as a picture of its style. Approached on the land side it stands at the end of a vista screened from the meadow in front by a wrought-iron clairvoyée, with piers supporting cut-stone finials. The house is reached through a fine pair of wrought-iron gates beneath a scrolled and initialled overthrow. These are hung upon heroic piers with cut-stone caps and bases, and large finials in the form of birds as a rebus for the owner's name. No such entrance gates apparently exist elsewhere in America, though they are familiar in English estates of the period. The Westover screen is singularly unchanged except for the modern wrought-iron infill of the flanking bays, and the covering of the piers with a cement coating. At the ends of the river walk are two companion gates having brick piers with stone caps and finials, though the latter are in part restorations. Here the gates have overthrows with the Byrd arms in the form of cast ornaments. At present, the question of the period of the ironwork is undecided, but it is a temptation to believe it was of these gates that William Byrd II was writing in his diary on May 17, 1711.[125] He recorded: "I took a walk to see Mr. G-r-l put up the gates but was driven in again by the rain." And: "In the afternoon it rained very hard so that my people could not proceed to put up the gates." On the previous day: "Mr. G-r-l went about hanging the gates and I took a walk to him."

A pair of gates at Grove Hall, Woodford, in London are almost exactly similar in design,[126] though the iron is heavier. The Westover gates are unquestionably the work of a London smith, and were probably made in the shop of Thomas Robinson; otherwise, by a man trained by Robinson. The designs of both the large and small Westover gates not only strongly partake of the character of Robinson's work, but their detail is almost entirely derived from it. The London origin is not surprising, since the normal source of imported worked materials to Byrd would be London. Indeed he may have known Robinson, who was the most prominent smith in London, and who had a shop at Hyde Park Corner.

Robinson's earliest known work is the beautiful railing, completed in 1697, in the Morning Chapel of St. Paul's Cathedral. He created a number of great clairvoyées in the style of that at Westover, some of monumental scale, such as those at New College, Oxford, and formerly at Carshalton, Surrey, respectively, 1711 and 1712. Several beautiful small-scale screens and gates by him also survive, and their resemblance to the Westover ironwork is more marked. Robinson was a native English smith, one of that great number which produced the superb array

WESTOVER. The north entrance gate, probably hung 1711. *Johnston.*

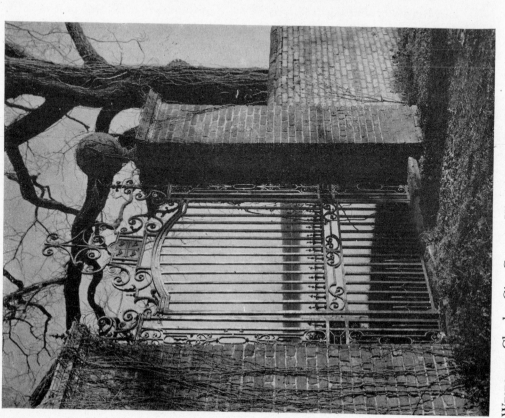

WESTOVER, Charles City County. West gate, one of two. *Author.*

of ironwork between 1700 and 1750. His style, however, was influenced by French precedent through Jean Tijou, apparently a Huguenot refugee. Tijou came to England with William and Mary in 1689 and immediately was set to work at Hampton Court Palace and St. Paul's. His most elaborate ironwork was heavy and overburdened with ornament, but his simpler things had great beauty. Robinson modeled his manner on the latter type of Tijou's work and produced a style of his own that is lithe and crisp with only occasional spots of well placed ornament. He has been called "the creator of the English style of smithing."

Although the Woodford gate has not been attributed to him, it has so much in common with his known works that there seems reason to consider it his product. It is not only an extraordinary repetition of the Westover main gate, but bears a design closely related to that of his gates at Hall Place, Bexley, Kent. This latter, and his known gates in Cheyne Walk, London, are the derivatives of the river gates at Westover.

The entrance gates at Westover are of the greatest simplicity and are formed of closely spaced verticals with arrow-pointed dog-bars at the bottom and a single lock rail topped by scrolled guard-bars. Each leaf of the gate is five feet wide and ten feet high. The gates are hung from masonry piers beneath a richly worked overthrow. Like the gates at Woodford, Carshalton, and Bexley, there is a horizontal motive of closely-spaced parallel bars with scrolls and ovolo at the gate-head. The overthrow itself is pyramidal in form, convolutions of scrollwork framing William Byrd's cypher and rising with stepped finials to a central motive enriched with acanthus leaves. There are no deviations of any importance between the Woodford and Westover overthrows except in the form of scrolls in the apex, and in the use of a coat of arms instead of a cypher in the English example. A departure from the common plan of the two is the triple division of the gate at Woodford, only the central panel being active, and this has a segmental head. Both the Westover and Woodford gates are hung from tall rectangular piers and have heraldic finials.

The entrance gates at Westover are unique in this country, but they are only the central motive of a screen that extends in thirteen bays across the entire forecourt. This screen is composed of a series of low masonry piers, now plastered, with cut stone caps and finials. Between them are iron railings, of recent installation, replacing wood rails. These latter, which show in old photographs,[127] were obviously not original, and whether the wrought-iron railings for which they were designed were ever set in place is unknown. The carved stone finials are the finest group in the country and were undoubtedly imported from England. They possess a variety of designs of acorn and vase types, all richly carved, on moulded bases and plinths. A clairvoyée such as this is rare even in England, where great numbers disappeared with the coming of the naturalistic school of landscape design. The richness of the stonework and the absence of a dwarf wall beneath both piers and railing is unusual in English examples. Forecourt screens were fashionable during the Restoration period, but most examples date from the period of 1710-20.

The arching of the gate-head at Woodford is followed in the Westover river gates, which are hung between narrow fixed panels next the gate piers, and beneath fine scrolled overthrows. The detail of this, as well as the finials of the fixed panels, is taken directly from the Bexley gate, as is also the scrolled lock rail. The overthrow is modified from the side finials at Bexley, and the Westover side finials form the Bexley central finials. All of these are G scrolls with leaf enrichments, leafed and turned top-knots. At Westover the fixed panels below the lock-rail are identical with those at Number 4, Cheyne Walk, and those above are an elaboration of this in the style of the Bexley gate.

The Westover gates are an amazing survival of a feature no longer possessed by any other American country house. In their dark modern paint they present exquisite silhouette patterns, but painted blue or green, as Celia Fiennes described, with gilt finials, they would be superb indeed.

Of the beautiful walled garden, in which stands the builder's monument, Beverley said: "Colonel Bird, in his garden, which is the finest in that country, has a summer-house set round with Indian honey suckles, which all the summer is continually full of sweet flowers, in which [humming-birds] delight exceedingly." [128]

As far as the date of the house is concerned, it probably was built soon after 1729, when Byrd wrote in a letter to a Mr. Spencer [129] in London: "In a year or 2 I intend to set about building a very good house." What the old house was like or exactly where it stood is unknown. If there was an earlier mansion it must have stood at least on the axis of the present one, for the west flanking kitchen building is almost certainly older, and before the Civil War was balanced by another, on the other side. The kitchen may date from the time of Thomas Stegge, Byrd's great-uncle, from whom Westover came to his father William Byrd I. The chimneys belong to walls earlier than the very old ones now standing, which latter could even be those of 1709 which Byrd himself had built. On April 5, 1709,[130] he wrote: "The brickmaker came this evening," and on the 7th: "The men began to work this day to dig for brick." In February, 1711, he referred to putting planks in the brick house, and on June 3, 1712, said: "The stonecutter came from Williamsburg to put up my marble chimney piece." The following day iron cramps were made and the workman "began to work in the library chimney." On the 23d he "found Mr. G-r-l here with the Dutch joiner. I settled accounts with the latter and got the first to put up the glass in the library." The wording of this sounds as if the library were a separate building and may have been one of the flanking buildings. This, or the old main house, must have had quite up-to-date windows, for on February 16, 1709, he wrote: "Mr. Anderson . . . promised to make me some [pulleys] for my windows." This, perhaps next to the Capitol and the Palace in Williamsburg, is the first reference to double-hung sash windows in Virginia. Byrd's marble mantel of 1711 may be the beautiful and unique marble bolection frame of the northwest first-floor room, for this is a late Stuart English piece and could hardly date from 1730 or after. When the new mansion was built this may have been moved to its present location.

To further complicate the dating of Westover as a whole, a notice in the *Virginia Gazette*,[131] copied by John Randolph of Roanoke, says: "On Saturday night last (7th) [January 7, 1748-49] the House of Wm Byrd, Esqr at Westover, Chas-City County took fire & was burned to the ground, with the loss of all the furniture, clothes, plate, liquore." A careful analysis of the interior of Westover almost disproves the report of the fire and establishes the woodwork as being original. If it were burned in 1749 the new interior must have been designed with reference to the same style book, for the influence of *Palladio Londinensis* and Gibbs is obvious. This is possible, but it would seem strange at that date to install a marble bolection fifty years out of style in England. The woodwork has the character of Sabine Hall and its period rather than Carter's Grove of 1753. The naïveté of the triangular panels, simulating pediments in the drawing room, and the top-heavy overmantel in the music room are more of 1730 than the middle of the century. There may have been a minor fire, or a fire in a minor building, but the architectural evidence indicates that the house did not burn in 1749.

The two façades of Westover, with their seven bays, recall Sabine Hall, but the all-brick quality of the wall areas and the strong focal points of the two superb stone doorways create a very different impression. This is especially true since Westover retains its vast steep hipped roof, which has a range of dormer windows in it. The doorways are a strong link with the Carter group, for they are executed with extraordinary fidelity from Plates XXV and XXVI in Salmon's book. On the land, or north front, the doorway is framed by beautifully proportioned and detailed Corinthian pilasters supporting a segmental pediment, and on the river front by the less graceful Composite order supporting a broken ogee pediment with a pineapple finial. The execution of every detail is so competently

WESTOVER, Charles City County. A detail photograph of the south door and its stone frame, and the plates from *Palladio Londinensis* that supplied designs for this and the north door. The wood door is not original, and once the full Salmon design may have obtained. *Johnston*.

WESTOVER, Charles City County. Left Wing may date from 1709 or earlier. *Metropolitan Eng.*

WESTOVER, Charles City County. South front. The tulip poplars were there in 1787. *Johnston.*

done that it may be the doorways were imported already worked from England. However, increasing knowledge of Virginia building makes it clear that most of the work was done at the site, the workmen themselves being brought over from England for the purpose. The exact adherence to the *Palladio Londinensis* plate would indicate this, perhaps, for in London the proprietors of the various shops were capable of making their own designs. The north door is particularly noteworthy for its beauty of detail, the well moulded bases, the fine fluting of the pilasters, and the masterly carving of their cap. The mouldings of the entablature and pediment and the carved modillions are also excellent. Perhaps as an essay in carving the south door is more important, but the graceful and clean-cut design of the former is more appealing. The rich capitals of the pilasters of the south door and the involved carving of the ogee pediment, with its modillions, terminal rosettes, and finial attest the technical skill of the carver.

Both doorways are of Portland stone, which was used for important features throughout the Colonial period in Virginia. The wood frames of the doorways are eighteenth century, but the doors and transoms are later. It seems probable that the openings were originally filled in accordance with Salmon's design which had, in Plate XXVI, the cross diagonal panels below two long and four short panels. Plate XXV had the glazed area above two short panels. The doorways are reached by broad flights of stone steps of pyramidal form.

The windows of Westover are unique in Virginia mansion building for their segmental brick heads. As has been observed, both Rosewell, the Shirley dependencies, and Nelson House have flat arches with segmental soffits, but at Westover true gauged-brick segmental arches are used. The two neighboring courthouses of Charles City and Chesterfield Counties were built with similar window heads. Early small dwellings often had ungauged brick segmental arches, and one medium-sized house, Belvedere, near Fredericksburg (built by the Daingerfields) has rusticated stone segmental heads. The sashes at Westover are partly original and have the top lights cut to conform to the arched head.

Nine over nine light sash was used with a smaller glass size in the second floor to give the characteristic diminution of the window openings. The dormers, which have hipped roofs with dentilled cornices, have sashes with the same number of lights, but of yet a smaller glass size. Some of the original broad-muntined sashes remain.

The brickwork of the walls is laid in Flemish bond with narrow rubbed dressings at the window joints and corners. The water table is double moulded in gauged brick, and the belt course at the second-floor line is an unmoulded gauged band laid in Flemish bond. Unfortunately, the walls were once painted red and the belt courses white. Remains of the paint still affect the appearance of the elevations, as do the metal caps of the pairs of tall end-chimneys.

One of the distinguished features of the exterior is the superb graduated slate roof which has been in place since the first photographs of the house were taken. Some claim has been made that this is slate from the Buckingham County quarries, up the James River. However, the soft variegated greys of the slates and the careful graduation of the courses, both uncharacteristic of Virginia slate, make it seem sure that this actually is Welsh. Slate such as this was ordered and received in Williamsburg for roofing the Palace in 1709.[132] Furthermore, if the roof is indeed original, it could not be of Buckingham slate, for those quarries were not opened until about 1800.

As has been observed, the plan of Westover shows the same interesting departure from the standard four-room-and-central-hall plan as noted in Leoni's Queensferry House in London, at Nomini Hall, Nelson House, Wilton, and Elsing Green. Although the entrance is actually in the center of the building, the hall itself is slightly off-center. The width of the hall includes the door and the window on one side of it; therefore, the rooms on the east side of the hall have three windows in their long exterior walls, and those to the west only two. This plan gives two pairs of rooms of unequal size, which provides for a greater variety of uses than does the usual four-equal-room plan. However, at Westover the two rooms to the west were apparently considered too small, and the partition between them was taken out in the alterations (c.1900), though on the second floor the old plan (in which there is a narrow longitudinal corridor) survives. It is interesting to note that the position of the chimneys parallels those of Sabine Hall, Wilton, and Elsing Green.

The hall is paneled and has a moulded chair rail and a full cornice. On the west wall the stair ascends to the north with a long initial run, then turns on a short cross-run and returns toward the south. The balustrade and stringer is all of mahogany, having a moulded handrail, scrolled at the newel, turned and spiraled balusters, as at Sabine Hall, and brackets carved with the tight scrolls and leafage. This stair and that of Shirley are the only two major stairs that ascend to the third floor, and, together with the Governor's Palace, are the only mansions with habitable attics.

Though the stair and wall paneling are fine, they are paralleled in other houses, but the superb enriched plaster ceiling is unique and is an outstanding example of its period. It is not as large as that of the drawing room, but it is more complete, and gives more the air of having been

WESTOVER, Charles City County. Balustrade. *Metropolitan Eng.*

WESTOVER, Charles City County. Stairway and ceiling. *Johnston.*

WESTOVER, Charles City County. Ornament of drawing room ceiling, looking east. *Author.*

Gibbs's derivative of drawing room mantel.

WESTOVER. Drawing room mantel. *Old photo.*

assembled as originally designed. In the eighteenth century, as today, plaster enrichments were often cast, then set in the ceiling and plastered up to, rather than being modelled in place. Washington ordered papier-mâché ornaments for a ceiling at Mount Vernon in 1757,[133] and the Westover ornaments were probably ordered in the same way.

In style the ceiling follows the French Rococo, popular in England in the mid-Georgian period. It is bordered by a rod-and-ribbon band which at the corners and at the center of each side is interrupted by large scrolled ornaments with leafage, masks, and vases. Enclosed by the border is a large center panel, edged by reverse curve scrolls, frilled with leaves and flowers, in the full Rococo style. Within this panel are four fine swags of fruit and flowers, but they are applied without any relation to the rest of the composition, and in spite of their beautiful modelling are detrimental to the general effect.

The most imposing room in the house is the great drawing room in the southeast corner of the building. Like all the first-floor rooms it is paneled to the ceiling, but it is further enriched by the doorways' being set off by Doric pilasters whose ogee caps are identical in profile with the Corinthian impost on Plate XIV of *Palladio Londinensis* and recall those of Christ Church. A curious treatment already noted, devised for the overdoors to simulate a pediment, is a large triangular panel, with two small filler panels above. This arrangement was probably inspired by the filler panels above the great marble mantelpiece. This other feature, projected on the chimney breast, is the center of interest in the room. It is probably the most monumental marble mantel of the period in the country, though it gives a curious feeling of incompleteness and can hardly be called beautiful. Before the alterations of about 1900 it composed a black marble overmantel field evidently jointed for a missing panel. This was above a fully moulded and carved architrave fireplace facing, with crossettes. The design was capped by a marble pediment supported on consoles. To compensate for the missing feature a mirror, framed in a carved marble border beneath a swag of fruit and flowers, has been inserted. The original design seems to be derived from Gibbs's *Book of Architecture*, in which Plate LXXI bears a remarkable resemblance to the Westover mantel, the only variations being the omission of pediment figures, pendants from the brackets, and the curve on the bottom of the architrave. This fine room does not depend on the mantel for its effect, which is obtained by the design of the paneling and by the stately range of tall windows in the south wall. These latter have window seats, paneled jambs, and moulded frames which, as in the drawing room at Sabine Hall, are tied to the cornice by cushion friezes.

The elaboration of the walls is echoed in the plasterwork of the ceiling.

WESTOVER. Drawing room, with west doorway. *Metropolitan Eng.*

WESTOVER. The drawing room, showing the south windows. *Author.*

WESTOVER. East wall and mantel of music room. *Metropolitan Eng.*

WESTOVER. Dining room, showing the marble bolection. *Author.*

This is covered with a pattern of baroque scrolls and leafage. Here while the individual pieces are good in detail, they do not seem to be correctly assembled, perhaps being intended for a smaller room, as the pattern seems broken to extend it. There is a double border of rod-and-ribbon ornament which turns the corners by intersecting single, large, baroque scrolls. At the center of each side of the ceiling is a motive of double C scrolls at the four center points and crossed branches of scrolled leaves at each corner. There are swags of fruit and flowers connecting them, and rococo motives as pendants from the corner·pieces. So far, the design is coherent and well executed, but the center field is powdered with scrolls, drops, and swags arranged as radii from the center, but disconnected and certainly not as disposed by the designer. In the center is a small six-pointed star of acanthus leaves.

The music room, to the north, suffers from its being slightly narrower than the drawing room, the resulting proportions being narrow and tall. Instead of minimizing this effect by suppressing the chimney breast, it was accented with vigorous overmantel pilasters, around the caps of which the main cornice was broken. The effect is not very good, though it is an interesting effort and somewhat reminiscent of the pilastered mantel at Tettington (1717; burned c.1928). This latter was apparently inspired by a plate in Joseph Moxon's *Mechanick Exercises,* published in London in 1703.[134] The overmantel is set on a marble mantel in the form of an architrave fireplace frame with crossettes at the head.

The smaller rooms (now thrown together) to the west are simply paneled, and between the chimneys there is a little entry which formed a vestibule for the kitchen door and a pantry for the dining room. This feature, either small or large, was indispensable to the Virginia mansion, though most examples have been destroyed by alterations. The mantel of the north chimney is the fine, small-scale, marble, roll-moulding, in grey-veined white marble, already spoken of. This is of the period of William and Mary and is apparently unique in this country. In the Great Hall of the College of William and Mary the restored mantel is in this form, though much larger, and of Ashburton marble, a heavily-fossilized grey English marble. The south chimney has a grey marble facing, channeled, with an arched haunch lintel.

However notable are the three mantels in the lower rooms, the group of four on the second floor are even finer, and together form the finest suite in America. They were probably all London made and brought over by William Byrd II.

At the time of the repairs and extensions of c.1900 the second-floor mantels were removed and new "Salem"-type pieces were inserted in their stead. However, after some criticism of this action, the old ones

WESTOVER, Charles City County. The four fine mantels of the second-floor chambers are undoubtedly of English manufacture. That of the northeast chamber (shown in above view) is a
facsimile in stone of the mantel which stands in the New River Company office in London
(see W. H. Godfrey, *History of Architecture in London* [Batsford, 1911], fig. 213), designed
in the style employed by Wren. The Westover mantel dates from about 1700-1710. *Brostrup.*

WESTOVER, Charles City County. Mantel of the northwest room, wood carved, c. 1730-40 (on previous page); mantels of the southeast and southwest chambers (above, below). These are the finest wood mantels of their period in Virginia (c. 1700-1730), and are richly carved in the style of Wren and Gibbons. These four mantels, removed in 1900 and replaced by modern ones, were reinstalled shortly after that date at instance of Joseph F. Biggs. *Brostrup.*

were replaced and the new ones sold.[135] This accounts for the tradition
that those in place are not the originals.

The mantel in the northeast room is of stone, the others being in wood
and painted. This one stone example, too, is painted, so the identity of
the Portland stone material is somewhat concealed. Around the fireplace
opening is a roll moulding, within a sort of an architrave, of receding,
unmoulded planes. This moulding breaks out into bold crossettes, in
the center of which are carved paterae. The outside edge of the stone
frame is moulded with a diminutive cyma and is also carved. At either
side of the composition are tall consoles, scrolled and feathered with
acanthus, and ornamented with cords and tassels. There is no counterpart of this in any of the fine masonry mantels of Virginia. Neither, however, is there a counterpart of the superb suite of carved wood mantels
in the other rooms.

The simplest of the group is that in the northwest room, and unfortunately this has lost its original marble or stone facing. However, the
wood backband, which is carved with egg and dart and mitred with
acanthus, remains. This frame supports a broad pulvinated frieze,
covered with scrolled foliage, and above is a fully-moulded and carved
cornice shelf. The same general scheme is followed in the southeast
room, where a new marble facing has been inserted. Here the backband
is bolder, but also carved with egg and dart, and has crossettes and superb
carved consoles at the sides. These are as fine as any American examples
and have broad scrolls frilled with baroque shell carving and enriched
with pendants of flowers and leaves. In this case the frieze is bellied and
carved with acanthus leaves, and in the center is a key block ornamented
with a child's head and a festoon and drops. A full cornice shelf also
occurs, with both cymatium and bed mould enriched. In spite of the
fact that these two wood mantels are extraordinary in their elaboration,
that in the southwest room is entirely unprecedented in this country.
It has paneled pilasters hung with high relief carving of flowers and
leaves issuing from scrolled and carved consoles. These support a frieze,
with blocks over the consoles carved with paterae, entirely filled with
full-relief scrolled leafage in the style of Gibbons. The cornice is a variant
of the fine carved examples of the other mantels. Set in the full-height
paneling of these upper rooms, the mantels form an incomparable series
in American architecture and give a finishing touch to the finest mansion
of its period, and the most complete in all its attributes.

A neighbor and contemporary of Westover is Berkeley, built in 1726
by Benjamin Harrison, husband of Anne, daughter of King Carter,
as the date and initials of both in the brickwork tell. It is curious that
two houses so much of the same age and size and of the same materials

could have so different an appearance. Westover gives a real feeling of growing from its low meadow by the river, but Berkeley stands high and a little awkwardly on its eminence overlooking the James River valley. The shorter length of the house, the lack of adjoining wings, and the use of a new roof type all contribute to this result. At the time of the writing of the insurance policy in 1800 there were two brick buildings twenty by forty-five feet on the south side, toward the river, but not those existing, which date from 1840-50.

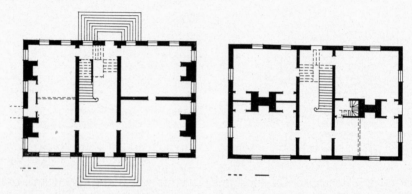

WESTOVER, Charles City County.   BERKELEY, Charles City County.

The mansion is two stories high, five bays in length, with a pediment roof and two tall ridge chimneys. The brick walls are of Flemish bond, the window jambs and corners are treated with narrow rubbed-brick dressings, and the openings with gauged, flat, brick arches. It has a beveled water table and gauged, flat, belt course. The present doorways have broad piers supporting pediments, all in gauged brick, but these are modern, and little of the originals remain. A fragment of a stone cornice in the basement suggests that they were of stone. An unusual feature of the house is the window sash, which, like few other Virginia houses of the period, is four lights wide with twelve over twelve light sash, as in the south second-floor windows of Nomini Hall. The sashes are new, but the openings are such that another arrangement with standard-size glass would be difficult. An old transom with lights of this size remains over the west door.

The use of a heroic pediment roof is extraordinarily significant here as the first of the style in Virginia and as the forerunner of a great company of a later period with and without porticos. It is probable that it was inspired by the roof of Gibbs's church at Derby, illustrated in his *Book of Architecture* on Plate XXV. This is really a reversion to the old gable, not at the time even quite superceded by the hipped roof. It is an interesting attempt to make a traditional and useful form stylish.

Church at Derby by James Gibbs. Perhaps the precedent employed in Virginia pediment roofs.

BERKELEY, Charles City County. Built 1726; first mansion with pedimented gable. *Dementi.*

All that was done was to lower the roof pitch and trim the gable ends with full cornices in an effort to make the building take on the appearance of a classic building. Claremont, a delightful traditional house across the James River, has the ends of a jerkin-head roof trimmed in this way, too, with interesting but unsatisfactory results. The pediment roof was superior in utility to the hip in that it gave useful end rooms in the attic without dormers, and ventilation where it was much needed.

The original plan of Berkeley has been modified by at least one alteration, or perhaps two, but the basement brickwork makes it apparent that the main elements have not been changed. Centering on the house is a hall twelve feet wide, and on either side two large, square rooms. Space for a small stair hall has been taken from that at the northwest corner. This latter change would seem to date from about 1800, when the house was largely retrimmed, but there is no indication as to the location of the earlier stair. From the typical practice of featuring the stair at this period, it may be assumed that the stair was in the central hall and probably ascended on the west wall, for the door to the south room on this side is set close to the exterior wall, in which position it might come under the landing. In the north end of the hall there are two doors on the west wall, one of which was closed by the alterations of about 1800. The closed door (right) would have entered the northwest room about on axis, but the other might have entered the chimney closet, in which a small service stair may have stood. In the longitudinal partition wall between the north and south rooms are the chimneys centering on the north-south axes of these rooms. Thus the house has the familiar center hall, ridge chimney plan of the second half of the eighteenth century. Two of its contemporaries have one of these characteristics in each; Sabine Hall the central axial hall, and Nelson House the two ridge chimneys, but the others have off-center halls and end chimneys. In Wythe House, Carter's Grove, Cleve, and Elsing Green, all after 1750, the characteristics of the Berkeley plan again appear.

The framing, and some fragments of eighteenth-century trim, indicate that Berkeley was altered, rather than rebuilt (which so complete a retrimming might imply) after a fire. In the basement the twelve by eighteen chimney girts and the four by twelve joists remain and seem to belong to the date of the building; and in the space east of the east chimney in the first floor, the floor and some trim also antedate the alteration. This latter condition not only testifies to the fact that the house has not been burned but clarifies the detail of the plan. At present, the two east rooms have arched passages between them on either side of the chimney, but on the old floor referred to can be seen the line of a thin partition on center of the chimney, with a trimmed door opening centered on it. This in itself would indicate a projecting chimney breast in each room, but there are sections of an old dado on the walls of this chimney passage, the chair rails of which are patched with re-entrant mitres at the line of the partition and at the chimney face. It would appear that the chair rail either carried around arched openings (like the later existing ones) or else around the inside of a closet, which also formed a passage. The detail of the paneled dado is unusual, the panel mould being formed by a quarter-round set against a filet, and the bevel of the panel being omitted. This is normally a late eighteenth-century form, but both the chair rail and base are formed with a cyma reversa and bead (in reversed positions, top and bottom), which is usually a very early profile. Only in the kitchen, which is now located behind the stair in the northwest corner, does any other eighteenth-century trim appear on the first floor, and this has much of the unorthodox detail of the east chimney passage. The panel mould becomes a cyma recta, and the panel is flat. The chair rail seems to have been changed, but the window trim is contemporary with the paneled dado and window reveals. For the trim of the openings an unusual architrave is used. The backband is a large quarter-round with a broad filet at the outside edge and a narrow one against the flat of the architrave. The latter is in two sections, broad toward the outside and narrow toward the opening, separated by a vertical break. The profiles seen in the kitchen and east passage reoccur in some of the second-floor woodwork, which is confined to paneled dados, moulded door and window frames, and later mantels. In short, while the elaborate fluted, reeded, and moulded trim of the first floor is certainly of the period of about 1800, that remaining of an earlier period is either an unfamiliar type of the period of the first building in 1726, or it is a replacement of post-Revolutionary date, when most of the profiles may be seen elsewhere. The only finish on the interior that indubitably belongs to the early period are the two fine mottled-grey marble facings of the east fireplaces on the first floor. These trim openings are just under forty-eight inches square, and are chamfered with quarter rounds on their inner face, with mason joints at the lintel. In the basement is a fragment of a large-scale moulded stone cornice showing a large cyma recta above a small cyma reversa. This may have been from a doorway or other such feature.

In the basement the brickwork is largely visible, though some has been plastered over. Only the exterior walls, hall walls, and chimneys seem to be original, all longitudinal walls and the stair partitions being later. All of the early brickwork is laid in English bond, but three brick sizes are used. Large rough brick with wide joints are employed in the chimneys, smaller brick with narrower joints in the walls up to the grade, and smaller above. The east chimney is pierced by narrow north-south passageways, the east one alone being visible and unchanged. This is two feet wide with full headroom, and is spanned by a pointed arch. It opens into the southeast room, but its companion passage opens into the northeast room and is faced over. In the west chimney there are two partly-blocked and plastered half-round passages opening into the north room, and the remains of what may have been a full-width arch in the south room.

It is fortunate that a superb Virginia house of the type and size of Berkeley remains complete with its woodwork. This is Nelson House (recently called York Hall) at Yorktown, probably built by Thomas Nelson in the second quarter of the eighteenth century. The date is unknown, but 1740 is usually accepted.

Nelson House, except for the four-bay south elevation, is almost the counterpart of Berkeley, and possesses a generally superior and more monumental architectural character. It has richer detail such as stone corner quoins, window sills, and keystones, a fine gauged-brick balustrade-type water table (as seen at Rosewell), deep flat window arches with segmental soffits, and a gauged belt course and fine pedimented doorway. Although in general the elements of the façades of Berkeley and Nelson House are the same, the effect of the latter is entirely different from that of the former. This is due to the strong verticals of the corner quoins (which like Cleve are received on pier strips in the basement wall) and the two tall tiers of equal window openings with the more familiar nine over nine light sash. The gauged and moulded all-brick doorway with simple piers and pediment may be, except for Stratford, the earliest of that fine series that includes Carter's Grove, the Treasurer's House in Williamsburg, and several churches, among them Abington and Ware in Gloucester County. Although the north doorway of Nelson House is original, that on the west elevation is modern and existed formerly as an untrimmed opening. The end elevations of the house are the most interesting and demonstrate the futility of trying to make the long elevation of a pedimented house the façade. Manifestly the plan would prevent the pedimented end from being the entrance front. Making the pediment traverse the length of the plan was shown to be undesirable at Belle Farm [136] in Gloucester, where the effect was ungainly in the extreme. It remained for the architect of the beautiful Randolph-Semple House in Williamsburg (c.1765-70) to solve this problem.

NELSON HOUSE, Yorktown. An early pediment-roof mansion. *Brady.*

NELSON HOUSE, Yorktown. Masonry detail, east elevation. *Brostrup.*

NELSON HOUSE. Detail of hall trim, northwest room door. *Author.*

NELSON HOUSE. Original stair; new balustrade and floor. *Tebbs.*

NELSON HOUSE, Yorktown. The Dining Room of the mansion, showing the unique, engaged Corinthian order, with archaic capitals. *Tebbs*

Even with the asymmetry of the east elevation and the lack of a focal feature this is the most interesting side of Nelson House. The masonry detail as well as the curious brown brick, which is unique in Virginia and may indicate its foreign manufacture, can be seen to good advantage here. This elevation derives great charm from the old chinaberry tree on one side, the giant box at the other, and the informal setting behind a garden wall close to the side street. The street traverses the depth of the garden and two fine story-and-a-half dependencies. The rear wall of the mansion, overlooking a walled entrance court, is now the main front of the house, but the symmetry of the four openings is disturbed by a vestibule built against the hall door.

The difference in scale between Rosewell and Nelson House is profound, but the work of the same hand is seen in both. Rosewell is tall, exquisitely fashioned, feminine; Nelson House is broad, substantial, and masculine. A comparison of the window heads will illustrate this contrast. In Nelson House the heavy sashes and cornice, the latter with big, closely spaced modillions, bear out this scale, as do the superb chimney stacks with richly moulded caps and steep weatherings similar to those of Carter's Grove. Useful dormers, installed at the time of the reconditioning of the house in 1920, detract from the original intent of the design.

Except for the balustrade of the great stair the interior of Nelson House remains almost intact. The stair apparently was damaged [137] during the active years of the Civil War in Yorktown, but is now restored.

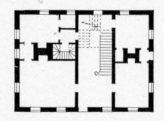

NELSON HOUSE, Yorktown. Diagrammatic.

As has been observed, the house has the Queensferry House off-center hall. There are two rooms on the east side with a lobby and service stair between them, and two square rooms to the west. These latter have an entry between them, in the thickness of the chimney wall. This was probably a pantry, for the kitchen stood farther to the west. The second floor repeats the first except that space for a stair to the attic is borrowed from the east rooms.

Like all the lower rooms, the entrance hall is paneled to the ceiling with ranges of panels above and below a balustrade-type moulded chair rail, and there is a fully developed cornice. The doors to the flanking rooms are set in deep reveals, paneled to match, with square panels set between two tiers of vertical panels and framed with fully moulded architraves. Although the hall floor is now laid in squares of black and white marble, the old wood floor was probably original. The stair ascends in three flights, an initial long run against the west wall, a short cross run on the south wall, and a final run on the east wall. The stair treads, risers, and stringer are original, the balusters and handrail being reproductions of the old. It is exceptionally broad and easy and has a particularly fine terminal scroll.

The present dining room (probably formerly the drawing room, since it is located away from the old kitchen) is the most elaborate room in the house. The walls here are not only paneled but marked off by a full-height, pseudo-Corinthian order. This curious order, somewhat like Plate LXXV in Batty Langley's *Builder's Director,* is composed of columns engaged about three-quarters of their depth. The resulting effect is much like a pilaster treatment, but it has novelty and considerable grace in spite of the fact that the proportions and detail are not particularly good. The capitals have single bands of tall acanthus leaves. The windows, doors, and mantel are framed by the orders. The marble mantel, with piers and frieze, is a copy of the original. This is true of all the others in the house, the new ones taking the place of slightly damaged originals. The northwest room is also paneled to the ceiling and has fluted pilasters marking the window and door openings and the mantel. The order was apparently Doric, but the capitals have been removed. Like those at Rosewell, the fireplaces here have curved jambs and smoke channels, and are apparently rebuildings of the originals.

Of a companion Yorktown house, the home of "Secretary" Nelson, built at the east end of town after 1744, de Chastellux observed: "a very handsome house, from which neither European taste nor luxury was excluded; a chimney piece and some bas reliefs of very fine marble, exquisitely sculptured." This structure was destroyed in the siege of Yorktown in 1781.[138]

Although no major houses of the period, other than Berkeley and Nelson House, have pediment roofs, there are a few minor buildings that do have them. The most important of these are the forecourt buildings at Shirley, Charles City County, probably dating from about 1740. These forecourt buildings at Shirley are perhaps the most complete in this country. They comprise two L-shaped stables or carriage houses flanking the north entrance to the courtyard and a kitchen and overseer's house which enclose the south sides of the court. To the south of these two, the mansion of c.1769 stands, terminating and enclosing the court.

SHIRLEY, Charles City County. The east dependency, one of a pair probably built about 1740 by John and Elizabeth Hill Carter to flank a new mansion which was not built until much later. The gable roof is in the style of those at Berkeley and the Nelson house, but with splayed eaves. The flat arches with segmental soffits are like those at Rosewell and the Nelson house. *Johnston.*

The two carriage houses to the north are one story high, with rather steep gable roofs expressed in the two ends as pediments. In each long elevation are tall window openings with grilles of horizontal wood bars. The south buildings are two stories high, also with pediment roofs, but here the eaves are splayed as at Christ Church, but in lesser degree. Both have inside end chimneys which appear above the pediment gables. The two buildings are five bays long with a center door in each long side. These doors are curious variants of the *Palladio Londinensis* design of Plate XXVII. They have six panels, two equal long tiers in the middle with a single long horizontal panel at top and bottom. The lower windows have nine over nine light sash, and the upper six over six, except the center window over the entrance door, which is widened a light, giving eight over eight light sash. This widening is the treatment seen at Rosewell, where the center third-floor windows have the same number of lights. The window arch is the same in form as that of Rosewell and Nelson House, with the arched soffit cut in gauged flat arches, but without stone keys. This detail also occurs in the carriage-house window heads. At the corners of the buildings are narrow rubbed-brick dressings. The water tables are gauged and beveled, and the houses have flat belt courses.

It is interesting to note the difficulties in which the designer was involved when trimming the splayed roof line with a modillioned cornice. A similar condition may be seen in the old shop east of the Paradise House in Williamsburg. In the larger buildings with pediment roofs the splay was suppressed.

The architectural evidence certainly links the Shirley of John Carter's period to the mansions under discussion. Simple as the forecourt buildings are, they yet show affinity to Berkeley, Nelson House, and Rosewell, as well as to Salmon's book. Since Carter was the eldest son of the "King" and heir to Corotoman, however, this is not surprising. During most of the lifetime of his brother-in-law, Edward Hill III, he and his family lived at Corotoman in a house he may have built (two houses seem to have burned on the site after 1726). When Hill died (c.1739), the Carters, however, were already domiciled at Shirley and must have lived in the old Hill house. This was built in the seventeenth century, according to tradition, and from the architectural evidence was modernized about 1725. In the personal knowledge of Mrs. Oliver, the present owner, the house was demolished about 1870 and the bricks used to build Upper Shirley.

There is no reason to believe that the early house was much different from Bacon's Castle, and Mrs. Oliver describes it as two stories high with two rooms on each floor. A sketch made by Fred E. Church in

1851 shows the present mansion with the forecourt buildings and the Hill house, the latter three stories high. This difference in height may be explained by the early eighteenth-century alterations. In these, it may be assumed that the old steep gable roof, concealed by a new third story and low hipped roof, was to be removed after the new roof was built (this was actually done at the Market Square Tavern in Williamsburg about 1900), but the work of removing the old roof was never completed. In substantiation of this theory it should be pointed out that the third-floor windows were blocked up and were not glazed. The drawing, which is in chiaroscuro, indicates the upper window openings with a white wash, but the lower ones glazed. Mrs. Oliver recalls that the windows were stoned up. The sketch further shows three bays, of a probable five on the south front, and a window on either side of the end chimney, on each floor. The window openings are indicated as having segmental heads, and the sash as three lights wide. Belt courses are shown at the floor lines. On the site is a pile of worked Portland stone, placed there as a marker at the direction of Mrs. Oliver's mother. Although these could not be separately examined, one was observed to be moulded in the form of a small-scale Doric capital. Under a venerable tree nearby is a large derelict stone moulded like the profile of the Tuscan cornice in *Palladio Londinensis*. Except for the missing crown mould this was apparently similar to the chimney caps at Rosewell, with a large-scale ogee bed mould. It may be questioned whether the Hill house of 1725-1870 had a cut stone cornice, or whether this member was for a gate pier or for a structure never built. This seems to be the sum of the information on the Hill house at present, but excavation and study may provide more data in the future.

The chronology of the Shirley buildings presents many problems. The facts presented concerning the Hill house effectually disprove the general misapprehension that it was incorporated in the present mansion. The date of its building and alteration can be only surmised. The latter may have been as late as about 1735, and that it was not completed could be explained by Hill's death. It would seem that on the accession of John and Elizabeth Carter an entirely different scheme was determined upon, a scheme which included a new house and subsidiary buildings, and the demolition of the old. For this the four fine forecourt buildings may have been built (off-center of the old house) and the mansion projected but never begun because of John Carter's death about 1742. At this time Charles Carter, the heir, was a child. Elizabeth Hill Carter married again, Bowler Cocke being her second husband, and together they lived at Shirley until her death in 1769. At this time Charles Carter came into the property, but Cocke continued to reside at Shirley

SHIRLEY, Charles City County. One of two stables at the end of the forecourt. *Johnston.*

CLEVE, King George County. Built c. 1750; destroyed, 1917. Early form. *W. M. Haussmann.*

until his death two years later. Up to this time Charles Carter and his family lived at Corotoman, but the architectural evidence indicates that he began the present house at least as early as his mother's death. This mansion belongs to a different group and will be discussed later.

At Nomini Hall the literary references outweigh the physical remains, but at Cleve, not far away, such is not the case, even though only shattered fragments of the house survive. Built about 1754 for Charles Carter, this was the fourth of the houses of the sons of Robert Carter. The great brick and stone walls survived the fire of about 1800, which claimed all the fine original trim, but it was the fire of 1917 that undermined the walls and necessitated their demolition. Photographs show the design of both long elevations, and drawings the plan and nineteenth-century trim.[139] After the last fire, the walls, except for the southwest corner, were demolished to the first-floor line. From here the basement remains complete and is partly covered by a modern house. The evidence of the walls, the derelict stonework in the grounds, and the photographs have allowed accurate restored elevations to be drawn, the roof form alone being conjectural.

Cleve was highly individual in its architectural decoration, the seven openings of the river front and the five of the land front being strongly accented by rusticated stone dressings which also occurred at the corners of the building. In detail, the window openings and doorways were trimmed with rusticated quoins and stepped arches with bold keystones. Such quoining was observed by Celia Fiennes, who wrote: "At Blyth was a very Sweete house . . . of Brick work Coyn'd with Stones and the Windows with Stone, all sashes." [140] The windows at Cleve had moulded stone sills, and the stone water table was also moulded. This broke out on piers in the basement wall to receive the quoin strips at the corners of the building. At the eaves was undoubtedly a large-scale modillioned cornice. That the roof was hipped and not originally gabled, as it was before the fire of 1917, was shown by the later brickwork of the gables, seen in the photographs. At the original break of the roof ridge were a pair of fine square chimneys with moulded stone caps.

The photographs of the house show that the brick work was very dark, but this may be due to a technical photographic defect, since the brick still at site is the characteristic soft salmon color of Virginia make. This color, with the grey-white of Portland stone, would have produced a more agreeable interplay of color than the pictures indicate.

The derivation of the design of rusticated stonework is much harder to determine than carved or moulded ornament because of the individualities the designer can introduce in the latter that he cannot in the former. Also, working the rusticated quoins and voussoir to different-

CARTER'S GROVE, James City County. View from northwest before changes of 1928, showing original dependencies. *Metropolitan Eng.*

sized openings often produces an effect different than the prototype. All of this makes it unreliable to attribute the rusticated trim to Plate XXVII in *Palladio Londinensis,* which shows rustication of this type.

Even if the fine original finish of Cleve has been gone for a hundred and fifty years, the floor plan survived the fire and even exists in part in the present basement. This is particularly interesting since it is more highly articulated than any other house of the period except Carter's Grove, which, except for being slightly larger, is almost an exact counterpart in plan of Cleve. The floor plan produced in both houses varying façades on the river and land sides, seven bays in the case of the former and five in the latter. On the river side was a broad entrance salon with large square rooms on either side, but on the land side was a narrower stair hall with two long rooms on either side the ends partitioned off for servants' lobbies.

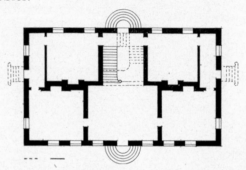

CARTER'S GROVE, James City County.

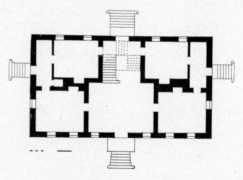

CLEVE, King George County.

This plan, seen more elaborately developed at Eltham Lodge, Surrey, was familiar in England and may have appeared in a style book. In fact, "Balveny House" in *Vitruvius Scoticus* has such a plan, but it is less successfully developed than the two Virginia houses and does not seem to have been their derivative. Cleve has lost its old landscape work, but

CARTER'S GROVE, James City County. South (river) front, above the great terraces. *Dementi.*

CARTER'S GROVE, James City County. North front showing original roof. *Metropolitan Eng.*

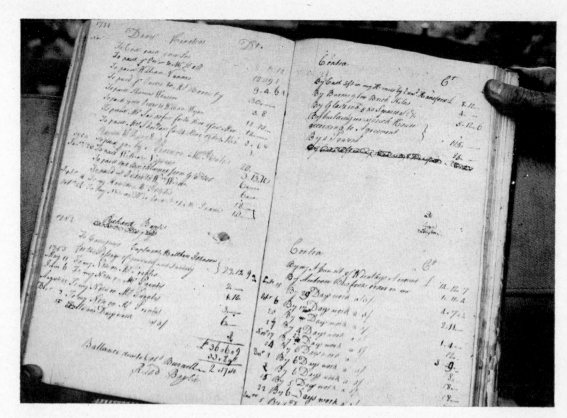

CARTER'S GROVE, James City County. Plantation account book of 1751-53 showing payments to, or in behalf of, David Minitree, Williamsburg, contractor-builder of the house, and Richard Bayliss, probably a joiner who came from England to complete the interiors of the house.

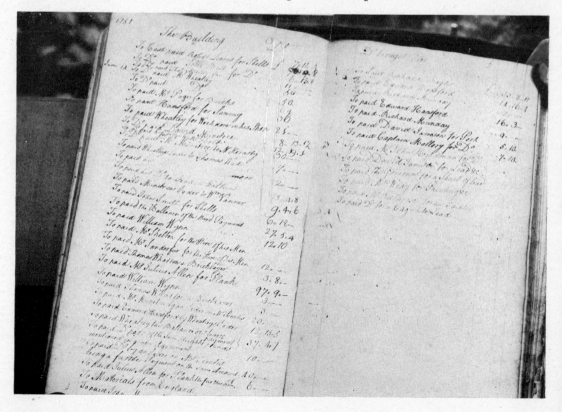

the site is a beautiful one near Port Royal on the Rappahannock River. It is opposite Gaymont and the site of Hazlewood, home of John Taylor of Caroline. On the river bank is a venerable cypress, and to the west is a curious canal-shaped pond, now thought to have been part of a tannery, but perhaps the "long water" of the old garden, like that at Middleton Place in South Carolina, and in numerous formal gardens in England, including that of Hampton Court Palace.

In Petersham, near London, is a charming example, paralleling Cleve and Carter's Grove, of an entrance salon from which opens, by means of a broad arch, a stair hall and its fine stair case.[141] Whether this, or any other London house, influenced the Virginia mansions is unknown. The superb finish of Carter's Grove was probably by Richard Bayliss, an English craftsman who came to Virginia apparently for the purpose, but of the Cleve interiors nothing is known. The well-executed, if provincial, trim of 1800 must have been the product of the hand of the local man who worked in the vicinity of Port Royal.[142]

The extraordinary parallel of the Carter's Grove plan to that of Cleve makes it seem certain that they were the product of the same designer. The fact, too, that the first was built for Carter Burwell, nephew of Charles Carter, builder of the second, makes the use of the same architect very probable. It is curious that even after the passage of twenty-five years since the building of Rosewell the same handbook was apparently used. The detail of the interior of Carter's Grove displays throughout parallels to plates in *Palladio Londinensis*. The relation of plans, the family connections, and the architectural detail all point to Carter's Grove as one of the group under discussion.

Fortunately, in this case the accounts of the builder, Carter Burwell, are extant and give many facts of the construction period.[143] This seems to have covered the years 1750-53, and the work was done by David Minitree of Williamsburg, to whom Burwell paid £115 personally in 1752 for "building me a brick House." A further gift of £25 "By a present" was made for work well done, as indeed it was. Preparations for financing the house were underway in 1748, when the assembly docked the "intail of certain lands, whereof Carter Burwell is seized in tail-male, and for settling other lands, of greater value, to the same uses."[144] Building was under way by February 21, 1750-51, when Burwell advertised in the *Virginia Gazette* as follows: "The Subscriber, being in Want of Oyster Shells, will give at the Rate of Three Shillings per Hogshead for any Quantity that can be delivered at his Landing by the last of March." These, of course, were to be burned for lime for the mortar.[145]

For many years Minitree has been supposed to be the architect of Carter's Grove and to have come from England especially to take charge of the work. This supposition was based, however, on an old misapprehension in reading the account book. In this latter the accounts of Minitree and Richard Bayliss with Carter Burwell are entered on the same page, but the payment in 1752 of £23/13/9 "To Cash paid to Captain Mathew Johnson for the Passage of yourself and Family," was on Bayliss' account and not on Minitree's. The latter apparently had long been domiciled in Williamsburg. A man of the same name worked on the construction of the Capitol at the beginning of the century,[146] but he seems to have died in 1712. He perhaps was the father of the builder. At the time of the erection of Carter's Grove, Minitree may have been along in years, for he seems to have deputized his son to represent him at the building. Burwell notes, in November, 1752, a payment of £8/13/12 to "Cash paid your Son." Of Minitree almost nothing is known except these facts.

Actually there is nothing to deny that he was the architect as well as the builder. The Williamsburg records, however, show that he was a workman and a contractor, but there is nothing to indicate that he designed his work as well. Unlike John Ariss, who is known to have studied abroad, there is no evidence that the Minitrees ever left Virginia. Perplexing as this lack of information is, the same is true of Richard Bayliss. Who was he and why was he brought from England? The most plausible explanation is that he was a skilled joiner, or woodworker, and came to execute the superb interiors of the house. However, the detail shows that he was not, at least entirely, responsible for the design, for exact parallels of various features relate the interior without question to *Palladio Londinensis* and to the houses of the group, even as far back as Rosewell. This implies that the influence of the architect was paramount and that if Bayliss did execute the interior he used details prepared by another.

From the years of its building until 1927 Carter's Grove stood almost untouched, complete and superlative in every quality. At this time, however, extensive alterations were undertaken, and these substantially affected the character of the building. The main building below the roof line on both exterior and interior stands relatively unchanged, however, and is an example of Virginia house building at its best. The mansion is of brick, two stories high below a hipped roof, with two ridge chimneys. It was flanked by two dependencies, standing free from the house at either side, and parallel to the main axis. These are a story and a half high, with end chimneys. The house has the varied fenestration of Cleve, with five openings across the land front and seven across the river front. The doorways, both centered on the façades, have fine gauged brick pedimented frames. The doors themselves are eight paneled with

CARTER'S GROVE, James City County. The south doorway, with pedimented door facing in gauged and moulded brick. This type was used in this group of houses as well as in churches such as Ware and Abington in Gloucester County. It was probably a substitute for stone, which was utilized at Westover and at Pohick Church, and in preference to wood, which was employed at Wilton. *Tebbs*.

moulded wood jambs and head. On the south, or river front, the brick
frame takes the form of a pair of narrow piers supporting a pediment,
but on the north the piers are lacking, the gauged brick frame supporting
the pediment. The gauging, moulding, and jointing of the brickwork of
the doorways is outstanding, as is that of the great double-moulded base
course.[147]

All the windows are of the same size, occurring in two equal ranges
on the first and second floors. They have broad rubbed jambs and dressings, as have the corners of the building, and deep flat arches richly
jointed. The belt course at the second-floor line is gauged, but
unmoulded, and is unusual in stopping short of the corners of the house.
Outstanding specimens of early brickwork were the tall ridge chimneys
much like those at Nelson House. They had full cornice caps above
moulded neckings and below steep splayed washes, similar to those
rebuilt. The only old stonework on the exterior was in the round flights
of steps on the north front, now rebuilt in different form. Of the exterior,
the principal woodwork is the fine modillioned cornice. In its original
form the roof was a hip of about forty degrees, with splayed eaves, which
were less exaggerated than those at Christ Church. This roof has now
been rebuilt on the lines of Westover, with the ridge raised eleven feet
and ranges of dormers inserted.

In enlarging the dependencies the south walls were taken down in
1928, the buildings increased in depth and the roof correspondingly in
height. Connections of nearly the same breadth were inserted, radically
changing the original composition, already affected by the higher roof
of the mansion and flankers.

The comparison of Carter's Grove before the alterations and Westover
was particularly interesting, showing as it did the progress from Queen
Anne to Georgian. The greater repose of the former and its more Palladian silhouette was due to the more horizontal line, broader wall surfaces, and lower roof slopes. The suppression of the tall end chimneys
and the substitution of lower, more substantial stacks at the break of
the hip was also in keeping with the trend of style.

The advance in period is more obvious in the plan of the house than
in the interior woodwork. The former, that of course of Cleve, with entrance salon and narrower axial stair hall is a finished and distinguished
composition. Technically and artistically the superb woodwork is no
less distinguished, but it is less advanced in style and recalls houses of
the beginning of the century in England. This is obvious when it is compared with that of Kenmore and Gunston Hall, both by contemporary
designers trained in England in the Palladian style.

The great suite of paneled rooms on the river front is the glory of

CARTER'S GROVE, James City County. Entrance salon, finest Virginia paneled room. *Tebbs*.

CARTER'S GROVE, James City County. Entrance salon showing staircase and its arch. *Tebbs*.

CARTER'S GROVE, James City County. East parlor, one of two matching paneled rooms. *Tebbs.*

CARTER'S GROVE, James City County. Detail of the fine carved wood stair brackets. *Tebbs.*

Carter's Grove and is as fine as any other in the country. The entrance salon to the south, with its adjoining stair hall, is one of the outstanding examples of American woodwork. In form the salon is a broad rectangle with a center door in the south side flanked by two windows. On axis with the door on the north side is a wide elliptical arch framing the stair. In each end wall is a door to the adjacent rooms. The walls, in common with the others of the suite, have high unpaneled dados with pedestal-type chair rail and base. Above this, reaching to the cornice, are ranges of panels moulded with the "bisection" panel of the other houses of the group. In the salon all the openings, except the windows, are flanked by Ionic pilasters standing on the dado, which breaks out to form pedestals. The shafts of the pilasters are fluted and the capitals excellently carved with Scamozzi's angle volutes ruffled with acanthus leaves and enriched with egg-and-dart bandings and fleurons. Above each of the pilastered openings a full entablature, with three-plane architrave, cushion frieze, and fully moulded modillioned cornice, occurs. Between the pilasters the soffit of the architrave is finely carved with guilloche ornament, the interlacing strapwork framing carved rosettes. To relate the rich treatment of the upper order, an applied Greek key fret was used on the chair rail. It should be observed that the field of the dado is unpaneled, thus denoting the more Palladian character of the period. The balustrade-type chair rail has given way to the pedestal type, current in mid-eighteenth-century English work.

The stair arch, like the one at Sabine Hall, is elliptical in form, and the moulded archivolt rests on imposts, the profiles of which are of the Ionic type seen on Plate XIV in *Palladio Londinensis*. Probably on account of their projection on the floor, the moulded bases were omitted at the arch. They actually were removed at Sabine Hall, perhaps for the same reason. The eight-panel doors of the earlier houses reoccur here, but with the wider lock rail popular at this later period. The jambs of both doors and windows are paneled, and the latter have paneled seats.

The stair ascends in a long initial flight on the west wall, then turns in two short flights before reaching the second floor. Great attention was lavished on the detail of the stair, even the dowels which fix the walnut nosings to the pine treads being covered with plugs in the form of fleur-de-lis. The landings, perhaps unique in America, are inlaid with a geometric pattern in walnut, like English examples of the period. Like them, too, they may once have been covered with leather, except on occasions of state.[148] Another American example was in the Clark-Frankland house in Boston, where the floor of the parlor "was laid in diamond-shaped figures, and had in the center a unique and curious tesselated design . . . encircling the coat of arms of the Clarke family." [149]

The balustrade of the stair is initiated by a fine open volute, or swirl, centered on a spiralled newel post, which is repeated in form at the landings and again for wall posts. The balusters are similar in turning to the type common to the whole group, but the spiral carving is omitted, plain shafts and vases being used as at the Wythe house in Williamsburg and Abington Church. The close parallel of the turnings of the heavier balusters of Rosewell to those of Carter's Grove is particularly interesting and significant. The brackets, too, being replicas of those at Tuckahoe, are precedented in other houses of the group. The consoles are feathered with acanthus leaves, to which five-petaled blossoms cling. Raking with the consoles is a moulded architrave, against which the paneled spandrel is received. As with most other Virginia and English mansions, the great stair terminated at the second floor, though it has now been extended to the third. A unique feature of the Carter's Grove stair is the broad brand of carved fret that defines the soffit of the old curved stair well.

The use of an order in the salon is repeated in the two south rooms, though the pilasters appear only as flanking the mantel and are Doric instead of Ionic. To conform to this change triglyphs and metopes occur in the entablature instead of the architrave and cushion frieze. However, the Doric cornice with triglyphs and metopes is replaced by a regular, fully moulded member with a dentil band. A distinguished feature of the southwest room is the beautiful mantel of white and Siena marble and the exquisitely carved frieze panel much like the old mantel at Rosegill. The fireplace opening is framed by an architrave in white marble veined in grey, with crossettes supporting a Siena frieze, and white and grey cornice. In the frieze are carved statuary blocks. These are certainly from a London shop and of the type Governor Tryon imported for the Palace in New Bern, North Carolina.[150] The southeast room is similar except that the metopes of the entablature are carved and a carved wood trim with crossettes frames the fireplace. All of these three rooms and the stair hall are now cleaned down to the wood and stained. The stain is effective, but from current English [151] and Virginia practice it can be assumed that the woodwork was originally painted.[152] This is true both from the point of view of period and from the fact that various woods, and not exclusively walnut or mahogany, were used.

The paneling of the two north rooms is of the earlier type with the dado and field both paneled, and a balustrade-type chair rail instead of a pedestal type. The overmantels are simply paneled. Until the changes of 1927-29, the ends of the north rooms were paneled off as service lobbies, enclosing a window in each side elevation. Before this change the mantels here, as at Cleve, were centered on the south walls.

Carter's Grove, James City County. West parlor, its paneling and marble mantel. *Met. Eng.*

Carter's Grove, James City County. West parlor after removal of the paint in 1928. *Tebbs.*

The careful restoration and repair of the incomparable woodwork of Carter's Grove allows the study and appreciation of Virginia woodwork at its finest development. With the external changes understood, the building as a whole can be considered as the final phase of the evolution of the Georgian mansion type from the high and impractical style of Rosewell to one that was harmonious with the country and eminently fitted to the needs and predilections of the Virginia planter.

Like its neighbor, Kingsmill, now gone, Carter's Grove stands at the top of a magnificent series of terraces looking out across fields and woods to the James River bluffs. After Carter Burwell II left it to build Carter Hall, in Clarke County, in 1790, Carter's Grove lost its landscape work except the row of great tulip poplars on the south side and the terraces. However, in recent years a fine garden and approach, which provide a sympathetic setting for the great house, have been developed.

A mansion which in mass and fenestration was closely akin to Cleve and Carter's Grove was Peckatone, Westmoreland County. It was built by Gawin Corbin about 1750, and stood until destroyed by fire on October 21, 1886. The only evidence that remains of it is a photograph taken after the fire. Even the ruins of the walls were recently removed for restoration work at Stratford. It is particularly regrettable that there is only a view of the south and east walls, so that it is impossible to tell whether the north wall had the varied fenestration seen at Cleve and Carter's Grove. Unfortunately, no drawings were made of the ruins before their removal. A description of the plan by a former resident suggests that it was similiar to Cleve and Carter's Grove.[153] The photograph, however, shows a fine brick façade of seven bays with tall lower window and short upper ones, all trimmed with rubbed brick facings, stone flat arches, and stone sills. The central doorway was trimmed to correspond. All the openings had excellent proportions and were well arranged in the elevations. The water table was of moulded brick. An interesting variation from Cleve was the irregular spacing of the windows, the wall between the end windows being broader than between the others. This unevenness probably was caused by the architect's drawing the windows flanking the door closer together to bring them within the broad central hall. Such was done at the Governor's Palace with marked effect on the elevation. In other houses where the same condition prevailed, the arrangement was made symmetrical by adjusting the spacing of the two flanking windows.

Little is left at the site of Peckatone; even the foundations have been partly washed away by the Potomac River, which is here eroding away the south bank. Of the outbuildings there remains a three-bay, two-story dependency with gable roof and end chimneys. It stood at right

PECKATONE, Westmoreland County. Built c. 1750. View after 1886 fire. *Courtesy Ethel Armes.*

PECKATONE, Westmoreland County. The east dependency as it is standing today. *Johnston.*

PRESTWOULD, Mecklenburg County. South front of mansion of Sir Peyton Skipwith. *Johnston.*

PRESTWOULD, Mecklenburg County. A view of the entrance hall looking north. *Met. Eng.*

angles to the mansion, closing the forecourt on the east. Although it
was built of brick laid in Flemish bond, the brickwork is not of high
quality and perhaps is of later date than the house. The flat arches of
the openings have been removed. There is no sign of the balancing
building, but to the west are remains of garden walls and of the barn.

Peckatone was somewhat more successful in design than was Sabine
Hall or Cleve in that the natural direction of the elevations was not
disturbed by strongly-accented stone trim. Even in the photograph of
the ruins the distinction of the design is obvious. The simplicity of the
façade, the vigor of the diminishing window openings, and the great
height of the fine chimneys are especially effective features.

According to descriptions it might seem that Eltham, the great house
of Burwell Bassett, was very much like Peckatone, but no evidence as
to the form of the building remains at the site. One of the dependencies
survived until recently when the brick walls were taken down for use
in the Williamsburg Restoration, unfortunately without record.

A far-distant early mansion that has elevations reminiscent of those
at Peckatone is Prestwould, Mecklenburg County, not far from the North
Carolina line. Under construction for a number of years, it was apparently finished about 1770, when the present interior trim was installed.
The builder was one of Virginia's few baronets, Sir Peyton Skipwith.
His wife, Lady Jean, is said to have laid out the garden, parts of which
still remain. The plantation continued in the family of the builder until
recently, though many years ago the elder branch became reëstablished
in England at the beautiful Georgian house, Honington Hall. Fortunately,
when Prestwould was sold it was purchased by a collateral descendant,
and much of the Skipwith furniture remains within it.

The unusual use of stone ashlar for the wall facing reduces the
resemblance of Prestwould to other Tidewater houses, but the long
elevations of seven bays, the diminution of the upper windows, and the
location of the chimneys definitely recall Carter's Grove, Cleve, and
Peckatone. However, the plan of Prestwould differs from existing Tidewater mansions in that it consists of six rooms, arranged in two files of
three rooms. The large central room on the south side is the stair hall
in which the stair ascends against the east wall and then parallel with
the north, but far enough out from it to allow a passage on the second
floor to the northeast room. The stair hall and the entrance salon to the
north have no fireplaces, the two chimneys occurring in the longitudinal
partition wall between the four corner rooms.

The woodwork of the interior is less interesting than the fine early
nineteenth-century wall paper and antique furnishings. The stair has
simple scrolled step ends, plain square balusters, set diagonally, and

square posts. The handrail has neither ramps nor easings, and consequently the stair lacks the flowing grace of the great Tidewater examples. Provincial qualities seen in the stair show also in the dados, cornices, and mantels. The latter principally follow one design, an architrave frame with crossettes, a pulvinated frieze, and cornice shelf. There is some polychrome work and marbleizing in the painting of the interior woodwork.

Prestwould has a commanding position on the high land overlooking the Roanoke River valley, and its long, low lines conform well to the site. It lacks architectural dependencies, but to the west is a large picturesque grouping of old plantation buildings arranged on a broad street that descends the hill to the west.

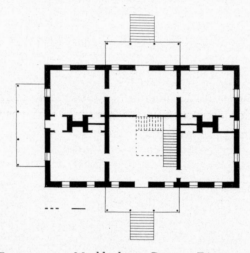

PRESTWOULD, Mecklenburg County. Diagrammatic.

Another house that does not definitely relate to any other but that has affinities to Carter's Grove and Cleve is Rocky Mills (now called Fairfield) which was built in Hanover County about 1750. It stood on the original site until 1928, when it was taken down and rebuilt in Richmond. The land in Hanover was granted to John Syme about 1727, but he died in 1731 leaving a minor son, who, through his mother's second marriage, became a half brother of Patrick Henry. The mansion was apparently built at the time of the marriage of John Syme II to Mildred Merriweather about 1750, though there is no documentary evidence concerning it. Both the architectural evidence of the masonry and woodwork point to this period and to the possibility that the house was built from finished designs by country workmen. It has much to relate it to Cleve in its exterior stone detail and to Carter's Grove in its interior wood detail, but it falls short of the latter in its execution.

PRESTWOULD, Mecklenburg County. South parlor showing the woodwork of c. 1770. *Met. Eng.*

PRESTWOULD, Mecklenburg County. The dining room showing the fine early nineteenth-century French scenic wallpaper. With Gaymont, Prestwould has the finest papers in Virginia. *Met. Eng.*

ROCKY MILLS, Hanover County. The east front before demolition. *From an old photo. HABS.*

ROCKY MILLS, Hanover County. The west front as rebuilt in 1929. *Chamber of Commerce.*

Its plan is strikingly like theirs, however, with a broad entrance salon and a narrower subsidiary hall beyond. There are two rooms of unequal size at either side. At Rocky Mills the stair was rebuilt in extensive interior alterations of about 1820. It now ascends from the salon (as rebuilt, in reverse of its location in 1928), but there is no evidence of its original location. This change diminishes the resemblance between the houses, as does the lack of servants' lobbies at the end of the long rooms.

The exterior has much to relate it to Cleve in the lavish use of stone quoining with brick walls, the corners of the building and jambs of the openings on three sides being trimmed with quoins. Both long elevations have five bays (lacking the variation of five and seven at Cleve) and there is an important central motive on each façade. One front, originally east, has an arched door (leading to the narrower hall) with a Palladian window above. The other has a low, square-headed door, now opening upon a new porch with stone columns, with closely spaced windows above and below, as at the Governor's Palace. Here, however, a pavilion was implied by placing an heroic pediment on the roof, over the grouped openings, as at Mount Vernon. This was removed many years ago and stored in the attic, but was replaced in the reconstruction and the wall advanced below to receive it. Extra windows were also cut in the wall on either side, making the present elevation seven openings long.

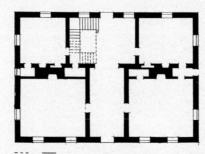

Rocky Mills, Hanover County. Before removal to Richmond.

The side elevations are unimportant, with a pair of windows on each floor flanking a very wide central wall pier. In one end elevation there is a small doorway slightly off axis, and in the corresponding elevation an untrimmed circular window. The roof is hipped with a comparatively low pitch, and tall square chimneys pierce the side slopes.

The striking feature of the exterior is the stonework, which is richly and carefully worked. The arch stones of the doorway and windows alternate long and short, the long ones treated with narrow intermediate members, as in the keystones of Rosewell and Christ Church. The typical windows have very broad quoins and stone flat arches with keys.

Although Peckatone and Prestwould resemble Carter's Grove, Cleve, and Westover in their possession of seven-bay façades, there is no definite evidence to link them to this group. There is, however, another mansion, a contemporary of Prestwould, that not only strikingly resembles all five designs but is a partial parallel to the plan type of Westover. It is U-shaped, however, with two wings to the north. This mansion is Elsing Green in King William County, built by Carter Braxton in 1758, as an inscribed brick records. A comparison of the Elsing Green and Westover plans shows that the halls are located in almost exactly the same relation to the center line and are the same width, but as Elsing Green is almost five feet longer than Westover the two south rooms are slightly larger. The drawing room to the east has much the proportion of that at Westover, but the lack of chimney closets in the latter house changes the aspect considerably. It is unfortunate that all of the original finish of Elsing Green was destroyed in the fire of about 1800, so that a comparison of the woodwork with that of the other houses of the group cannot be made.

In elevation the house is seven bays long on the river front, and is two full stories high beneath a hipped roof. Each side elevation is five bays long with a center door, and on the north front appear the two wings and the axial court. The latter has a center door with a window on either side, and the wings have a narrow window on either side of the chimney pier. Except for the narrower wing-windows all of the others have nine over nine light sash, with the upper slightly diminishing in size. The brickwork, regularly laid in Flemish bond throughout, has rubbed and gauged dressings and a moulded water table. The window arches of the first-floor windows are remarkable for their depth of six courses, equalled only by those at Elmwood, in Essex County (c.1774), but the splay is more moderate. The string course of gauged brick is unmoulded, four courses high, but the water table has the double moulded member of Westover and Wilton. Elsing Green, indeed, bears more resemblance in detail to Wilton than perhaps any other house. It is not similar to Wilton in general appearance, but the end elevations of the wings are very much like it. The same tall, narrow sashes and the square chimney stacks occur in both houses as well as at Chelsea. In the recent restoration a pedimented, gauged brick doorway (such as lines in the old brickwork showed once existed) was installed.

The unusual length and depth of Elsing Green give an impression of great size, which is accentuated by the site of the house on a high terrace overlooking the Pamunkey River. It is flanked by old, but probably not original, dependencies. These are a story and a half high, of brick, and parallel the long axis of the mansion. Because of its rather remote loca-

ELSING GREEN, King William County, 1758. South front facing Pamunkey River. *Author, HABS.*

ELSING GREEN, King William County. West side showing door to the long hall. *Author, HABS.*

Powhatan, James City County. *Author.* Elsing Green, King William County. *Author.*

Wilton, Henrico County, 1753. South or river front as rebuilt in Richmond in 1934. *Bagby.*

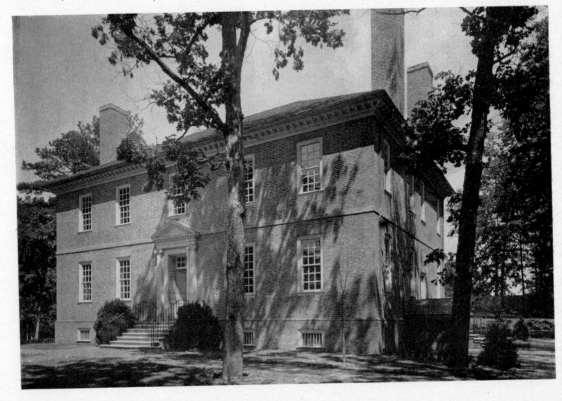

tion Elsing Green has not been fully recognized as a particularly distinguished example of its period. Its unusual qualities and its relationship to the other houses of the group, however, make it especially interesting.[154]

The resemblance between Elsing Green and Wilton (1753) has been commented on, and the close similarity in dates makes this resemblance seem reasonable. However, although the parallel in planning between Elsing Green and Westover is obvious though incomplete, the parallel between Wilton and Westover is more nearly exact than between any other two Virginia houses. The disparity of nearly twenty-five years here makes this parallel remarkable, but their fairly close proximity, on the north bank of the James, near City Point, may explain it. William Randolph III knew Westover and perhaps desired a replica of it, at least in plan.

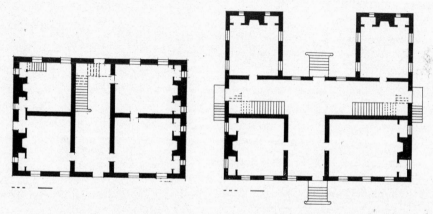

WILTON, Henrico County.　　ELSING GREEN, King William County.

Wilton formerly stood in Henrico County near Curles Neck, but it was demolished and rebuilt in Richmond in 1934. It was originally built for Randolph in 1753, the precise date being established by an inscription on the back of one of the cornices. This records that "Samson Darril put up this cornish in the year of our Lord 1753."[155] Such authentic dating of early houses is rare, but in this case it substantiates the date of 1754 usually ascribed to the house before the discovery of Darril's inscription. It should be recalled that it usually took five years to build a large house.

The difference in the fenestration and in the roof treatments of Wilton and Westover somewhat obscure the extraordinary parallel between the two buildings. They are within an inch of the same length, both being slightly over sixty-four feet long. In depth Wilton is forty-three feet, five inches (the precise depth of Carter's Grove), but Westover is just under two feet narrower.[156] The story heights are nearly identical, as is the dimension from grade to the underside of the cornice of about thirty-two feet. In both houses the windows of both stories have nine over nine light sash, with diminished glass size in the upper story. The segmental arched heads and narrow rubbed brick dressings of Westover give quite a different effect than the deep, flat arches and broad dressings of Wilton.

Both houses have double-moulded brick water tables, flat gauged string-courses, and fine wood cornices displaying both dentils and modillions. The introduction of connections to the wings at Westover prevents the observation of the end elevations as whole designs, but the four window openings, divided in either side pair by the breadth of the chimney stack, is identical with the Wilton arrangement. In the latter house, however, windows two lights wide were used instead of the familiar three.

Westover and Wilton are the only major Virginia houses of their period and scale with pilastered doorways of a material contrasting to the walls. The superb stone doorways of the former have already been discussed. Those at Wilton certainly follow them, but are less well designed, and in spite of the easily worked wood of which they were built are less skillfully executed. Also unlike Westover, there is no variation in the design of the two elevations, both doorways having moulded architrave frames flanked by Ionic pilasters, which support pediment heads. The latter are composed of three-plane architraves, cushion friezes, and pediments, enriched with modillions. The capitals of the pilasters have angle volutes in Scamozzi's style, but without the fleuron, or center rosette, usually associated with this form of cap. Derelict Rosewell capitals, now at Shelly, have all the peculiarities of those at Wilton, but in the latter the floral carving and feathering of acanthus is omitted.

The towering roof of Westover is replaced at Wilton with a low-pitched hip, much like the old one at Carter's Grove but lacking its graceful splay at the eaves. The Wilton chimneys are in the same location as those at Westover, in the end walls, but their greater girth and more reasonable height (due to the lower roof ridge) make them relate better to the structure of the house. The exterior of Wilton, though distinguished and notable, does not have the charm of Westover. This may be due both to the more mid-Georgian quality of the design and to the lessening of the influence of Wren's style in the last houses of this first group. This same phenomenon can be observed in the interior, where the magnificent woodwork, in spite of its many similarities, has

WILTON, Henrico County. A detail of the east entrance. *Bagby.*

WILTON, Henrico County. The south doorway, in wood. *Bagby.*

WILTON, Henrico County. Hall looking south showing the stairway. *Brostrup*.

lost some of the warmth and richness of the Queen Anne tradition and taken on the more academic properties of Georgian work.

In plan Wilton not only presents a very remarkable parallel to West-over but exhibits the characteristics of the Sabine Hall, Nomini Hall, and Nelson House group. The only deviation from Westover is that the off-center hall is moved slightly toward the center line, giving needed space in the narrower rooms. Also because of the increase in the depth of the house, the south rooms at Wilton are considerably widened. Thus there is a wide hall with two small rooms to the east, and two large rooms to the west.

The plan of Wilton is almost a repeat of Westover, but the house is not similarly orientated; in fact it is exactly the reverse. The stair is at the opposite end of the landward entrance, ascending to the south on the left-hand side. At Westover the land entrance door is under the second run of the stair, with the latter ascending on the right-hand wall, toward the north. This might mean that in the former house the most used means of approach was from the road, and of the latter, from the river.

The stair halls are very much alike both in the design of the stairs and in the paneling. At Wilton the stair balustrade is of turned and spiraled walnut balusters like those employed in most of the other houses of the group, and as at Sabine Hall the minor posts are omitted. Unfortunately, a variation occurs in the consoles of the stringer, those here being merely scrolled and pierced rather than carved as in the other stairways. The ascent of the stair is the normal one of one long initial flight, then two short flights. Here the header was set back from the top riser to give adequate headroom below. It may be recalled that both at Mount Vernon and Carter's Grove this was done at the well by a quarter-circle curve, a more interesting treatment than the straight header here. All the walls of the Wilton hall are paneled to the ceiling, displaying fine ranges of panels, short below and tall above the balustrade-type chair rail.

Almost all the walls of the first- and second-floor rooms are covered by this same fine, quiet type of paneling. However, the two north rooms of the first floor have the additional enrichment of Classic orders. In the northeast room the mantel is flanked by Doric pilasters with entiasis supporting a full but disproportionate entablature, and the fireplace is framed by a marble facing. The jamb pieces of the facing are paneled, and the lintel piece, arched on the soffit, has a continuation of the panels which are shaped to the soffit. Such marble facings were probably much more usual than now appears, and are more often seen in English houses of the period than in Virginia. There was a set at Ampthill, formerly one at Scotchtown, and there were interesting examples in

WILTON, Henrico County. Drawing room, one of the elaborate rooms of the period. *Brostrup.*

WILTON, Henrico County. Dining room. All the rooms are paneled to the ceiling. *Brostrup.*

Wheatland, in Williamsburg, one grey and one pink. In the west room of the Blair house in Williamsburg is a white marble facing worked with rectangular panels with demi-roundels. The west rooms at Wilton have richer facings with scrolled soffits in the style of the mantel in the Bull Head Room in the Carter-Bland house in Williamsburg, but they are more richly paneled.

The Wilton drawing room, at the northwest corner of the house, is a fine and unspoiled room of its period, now repaired and cleansed of the nineteenth-century decoration that once marred it. It alone of the major houses of its period has the chimney breast flanked by arched recesses as at the Randolph-Tazewell house, Chelsea, and Toddsbury, and it has much in common with all three. The fireplace, framed by the marble facing, has overmantel paneling formed by three tall panels above three horizontal panels (as once also at Scotchtown), and flanked by full-height pilasters. These define not only the mantel motive but also the arched recesses, beyond which are pilaster responds. In form the pilaster capitals are almost unique, the only parallels apparently being those in the dining room at Ampthill and in the reredos of St. John's, King William County. Undoubtedly the designer was attempting to obtain the effect of a Corinthian order without the expense of carved acanthus leaves and volutes. He therefore employed a moulded cap above a plain member as wide as the bell of a Corinthian cap and banded at the height of the first row of leaves with a second necking. The result, while unorthodox, is interesting and even graceful. The pilasters support a full entablature with pulvinated frieze and dentilled cornice and the effect of richness is increased by the entablature's breaking out over the pilasters and keystones of the arches.

In the imposts of the arched recesses a profile from *Palladio Londinensis* is used; this is the Corinthian type from Plate XIV. This richly moulded member receives the arched trim, which is broken at the center by a large key. Within the reveal of the alcove the walls and window jambs are fully paneled. The window openings of the north wall, and the doorway of the east are framed, like the other openings, by pilasters. The south wall is treated with ranges of panels. It should be pointed out that the panel mould is the "bisection" type seen in the other houses of the group. Elsewhere, as at Westover and Ampthill, bead and beveled paneling is used together with another panel mould. The latter has a curious profile employing a cyma reversa, and with a bevel which is coved out to the face of the panel.

At Chelsea, the home of William Randolph's sister Mrs. Bernard Moore, the parlor is a simplified rendering of the Wilton drawing room. The pilasters, of a simple Doric order, with fluted shafts, extend up to the soffit of the cornice, the frieze and architrave of the entablature being omitted on account of lack of sufficient height. In one respect this room is superior to that at Wilton: the side walls are identical, each having a pair of windows, framed by pilasters, so that the order is continuous around the whole room. Harewood has a more academic rendering of this same arrangement.

The southwest room at Wilton has a paneled overmantel flanked by Doric pilasters beyond which are doors to the chimney closets. Here again a marble fireplace facing appears, almost a mate to that in the front room. In the room above there is a dark marble facing, slightly arched, which has in the center a carved roundel much like an example at Mawley Hall in Shropshire.

On its original site the house stood within a walled area, the foundations of which still remain. On the approach, or northeast side, was a court one hundred and seventeen feet deep and slightly over one hundred and sixty feet wide. On the river side this widened out to over one hundred and eighty feet wide and decreased to fifty feet deep. The widening was managed by twenty-foot breaks in the side walls, one hundred and five feet from the north wall. At the river side the court was defined by a terrace five feet high, rather than by the wall.

The setting was completely symmetrical except that it was slightly off-center, and two buildings were probably built against the walls at sometime after the original completion. These were both twenty by forty feet, but the eastern one was built outside the wall and north of the break and the western one inside the wall and south of the break. At the north end of the court were two structures sixteen by twenty feet, built against the outside of the side walls and lining with the front wall. These buildings all seem to have been of frame and of informal design. Another building of the same type stood outside the wall southeast of the house, and this building shows in old photographs of Wilton. There were two penetrations in the walls; a nine-foot gate in the center of the north court and a narrower one just south of the house in the east wall. Both of these openings had piers seventeen inches square, and the foundation of another of the same size exists at the terrace end of the eastern wall. There was a gravel bed six feet wide on the center line of the terrace, indicating steps at this point.

The foundations denote a fine typical setting for the house, and it is hard to believe that originally it was not planned to be entirely symmetrical, with masonry dependencies more distant than those of which the foundations were found. It seems especially possible that the kitchen was meant to be on axis with the east gate and at a convenient distance from it. The recent kitchen was so close to the gate as to suggest

Wilton, Henrico County. Mantel treatment of the northeast room. *Brostrup.*

that it was built after the wall was destroyed. Even a record of the formal settings of Virginia mansions is so rare that it is especially fortunate that that of Wilton could be excavated and recorded.

Although the demolition and rebuilding of Wilton deprive it of the significance it would have had on its original site, it has been superbly rebuilt and the interior woodwork, cleaned, repaired, and re-erected, is even more significant. It is a rich study in the final phase of that great period of English woodwork that Wren inaugurated nearly one hundred years before. Its neighbor on the new site, Ampthill, which was also one on the old, supplements this study with its less elaborate and smaller-scale interiors by the same hand.

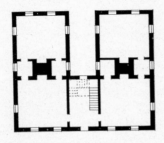

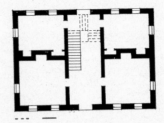

AMPTHILL, Chesterfield County.   WYTHE HOUSE, Williamsburg.

Built before 1732, Ampthill was enlarged twice and refinished about 1750. Before its removal to Richmond its brick walls and original roof framing told its story. As first constructed it had a central hall with one room on either side. Later, as originally provided for, two wings were built against the rear wall, each containing one room, with an open court between, as at Elsing Green. The house at this time was two stories high, surmounted by a hipped roof, and had two chimneys in the center wall. About 1750, probably after the death of Henry Cary and the succession of his son Archibald, Ampthill was enlarged by roofing over the court and changing the location of the stair. This alteration not only provided a larger hall but also gave access to all four wing rooms without traversing the front rooms, which was undoubtedly the reason for the alteration. The development of the roof plan to the present hip on hip has been studied elsewhere.[157]

All of the elevations are smaller in scale than those of Elsing Green, and the house, lacking the cross hall, has no side entrances. The side elevations therefore became purely secondary and had the windows arranged in an unarchitectural manner. The front, originally and after the alterations of about 1750, was five bays long with a center door.

The windows were longer on the first floor than on the second, but the early sash did not remain at the time of the removal of the house in 1929; so the design of the lights is unknown. There seems to be no explanation for the curious fact that of the major Virginia houses Ampthill alone has walls of English bond rather than the usual Flemish. This is one reason for thinking that the house may be older than the attributed date of 1732, and another is the rather archaic plan. Ampthill, otherwise, has brickwork characteristic of the simpler building types. The rubbed dressings are one brick deep; the flat arches of the windows are four courses deep downstairs and three upstairs; and the water table is a simple splay. An unusual feature lay in the use of glazed headers in the gauged-brick string course, which was laid in Flemish bond and was unmoulded. The fine cornice of Ampthill has modillions and dentils. Even though the old stone steps were not in place in 1928, fragments of them, found nearby, were of the paneled face riser type seen at Scotchtown and at the Archibald Blair house in Williamsburg.

At the time of the 1750 alterations the old house was given added importance by the erection of dependencies flanking and parallel to the mansion. That to the right, or approximate north, was the kitchen, and that to the left was the ball room, the latter having fully paneled walls. They were entirely detached from the house, though in the re-building they have been joined by passages, and were rather like the river-front dependencies of Stratford. Each was three bays long, with a center door under a transom, flanked by a large window on either side, and with a modillioned cornice and hipped roof. At the end away from the house was an end chimney in each building. These had handsomely offset caps and apparently gauged-brick washes. The chimney pier was flanked by a narrow window on either side, two lights wide and six high, as at Wilton, Chelsea, and Elsing Green. Before 1750 the court side displayed its deeply recessed doorway and ends of the wings, with pairs of almost-overlarge windows recalling Dutch work of an earlier period and the Wren house at South Croydon, Surrey.[158]

For all of its interest, the exterior of Ampthill had less academic character than almost any other major house and more the character of the preceding period in England. Except for the narrowness of the hall and a somewhat smaller scale, this was not true of the interior, which was handsomely paneled. On its new site this can better be appreciated, for it has been carefully repaired and cleaned down to the original paint. The whole first floor is paneled to the ceiling, with broad panels below and above a balustrade-type chair rail. This moulding is interesting as having the same form as that at Wilton and Westover with two torus moulds separated by a cove, rather like an Attic base upside-down.

The typical cornices are fully moulded but unenriched, except in the dining room.

The stair now ascends as it was rebuilt in 1750, starting in the old court and ascending in one long run toward the front, or river (now land) door. Although not as fine as the Wythe house in Williamsburg, it resembles it in the lack of a terminal swirl and the use of a square plain newel. Like it, too, the Ampthill stair has simply-scrolled brackets but richly-turned balusters almost identical with them. Except for the lack of spiraling on the shaft and vase, these, together with the Carter's Grove balusters, are of the Sabine Hall type.

The present dining room has the finest of the interior finish, and this is treated with pseudo-Corinthian pilasters flanking the mantel. This latter had been replaced, but originally was apparently a marble facing, as existed elsewhere in the house, and as at Wilton. The over-mantel is paneled, also as at Wilton, with a large rectangular panel framed by narrow panels at the sides and bottom. The pilasters support a full entablature that carries around the whole room, the two lower members being interrupted at the windows. The cornice has a dentil course and rests on a pulvinated frieze supported on an architrave. This, of course, is the scheme of most of the houses of the group, but here the detail is simpler and the scale smaller.

Ampthill seems to have been built by Henry Cary, Jr., who with his father was active in building many of the more important buildings in Williamsburg. From the evidence of Ampthill itself it does not seem that they were architects, but rather contractors, and curiously enough the house has little in common with existing Williamsburg structures. Henry Cary, Jr. came to Chesterfield County in 1727, and three years later was in suffcent funds, from the sale of some property, to start building. This evidence supports the traditional date of the house, but there seems to be no documentary confirmation. On his death in 1750, Henry Cary left Ampthill to his son Archibald Cary, who figured in the events in Virginia leading to the Revolution. When he came into the property he apparently embarked on the alterations to the old house and built the flanking dependencies. Thus, although the mansion itself was probably designed and built by Henry Cary, Jr., the extensions and alterations of about 1750 were carried out by another, obviously the architect of Wilton, its neighbor.

Apparently, the last mansion of the group is Wythe House in Williamsburg, which is usually dated 1755. It is a particularly significant structure in this study, for in its fabric are parallels to the other houses under consideration, and it was the home of Richard Taliaferro himself. Very little is known of Taliaferro and his life, and research in the subject

AMPTHILL, Chesterfield County, on original site. Rebuilt in Richmond in 1929. *Met. Eng.*

THE WYTHE HOUSE, Williamsburg. East front, built by Richard Taliaferro c. 1755. *Peterson.*

AMPTHILL. The staircase and paneling of the hall, as it was enlarged about 1750. *Bagby.*

AMPTHILL. Paneling of the northwest room. The east rooms have pilaster treatments. *Bagby.*

is made difficult by the fact that there were several members of the same name in the family. Richard was the son of Francis and grandson of Robert Taliaferro of York and Gloucester Counties. The latter was the first of the name in Virginia, and received a grant of land in Gloucester as early as 1655. According to the death notice of Richard Taliaferro in the *Virginia Gazette* of July 3, 1779, he was then in his seventy-fourth year, but there is no mention of his birthplace. However, he was long domiciled in Williamsburg, for he was appointed a justice of the peace of James City County at a Council at the Capitol there on December 15, 1737, and on June 10, 1740, was appointed sheriff. Taliaferro, variously styled Major and Colonel, was chosen a member of the Committee of Safety on November 25, 1774, and was later a senator in the Virginia Assembly. His wife was Elizabeth Eggleston.

A member of a distinguished family (whose name in the land-grant is spelled Toliver, as it is pronounced), he was a man of means who not only possessed the finest town house in Williamsburg but nearby a plantation, Powhatan, with a large brick dwelling upon it. The former mansion, now known as Wythe House, he apparently lent, or occupied in common with, his son-in-law George Wythe and his daughter Elizabeth. His will refers to Wythe's tenure of the house. It reads as follows:

"In the Name of God Amen. I, Richard Taliaferro, of the Parish and County of James City, being aged, but of sound mind and memory, do make my last will and testament as followeth. . . .

"I give and desire my House and Lotts in the City of Williamsburg, situate on the West side of Palace Street, and on the North side of the Church yard, to my Son in Law, Mr. George Wythe, and his wife, my daughter Elizabeth, during their lives, . . .

"I give to my Grand son Richard Taliaferro my negro Boy Sam, . . .

"All the rest residue and Remainder of my Estate real and Personal, I Give and Devise to my son Richard Taliaferro and his heirs forever. . . . And I do hereby constitute and appoint my Son in Law the said George Wythe, and my said son Richard Taliaferro, Executors of this my last Will and Testament, hereby revoking all former Wills by me made. . ."

Dated February 3, 1775.[159]

Wythe's distinguished achievements as attorney, justice, reviser of the laws of Virginia, and signer of the Declaration of Independence have caused the house to be known by his name, but he apparently never owned it. The loss of the James City County records in the Civil War prevents verification of the date, but the architectural characteristics would tend to confirm the traditional date of 1755. There is apparently no record of the building of Powhatan, but it seems rather earlier in period. It is probable that both houses were designed and built by Taliaferro, for he is known to have worked both as an architect and builder. Thomas Lee, in a letter cited, apparently called him "our most skillful architect." That he also worked as a contractor is shown by the records of William and Mary College, where he did some work on the grounds, and on the President's House in 1756, and by John Blair's diary. Previous to that date, Taliaferro, in 1749, together with James Wray, had surveyed the Palace and estimated the cost of the alterations and repairs. This seems to be the sum of present knowledge of his life and activities. Any connection he may have had with the mansions of the group must, at least for the present, be based on surmise and by comparison of his own houses to them. He is sure to have known the owners of all of them, for they came constantly to Williamsburg, the Capital of the Colony. Almost all of them were at one time or another members of the Assembly or Governor's Council, and must have been associated with Taliaferro, who in 1737 had sat with Carter Burwell on the Committee of Peace.

It is possible that Taliaferro received his architectural stimulus, if not actual training, from a sojourn in Great Britain, as John Ariss is known to have done at a later date. In this case he may really have been responsible for the design of Rosewell, Christ Church, and Sabine Hall; but if not, he may have participated in the building of the structures under an English architect or builder. The more formal and highly articulated planning of these buildings of the group, and the greater elaboration of their architectural detail, suggests the latter course. However, it may have been merely a period of transition between building in a manner not extravagant for England but over-extravagant in the Colonies, and to one normal to the fortunes of Virginia planters. It is known that the building of Rosewell, the most English of all American houses, impoverished Mann Page's estate, though Robert Carter's fabulous wealth apparently sustained the building of Corotoman and Christ Church and provided means for building his children's houses as well. The mansions subsequent to Sabine Hall are more indigenous in their planning and decoration, and though simpler than Rosewell and its English equivalents, are more elaborate and spacious than mansions of the period in other areas of the eastern seaboard.

Wythe House is the most unassuming of the group, being smaller in size and simply finished. However, it was carefully designed and has characteristics of the other houses. It is of brick, laid in Flemish bond, and is two full stories high, below a low hipped roof. The façade is five bays long with a center door, and the chimneys occur, as at Carter's

Grove, in the end slopes of the roof. The windows have nine over nine light sash throughout, but the glass size in the sash of the upper windows is greatly reduced, and the whole opening becomes smaller.

The diminution of the upper windows is a characteristic of the building that relates it to the others of the group. This variation also occurs at Westover, Elsing Green, Nelson House, and Wilton. In the first two examples the windows are narrower as well as shorter in the second story, but in the latter two the width is the same, the upper only being shorter. This, of course, means that a differently proportioned sash light was used. At Carter's Grove the windows are the same size in both stories. It is easy to see that the diminution was an effort to increase the scale of the buildings. How successful the refinement was can be seen at Wythe House, where a structure of only moderate size has the importance of a much larger one. Decreasing the light size in both dimensions has a tendency to increase the height of a building, as can be seen at Wythe House; but maintaining the same width, with a lesser height, would tend to preserve the normal height of the structure while increasing the scale. Of all of the Carter group, only Sabine Hall and Cleve (and of course Rosewell) used the very generally employed device of sash of fewer lights in the upper floor. In the mansions attributed to John Ariss this form of diminution is consistent. The significance of the design of the fenestration in the Carter group can be appreciated, therefore, and the close association of Wythe House to them can be understood.

The windows of Wythe House, with their broad muntins and wide frames, give interest to a very conservative façade. The doorway is unenriched except by its fine paneled double doors and transom. However, the chief beauty of the building lies in its good lines and fine brickwork. This latter is quiet and rather uniform, with a simple beveled water table and an unmoulded belt course, both in gauged brick, as are the flat arches. The windows, doors, and corners of the house have rubbed dressings, and at the eaves line is a modillioned cornice. None of these features is individual enough to show a special origin, but in the chimneys can be seen an exact parallel to those of Powhatan and the Treasurer's House in Williamsburg, and a relationship to those of Stratford, Carter's Grove, and Nelson House. The form of this group of fine chimney caps is unique in Virginia. In the first three examples the caps have three offset courses below a fascia two courses high. This is surmounted by a steep gauged wash four courses high with a gauged band two courses high at the top. At Nelson House the offset courses are replaced by a gauged and moulded profile approximating a full cornice. This was repeated at Carter's Grove except that a true cornice profile was used, and it was supplemented by a moulded necking four courses below it, thus increasing the importance of cap and shaft.

In plan Wythe House has the late eighteenth-century standard central-hall-and-four-room arrangement. This might mean that it would not be individual enough to relate without question to the plans of the group, were it not for the curious placement, side by side, of the fireplaces of the central chimneys. Although this may have been the original arrangement at the Governor's Palace, it was actually the case at Carter's Grove and Cleve. The extra length of these houses allowed an axial arrangement of both front and back fireplaces, which at Wythe House was not possible. The wide central hall has a fine stair ascending in one long run, as at Ampthill, on the south side of the hall, the house facing east. Like the exterior of the house, the stair is well designed, but the architectural features are unusually simple, in fact almost recalling the "elegant" simplicity of some of the great Quaker houses of Philadelphia. The hall has no paneling except the stair spandrel (it should be noted this has the "bisection" panel mould). For finish it has only a moulded chair rail on a plaster-board and a single crown mould at the ceiling line. However, the stair has a beauty that comes from fine materials and well-studied detail. As at Ampthill, the newel post is square, there are no ramps in the well-moulded handrail, and it is received against the face of the gallery post, which has a fine turned pendant. The stair is, of course, of the open string type and has simply, but suavely scrolled brackets at the stair ends, above a moulded string piece. Of walnut, the balusters are richly turned with the same profile used at Ampthill, Carter's Grove, Abington Church, and as seen in some fine derelict balusters in a cottage near Rosewell. This design, as has been observed, is a simplification of the turned and spiralled balusters of most of the houses of the group. It may be that Palladian influence caused the omission of the spiralling of the shaft and vase. The result is certainly good, and what the balusters lose in richness they gain in strength. If Richard Bayliss were indeed brought from England to do the interiors of Carter's Grove, he may be responsible for this change and for the generally more academic quality of the woodwork there. Except for the stair there is apparently no important original woodwork, and apparently there was none, though fragments of marble mantels were found, and these formed the basis of the new ones now in place. Plaster dados occur throughout, with chair rails on plaster-boards and single moulded cornices. When the writer first knew the house before the renovations of 1927, the mantels were hardly more than moulded architraves with, perhaps, cornice shelves, but these were changed at that time. However, the stair shows that the simplicity was by design, and it also shows the indubitable relationship to Carter's Grove and its kindred mansions.

The Wythe House, Williamsburg. A detail of the stair balustrade and brackets. *Met. Eng.*

Weyanoke, Charles City County. Unusual example of Chinese trellis stair design. *Johnston.*

At Powhatan, because of the firing of the house during the Civil War, there is nothing but the brickwork of the original structure remaining. This has the same beauty and simplicity as Wythe House, with a beveled water table, a flat belt course of gauged brick, and deep flat arches over the openings. The house is five bays long, with a center door. The chimneys occur in the end walls, and like those at Westover are inordinately tall, indicating that the old hipped roof was steeply pitched. In the attic this pitch can be confirmed by the old line in the brickwork of the chimneys. The generally more satisfactory appearance of these chimneys, the fine bonding of their shafts, and the corbelling and gauging of their caps suggest that those at Westover may have been rebuilt at some time. This is also suggested by their simple, square plan, which lacks the shafted inside flue of Powhatan.

Like those at Carter's Grove the window openings of Powhatan are uniform in size, without diminution, and would have had nine over nine light sash, but these, of course, were lost in the fire. It is interesting to note that Powhatan, of all the houses of the group, has all of the header brick glazed; so there is an all-over pattern like that at the Governor's Palace and other early buildings. The date of the house may well be before 1740.

It is unfortunate that so little explicit information regarding the design and construction of the great brick houses from Rosewell to Elsing Green remains. Their family relationship is clear, but it may remain a question in many students' minds if the relationship were not as much a result of geography as authorship. In traditional building both factors are equally important, but in academic architecture this is not so. The persistence of certain stylistic mannerisms and derivation from the same publication make the question of authorship paramount. In these Virginia mansions, the finest group of brick Georgian structures outside of England, the mark of the same designer can definitely be seen, and the circumstantial evidence, as well as one brief literary reference, indicate that this was Richard Taliaferro, distinguished citizen and architect, of Williamsburg.

On the edge of the stream of formal architecture in Virginia there are structures that are the work of master builders in which the correct detail of English handbooks is applied to purely traditional buildings. The result is a great number of excellent houses that have more native quality than formal designs, and in domestic architecture constitute a group of charm and livability. Outstanding examples are medium-sized dwellings such as Toddsbury in Gloucester; Claremont; Four Mile Tree in Surry County; and larger houses such as Ditchley, Northumberland County; Weyanoke, Charles City County; and Hillsborough, King and

Queen County. The smaller houses all have roofs of the jerkin-head or the useful-gambrel types, with resulting informal exteriors, but all have excellent and rather formal interior woodwork employing academic detail. The larger houses are two stories high with hipped roofs, and although two are of frame construction, Ditchley is of brick. All have a more architectural character than do the medium-sized dwellings.

The field that this group covers is so extensive that its discussion is a work in itself. There is, however, one house in this category whose architectural qualities are so marked that it must be included in this study of its more stylized contemporaries. This is Gunston Hall in Fairfax County, built in 1755-58 by George Mason on traditional lines, with fine and elaborate architectural detail by William Buckland.[160] The latter came from London to the Colony in 1755 with Thompson Mason, under an indenture of four years, specifically to assist in the construction of the house. After the completion of Gunston Hall, Buckland apparently stayed in the vicinity for several years, but later settled in Annapolis, Maryland, where he designed a number of distinguished and beautiful mansions. An exhaustive study has been made of his life and works, and has produced many interesting facts concerning Buckland's career and his buildings.[161]

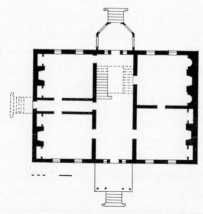

GUNSTON HALL, Fairfax County.

By good fortune his annotated indenture papers were discovered in the Maryland archives. In Buckland's own writing is a statement that he was born in the parish of St. Peter-in-the-East, in Oxford, England, on August 14, 1734, and that in 1748 he was apprenticed to his uncle, James, a bookseller and joiner of London. He therefore had seven years' training in the center of all British art, undoubtedly working on important buildings under competent supervision and with all the current architectural publications for reference. He even may have worked on Honington Hall in Oxfordshire,[162] which has much in common with Buckland's work at Annapolis and which was extensively altered before 1750. It not only possesses many of the same exterior details as Gunston, including the demi-octagonal porch with a Doric order, but the curious and perhaps unique window shutters, with octagonal panels, found also in Annapolis in the Hammond Harwood and Paca houses.[163]

Even if Buckland were only the elaborator of a traditional scheme, his work at Gunston Hall is proven by documentary evidence rather than by the structural evidence of the house itself. At the expiration of his indenture George Mason endorsed the paper with the statement that Buckland had done all the joining and carving in the house. It does not seem that Mason had another architect, for Buckland's is the only part of the building that has academic architectural character. It would be interesting to follow the statement on the indenture with an analysis of the beautiful and elaborate interiors and to identify them with plates in various books. However, even Halsey with his superb collection of architectural books of the period was unable to do so. It probably could not be done without consulting all seventeen volumes in Buckland's library, many of which are unobtainable in this country. Such a number of costly architectural works in Buckland's time must have been exceptional. Other architects working in Virginia seemed to derive their precedent from only three or four books.

Gunston Hall, in spite of its not inconsiderable size, is really a large cottage in architectural effect. It is one story high above a usable basement, and has a gable roof with dormers and two pairs of end chimneys. In plan it is simply the central-hall-and-four-room type familiar throughout Virginia, and indeed familiar to the country after 1750. There can be no doubt that George Mason himself was responsible for the use of this Colonial type, for it must have been at least a novelty to Buckland, who had been working in the current style in England. Evidently George Mason was willing to give his assistant freedom in the selection of the style of the detail, once he had established the form. It is the detail that sets the house apart from any other of its period and bestows upon it a real architectural quality.

Built of brick, laid in Flemish bond, it has stone quoins at the corners and a stone water table, as well as keys to the flat arches and chimney caps. It is simply five bays in length with center doors, both of which are protected by wood porches of unusual and interesting form. That of the land front has two pairs of Doric columns supporting an arched central bay. This creates the familiar Palladian motive, which is here covered by a broad pediment. All of this is beautifully executed with classically

GUNSTON HALL, Fairfax County. A traditional type with fashionable trim of 1758. *Brostrup.*

GUNSTON HALL, Fairfax County. Entrance hall showing double arch and stairway. *Met. Eng.*

proportioned columns and mouldings. The river-front porch may have been derived from an engraving of a Roman coin. This shows a similar feature in the Temple of Tyche in Eumeneia. It is an engaged octagon with five of the eight faces exposed. Each one of these is pierced by an arched opening with moulded imposts and keys. Aside from the porches and stone trim, the exterior has little detail except a good modillioned cornice across the two fronts, which at the gable ends becomes a cove and ascends the rake in place of a barge board.

On the interior, Buckland, who at first was perhaps primarily a carver, created rooms of outstanding richness and beauty with door and window trim unparalleled in elaboration in Virginia. These he derived or adapted from the great style books of the period. These books he possessed in unusual number, due, apparently, to his uncle. In the hall the source of the designs is less apparent than in the rooms themselves, for here the trim is simpler. In form the hall is a broad passage extending from door to door, but divided near the middle by a curious double arch. Each of the arches is elliptical, and the spandrel between them is a pendant decorated with a single triglyph and baroque scrolls, from the spring line of which hangs a carved drop. This somewhat bizarre motive may have been inspired by that at Tulip Hill in Maryland, which is apparently the only other example in the area, though others occur on a smaller scale in New England. The double arch frames the stair, which ascends in the customary way in one long initial flight and two short ones. It lacks the deep treads of the usual Virginia stair, and in consequence has only two balusters to each step. These, however, are unusually heavy and rich, and may be from Plates LXII and LXIV in Swan's *British Architect*. Each baluster comprises a vase turning below a tall tapered shaft. Both turnings are supplied with a base and cap and are separated by a rectangular block. The variation from the usual is in their weight and in the definite subordination of the vase to the shaft, which here is fluted. Except for the balusters at Christ Church in Lancaster, no other fluted examples seem to remain in major Virginia buildings, and none the width of those at Gunston Hall, which resemble, rather, Philadelphia balusters. The use of two to a tread is unusual, three being normally employed. The brackets are carved with simple acanthus scrolls, the rosettes of which seem to have been removed.

The house is unique in Virginia for its two principal rooms, one of which is in the so-called Chinese Chippendale style and the other in baroque Palladian. In both cases the mantels were replaced during the Victorian period, and those now in place were designed at the time of the restoration on the lines of the door and window trim. Both rooms show in various ways Buckland's immaturity as a designer and the re-

GUNSTON HALL, Fairfax County. A detail of the stair balustrade and brackets. *Met. Eng.*

GUNSTON HALL, Fairfax County. Chinese Chippendale Room, by William Buckland. *Met. Eng.*

GUNSTON HALL, Fairfax County. Palladian Room, the doorway, with stair beyond. *Met. Eng.*

GUNSTON HALL, Fairfax County. Palladian Room. Detail of trim and window frames. *Met. Eng.*

strictions of a building perhaps already begun when he reached this country. The small size of the rooms and their unimaginative planning prevented the effects he was later to achieve in his Annapolis work. In spite of these drawbacks, the interiors of Gunston Hall stand as a monument to his ability as well as to its statesman-builder.

The Chinese Chippendale room, the only one of its type in Virginia, has great individuality and distinction. The doors and windows are trimmed with broad, shallow roll mouldings. At the head of each an entablature occurs, the frieze being carved with strapwork, and the cornice supporting a cresting of concave scallops. It is these latter that give the room a suggestion of Chinese style. It is a suggestion such as this that was characteristic of the style, and sounded a note that was to be carried out by trellis-back chairs, pagoda-roofed pier tables, scenic wall paper, and oriental porcelains. The dado here is sheathed, with moulded cap and base.

The Palladian room is perhaps the most important example of carved decoration of its period in the country. The chair rail, base, pilasters, and entablatures of both doors and windows are elaborately carved, as is the trim of the arched-top cupboards. All of this trim, except the field of the dado, is painted, but the walls themselves are sheathed vertically in natural pine, evidently as a backing for fabric. The marks of the tacks which actually fixed it to the sheathing may be seen where the borders were applied. Fabric-hung walls were not entirely unfamiliar in Virginia as evidenced by advertisements in the *Virginia Gazette*.[164]

The trim of all of the openings is extremely rich, each of the doors having classically proportioned Doric pilasters supporting a full entablature and a broken pediment. The pilasters are fluted and have full Attic bases, both toruses of which are carved. The capitals have the fascia decorated with continuous fluting, the arisses being delicately fretted. The crown mould is enriched with water-leaf ornament and the main ovolo with egg and dart above a band of bead and billet. The moulding of the necking is also carved.

The architrave of the door and window heads is rudimentary, but the vertical face is made more important by the use of an elaborate leaf carving covering the soffit and forming, in effect, a continuous corbel. Strap carving of interlacing diagonal lines fills the frieze, thus producing a sort of fret. The window shutters are paneled, and the narrow casing that receives them, inside the pilasters, has a sort of lambrequin in an applied fret across the top and down the sides for a foot or so. The narrowness of the windows and the height of the embrasure impart a somewhat over-tall effect. The cupboards are also over lofty, but the open work at the head makes the effect more agreeable. Here the pilasters receive a band of the entablature, and each one-half of the broken pediment. The space in the tympanum above the arched head is continuous with the sheathed walls, and in the center is set a scrolled and carved keystone. The cupboards themselves are apsidal in plan with a semi-dome at the head and no decoration other than the scrolled shelves. The main cornice itself is of almost maximum richness, having the cymatium, modillions, and three-part bed mould all decorated. Leaf ornament occurs on the corona and the cyma of the bed mould, the modillions are carved and scrolled, and between them the soffit of the cymatium is enriched with rosettes. The ovolo of the bed mould is carved with egg and dart, and below it is a dentil course. Only the Philadelphia cornices with their baroque carved friezes can compare with this superb crowning feature.

The dado around the entire room is sheathed, except at the pedestals, where the panel mould is carved with leaf ornament. The base is formed of a carved cyma-recta run with acanthus leaves below a carved quarter round. The chair rail has the fascia covered with a Greek key fret, the upper mould being carved with a water-leaf design.

There is a lapse of several years between the expiration of William Buckland's indenture in 1759 and the beginning of his residence in Annapolis about 1770. Nothing seems to be known of his activities during this time, but it is obvious that a man of his talents, with the backing of his distinguished patron, would have been kept busy. He is said to have built the Ballendine house at Occoquan,[165] but it is a traditional stone building possessing none of the architectural quality with which he would have endowed it. That he might have worked with John Ariss on Mount Airy, in Richmond County (1758-62), is speculation, but it is a surmise that is prompted by the superb fragments of carved bed moulds that survive from the finish of the office. The problem of qualified craftsmen must have followed the architects and builders of the Colonial period, and the infrequent availability of them would explain the wide differences in quality between the trim of related houses. Perhaps the most likely place for him to busy himself was at Dumfries, only a few miles from Gunston Hall, though the style of the two known mansions there was more in the style of James Wren, the builder of Pohick Church, Christ Church, Alexandria, and Falls Church. Dumfries was a prosperous port, and both George Mason and John Tayloe were among the founders of the town in 1759. In it lived a distinguished group of merchants and gentlemen. Among them was Major Fouchee Tebbs, who built the fine mansion on the side of the hill which, after a long period of dilapidation, fell a victim to the great storm of 1933. This mansion and the old hotel were the only buildings of architectural character that survived the decay of the town, the decay which followed the silting of the harbor, the removal of the county seat of Prince William to Manassas, and the devastating fire of 1833.

The two houses were large-scale brick structures with cut-stone trim, but the Tebbs house had certain immaturities in design that suggest it may have been the earlier of the two. Little evidence as to its date, except a fire-back dated 1762,[166] which stood in place until the interior woodwork was removed about 1920, seems to remain.

The front of the house, which was situated on a steep hill, was really three full stories high, though the first floor was treated as a basement and the principal floor lined with the grade in the rear. The house was five bays long but only two deep, and was covered by a rather low hipped roof. At the break of the hip the chimneys, almost square shafts with moulded stone caps, occurred. The façade was symmetrical with corner quoins, a stone belt course, and a fine modillioned wood cornice. There was an arched center door framed with cut-stone pilasters supporting a moulded archivolt. As has been observed, this motive was used also at Kenmore in the entrance to the great drawing room, and cannot be considered entirely successful, since the archivolt covered only one half of the pilaster cap. If the Tebbs house door had been protected by a pedimented hood resting on corbels, as perhaps was intended, the design would have been much improved.

Approaching the door was a long flight of stone steps which splayed out toward the bottom. Strangely enough, they were not provided with wrought-iron railings which, on account of the height of the steps, would seem indispensable. The whole basement wall was of coursed stonework, and the window openings were spanned by stone flat arches. The upper windows, which were graduated in height from the first to second story, were untrimmed except for stone flat arches with fluted keys. These, however, were employed only on the façade, brick flat arches being used on the other elevations. An unusual feature of the front wall was that, like the old hotel, it was laid in all-header bond, though Flemish bond was used elsewhere. Except for one or two minor structures, there seem to be no other Virginia examples of all-header bond extant, though many may be seen in Maryland. In Annapolis especially, this bond was a favorite. In England it was seldom used, a rare example being at "The Old Hall" at Ormsby St. Margaret, and dated about 1735.[167] A feature of the exterior of the Tebbs house was the main cornice, which was well moulded and enriched with modillions. Except for this and some of the sash, with its narrow staff bead, there was no early exterior woodwork surviving.

In plan, the house had a central stair hall with one large room on the left and two smaller on the right. This arrangement, with symmetrical chimneys on the roof, was managed by carrying the flues of the north or right-hand chimney at an angle to come out of the roof at the correct location. The stair ascended the right-hand wall and returned toward the front from a rear landing. This prevented access to the right rear second-floor room, to which there was a supplementary stair. The basement rooms were used also, probably for service and merchandise. If there were dependencies, no evidence of them remained.

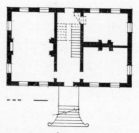

TEBBS HOUSE, Dumfries.

The interior woodwork was distinguished, but had little carved ornament. All of it was removed before the time the house was seen by the writer, but much of it is preserved elsewhere. The great south room was the important one of the house, and this had a dado with pedestal-type base and chair rail. At the ceiling line was an excellent, fully-moulded cornice with a band of Wall of Troy dentils. There were two windows in each of the three outside walls, and between the two in the long south wall was a cupboard, the reveal of which was gained from the thick brick wall. This, as well as the windows, was set on the chair rail, and also like them was trimmed by a moulded architrave. There is remarkable similarity between these cupboard doors and those in the Blue Room at the Carlyle house in Alexandria. Each of the double doors has a single panel arched at the top. The mantel of the Tebbs house is of the familiar Palladian type, with a marble facing framed by a backband, broken out in crossettes at the head. The frieze, with scrolled brackets, above the mantel supports a full cornice-shelf. The overmantel panel also has crossettes and is supported by a carved frieze and pediment. This forms a conservative but handsome room of its type. It is interesting to observe that both the upper and lower halls had small, plaster, cove cornices with moulded cymatiums and neckings. Perhaps unique in Virginia was the framing of the great-room floor, which had girders running from north to south, with smaller perpendicular members above and below them. This was evidently a recognized structural form and is referred to in Nicholson's *Encyclopedia of Architecture* as a "carcase" floor.[168]

TEBBS HOUSE, Dumfries, Prince William County, c. 1760; destroyed 1933. *Columbia Hist. Soc.*

OLD HOTEL, Dumfries, Prince William County. Survivor of a Georgian town. *Brostrup, HABS.*

TEBBS HOUSE. Basement wall, window arch, and water table. *Author.*

TEBBS HOUSE. Doorway with cut stone pilasters and arch. *Author.*

OLD HOTEL. Header bond unique in Virginia. *Brostrup, HABS.*

TEBBS HOUSE. Upper wall with bonding and stone trim. *Author.*

Unfortunately, the old hotel has no early interior trim, but the exterior effect is good in spite of the addition of a porch and the replacement of the old small light sash. The building is deeper, and perhaps longer, than the Tebbs house, and it is more successful in its proportions. The façade is also five bays long with a center door and a low hipped roof. Here the side elevations are three windows deep with two chimneys in each end wall. The front wall is laid in header bond with rusticated stone quoins at the corners, and has a fine rusticated stone doorway. The window openings are spanned by brick flat arches with stone keys, and the basement wall is of random ashlar below a moulded stone water table. The main cornice is of wood, fully moulded, with modillions.

As has been observed, the architecture of the fifty years following the erection of the Governor's Palace was more in the style of Wren than of the Burlingtonians, who succeeded him about 1710. It is only in minor ways that any of the mansions discussed up to this point betray the approach of a new style. In fact, except for a few outstanding buildings, those that were to follow were so tinctured by tradition that the two phases of Virginia Georgian blended together and left no sharp line of demarcation between them.

REFERENCES

1. Philip Alexander Bruce, *Economic History of Virginia in the Seventeenth Century . . .*, II, 569.

2. *Journal of the House of Burgesses,* April 30, 1706: *Resolved* That a duty of twenty shillings per head be laid upon Negros imported toward defraying the Charge of building an house for the Governor."

3. *William and Mary Quarterly,* X, 140.

4. Francis Price, *Builder's Dictionary,* under "Building."

5. Frances Benjamin Johnston and Thomas Tileston Waterman, *The Early Architecture of North Carolina,* pp. 82-83.

6. *Virginia Magazine of History and Biography,* XXXVI, 343.

7. Manuscript in the Library of Congress.

8. Christ Church Parish Book (Middlesex County), 1663-1767. Photostat Virginia State Library, p. 107.

9. Philip Slaughter, *The History of Truro Parish in Virginia,* p. 53.

10. Benjamin Duvall Chambers, *Old Chapel and the Parish in Clarke County, Virginia . . .*, p. 59.

11. Colonial Office 5, Vol. 1327, p. 127. Transcript Library of Congress; Thomas Lee to Board of Trade November 7, 1749. "The Gover⁽ˢ⁾ hous, gardens &c, has been Viewed & examined by our most Skillful Architect & he reports that the necessary repairs will cost £1259 . . . ."

12. Architects' Emergency Committee, *Great Georgian House of America,* I, 15.

13. Lloyd, *A History of the English House,* Figure 188.

14. *Virginia Magazine of History and Biography,* XXXVI, 343.

15. William Waller Hening, *The Statutes At Large; Being a Collection of All the Laws of Virginia from the First Session of the Legislature in the Year 1619,* III, 285.

16. Lyon Gardiner Tyler, *Williamsburg, the Old Colonial Capital . . .*, p. 213.

17. *Country Life* (London), Vol. 74, Nos. 1924-25, December 2, 1933, pp. 587-93; December 9, 1933, pp. 624-30.

18. Lawrence Edward Tanner, *Westminster School, a History.*

19. See Jefferson drawing on page 396.

20. Gooch Papers Transcripts, February 4, 1749-50. Virginia Historical Society.

21. For details of Wren's life see Lena Milman, *Sir Christopher Wren,* and *Dictionary of National Biography.*

22. Tipping, *English Homes, Period IV,* I, 1-22.

23. Samuel Pepys, *The Diary of Samuel Pepys . . .*, VIII, 268.

24. Tanner, *Westminster School,* p. 84.

25. Pepys, *Diary,* V, 332.

26. Tunstall Small and Christopher Woodbridge, *Houses of the Wren and Early Georgian Periods,* p. 117.

27. Historic American Buildings Survey.

28. *Ibid.*

29. Blomfield, *A History of Renaissance Architecture,* I, 120; II, 285.

30. Hugh Jones, *The Present State of Virginia,* p. 36.

31. Henry Howe, *Historical Collections of Virginia,* pp. 328-29.

32. Small and Woodbridge, *Houses of the Wren and Early Georgian Periods,* p. 125.

33. Celia Fiennes, *Through England on a Side Saddle, in the Time of William and Mary*, p. 304.

34. William Byrd, *The Secret Diary of William Byrd of Westover*, p. 429.

35. *Virginia Magazine of History and Biography*, XXXII, 118.

36. Tipping, *English Homes, Period IV*, I, 104.

37. *Ibid., Period V*, I, 270.

38. Fiennes, *Through England on a Side Saddle*, p. 18.

39. *Ibid.*, p. 44.

40. Journal of the House of Burgesses, 1712-26, p. 297.

41. Waterman and Barrows, *Domestic Colonial Architecture*, p. 143.

42. Architects' Emergency Committee, *Great Georgian Houses*, I, 158-59.

43. Tipping, *English Homes, Period V*, I, 267.

44. Lloyd, *A History of the English House*, pp. 408-09.

45. Journal of the House of Burgesses, 1712-26, p. 297.

46. Lloyd, *A History of the English House*, Figure 792.

47. *Tuileries Brochures*, I, 31.

48. Tipping, *English Homes, Period IV*, I, 48-49.

49. Fiennes, *Through England on a Side Saddle*, p. 232.

50. *Ibid.*, p. 66.

51. *Ibid.*, p. 295.

52. Mervyn Edmund Macartney, *English Houses & Gardens in the 17th and 18th Centuries*, Plate III.

53. Ledger of Humphrey Harwood, August 7, 1787. Manuscript at Williamsburg.

54. Journal of the House of Burgesses, 1712-26, p. 297.

55. Fiennes, *Through England on a Side Saddle*, p. 307.

56. On September 20, 1795, Washington ordered for Mount Vernon "1 Mahogany Close Stool Case in the Newest taste wt. place for Chamber pot & ca." John Clement Fitzpatrick, editor, *The Diaries of George Washington, 1748-1799*, II, 331.

57. Robert Alexander Lancaster, *Historic Virginia Homes and Churches*, p. 335.

58. Historic American Buildings Survey (photo).

59. *Ibid.*

60. Samuel Gaillard Stoney, *Plantations of the Carolina Low Country*, pp. 119, 170.

61. *William and Mary Quarterly*, 1st Series, XII, 24.

62. Historic American Buildings Survey (photos).

63. Grymes was the third generation of the family in Virginia. He was at William and Mary Grammar School in 1704, Sheriff in 1724-25, and a Burgess in 1727-28. He married Frances Jennings, daughter of Edmund Jennings (1659-1727) who was a resident both of Rippon, England, and of Rippon Hall, York County.

64. Historic American Buildings Survey.

65. Fiennes, *Through England on a Side Saddle*, p. 298.

66. Lloyd, *A History of the English House*, p. 164.

67. Downman-Ball Letter Book. Manuscript Division of Library of Congress.

68. Historic American Buildings Survey. (Demolished about 1941.)

69. *Ibid.*

70. William Salmon, *Palladio Londinensis: or the London Art of Building*, p. 49.

71. *Ibid.*

72. Georgian Society, *Records of Eighteenth Century Domestic Architecture and Decoration in Dublin*, Vol. II, Plate XXVIII.

73. Salmon, *Palladio Londinensis*, p. 69.

74. *Ibid.*, p. 69.

75. Historic American Buildings Survey.

76. Waterman and Barrows, *Domestic Colonial Architecture*, p. 48.

77. John Evelyn, *Diary and Correspondence of John Evelyn*, II, 48.

78. Historic American Buildings Survey.

79. Joseph Moxon, *Mechanick Exercises Or, The Doctrine of Handy-Works*, p. 102.

80. Edward M. Riley, *The History of the Founding and Development of Yorktown, Virginia, 1691-1781*, pp. 80-85.

81. See Frances Stackhouse Acton, *The Castles and Old Mansions of Shropshire*; Stanley Leighton, *Shropshire Houses, Past and Present*.

82. *Tuileries Brochures*. I, 67-71.

83. Tipping, *English Homes, Period V*, I, 139-54.

84. Sir Henry Wotton, *The Elements of Architicture*, p. 70.

85. Fiennes, *Through England on a Side Saddle*, p. 155.

86. Tipping, *English Homes, Period IV*, I, 63-112.

87. *Ibid.*, pp. 141-56.

88. Wotton, *The Elements of Architecture*, p. 78.

89. Richard Blome, *The Gentleman's Recreation*.

90. Margaret Jourdain, *English Interiors in Smaller Houses, from the Restoration to the Regency, 1660-1830*, p. 84.

91. Salmon, *Palladio Londinensis*, p. 49.

92. *Ibid.*, Plate XXI.

93. Drawing at the Society for the Preservation of New England Antiquities.

94. Colonial Offices, vol 1327, p. 127. Manuscript Division, Library of Congress.

95. *William and Mary Quarterly*, 1st Series, VII, 145.

96. *Ibid.*, 2nd Series, VIII, 239.

97. *Ibid.*, 240.

98. Seen by the author.

99. Tipping, *English Homes, Period IV*, I, 420.

100. Acton, *The Castles and Old Mansions of Shropshire*, p. 56; Leighton, *Shropshire Houses*, p. 19.

101. *Virginia Magazine of History and Biography*, XXXIV, 104.

102. *Ibid.*, VI, 1.

103. *Ibid.*, XXVI, 209; XXIX, 352.

104. Tipping, *English Homes, Period IV*, I, Plate VII.

105. Hening, *The Statutes at Large*, III, 421. Act of October, 1705, confirming the Act of April, 1699.

106. *Virginia Magazine of History and Biography*, VI, 1.

107. Hening, *The Statutes at Large*, V, 278.

108. Mutual Assurance Society of Virginia (microfilm). Virginia State Library.

109. *Richmond Times Dispatch*, March 26, 1916.

110. Carter Burwell's Account Book, January 14, 1751, at Millwood, Virginia.

111. Salmon, *Palladio Londinensis*, Plates XXIII and XXVII.

112. Waterman and Barrows, *Domestic Colonial Architecture*, p. 163.

113. Richard Neve, *The City and Country Purchasers and Builders Dictionary*, p. 36.

114. Anne Page Saunders, *Leonora and the Ghost*, pp. 1-2; also *Southern Literary Messenger*, X, 41, January, 1844.

115. William Fitzhugh Letter Book, 1682. Manuscript Division, Library of Congress.

116. Fiennes, *Through England on a Side Saddle*, p. 306.

117. The original alteration drawings are preserved in the house.

118. Mutual Assurance Society of Virginia (microfilm). Virginia State Library. (The buildings are not dimensioned but are shown symme-

trically and noted as "brick covered with wood," 162' distant).

119. Fiennes, *Through England on a Side Saddle*, p. 43.

120. Louis Morton, *Robert Carter of Nomini Hall*, p. 31.

121. Robert Carter's Letter Book. Manuscript Division, Library of Congress.

122. Philip Vickers Fithian, *Philip Vickers Fithian, Journal and Letters, 1764-74*, p. 129.

123. Waterman and Barrows, *Domestic Colonial Architecture*, p. 77.

124. Robert Carter's Letter Book, March 5, 1775. Manuscript Division, Library of Congress.

125. Byrd, *The Secret Diary of William Byrd*, p. 345.

126. Gardner, *English Ironwork of the XVIIth and XVIIIth Centuries*, Plate XLV. See also other examples cited and further information.

127. Lancaster, *Historic Virginia Homes and Churches*, p. 81.

128. Daniel Fenning and J. Collyer, *A New System of Geography*, p. 661.

129. *Virginia Magazine of History and Biography*, XLVI, 244.

130. Byrd, *The Secret Diary of William Byrd*. References under dates cited.

131. *William and Mary Quarterly*, 1st Series, XX, 17.

132. William Keith, *The History of the British Plantations in America (1710)*, pp. 170-72.

133. Fitzpatrick, *The Diaries of George Washington*, II, 157.

134. Moxon, *Mechanick Exercises*, p. 79.

135. Dr. Paul Howle, Richmond.

136. Historic American Buildings Survey. (This house was demolished about 1930 for re-erection in Williamsburg, but is not now rebuilt).

137. Mrs. Edith Dabney (Tunis) Sale, *Interiors of Virginia Houses of Colonial Times*, p. 92.

138. (François Jean) Marquis de Chastellux, *Travels in North America in the Years 1780-81-82*, p. 220. See also Riley, *Yorktown*.

139. Waterman and Barrows, *Domestic Colonial Architecture*, pp. 111-16.

140. Fiennes, *Through England on a Side Saddle*, p. 57.

141. Small and Woodbridge, *Houses of the Wren and Early Georgian Periods*, p. 95.

142. *Journal of the American Institute of Architects*, June, 1915, III, # 6, 234-40.

143. Carter Burwell's Account Book at Millwood, Virginia.

144. Hening, *The Statutes at Large*, VI, 212.

145. *William and Mary Quarterly*, 1st Series, XII, 77.

146. Legislative Journals of the Council of Colonial Virginia, I, 493 (1710).

147. Waterman and Barrows, *Domestic Colonial Architecture*, p. 103.

148. Lloyd, *A History of the English House*, p. 475.

149. Fiske Kimball, *Domestic Architecture of the American Colonies and of the Early Republic*, p. 132.

150. Johnston and Waterman, *The Early Architecture of North Carolina*, p. 33.

151. Jourdain, *English Interiors in Smaller Houses*, p. 130.

152. *New Oxford Dictionary* under Paint: "a modern fashionable house ...daubed over with oil and paint." (1753).

153. Description to C. G. Lee, Esq.

154. Frederick Horner, *The History of the Blair, Banister and Braxton Families*, p. 165.

155. Architects' Emergency Committee, *Great Georgian Houses*, II, 116. (Photograph of inscription).

156. Waterman and Barrows, *Do-*

mestic Colonial Architecture, pp. 70, 117.

157. *Ibid.*, p. 44.

158. Lloyd, *A History of the English House*, p. 232.

159. *William and Mary Quarterly*, 1st Series, XII, 124-25.

160. Harry R. Connor, *Gunston Hall, Fairfax County, Virginia*, pp. 227-46.

161. By the late R.T.H. Halsey, to whom the author is indebted for all information as to precedent used at Gunston Hall.

162. Tipping, *English Homes, Period V*, I, 255-80.

163. Architects' Emergency Committee, *Great Georgian Houses*, I, 158-59.

164. *Virginia Gazette*, December 28, 1769.

165. (Writer's Program, Virginia), *Virginia, a Guide . . .*, p. 344.

166. Lewis Augustus Coffin, Jr., and Arthur C. Holden, *Brick Architecture of the Colonial Period in Maryland & Virginia*, p. 48.

167. Nathaniel Lloyd, *A History of English Brickwork*, p. 238.

168. Peter Nicholson, *Encyclopedia of Architecture*, I, 77.

MOUNT VERNON, Fairfax County. Colonial Palladian Architecture. *Johnston.*

4. THE MID-GEORGIAN PERIOD 1750-1765

Palladio's Monumental Style; Mansions with Connected Dependencies

THE FIRST half of the eighteenth century in Virginia mansion building was substantially a continuation of that style which Wren had initiated in England and which reached its flower in the years of Queen Anne's reign. Even in England smaller manor houses were often built in this style long after the beginning of the Palladian revival under Lord Burlington. It is not surprising, therefore, that little disturbance occurred in the manner in which the Virginia planters housed themselves until the middle of the century, and that Carter's Grove, built in 1751, was more Queen Anne in style than it was Mid-Georgian.

There was more than just lag in transmitting the new fashions from England. Palladian was essentially a monumental style, utilizing classic trim and highly articulated planning. Both of these were beyond the means of the Virginians, whose fortunes were modest compared with the fabulous wealth of the English nobles. They therefore continued to build their plantation houses with relatively simple plans and to construct their elevations in native materials, brick, stone, and wood. If cut stone was employed, it was usually done sparingly, and was sometimes imported English stone and sometimes from the Aquia Creek quarries.

Even in the great building years from 1750 to the Revolution, the essays in Palladian design in Virginia were unassuming when compared to the English examples. The cost of the great stone columns and pediments was prohibitive, and even though the trim of the Virginia houses was sometimes highly stylized, it was never more than the type of architectural feature that could be conveniently shipped in the hold of a ship out of Bristol together with other supplies coming to the Colonies. The relatively small scale of Virginia Palladian is the reason for its charm and livability, and the ingenuity the designers used to attain an effect of dignity and size is a source of never-ending interest and admiration. Its translation to Virginia is apparently due to one man, a gentleman and architect, John Ariss of Westmoreland.

Even the name of this most important figure in the history of American Georgian architecture has been lost for over a hundred years. Only through an advertisement which he inserted in the *Maryland Gazette* of May 22, 1751, has a partial recovery of his career been made possible. This reads:

"John Oriss,—'By the Subscriber (lately from Great Britain) Buildings
of all Sorts and Dimensions are undertaken and performed in the neatest
Manner, (and at cheaper rates) either of the Ancient or Modern Order
of Gibbs' Architect and if any Gentleman should want plans, Bills of
Scantling or bill of Charges, for any Fabric, or Public Edefice, may have
them by applying to the Subscriber at Major John Bushrods at Westmoreland County, Va., where may be seen a great variety and sundry Draughts
of Buildings in Miniature, and some buildings near finished after the
Modern Taste.' John Orliss."

This advertisement is in itself extremely informing in that it indicates
that Ariss had an acquaintance with British architecture, shows that he
provided plans as an architect would and that he was not merely a
builder, and indicates that he actually had buildings under construction.
Also valuable is his reference to his use of the publications of Gibbs,
the distinguished British architect of the period. The advertisement
indicates that Ariss was possessed of British style books or a group of
drawings of structures of the type. It seems from a study of his buildings
that the two publications he used most were James Gibbs's *Book of
Architecture* and William Adam's *Vitruvius Scoticus*.

Lastly, his reference to his residence at Major Bushrod's (Bushfield)
in Westmoreland County, Virginia, identified Ariss as the advertiser,
establishing his family connections and permitting the tracing of his
career. Bushfield was property purchased by the Bushrods from the
Spencers.

John Ariss was born about 1725, probably at Albany, Westmoreland
County, to John and Frances (Spencer) Ariss. His mother was the
"daughter and sole heir of John Spencer,"[1] and granddaughter of the
Honorable Nicholas Spencer of Cople Parish, Westmoreland. Spencer
was a distinguished Virginia figure, having emigrated there in 1657
from Cople, Bedfordshire, England. He returned to England, where he
inherited large estates from his father, and died in 1699. During his
years in Virginia he held a number of important offices, including that
of a Burgess, Secretary of State, President of the Council, and Acting
Governor (1683-89). With John Washington he patented the Mount
Vernon estate in 1674 and purchased Albany in the same year. John
Spencer was a man of wealth, and possessed considerable lands in
Westmoreland as well as "that moiety of 5,000 acres held in joint tenancy
with Captain Lawrence Washington." [2] This reference to the Washingtons
is an important one, and the joint tenancy referred to perhaps resulted
from a family connection, for there are Spencers in the Washington
genealogy. References to constant associations with the Washington
family appear throughout the life records of John Ariss, the younger.

The exact date of his birth has not been established, but he is referred to as a minor in his father's will, probated in 1730,[3] and in 1743 he chose his brother Spencer "Ayres" as his guardian,[4] showing he had not then reached his majority. These seem to be the only records of him before his advertisement of 1751. It can be assumed that on his coming of age he went to Great Britain, and in addition to observing fine buildings may even have served an apprenticeship with an architect there. Although it is possible that he visited his mother's family in Cople, the last parish record dealing with the Spencer family there was dated 1707.[5] A chalice was presented to the church by a William Spencer about 1700.[6]

The records concerning Ariss from 1751 on concern his places of residence and public activities rather than his personal life. Up to the present time no personal letters or memorabilia of his have been found. The public records show that he was a resident of Westmoreland County until about 1755,[7] of Richmond County until about 1762,[8] and of Berkeley County from about 1770[9] to his death in 1799.

It seems possible that Ariss inherited his architectural talent from his father. The latter is described as a builder in various genealogies of the family,[10] though writers may have confused the two men. The son certainly embarked on his architectural career at an early age, for he could not have been over twenty-nine when his advertisement appeared, and he might have been seven years younger. Also, he mentions buildings nearly completed, showing that he had been practicing for at least a year or more at that time. In 1753 he was one of a committee to inspect the construction of a new church in Cople Parish in Westmoreland,[11] and in 1772 a member of another committee to inspect the chapels in Frederick, Norborne, and Beckford Parishes.[12] His interest in the Episcopal Church is made clear in his will (probated September 22, 1800), and the fact that he served the Church in an architectural capacity is confirmed by the vestry book of Truro Parish, which shows that he was paid for a plan of Payne's Church in 1769.[13] In 1773 he presented a plan and specification for a proposed rebuilding of Cunningham's Chapel in Berkeley County.[14]

These two are the only buildings of which Ariss can be conclusively shown as the architect. One is destroyed, and the other apparently was never built. From the resemblance between them and Payne's Church, of which photographs survive, it would seem that he may have designed Lamb's Creek Church,[15] King George County, and Little Fork Church, Culpeper County.

Ariss' great work was undoubtedly in domestic architecture, and here, while the evidence of his authorship is circumstantial, it is so strong as to be convincing. Before his name had come to the author's attention, he had already segregated the houses, now believed to have been by Ariss, into two groups, informal and formal. Of the former there are Sara's Creek House, Gloucester County; Kenmore in Fredericksburg; and Harewood and Locust Hill in Jefferson County. To these may be added Fairfield in Clarke County, and in Maryland (where his advertisement appeared), Ratcliffe Manor and Pleasant Valley, both in Talbot County.[16] In the formal group are the Carlyle house in Alexandria, Mount Airy and Menokin in Richmond County, Mannsfield in Spotsylvania County, Mount Vernon in Fairfax County, Blandfield and Elmwood in Essex County. These, in contradistinction to those in the previous group, are buildings conforming to British Palladian rather than to the more familiar Virginia Colonial. The rare Georgian architectural design book *Vitruvius Scoticus*, previously mentioned, proved to be the source of the designs of all these houses. It also showed that Ariss' two groups were substantially one and had emanated largely from this one publication, which illustrates mainly the work of William Adam (father of the more famous Robert) who practiced in Scotland at the beginning of the eighteenth century. Adam was associated with Gibbs, and the authorship of some of the buildings may be attributed to either. The style of the latter is purer and more like the Virginia buildings, though Gibbs's own design book does not seem to have been used here as much as Adam's, probably because of the overlarge scale of the buildings. As the more famous of the two, it was Gibbs to whom Ariss referred in his advertisement, rather than to Adam. It should be noted that one of the Gibbs's designs was obviously used for the river front of Mount Airy.

The fact that the origin of this group of buildings is in *Vitruvius Scoticus* makes it seem reasonable that they were the work of one man. When the evidence indicates that Ariss was a resident in the vicinity at the time of their erection, there is considerable reason to believe he was their architect. It cannot at present be proved that he owned Adam's book; recourse to the inventory of his estate shows the listing of three books and no titles.[17]

Vitruvius Scoticus, published in Edinburgh in 1750, is described in the subtitle as "Being a Collection of Plans, Elevations and Sections of Public Buildings, Noblemen's and Gentlemen's Houses in Scotland, Principally from the Designs of the late William Adam, Esq. Architect." The publishers were Adam Black and J. J. Robinson. As might naturally be expected, the Scotch buildings are of a larger scale than the Virginia counterparts, but in two of the houses illustrated the designs of the façades of Mount Airy and the Carlyle house are seen. These are Haddo House in Aberdeenshire, built for, and now the seat of, the Lords Aberdeen; and Craigiehall, now owned by Lord Roseberry and built for

Charles Hope, an ancestor. In these two houses is seen most clearly the striking kinship of the Virginia and Scotch structures. William Adam practiced architecture in Edinburgh during the second quarter of the eighteenth century, his death occurring on June 24, 1748.[18] He was the father of a remarkable family, the most famous of which was Robert Adam, the creator of the style which has come to be known as Adamesque. With Robert, his brother James practiced architecture in London, but John took over his father's practice in Edinburgh.[19] Robert had gone to Italy with his brother James, and part of the time traveled with the French architect, Clérisseau, who was later Jefferson's friend and associate in the design of the Capitol at Richmond.

The usefulness of *Vitruvius Scoticus* to a Colonial builder over other style books of its period is occasioned by the number of plans and elevations it shows of mansions small enough to be adapted to their more limited means and requirements. The sister volume, Colin Campbell's *Vitruvius Britannicus*, illustrates vast Palladian country houses almost entirely unsuitable to American adaptation. An interesting feature of the use of Adam's book in the Virginia houses is that in no case is it slavish. Schemes of façades or plans were modified, and unsuitable features were either replaced by others found in other plates, or a substitute was designed by the architect. Among the Virginia houses derived from the same plate there are intelligent and interesting variations.

In studying the Virginia houses in question chronology should be considered, especially in reference to Ariss' places of residence. These are as follows:

Virginia		*Ariss' Residence*	
Carlyle House, Alexandria	1752	1751	Westmoreland County
Kenmore, Fredericksburg	1752		
Harewood, Near Charles Town	1756		
Mount Airy, Richmond County	1758		
Mount Vernon, Fairfax County	1757-87		
Mannsfield, Spotsylvania County	c.1760-70	1762	Richmond County
Camden, Caroline County	c.1760-70		
Blandfield, Essex County	1770	1769	Berkeley County
Fairfield, Clarke County	c.1770		
Elmwood, Essex County	c.1774		
Menokin, Richmond County	1776		
Locust Hill, Near Charles Town	1785		
Sara's Creek House, Gloucester County	Undated		

This chronology shows ten-year gaps in Ariss' places of residence. Considering the length of time required to build a large house at that period (about five years), he could not have been resident at each place during the whole period of construction. It seems that he may have been designed, and supervised, from Westmoreland, the Carlyle house, Kenmore, and perhaps Harewood. The first was accessible from the Potomac River, the second from the Rappahannock, but the third was a considerable journey over the Blue Ridge. With the Mount Airy commission Ariss probably moved there to take charge of construction, for it was in 1762 (when the house would have been about finished) that he relinquished his lease on a place in Richmond County. He may then have undertaken Mannsfield and supervised it either on the spot or from Westmoreland County, in which latter case he could have reached Blandfield as well. The move to Berkeley took place before 1769.[20] The reason for the move is not clear, unless it was to supervise Harewood and Fairfield. Mount Vernon, Blandfield, and Elmwood would probably have occasioned journeys to Tidewater.

Literary references lacking, the structures will have to speak for themselves. The earliest of them (excluding the possible Maryland examples) is the Carlyle house in Alexandria. The carving of the keystones bears the date 1752 and the initials of the builder, John Carlyle, as well as the family arms. Since the family records were lost in the Civil War, nothing further is known of its construction.

Less highly articulated than Mount Airy, and less well preserved, its nearest compeer, the Carlyle house, has fewer features that can definitely be ascribed to Adam's book. Even at that, however, the source of the design can be seen clearly in Craigiehall,[21] Midlothian, Scotland. Both houses are similar in elevation, two stories high and six bays long. The two central windows are contained within a pavilion, giving a pier on the center of the building, an unusual condition. The pavilion at the Carlyle house probably once was pedimented, though now the pediment is missing.

It would seem that the entire roof was rebuilt when the roof space of the house was altered to provide attic rooms in the mid-nineteenth century. In rebuilding, a straight hip was used instead of the hip-on-hip found at Craigiehall, Blandfield, and Menokin. Another alteration that affects the similarity of the Carlyle house and its prototype is the rebuilding of the doorway. This is now a wide ellipse, all of the woodwork being of the nineteenth century. This was probably once a Palladian motive such as that at Gartmore House,[22] for there is not sufficient room for an arrangement like that at Craigiehall. The carved keystones, one now reused in the post-colonial doorway, would have fitted into a pair of Palladian motives on east and west façades. There is one other important departure in the designs, Craigiehall having the water table raised to the sill of the first-floor windows, the Carlyle house having it in normal position. The quoining of the corners and framing of the

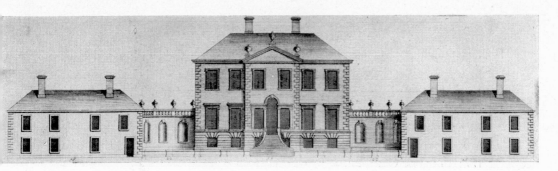

CRAIGIEHALL, Cramond Bridge, Midlothian, Scotland. William Adam, architect. Built c. 1725.

THE CARLYLE HOUSE, Alexandria. Conjectural restoration. *Perspective, author; rendering, Collins.*

CRAIGIEHALL, Cramond Bridge, Midlothian, Scotland. General view, 1936. *Inglis, Edinburgh.*

windows with masonry architraves are common to both houses. It should be noted that there are several changes in the Craigiehall elevations, these taking place between the design and structure. The Carlyle house once possessed dependencies and connections, but they were destroyed in the nineteenth century. An old drawing in *Harper's Magazine* shows the dependencies as small pedimented pavilions,[23] not unlike one still remaining at Camden.

The examination of the two plans shows strong similarities in the Carlyle house and Craigiehall, though the latter is the deeper of the two. This difference has considerable effect on the plan, giving a suite of three rooms at Craigiehall to one side of the hall, while at the Carlyle house there are only two, perhaps once divided by a lateral hall reaching the wings. The disposition of the other side, a large drawing room with a smaller room at the end, is similar in both houses. This latter arrangement also occurs at Mount Airy.

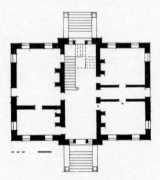

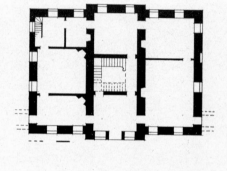

CARLYLE HOUSE, Alexandria.   CRAIGIEHALL, Midlothian, Scotland.

At Craigiehall the stair is placed in a square stair hall behind the entrance hall and in front of a room balancing the entrance hall at the rear. This latter has no exterior doorway but two windows, centering on those above. At the Carlyle house the stair was rebuilt and retrimmed at the time the alterations were made, so that its present location is not necessarily the original one.[24] The restricted space here, however, would suggest that the Craigiehall arrangement would probably not have prevailed, though the floor framing exposed in the basement might indicate it.

It is unfortunate that no clue remains as to the appearance of any of the stairways of Ariss' monumental Virginia houses. The Craigiehall stair rail is of wrought iron in a design of acanthus leaves and vines in continuous convolutions, but it is more likely that the Virginia stairs were of wood with turned balusters. In Scotch houses of this period

The Carlyle House, Alexandria. Blue Room mantel. *Met. Eng.*

The Carlyle House, Alexandria. Blue Room doorway. *Met. Eng.*

the stairs were often built of monolithic stone steps cantilevered out from the wall, each step leaning on the one below and having wrought-iron balustrades.

The second-floor plans of Craigiehall and the Carlyle house are more marked in their similarities. The plan is traversed lengthwise by a narrow corridor leading to a room in each corner, and where this intersects with the stair hall the corners of the partition walls are rounded off in plan, thus facilitating circulation. In the central area there is a room over the entrance hall in both houses, but that in the rear is omitted at the Carlyle house on account of the stair treatment, though originally it may have been included.

The finish of the two north first-floor rooms at the Carlyle house is original. That to the west was probably a small reception room and is simply-trimmed, with a cornice and dado and mantel, the latter with stone (or marble) facing, framed by a moulded wood backband with crossettes. That to the east, the Blue Room, is fully paneled. The dado has a moulded base, a plain field, and a moulded chair rail enriched with a Greek key pattern after an example in Gibbs's *Rules for Drawing*. The area above the dado is divided into vertical panels which are moulded and beveled. At the ceiling is a modillioned cornice with carved rosettes on the soffit between the modillions. The two doors to the hall have overdoors of broken serpentine pediments above pulvinated friezes, but from the way they are applied over panels it is doubtful if they are original. The doors themselves are not original, and the openings have been raised. The west is old, but irregularities in the trim raise doubt as to whether the opening has always been there. The cupboard in the north wall of the Blue Room was probably inserted when the wings were removed. It is obviously not part of the original design, but is old and similar to one formerly at the Tebbs house at Dumfries. It has two long panels cut to a semicircular termination at top and bottom.

The Blue Room mantel treatment is interesting, though unsatisfactory. Little fluted Doric pilasters above the mantel shelf were originally intended, no doubt, to support a pediment, but lack of height prevented this. They stop an inch and a half below the main cornice, without performing any function except framing the overmantel panel, which is formed by an architrave with crossettes at the top. The mantel has a marble facing contained within a wood backband which is moulded and carved with egg-and-dart ornament. Restricted space here spoiled a design probably intended to have been much like the fine mantel treatments in the ball room at Gadsby's Tavern, Alexandria.[25] Except for the windows of these rooms, all framed with architraves and possessing window seats and paneled shutters in the reveal, no other original woodwork except the paneled stair spandrel seems to remain in the house.

The stone cornice across the front of the Carlyle house is a feature unique in Virginia, though Mannsfield and Mount Airy may have had such at one time. The bed mould and fascia are of cut stone with moulded wood cymatium. The cornice on the sides and rear is of wood, at a different level, and apparently dates from the rebuilding of the roof.

The evidence of the carved date points to the fact that 1752 was probably the year in which the stone was set in place. Judging from the fact that construction at the time was leisurely and protracted, building may have begun about 1750, or two years after John Carlyle became possessed of the two lots on which he built it, and may have been finished about 1754. When William Beverley wrote to his London agent, Samuel Athaws, for plain grey marble mantels in 1771, he said that a reply in eighteen months' time would suit him, indicating the unhurried way in which the great houses were built.

Mount Airy, built by John Tayloe on his ancestral estate, is often dated 1755, but a reliable nineteenth-century book gives the date as 1758.[26] It would have been built, therefore, in the later fifties. This mansion ranks with the finest houses of the Colonial period in this country. It is built of a local dark brown sandstone, poorly consolidated and verging on a grit. This is in random coursings, perhaps originally plastered, with trim of cut Portland and Aquia Creek stone.[27] Standing complete, save for its interior trim, which was lost in the fire of 1844, it retains its connections, dependencies, and minor flanking outbuildings. Its superb situation on the ridge overlooking the Rappahannock River Valley, and its carefully graded landscape setting enhance its architectural effect.

The semicircular forecourt is raised by a low terrace above the entrance drive, and is reached by cut and moulded stone steps, flanked by elaborate carved stone vases on pedestals. The square dependencies have hipped roofs pierced at the apex by stone chimneys with moulded caps. The connections to the house are quadrants, with shed roofs concealed from the front. At the junction with the house, the roofs of the connections are stepped up to allow entrances to the main floor of the house. The main block is two stories above a high basement, with a central pedimented pavilion. This latter contains a recessed loggia at the entrance, with Doric pilastered piers, reached by a broad flight of steps (now granite replacements) between stone ramp walls. Above the entrance loggia there are three windows framed by moulded and eared stone architraves, resting on a cut-stone pedestal over the modillioned cornice of the loggia itself. The pavilion is rusticated with square sunk channels, the corner quoins being V-sunk. The corners of the main

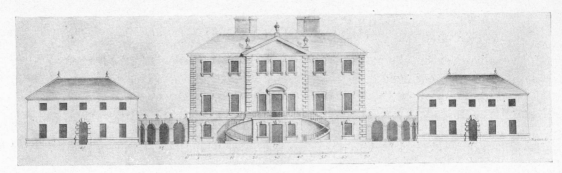

HADDO HOUSE, Aberdeenshire, Scotland. From *Vitruvius Scoticus*. Designed by William Adam.

MOUNT AIRY, Richmond County. North front inspired by design of Haddo House. *Johnston.*

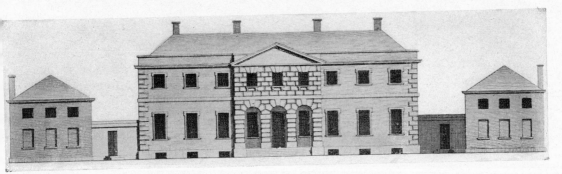

Plate LVIII (a design for a gentleman in Dorsetshire) from Gibbs's *Book of Architecture*.

MOUNT AIRY. South front derived from Plate LVIII, Gibbs's *Book of Architecture*. Johnston.

house and dependencies have similar quoin treatment. On the garden façade the triple loggia reoccurs, but with arched and rusticated openings and piers. Across the pavilion the second-floor line is indicated by a modillioned cornice. The rustication is continued across the upper part of the pavilion, the three windows lacking trim except for the flat arches over them.

The pairs of windows flanking the pavilions on front and rear walls have moulded architraves and sills, and the wall spaces in which they are pierced are laid off with a cut-stone belt course at the second-floor line and boldly moulded water table similar to those at the Carlyle house and Mannsfield. The present hip roof replaces a hip-on-hip, as at Bland-field. The four chimneys had moulded stone caps which, calcined by the fire, have been plastered.

The main front shows, without doubt, the derivation of the design in Haddo House, Aberdeenshire, Scotland.[28] Although in scale the latter is larger than Mount Airy, all of the architectural features are similar, except for the entrance motive. Tindwall and Belhaven houses, as well as a mansion for the Duke of Montrose, have reminiscent elevations. Features illustrated in *Vitruvius Scoticus*, also used at Mount Airy, are the recessed loggia with square pilastered piers, as at Hamilton Church and Newliston, and pavilion windows set on a continuous pedestal, as at Saughton and Drum House. The south front is undoubtedly inspired by Gibbs's design [29] for a house "for a Gentleman in Dorsetshire," already referred to. That this plate actually was used is a strong link in the chain of evidence identifying Ariss with these houses, for Gibbs's style was specifically referred to in his advertisement. The square two-story dependencies of Mount Airy are very similiar to those at both Newhall (East Lothian) and Drum House, the former having the same fenestration to the approach. The fenestration varies on the east, north, and west walls of the Mount Airy dependencies, and it is not known to the author that this is so in the Scotch examples. The pent roofs of the connections correspond to those at Dumfries House.

In the lower part of the east wall of Mount Airy there is a large Palladian window, a simpler one above having an elliptical center motive. At Drum House, Midlothian, a Palladian window occurs, identical in detail with the lower here, but at Hopetoun there is one which has a cornice at the spring of the arch. The elliptical arch of the upper window at Mount Airy is precedented by similar openings in Hamilton Church. Broad entrance steps, such as those of the two Virginia examples, are unique in the state in that they are enclosed at the ends by ramp walls, but this was a frequent device in the buildings illustrated in *Vitruvius Scoticus*, an example being at Arniston.

MOUNT AIRY, Richmond County. A lithograph by Pendleton of Boston, view before 1844 fire.

MOUNT AIRY. Detail, south loggia. *Author.*   MOUNT AIRY. Detail, north loggia. *Met Eng.*

HADDO HOUSE, Aberdeenshire, Scotland.

MOUNT AIRY. View of east elevation. *Author.*

MOUNT AIRY. West pier, forecourt. *Author.*

MOUNT AIRY. East pier, forecourt. *HABS.*

In addition to the five units of the main group, mansion, connections, and dependencies, there were two further subsidiary buildings, one of which is still extant. This was the office (though now much altered) and stands about fifty feet beyond the east dependency and in advance of it, the front wall of the latter lining with the rear wall of the office. A balancing building apparently stood to the west. The office is square in plan, of stone, with a low hipped roof. At present, the close relationship of the two minor dependencies is not apparent, but before the fire of 1844 it was emphasized by railings and gates. Those on the east side show in a lithograph that predates the fire.[30] Also shown are the elaborate stone vases on pedestals, flanking the gate. Fragments of these still remain on the east terrace. The stone bases or shafts, which supported the wrought-iron screens and gates, show vaguely in the lithograph.

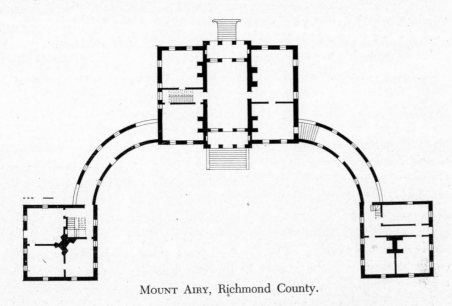

MOUNT AIRY, Richmond County.

In plan Mount Airy has a broad entrance salon that extends the entire depth of the house. At either end are center entrance doors flanked by full-height windows. This entire inner entrance wall was rebuilt after the fire, but the form of the original north loggia entrance is preserved in Pendleton's lithograph, which shows a triple arcade, though the sash and doors are omitted. To the east of the salon are a pair of drawing rooms divided by a narrow cross-hall, which has probably been altered in width. On the west side this hall is omitted, the space being thrown into the dining room in the southwest corner of the building. At present there is a hall in the northwest corner, with a nineteenth-century spiral stair. The plan of Dumfries House is reminiscent of that of Mount Airy.

The central salon of the latter, however, was divided in the plan of the former by a partition which created a large entrance hall with a screen of columns at the inner end, beyond which lay a smaller room. The location of the stair at Mount Airy is still a question, for its present position in the northwest corner may not be original. Authorities have placed it in the hall dividing the side rooms to the east. This is the location attributed to it by tradition, and this is the position it has on the Dumfries House plan in *Vitruvius Scoticus*. The existing basement walls, however, allow only six feet in the clear between them, obviously too narrow a space for a passage and stair. The partitions above may have been off-center with the basement walls, and the fact that the chimney foundation of the northeast room is off-center to the north makes it seem that at least the north wall may not have been directly over the wall below. Spreading the hall partitions would open the sidelights of the Palladian window, which are at present closed and filled with false black glazing. Such a window was used in the same position at Dumfries House.

It is regrettable in the extreme that the fire of 1844 should have taken all of the magnificent interiors that Mount Airy must once have possessed. The present mantel shelves were made of sections of cornice bed mould taken from the office, the further outlying building to the east. These are composed of three members, a Wall of Troy dentil band between an ovolo, carved above with egg and dart, below this a cyma, worked with Greek water-leaf ornament. This carving is so reminiscent of that at Gunston Hall as to suggest that Buckland worked at Mount Airy, on the interior, after completing his work for Mason and before settling at Annapolis. It can be surmised that the finish of the house itself was as rich as any of the period, though it may not have been fully paneled, but finished like Kenmore. The dependencies possess simple woodwork contemporary with the house. In the east building there is a very interesting group of stone mantels.

The sash in the dependencies was changed to conform to that in the main house after the fire, but the frames are original. Here the wide box frame was used, but owing to the narrowness of the openings in the house it may be considered that a narrow setback frame was used, as in the Orangery,[31] still standing in ruins on the grounds, and as at the Carlyle house.

At Craigiehall the sash is four lights wide, and it is probable that it was also of this type throughout the entire group of Virginia houses, except Menokin and perhaps Blandfield. A significant piece of evidence may lie in a derelict sash found in the basement of Camden, in Caroline County, on the Rappahannock River. This is four lights wide and three high, with eight by ten glass and wide muntins. The date would seem to be about 1765. This sash would fit the Mount Airy and Mannsfield openings.

In the study of Camden lies an interesting problem. The present frame house is said to be the result of a complete rebuilding just prior to the Civil War, in the romantic Italian Villa style. That there was an earlier house on the site is well known, and it is probable that the old house was at least in part incorporated in the new. The foundation plan is reminiscent of Mannsfield, and the whole wall up to the sill is of stone, like the other houses of this group excepting Blandfield. The overall dimensions are forty-eight feet ten inches by seventy feet nine inches, comparing closely with Mannsfield, which is forty-eight feet by sixty-eight feet. The plan differs from the Carlyle house in that the chimneys are in the outside end walls; otherwise it is similar. It has a large drawing room and a smaller reception room to one side, and across a central hall a pair of equal rooms. An interesting feature is the southwest chimney, which is set into the room from the end wall to allow a narrow room between it and the end wall, such as the evidence points to at Mannsfield. At this point there may have been an outside entrance or one to a connection. Two mannerisms of the plan have precedents in *Vitruvius Scoticus*, and these make it seem that perhaps the superstructure of Camden was retrimmed rather than rebuilt. These are the convex, rounded corners of the upper cross hall and the concave, rounded corners of the entrance hall, as at Dunn House.

Several paneled doors of the period of the window sash are still in the basement at Camden. On the porch is a beautiful pair of wrought-iron brackets, evidently intended as part of a marble-top console table. To the east remains a pedimented dependency of the period, now much altered. This has a modillioned cornice and a sheathed pediment with a roundel in the tympanum. Further afield recently stood a ruined cabin built of dovetailed plank; this is of interest for its structure.

The great drawing room of Camden retains its fine furniture, rugs, hangings, and ornaments of the period of its rebuilding by John Pratt and is an important example of Victorian decoration in Virginia. The rebuilding was designed by N. G. Starkweather of Baltimore, and his drawings are still preserved in the house.[32]

Blandfield, a contemporary and neighbor of Camden, was erected by William Beverley almost twenty years after the keystone of the Carlyle house was carved. This is authenticated by the letter [33] of William Beverley, the builder, dated 1771, ordering plain grey marble mantels from London for his new house. The difference in date and type of masonry causes an effect so different from that of Mount Airy that a kinship is not immediately obvious. A study of the designs makes the relationship clear, however, especially when Mannsfield is also considered. The latter has the same narrow rectangular dependencies with central chimneys, though the curved passages are absent at Blandfield and straight connections take their place. The pavilions, the group of three central windows, and the arrangement of the chimneys certainly relate the façades of Mount Airy and Blandfield.

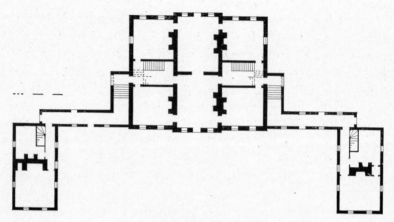

BLANDFIELD, Essex County.

DRUM HOUSE, Midlothian, Scotland.

If the resemblance stopped there, it might be explained as the simple influence of the former on the latter, but the unusual forecourt layout of Blandfield has a counterpart from *Vitruvius Scoticus* in Drum House. The latter is much larger in scale than the former, so the room disposition is naturally different; but the advance buildings have the same relation to the mansion, and the connections join in the same way. This is significant,

BLANDFIELD, Essex County. North front. The porch woodwork and sash are of 1854. *Met. Eng.*

BLANDFIELD, Essex County. Mansion, forecourt, and dependencies from southeast. *Layton.*

MANNSFIELD, Spotsylvania County, c. 1760-70. Perspective of foundation. *Barnette, HABS.*

MANNSFIELD, Spotsylvania County. A photograph from the northwest, after 1863 fire. *Brady.*

as the treatment of the uncurved connecting passages here is unique in Virginia in that they are built against the back wall of the dependencies instead of at the side. The pavilions at the junction with the main building are centered on the house, as at the Carlyle House, instead of on a plane with the forecourt, as at Mount Airy. In plan the house has a pair of entrance salons, one beyond the other, with two rooms on either side, separated by stair halls. The chimneys are in the transverse center walls.

Of brick, Blandfield has a much more familiar Virginia character than its stone fellows. The present effect of the elevations is injured by the loss of the original sash, for which glass lights of a larger size have been substituted, and by the addition of porches of Classic Revival style. Even with these changes it more perfectly shows the original aspect of the buildings of this group, as it retains its original roof. Mount Airy, it was noted, has lost this featue. It might be expected that, since Blandfield has never been burned, it would have retained its original finish. Yet at the time of the mid-nineteenth-century renovations all this was removed, leaving no clue to the design of the interiors. Since the house was pillaged in the Civil War, it is bereft of much of its eighteenth-century furniture. Fortunately, the builder's letter books remain, but save for the letter referred to concerning the mantels, little reference to the construction of the house is made. Ariss, the presumed builder, may have been directing construction from the site itself, thus obviating the necessity for correspondence. For the decoration of Blandfield Beverley ordered wall paper from London on July 16, 1771, in an invoice to Samuel Athaws. These papers included "Pea green flowered ... yellow ... Stucco color large patterns of pillars and galleries ... The borders to be of paper," and also "white lead, light stone color, bright olive, dark chocolate, and whiting." Spared the disasters of the alterations and of the war, Blandfield would have been an unusually valuable example of the architecture and decoration of the period.

Until recently Mannsfield was only a memory, the house having been destroyed in the Fredericksburg campaigns. An excavation of the site, undertaken in 1934, revealed the entire plan of the mansion and its immediate dependencies. The main block was divided into four rooms, with a stair hall behind an entrance salon. The chimneys were placed in the longitudinal partition wall, the fireplaces in the two north rooms being offset toward the hall, evidently to allow pantries between them and the connections. This arrangement is indicated by the stone piers in position to support the partition-bearing beam.

The dependencies were placed with their long axes to the approach and were connected with the mansion by quadrant passages. Both dependencies were divided by a cross wall forming two unequal rooms. The east building was the kitchen and the west the laundry.

Foundations remain for the front steps, which comprised a long flight with a platform at the top. The sub-structure of this latter covered the lower part of two windows, spaced, as at Craigiehall and the Carlyle house, with a pier on the center of the building and contained within a projecting pavilion of V-sunk, rusticated stone. The entrance salon was about sixteen feet by twenty-four feet and may have had a marble floor, as this area is above the vaulted cellar. Remaining in place in the stair-hall area is a flight of stone steps to the basement, indicating that the main stair ascended on the left toward the rear wall.

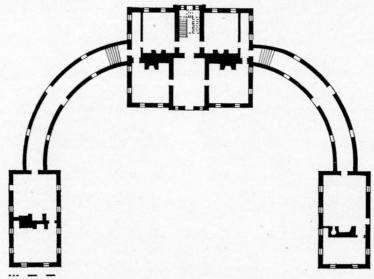

MANNSFIELD, Spotsylvania County.

An old photograph of the house after the fire exists, but it is faded.[34] This photograph shows the building from the northwest, and the super-structure agrees with the evidence of the foundation. The rear pavilion apparently was rusticated, and the corners of the house had rusticated quoins. The windows were framed by a raised stone band, as as Mount Airy, with similar base and band courses. The fenestration of the west wall is not clear but seems to have been four windows spaced evenly across the wall. Unfortunately, since in the photograph a tree conceals the rear entrance, its design can only be surmised. Aside from this feature, the evidence of the photograph and of the foundations made it possible to determine that the house was probably inspired by the plate of Balveny House in *Vitruvius Scoticus*.[35] The major difference seems to lie in the narrowing of the north pavilion at Mannsfield. The south or front pavilion corresponds in width to the entrance salon, and although the stair hall behind it is narrower, the north pavilion does not express this width but is slightly wider. The resulting elevation could not have been as satisfactory as the main façade, where the broad pavilion occurred.

The exact design of the façade cannot be determined without question, but its general characteristics can be. The basement wall contains the original openings which can be expected to have carried through the first and second stories; thus the fenestration can be presumed, except for the center window. The width of the pier, however, is so great that it seems doubtful that it would have been used in the superstructure. The window may have been omitted because it was planned to have a vaulted wine cellar behind it, and in fact the latter was built, but it was so wide it blocked even the flanking openings. Using three windows in the second story produces an arrangement not unakin to that of Mount Airy, but the recessed loggia and rich trim of that house were omitted. The rusticated stonework of the basement and derelict flat arches are also like those at Balveny. There is no evidence at the site that would contravene the assumption that the plate of this house was used as inspiration for the façade of Mannsfield. It is probable that the parapet was omitted, as it seems to have been in all Virginia work except Rosewell, and that the roof was composed of the more graceful pitches of Blandfield and Menokin.

Very little is recorded of life at Mannsfield, but in his journal Benjamin Henry Latrobe, the architect, mentioned being entertained there. On July 19, 1796, dated at Rippon Lodge, he wrote: "I dined with Mr. Minor at Mr. Man Page's at Mansfield where I met several gentlemen of the town and of the neighborhood. Mr. Page's house is of stone of a good but coarse grit in the style of the Country Gentlemen's house in England of 50 years ago. It is a tolerably good house but the taste is indiferent."

At this time young Page's fortune was impaired, for Jefferson wrote to Philip Mazzie on April 24 of the same year: "...Our friend M.P. is embarrassed, having lately sold the fine land he lives on ..." [36] However, the insurance policy, number 150, dated June, 1806, was issued to Mann Page, and the house was noted as recently repaired. This policy gave the dimensions of the building as fifty-one by sixty-nine, with a porch nine by twelve. It referred to the right advance building as the kitchen and the left as the laundry.[37] In 1808 the entire estate passed out of the hands of Page.[38] In 1811 William Bernard acquired the property, and his son Alfred N. Bernard was living there during the Civil War when the mansion was destroyed. The particulars of its destruction in the spring of 1863 are unknown, but the events concerning it are as follows:[39] "On December 12, 1862, General W. B. Franklin's left Grand Division of the Army of the Potomac crossed to the south bank of the Rappahannock. During the Battle of Fredericksburg, which followed on the thirteenth, the mansion was used as a temporary hospital for the Union Corps engaged in the Hamilton's Crossing action. General Franklin set up his headquarters in a nearby grove.

"The circumstances surrounding the destruction of the Mansion are unknown. All that can be said is that the house served as a hospital for the Union forces on December 13, 1862, and that it was in ruins when artillery units of General Sedgwick's Sixth Corps occupied the adjacent fields in May, 1863, during the Chancellorsville Campaign."

Mannsfield, Mount Airy, and Mount Vernon were the three great houses of the period with quadrant connections between the house and the dependencies. Although Latrobe never seems to have visited Mount Airy, he immediately discerned the resemblance between the other two and wrote of Mount Vernon in his journal: "The general plan of the building is at Mr. ManPage's at Mansfield near Fredericksburg, of the old school." [40]

Latrobe continues his observations by writing: "Mount Vernon becomes visible between two groves of trees at about a mile's distance. It has no very striking appearance, though superior to every other house I have seen here. The approach is not very well managed but leads you into the area between the stables ... It is a wooden building, painted to represent chamfered rustic and sanded. The house is at the north end, and a study, etc., etc., at the south. The whole of this part of the building is in a very indifferent taste. Along the other front is a portico supported by 8 square pillars, of good proportions and effect. There is a handsome statuary marble chimney piece in the dining room (of the taste of Sir William Chambers) with innilated columns on each side. This is the only piece of expensive decoration I have seen about the house, and is indeed remarkable in that respect. Everything else is extremely good and neat, but by no means above what would be expected in a plain English Country gentleman's house of £500 or £600 a year. It is, however, a little above what I have hitherto seen in Virginia. The ground on the west front of the house is laid out in a level lawn bounded on each side with a wide but extremely formal serpentine walk, shaded by weeping willows, a tree which in this country grows very well upon high, dry land. On one side of this lawn is a plain kitchen garden, on the other a neat flower garden laid out in squares, and boxed with great precision. Along the north wall of this garden is a plain greenhouse. The plants were arranged in front, and contained nothing very rare, nor were they numerous."

The influence of *Vitruvius Scoticus* is not as apparent at Mount Vernon as in the other houses of the group, but this is due to the fact

MANNSFIELD, Spotsylvania County. A restored bird's-eye view from the southeast. *Perspective by Author; rendering by R. E. Collins.*

MOUNT VERNON, Fairfax County. *All photographs Mount Vernon Ladies Association. Johnston.*

MOUNT VERNON, Fairfax County. West front. Enlarged twice; completed in 1787. *Johnston.*

that the house reached its present form through various alterations rather than from one definitive plan. The use of rustication (even though it be of wood siding), over the whole exterior is unprecedented by any other mansion in the south, though several, including Drum House, are shown in Adam's book. Also the form of the Banquet Room, added in the 1773-87 alterations, is probably derived from Adam's designs at Yester and Castle Kennedy, and the arcaded passaged from Haddo. Mount Vernon is one of the few buildings with which Ariss' name is associated. This is in a literary reference not now available for quotation, though its correctness is vouched for by a descendant of Bushrod Washington, who possesses books from both his library and from that of the Throckmorton family.[41] This latter may include items from Ariss' library, which from his grandson Ariss Throckmorton descended to an heir who bequeathed them to the present owner. It was the latter who confirmed to the author his surmise that Ariss had provided the drawings for the alterations.

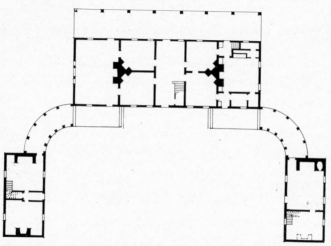

MOUNT VERNON, Fairfax County.

A study of Mount Vernon[42] must begin with the earliest house, for part of it may be incorporated in the present structure. Just when it was built has not been determined, but it may have been before 1700.[43] The land was patented in 1674, but although there is no record of the building of a house on it at that time, the patent required one to be built in three years.[44] Some historians have held that this house burned in 1739, but there is reason to believe that it did not and was enlarged by Augustine Washington and deeded in 1740 to Lawrence, half brother of George. He lived at Mount Vernon until his death in 1752, except for the period of the journey of the two brothers to Barbados in 1751 and Lawrence's sojourn there of nearly a year. In the foundation of the present building is a facsimile of the cornerstone, marked "L W," and crudely carved, believed to be from the earliest house with the initials of Lawrence, grandfather of George.

In plan this structure was, as has been noted, similar in its elements to other houses of the vicinity. It was about thirty-three feet deep and forty-seven feet long with a central hall, off-center to the south, and two rooms on either side. Those at the east were narrower, and the two north rooms were slightly longer. All four rooms were heated by two end chimneys with corner fireplaces. Since the house was only a story and a half in height, the upper rooms were within the roof and lighted by dormer and gable windows. The effect must have been similar to that produced by nearby weather-boarded houses which still stand, especially Rippon Lodge.[46] There is a tradition, in fact, that Richard Blackburn of Rippon also built Mount Vernon, but in view of its simplicity it can hardly be that he was in any sense the architect. If he had anything to do with the construction, it was probably equivalent to the good offices of George William Fairfax in overseeing the alterations in 1758.

Unfortunately, there is not sufficient documentary evidence to determine in full detail what was done to Mount Vernon in the way of alterations in 1758, but what there is, together with the additional evidence, tends to show that the roof was raised a full story and that the whole interior and exterior were retrimmed. Why Washington altered the old house rather than build anew is unknown. It may have been the desire to take his bride there without waiting several years for the construction of a new dwelling, or it may have been sentimental attachment for his much-loved brother's home. The house, built on traditional lines, was old-fashioned, perhaps being that of about 1674, or one built by Augustine Washington between 1726 and 1735. In this latter case it may have been built on the foundations of the earlier house. At best it was little more than a farm house.

It has seemed to previous writers that the completed building of 1759 was hardly more architectural than it had been before the alterations. However, a careful examination of the finish indicates that this is not the case, and that within the confines of the old work, which was small in scale and asymmetric, a definite attempt was made to formalize the fabric. This is probably the time that Ariss entered the scene. His work during this period certainly relates him to Mount Airy, on which, in fact, he may have been working at the same time.

The most striking similarity between the two houses in question is in the use of rusticated work in both houses, in cut stone at Mount Airy, and in channelled wood-siding at Mount Vernon, sanded to represent

DRUM HOUSE, Gilmerton, Edinburgh, Scotland. Drawing, William Adam's *Vitruvius Scoticus*.

BALVENY HOUSE, Banffshire, Scotland. Perhaps the precedent for Mannsfield and Mount Vernon.

Mount Vernon, Fairfax County. South dependencies and the plantation street. *Johnston.*

Mount Vernon, Fairfax County. The great house from northeast, showing portico. *Johnston.*

MOUNT VERNON, Fairfax County. Detailed view of the portico, completed in 1784, for which Washington priced White Haven stone paving in 1785. Precedent for the portico, which is unique of its period, is unknown. Piers seem to be detailed from examples in Langley's *City and Country Builder's Treasury*. Horizontal wood sheathing of the walls is cut to resemble rustication and painted and sanded to give the appearance of stonework. *Johnston.*

Mount Vernon, Fairfax County. Detail of central motive of west front. The original house was a story and a half high and embraced the five central openings of the first floor. In the 1757-58 alterations the house was raised to two stories, and in 1776-79 was lengthened from five to nine bays. The pediment was added in 1778, and cupola finial in 1787. *Johnston.*

Plate XXXIII, Langley's *City and Country Builder*. Model for the Mount Vernon doorway.

MOUNT VERNON, Fairfax County. Entrance hall, stair, and pedimented doorways. *Johnston*.

stone. At the former it was only employed as a whole wall treatment in the pavilion of the river side, as in Gibbs's "House for a gentleman in Dorsetshire," but at Mount Vernon is was used over the entire wall surface, as in Yester and Somervel Houses in Adam's book. In stone designs it is a simple matter to emphasize a feature or pavilion with rusticated work, as plain ashlar can be used for the walling. In a frame building this is not true because against the rustication either weather-boards or matched boarding (such as in the end wall of the kitchen to which Washington objected in 1775)[47] fail to maintain the effect of stone. That to achieve this latter effect was patently Washington's desire is demonstrated by the painting and sanding of the wood finish. Washington completely encased all walls in rusticated boards, and under some light conditions the house does really seem to be of stone. It has been thought that the entire exterior finish was applied in the 1773-87 alterations, but this is disproved by the existence of fragments of this finish against the old north wall above the Banquet Room ceiling. The joints in the east and west walls at the line of the chimneys can also be plainly traced. It is interesting to note that the extra height of the Banquet Room was concealed on the exterior by false upper windows.

The house thus formed would have been two full stories high with all rusticated walls, a modillioned cornice (perhaps part of that now in place), and probably a hipped roof. The chimneys were only partly inside the finish of the end walls. The river, or east front, would have been comparatively symmetrical in spite of the fact that the building was longer from the center to the south end than to the north, for there was not wide disparity in the spacing of the openings. The focal point was the doorway, probably then as now, with an architrave frame supporting a frieze and pediment, but the effect of this fine doorway is changed by the nineteenth-century doors. These were probably inserted by John A. Washington on his accession to the property in 1829, or by Jane, his wife, who inherited it in 1832. A curious feature of this elevation is that there is no window opening above the door in the second floor, but this is due to the arrangement of the partitions, the attic stair hall and a small bedroom occurring here. In spite of the fact that the asymmetry of the east wall was not noticeable, that of the west wall must have been even more obvious in the five-bay façade than it is now with the building extended. The asymmetry is caused not only by the off-center door but by the location of the stair between it and the pair of windows in the dining room.

The Mount Vernon of 1759, more than any other house in *Vitruvius Scoticus,* must have recalled Balveny, and therefore its derivative, Manns-field, in Virginia, as has been observed. This similarity was commented upon by Latrobe in his journal. However, Mount Vernon, in both its initial and final stages, was much less architectural than Mannsfield, the difference being due to the difficulties of formalizing the old fabric. Perhaps as an attempt to distract attention from the uneven fenestration, a highly architectural doorway was employed in this front. This door has engaged Tuscan columns, on high plinths, supporting an overdoor consisting of an architrave, frieze, and pediment, the three horizontal members of which are cleft by a large winged keystone. The door opening is framed by a bold, narrow moulding and is filled with a fine eight-panel door similar to those in Scotchtown from *Palladio Londinensis*. The design of the doorway, apparently derived from Plate XXXIII of Langley's *Builder's and Workman's Treasury of Designs,* was itself a modification of the two examples illustrated. The columns were fortunately shorn of the rusticated blocks shown on the plate.

The date of this doorway is doubtful, for the same source was used for the design of the great Palladian window in the north end, which dated from the 1773 extension. Much, however, of the interior detail that seems to date from 1759 was due to this publication, so it is more than possible that the *Builder's Treasury* was used in preparing the design for both alterations.

Since the 1759 house was considerably shorter than the present one, the existing forecourt buildings would not have fitted it, but it is probable that a not very dissimilar arrangement existed. In fact, it is possible that some part of the outer dependencies flanking the forecourt were those referred to when Washington agreed in March, 1760, to give Mr. William Triplett £18 "to build the two houses in Front of my House (plastering them also), and running walls for pallisades to them from the Great House and from the Great House to the Wash House and kitchen also." [48] Where the latter two buildings were located and how they related to the mansion is not entirely clear, but they are reputed to have stood on the east side of the house. This would have produced an arrangement like that of Kedelston, in Derbyshire, by Robert Adam, but the prototype of both would have been a villa by Palladio on the Brenta. [49]

The two front buildings at Mount Vernon were doubtless much the same in effect as the present inner dependencies, but somewhat closer together and smaller. The use of the term "pallisade" for the connections certainly connotates nothing more than formalized fences rather than covered passages. There is a possibility that decorative arcaded walls were used, for such occur at Mavisbank House near Edinburgh and are illustrated in *Vitruvius Scoticus*. The more usual form was a railing on a dwarf wall, as once used at the Governor's Palace in Williamsburg.

An examination of the interior will reveal that three of the lower rooms are paneled, these being the hall, the West Parlor, and the Small Sitting Room. In the case of the first two, the panel mould is formed of a large cyma, a bevel and bead. As far as the cyma is concerned, it is an unusual form, and the rare examples of it seem to date from after 1750. Another feature, common to both rooms, that would place them after the middle of the century are the pedestal-type chair rails. This variety has a flat top, with the outside face moulded like a simple cornice. It superceded, about 1750, the old type that was like half of a stair hand-rail. As has been observed, this was the old form used from the time of Wren to the period of the Revolution, but in unimportant rooms rather than in fine ones as the style progressed. This latter was the profile used in the Small Sitting Room, together with the plain bead-and-bevel panel mould commonly used in Virginia from the beginning of the eighteenth century. The occurrence of these two features with a typical unenriched cornice makes it more than possible that this room is the sole survivor of Lawrence Washington's house of 1743. This conclusion is strengthened by the use of paneling in the dado, corresponding to that above the chair rail, a practice that was employed less frequently as the period progressed. In the work before about 1750 it was characteristic, but after this date sheathed dados such as those in most of the other rooms at Mount Vernon were employed in stylish rooms.

If this reasoning is correct, the woodwork of the Small Sitting Room dates from 1743, and that of the hall and West Parlor from 1759. It is obvious that that of the Banquet Room and Library is of the period of 1773-87; so only the finish of the Music Room and the Dining Room is in doubt. The former is very simple, having a plaster dado with a flat base. The chair rail is capped by a cyma, similar to the backband of the door trim, and the base is advanced from the wall by a quarter-round. There is a simple wood cornice, composed of a crown mould planted on a plaster-board, which is paralleled on the ceiling with a strand of enriched plaster work accented with small roundels. The mantel of wood is composed of stone facing inside an architrave frame surmounted by a pulvinated frieze and cornice shelf. Each of the elements of this room is probably of the period of the Banquet Room, into which it opens, and it was evidently retrimmed to conform in style to the latter between 1778 and 1787.

There is no question about the period of the mantel and ceiling of the Dining Room, for on August 20, 1775, Washington wrote from Cambridge to Lund Washington, his cousin and factor at Mount Vernon: "I wish you would quicken Lamphier and Sears about the Dining Room Chimney Piece (to be executed as mentioned in one of my last letters) as I wish that end of the House compleatly finished before

I return." [50] Lund reported this work done before the end of the year. Washington's specific reference to the mantel suggests that the dado was already in place, which would explain the use of paneling below the chair rail in a plastered room. The sumptuous chimney-piece and ceiling, both of which are highly enriched, are among the most elaborate of their period in America.

The second-floor rooms, except Washington's own bedroom, over the Library, have nearly identical trim. All have plaster dados with flat chair rails and bases. The former feature is capped by a projecting piece, run with a half-round set against two filets. Each room has a slightly different mantel design, the variations occurring in the frieze and shelf. All have Aquia stone facings with wood backbands, the latter a quarter-round with a broad filet at the outer edge and a narrow one against the stone facing. In each case there are lateral crossettes, but the friezes all differ; the northeast room has a flat paneled frieze, the northwest is pulvinated, the southwest is bellied, and the southeast is flat with a panel and scrolled ends. The crown of the cornice shelf is the same in each room: a cyma-recta above a fascia, but there are slight variations in the bed moulds. Scrolled consoles occur in the southwest room below the crossettes. Although this woodwork is unimportant, it is interesting, and probably dates from the raising of the house in 1758. When this was done, the ceiling downstairs may have been slightly lifted, for the old plate is said to remain below the new second-floor girt.

The finish of Washington's bedroom is abjectly plain, and in the form of trim there are only a narrow cornice and simply-cased mantel, However, the hall, outside, has a fine walnut rail around the stair well with balusters turned to match those in the main hall.

The finish of the 1759 rooms is perhaps the most satisfactory of the house; it is in good scale, well designed, and well executed, conditions which are not entirely true of the 1773-87 work. In spite of its relatively small scale, the hall has a good deal of real English Georgian character and possesses repose and dignity. Above the unpaneled pedestal dado the walls are covered by a series of tall panels capped by a cornice with "block" modillions. The detail of the paneling has been referred to, and the cornice is apparently taken from a detail in Langley's *Builder's and Workman's Treasury of Designs*. This is an unusual cornice type, though shown in Palladio, the modillions being larger than ordinary and cut to an ogee profile instead of the usual console form. This is also the type used for the exterior cornice. Other Virginia examples are in main cornices of the Blandfield dependencies and in the Treasurer's house in Williamsburg. In the Mount Vernon hall it is curious to see this cornice form adapted to the under side of the rake of the stair. At one time it returned against the sides of a beam in the center of the hall.[51] The side walls of the hall are balanced by a pair of doors on either side, near the middle. Each doorway is framed by a fully-moulded architrave supporting a flat frieze and broken pediment. It was probably for these latter that Washington ordered from England four "bustos;"[52] and it easily may have been that the pediments, since they come against the panel moulds, were added to the doorways at this time.

A rather irrelevant ornament of the hall is the elaborate entablature supported on consoles of the east door. The frieze is filled with strap ornament after the style of a border for a ceiling, illustrated by Langley in the *Builder's Treasury*. Also shown elsewhere are carved and scrolled brackets similar to these examples which flank the moulded architrave of the opening and support the cornice. The doors now in place, as has been observed, are of nineteenth-century origin.

In spite of the interest of the side walls, the stair is of course the main feature of the hall. It ascends against the south wall in a long initial flight to a landing against the west front. From there it ascends in two short flights to the second floor. Because of the small scale of the house, it was evidently found difficult to gain headroom under the header. This timber was therefore set back far enough from its usual location at the line of the top riser to attain ample height, and the re-entrant corner thus formed was very agreeably softened by curving the gallery floor-line. The design of the stairs is unusually fine. It is at the same time simple, substantial, and graceful, and gains richness through its walnut balustrade and stringpiece. The balustrade is initiated by a large swirl at the newel, and the handrail then continues, by beautifully-executed ramps and easings, over the turned minor posts to the wall post at the second floor. The handrail is of the normal type, but the balusters are almost unique in the state for their simplicity. Each consists of a long shaft showing an entiasis, with a short vase at the bottom and a delicate Tuscan cap. These balusters are undoubtedly the work paid for by Washington on August 10, 1759, which he noted in his account book as "By Going [Gawen] Lamphire in full for Turnery, 17.14.7½." The simplicity of the turnings may be accounted for by Lamphier's residence in Alexandria, where even in fine buildings, such as Gadsby's Tavern, the balusters were often merely shafted without vase or supplementary turnings other than narrow vase and cap moulds. The Mount Vernon string piece is equally lacking in elaboration, possessing a simply moulded rake and a series of fine broad brackets, entirely unornamented except for their scrolled soffits. The only ornament on the stair is a large-scale Greek key fret. This is applied to the fascia of the second floor of the stair well, but is now in poor condition. The respond of the balustrade against the

Plate LXXXI.

These Cornices are
described at large
in Plate II.

Precedent from Langley's Treasury for Library mantel.

MOUNT VERNON, Fairfax County. Stairway of 1759. Troubridge.

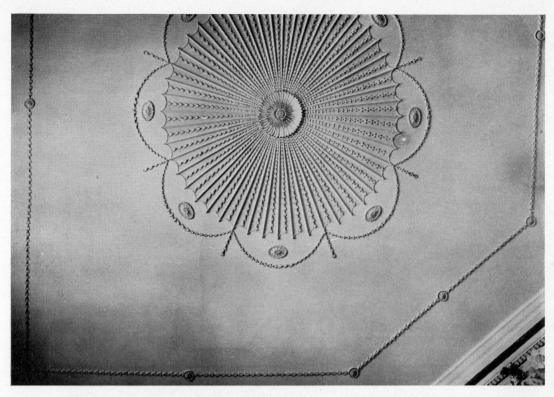

MOUNT VERNON, Fairfax County. West Parlor ceiling, in the style of Robert Adam. *Johnston.*

MOUNT VERNON, Fairfax County. West Parlor, trim of c. 1759; ceiling of c. 1770. *Johnston.*

wall is sheathed, but the spandrel of the first flight of the stairs is filled with one large triangular panel. The stair is notable even in a state where the finest and most elaborate of all American examples occur. It seems in a way more expressive of Washington than any feature of the house, having the reserve and distinction he himself so superbly displayed.

Immediately opposite the first flight of the stair is the beautiful West Parlor, paneled to the ceiling on all walls and with a full-height frontispiece mantel and two Ionic doorways. All of this work may date from 1759, for the mantel is inspired by Plate LI of Swan's *British Architect* (1745), and the doorways by Plate CCCXLIX, Langley's *Ancient Masonry* (1734). The parallel of the latter is exact, with fluted Ionic pilasters supporting a moulded architrave, pulvinated frieze, and angle pediment. The latter feature is enriched with modillions, and the six-paneled door is framed by an ovolo, carved with egg and dart. All of the members are well designed and executed. One of the doors enters the hall, and the other, diagonally opposite, leads into the Banquet Room. The angle chimney breast displays the mantel to good advantage in spite of the small size of the room. Although it is based on the Swan design, there are many variations, especially in proportion. In both of these the fireplace opening is framed by a full architrave which at the jambs is buttressed by carved consoles. The cornice-type mantel shelf is supported on consoles, and above it, resting on a moulded base, is an overmantel panel framed by an architrave broken out into full crossettes at the top and buttressed by baroque consoles. The Mount Vernon mantel, in addition to a rococo scroll finish above the panel, has a broken serpentine pediment with a carved cartouche bearing the Washington arms. The proportion is certainly superior to the original design, the lower part being broadened out, the frieze reduced in height, and the overmantel expanded considerably. The use of a pediment, too, is helpful and gives a suitable finish to the design, in spite of the fact that it is applied to the paneling without advancing the frieze. The precedent of Swan's plate being early enough to allow its use in the 1757-59 alterations, it is particularly significant that at this time Washington ordered a "landskip" of exact size of that now in place in the overmantel.[53]

Various simplifications were made in translating the design to Mount Vernon. A marble facing with a carved wood backband took the place of Swan's fully moulded architrave, and simple scrolled consoles supplanted the extremely elaborate ones of the original. Likewise, the brackets under the shelf were carved with fish-scale ornament in place of scrolls and leaves, and the frieze with rather heavy scrolls of leafage instead of Swan's festoon. In the overmantel the changes were less extensive—except for the proportioning, the same consoles and panel form being retained, only a scrolled baroque inner panel being omitted.

Although the enrichments of this mantel cannot compare in beauty of execution to those of the Dining Room mantel, there is much fine running ornament in the backbands of the architraves, the mouldings of the cornice shelf, and the detail of the pediment. Only in the lower consoles is the carving actually crude, even though that of the upper consoles is far from matching the brilliant dexterity of that of the Dining Room workmanship. However, there can be no question of the superior suitability of the West Parlor mantel, well scaled to the room, and quite free of the somewhat ostentatious character of the other.

The architectural features of the room are well displayed against the simple broad panels of the wall. The fine ornament of the former is related to the cornice and chair rail by dentils in the bed mould of the former and a Wall of Troy fret applied to the fascia of the latter.

An unusual feature of the fireplace is the fine Georgian cast-iron fireplace lining of 1787. Few of this period survive, though many highly ornamental Pennsylvania and New Jersey examples of a later date remain. This has plain fields with a moulding accenting the top line, which ramps up in a curve on the jambs from a lower back-plate. Centered on the backplate is Washington's cypher and crest in a beautifully designed relief.

A really fine Adamesque ceiling, undoubtedly dating from the period of 1773-81, completes the room. It is simpler than any at Kenmore or than the Mount Vernon Dining Room, but is certainly more adapted to the material than any of them. It has a large centerpiece, composed of rays of a sunburst between which are strands of diminishing husks. Encompassing the whole motive are scallops of diminishing husks which form a series of eight lunettes, in which are set oval medallions. The perimeter of the room is encompassed by a band of husks and medallions.

Of the other rooms, the Sitting Room, in the southeast corner, is most like the West Parlor, though it lacks the interest and fine detail of the latter. As has been observed, it is probably the only room of Lawrence Washington's time. The room is paneled above and below the chair rail, which, like the full cornice, is simply detailed. The chimney breast has another frontispiece mantel, which resembles those of the Library and Dining Room, though unlike them, it has no carving. The mantel itself has a full architrave frame with crossettes, a pulvinated frieze, and a cornice shelf, fully moulded with a dentil band. The overmantel, resting on a moulded plinth, is formed by a large panel with four crossettes and a delicate parallel border framing the field of the panel. Nothing in this motive is foreign to Virginia, and it resembles much of such work in minor houses, though the derivation of the type is undoubtedly from style books of the period.

Mount Vernon, Fairfax County. Small Sitting Room, perhaps dating from 1743. *Johnston.*

Mount Vernon, Fairfax County. The north wall of the Library, dated after 1773. *Johnston.*

MOUNT VERNON. The Dining Room mantel. *Johnston.*

Plate L. Swan's book. Source of Dining Room mantel.

MOUNT VERNON. The West Parlor mantel. *Johnston.*

Plate LI, Swan's book. Precedent for West Parlor mantel.

The Dining Room is more reminiscent of the work of the period in Philadelphia than in Virginia, and this may be due to Sears, whose origin is unknown. The lack of work of this character in Alexandria makes it seem unlikely that Lamphier was responsible for the enrichments. Although the parlor mantels of the Powell and Blackwell houses in Philadelphia [55] eclipse this room in elaboration, it bears striking resemblance to them, especially the latter with its low studded ceiling. The paneled dado, too, may be due to Philadelphia influence, as both of these two houses have them.

The mantel is, of course, the cynosure of the room. It has the same general form as that of the West Parlor but is derived from Plate L of the *British Architect*. The facing of the fireplace is Pennsylvania blue-mottled marble and is framed by a richly carved backband, which breaks out in the crossettes at the head. Below the break in the jamb is a superb console of tall acanthus leaves rising from a shell. The frieze brackets are also ornamented with acanthus, a broad leaf covering the whole face of each one. The sides are carved with leaves and scrolls. Between them the frieze is covered by an extraordinary band of rococo decoration, almost exactly copied from Swan's design, occupying the entire space. Supported by the frieze bracket is the elaborate cornice shelf, every member of which, except the fascia, is enriched. The two cymas of the corona have leaf ornament, the ovolo of the bed mould, egg and dart, and below the dentil band another line of water-leaf. The backband of the overmantel is carved and edged with a rope mould. The raised moulding of the inner panel is carved with ribbon-on-reel, and from the upper crossettes of the outer frame hang pendants of diminishing motives. To complete this feature there are further undulating baroque ornaments below and above the panel. Placed as it is at an angle, and because of its large scale, this fine frontispiece loses much of its effectiveness, but it is outstanding of its type.

The rich effect of the mantel is accentuated by the magnificent enriched plaster ceiling and frieze. The latter is composed of a band of scrolled leaves bordered at the bottom by an ovolo bearing egg-and-dart ornament, and at the top by a series of rosettes and scrolls set in an angle, simulating a corona. The ceiling is well designed and adapts itself to the unorthodox shape of the room. It has a circular center piece composed of sixteen spokes of husks radiating from a large rosette and enclosed by a circle of similar husks. These are again used in a series of inverted festoons, beyond which the rest of the area of the ceiling is taken up by delicate convolutions of foliated tracery. This is the ceiling Lund Washington said was as good as any at "Colonel Lewises but less work on it;" [56] and whether or not he was right, it shows extraordinary

MOUNT VERNON. Detail of Banquet Room ceiling, design of agricultural symbols. *Johnston*.

MOUNT VERNON, Fairfax County. Dining Room ceiling. Well designed for the space. *Johnston*.

MOUNT VERNON. Banquet Room chimney piece. The superb marble mantel, gift to Washington of Samuel Vaughn of London, is the finest extant in Virginia, and the only example with an inlaid hearth. *Johnston.*

mastery of the medium by the artisan and considerable ingenuity of design.

A comparison of the Dining Room mantel with the Library mantel makes clear the vast difference between the work of an average workman and that of a brilliant craftsman. From the Library mantel the dash and sparkle is gone, and a subdued decorousness takes its place. The Library, commenced in 1773 and finished in 1774, has plaster walls, a simply moulded base and chair rail, and an excellent fully moulded cornice, enriched only by a Wall of Troy dentil course. A feature of the room is the series of four tall glazed bookcases on the east wall. These have paneled cupboards underneath and paneled extensions at either end; the extensions contain, to the north, a door to the stair, and to the south, a door to the large closet under the stair. Only the north end is original, the cupboards having been added shortly after the date of the building to fill a setback caused by the greater width of the stair hall than of the stair itself. Behind them the old dado mouldings can be seen, but the cornice was carefully moved forward to the new line, as can be seen by the mitre in it near the door. The cupboard doors, two lights wide and six high, are given a decorative quality by the interlacing muntins in the top pair of lights.

The north wall is occupied by a very broad chimney breast flanked by narrow paneled cupboards. The unusually broad chimney-face has centered in it the frontispiece panel flanked by broad panels, above and below a chair rail. The profiles are more architectural than the rest of the room, the dado taking a pedestal form, the paneled face perhaps being an effort to establish a relation to the Sitting Room.

The mantel motive itself is reminiscent of that in the drawing room at Menokin, though more scholarly in detail and distribution of the elements. A broad Purbeck marble fireplace-facing has an uncarved backband with crossettes at the head, from which hang long pendants of diminishing husks. The frieze has the same fish-scale brackets seen in the West Parlor, and between them, with responds beyond as well, is a band of guilloche with both large and small circles filled by rosettes. The cornice shelf matches the main cornice at smaller scale. In a large sunk overmantel area is set a projecting panel with four crossettes enriched with pendants against the outside, and with large rosettes in the corners. A raised beading defines the rectangular inside panel. The whole upper motive is supported by a boldly moulded base, set on the mantel.

Although lacking the elegance of the two west rooms, the Library has the homely qualities of a much-used room, and with it Washington as the country squire is most closely identified.

The Banquet Room, commenced in 1776 and finished in 1786, is one

of the handsomest rooms of the period and, while not as fine architecturally, it is reminiscent of the drawing room in the Miles Brewton
house in Charleston,[57] South Carolina, and the ball room of Hampton
on the Santee in the same state.[58] Both of these rooms are a decade
earlier than the Mount Vernon room, but except for their more elaborate
and extensive woodwork, they have much the same mid-Georgian
flavor. Hampton is a remarkable parallel to Mount Vernon in that the
early house has been added to in the same way Mount Vernon has, with
the ball room in the same location. It, too, has a two-story porch, but
an extraordinarily beautiful one of hexastyle portico form. Like Mount
Vernon, the South Carolina rooms are long rectangles with high coved
ceilings.

The form of the Mount Vernon room may well have originated with
Vitruvius Scoticus, for in it are illustrated several rooms of this form,
such as at Yester, with fine plaster decorations. If the woodwork had not
been enriched with rather extraneous composition ornament, the effect
would have been more that of Hampton. However, even at the expense
of making a transitional Georgian-Adamesque room of it, the decorating
of the ceiling with its beautiful plaster work of the latter style is hard
to regret.

The Banquet Hall has a projecting chimney breast on the south wall
flanked by two doorways, and on the north wall on axis with the fireplace
is the great Palladian window. The mantel is a magnificent marble piece
with free-standing Ionic columns supporting a frieze enriched with bas-
reliefs. It was the gift of Samuel Vaughn of London, and is the most
elaborate of its period in the country. It is unique in having an inlaid
marble mantel. The end walls have one small exterior door and a
normal eighteen-light sash window. The length of the room is thirty-
one feet, the width twenty-three, and the height just over sixteen. The
cornice is depressed almost two feet to allow a fine cove to surmount it.
Like the Music Room, the Banquet Room is entirely plastered and has
wood mouldings and trim. There is an unpaneled dado of pedestal
form below high, plain walls which are crowned by an enriched plaster
cornice, below the cove. The doorways have architrave frames and are
surmounted by entablatures. Both the dado and door-frame mouldings
are intricately decorated with over-fine composition ornament which is
quite unrelated to the detail of the mouldings.

Leaves and an inverted band of egg and dart enrich the base, and the
chair rail has a fluted fascia below a cove. This latter is treated with tiny
radial medallions and pendants of leafage above a water-leaf bed mould.
The back band of the door and the crown mould of its entablature have
the same profile and ornament as the top mould of the chair rail. An

intermediate member of the architrave is enriched with leaf ornament, and the fascia of the cornice with a Greek fret, in scale normal to the woodwork. The frieze is decorated with a band of intricate ornament comprising an urn in the center, issuing from scrolled leaves. These originate in flanking roundels which enclose symbols of agriculture. The remaining length of the frieze is taken up by a festoon of husks at either end enclosing a medallion and terminating in a pendant. The doors themselves are of familiar six-panel type common to the house.

The ornament is somewhat out of character with the doorways, and it is pronouncedly so in the great Palladian window. Here the wide paneled piers that divide and flank the openings are treated with thin pendants of Adamesque ornament both above and below the dado, and the frieze of the entablature with delicate festoons. All of the mouldings of the piers and entablatures are further ornamented, as is the archivolt of the central arch. This latter extends into the cove, creating a penetration.

The main cornice is detailed in the style of the ceiling and is excellent in effect and in relation to its detail. It has a shallow projection in the character of a pedestal cap, and the bed mould is decorated with leaves, dentils, and egg and dart, and the crown mould by fluting and medallions. Below the cornice is a fine frieze of modified anthemions, alternating with foliated vases, defined at the bottom by a bead moulding.

The cove itself has a series of delicate, large-scale festoons of diminishing husks tied with ribbons at the intersections, long pendants of matching husks, and in each of the spandrels of the festoon is a small medallion.

The ceiling design, within a border of vines looped to a central stem, consists of a large centerpiece of scrolled foliage outside a sunburst, and four large equal panels, in each corner of the ceiling, containing great wreaths enclosing further agricultural symbols. The good design, low relief, and excellent modelling of the ceiling make it the outstanding example of its period in this country.

The transformation of Mount Vernon, even if it was in two stages, from the cottage of 1742 to the mansion of 1787 was no mean feat, and both Washington and his architect acquitted themselves well. Seen from the old gatehouses, across the vista cut through the woods, the house is the perfection of Colonial architecture, with the rustic elegance of a Palladian design translated into wood three thousand miles from London. The white mansion in its beautiful setting of green lawns sloping to the river, and with its streets of plantation buildings, makes an unforgettable picture.

As has been pointed out, Mount Vernon as it stands today is an

MOUNT VERNON, Fairfax County. Banquet Room: mantel. *Johnston.*

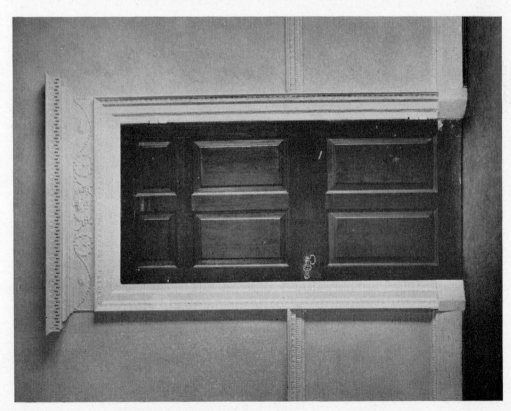

MOUNT VERNON, Fairfax County. Banquet Room door. *Johnston.*

MOUNT VERNON. The Banquet Room window. *Johnston.*

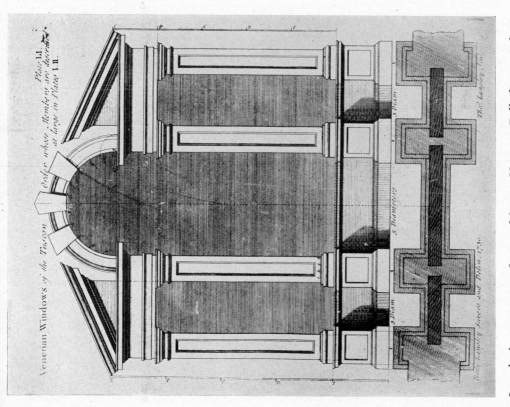

Langley's prototype of great MOUNT VERNON Palladian window.

architectural design that resulted from a series of skillful alterations and additions rather than from one clean-cut operation. There were inevitably artistic and functional difficulties, as those encountered in the rebuilding of Ashburnham House, for example. If, as it seems probable, the Governor's Palace in Williamsburg was the perfecting of the Ashburnham scheme, so it seems that Elmwood in Essex County is the perfecting of Mount Vernon. The preparation of the final designs for extensions to the latter must have been complete by 1773 when the Library end was under construction, and it appears that Elmwood was begun shortly afterward. Tradition and the architectural evidence both point to this date, but all documentary confirmation is lacking.

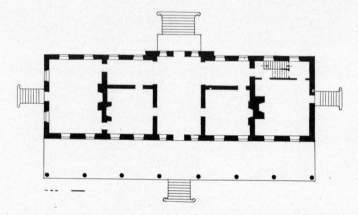

ELMWOOD, Essex County.

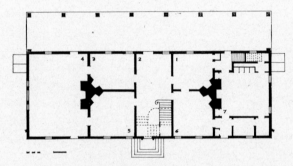

MOUNT VERNON, Fairfax County.

The relationship of Mount Vernon to Elmwood, which was built of brick and has no dependencies, is made evident only by close study of its plan, elevations, and details. Of the major mansions of the state, the two house alone have long, comparatively narrow plans instead of relatively square ones, such as those of Mount Airy and Carter's Grove. Elmwood is exactly one hundred feet long, and Mount Vernon only a few feet shorter, and both are about thirty feet deep within the walls. They both have central halls, but at Elmwood this hall is on the center axis, and from it corridors extend across the north front to the drawing room on the west side and the dining room entry on the east. The stair was removed entirely from the central hall and located to one side, but exactly where is a problem, for it was removed in the extensive alterations of 1852 and placed in a stair tower. Family tradition has it that it stood in the east corridor, but it seems very possible that it was in the dining room entry, like the Library stair at Mount Vernon. Nothing is known of the stair trim except details gained from a few of the balusters, which are preserved in the attic. These have tapered shanks above vase turnings.

The north corridors obviate the necessity of traversing one room, as at Mount Vernon, to get to another, but reduce by two the number of rooms on the first floor. The two center rooms, the library and music room, can be entered from both the hall and corridor. The mantels face the hall and there are a pair of windows in the south walls. The drawing room occupies the whole west end and has a range of three openings in the west wall (the middle, an exterior door), and a pair of windows in each end wall. The chimney breast is against the east wall, and is flanked by a door to the hall and one to the library. The exact original arangement in the dining room is not sure, for it was involved in the Victorian alterations, but it probably was much as at present, except for its trim. It occupies the southeast corner, with an entry to the hall and a pantry on the north side.

On the second floor a corridor extends from chimney wall to chimney wall, and there is a range of five bedrooms on its south side. The arrangement of the basement is much the same.

The great north façade is now sadly shorn of its original character by the nineteenth-century alterations which involved reglazing the windows, lowering the sills of the first- and second-floor windows, and adding the cumbersome Italian-Villa-style stair tower to the left of the entrance pavilion. In its original state the building must have been unusually beautiful, with the long series of windows flanking the pavilion with its Palladian window and open tympanum. Now the brick is painted brown, but the original pink color foiled by the white sashes and cornice would have given the house the gaiety and charm it now so signally lacks.

The façade seems to be definitely a development of that of Mount Vernon, perhaps influenced by the design of Murray House shown in Plate CXIII in *Vitruvius Scoticus*. As in the latter house, the pavilion is only one broad bay in width, but like Mount Vernon it is flanked by rows of four windows on either side. The awkward problems which prevented the Mount Vernon pediment from being properly supported on a pavilion were not present here, for the bay is advanced a foot or more from the main wall. Particularly notable is the brickwork of the façade, laid in Flemish bond, of unusual regularity, with richly-worked window arches, belt course, and water table. These features almost exactly parallel those of Blandfield, which was probably hardly finished when Elmwood was begun. The water tables of both are double moulded with a scotia above a torus, and are raised to about five feet above the grade, giving full basement windows. The corners of the building and jambs of the windows are rubbed a full stretcher and header in depth, and the gauged flat arches are six courses high. Like the arches at Blandfield, the splay at the jamb line is forty-five degrees, a considerably greater angle than that of any other Virginia example. The somerings, or horizontal joints, are well arranged and give a rich pattern. Fine as these arches are as examples of bricklayers' art, they are eclipsed by the superb complex of the Palladian window. Here the flat arches of the sidelights merge into the half-round of the center opening without affecting the structural integrity of the arch function of all three elements. This is apparent by the perfect condition of the brickwork of the pediment above. An interesting feature of this latter is its open tympanum form, the earliest example of such a use later appearing at Woodlawn,[59] in Fairfax County. The main cornice returns under the haunches of the pediment to allow the blind arch of the Palladian window to extend above it. It may be that this form, which is certainly unusual, was inspired by Plates XXIII and XXIV in *Vitruvius Scoticus* of Yester House, the sole example in the book, or by Gibbs's open pediments on brackets such as Plate LXXI, which inspired the Westover mantel. Unfortunately, there is no evidence of the original design of the doorway, which is now bereft of all trim and appears as three square-headed brick openings, but it may have followed the design of Drum House, in Adam's Plate XXXVIII.

In detail the main cornice is unusually rich, being fully moulded with both modillions and dentils. It extends around the entire building and supports a low hipped roof broken only by two large chimney stacks, near the break of the hip, and by the pavilion projection. The fact that the south, or rear wall, possesses the full decorated cornice and that it is undisturbed at the returns of the end elevations indicate that the original full-length porch did not rise two full stories, as the Mount Vernon porch does. This is further substantiated by the presence of gauged arches over the second-floor windows and the lack of them in the lower windows, where they are supplanted by single-tier rowlock arches. Since the old porch disappeared in the 1852 alterations, its exact form

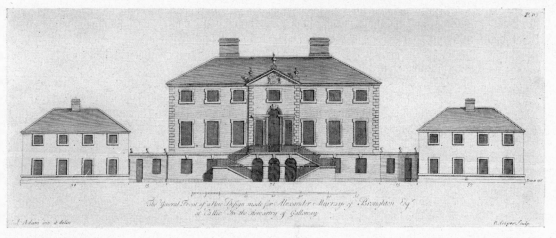

Mansion of Alexander Murray of Broughton, in Galloway, Scotland, from *Vitruvius Scoticus*.

ELMWOOD, Essex County, Virginia. The culmination of the mid-Georgian period. A huge house one hundred feet long, which once may have had dependencies. It has many similarities to Mount Vernon and seems to be a development of it. *Haussmann.* (Victorian additions omitted.)

ELMWOOD, Essex County. The south front, once traversed by a one-story porch. *Met. Eng.*

ELMWOOD, Essex County. Drawing Room, one of the latest paneled rooms in Virginia. *Met Eng.*

can only be assumed. This elevation being unbroken by a pavilion, it probably was eleven bays in length, though there may have been some special treatment in the center when the bays are of a different dimension. Some derelict Greek Ionic wood columns are now in the basement, but these are from the altered porches from both front and back, which were four bays in length, and were recently removed.

The end elevations of the house are without architectural features, being merely two bays in depth with an inconspicuous door inserted between the two lower windows. The end rooms do not seem to have been reached from covered passageways or to have communicated with formal dependencies, though the latter may have existed. The site of the kitchen, abreast of the house and to the east, is still pointed out.

The approach to Elmwood is across the broad lowlands of the Rappahannock from near venerable Vauter's Church, and up the low ridges that define the valley. Approached from the west, the north front faces open meadows falling away to the wooded slopes. The wide north terrace, once traversed by the drive, had a row of fine walnut trees at the brow of the meadow slope opposite the façade, but these recently have fallen. There are, however, fine specimen trees in the south garden, once part of the design of a vast parterre. Some of the design, such as the axial box walk with circular centerpiece, and cross walk of crape myrtle and other flowering shrubs, can still be traced. The great beauty of the garden, however, is in drifts of thousands of daffodils, narcissus, and blue bells that cover the garden floor in the spring, and in the dogwood and redbud blossoms in the surrounding woods.

Although the interior suffered severely from the Victorian changes, it still retains the major part of its original trim. The hall, however, has lost all except the elliptical arches and supporting pilasters that frame the openings to the north corridor windows, and the Doric entablature at the ceiling line. This latter is of wood with triglyphs, and metopes filled with rosettes. The whole is now unfortunately polychromed. The corridor arches are of wood with paneled soffits, moulded archivolts, and fluted Doric pilasters. Such arches of elliptical form are characteristic of the region and reoccur at Gaymont, Brooke's Bank, Nanzatico, and elsewhere, and show that the craftsman working under the architect was allowed certain liberties, also seen in the detail of the overmantels. In the hall, as throughout the house, all the window trim has been altered, but fortunately this and the removal of the mantels and doors are the only changes in the drawing room and library. The music room still retains its fine mantel. The dining room and all the bedrooms save two were entirely retrimmed.

ELMWOOD, Essex County. Library mantel. *Author, HABS.*

ELMWOOD, Essex County. Northwest corner. *Author, HABS.*

ELMWOOD. The overmantel of drawing room. *Author, HABS.*

LANGLEY's Plate LXXV, basis for drawing room overmantel.

The library, to the east of the central hall, is paneled to the ceiling above a sheathed pedestal-type dado. The arrangement of the panels in groups of three, one wide flanked by two narrow, is extremely unusual and is useful in the hanging of paintings. Now, however, the walls are covered by nineteenth-century bookcases, from which the books have recently been removed by gift of the owner to the University of Virginia. The focus of the room is the beautiful pedimented overmantel, now unfortunately bereft of the mantel on which it once rested. It is formed by a large panel framed by an architrave with crossettes, supported at the side by broad scrolled consoles, and surmounted by a frieze and pediment. The consoles are of an unusual form, the lower volute being worked with an intricate scroll, without the carved leafage usually seen in such features. Between the backband of the architrave and the beading of the panel is a band of fret work. The angle pediment is enriched with arched corbels in place of modillions, and the same treatment on a larger scale is repeated in the main cornice. This mantel seems to be based on Plate LXXVIII of Langley's *Builder's Treasury.*

The balancing music room, in contradistinction to the library, has plastered walls above a similar sheathed pedestal-type dado. The main cornice is the familiar modillioned type, with dentilled bed mould. Again the mantel motive is the feature of the room, and here the full beauty of the complete design can be appreciated. The fireplace is framed with a pink marble facing, with a carved backband broken out in crossettes at the head. The frieze is interrupted at either end by a bracket which supports the cornice shelf. These brackets are reminiscent of those of the West Parlor of Mount Vernon in their simple scroll shape, and particularly in the fish-scale ornament that covers their broad faces. Also as at Mount Vernon the cornice shelf is elaborately carved, the bed mould having, in addition to dentils, its upper moulding carved with egg-and-dart ornament. The fascia is enriched with an elaborate Greek key fret carved and applied.

The overmantel, inspired by Langley's Plate LXXXVI, has a high panel, with crossettes at each corner, the architrave of which has the backboard carved and the fascia covered with a pierced fret. A curious feature of the design is the small-scale entablature that traverses the head resting in the crossettes. The length between them is slightly projected and is crowned by a low pediment, a use that reoccurs in the drawing room and is precedented by Plate LXXV of Langley's *Builder's Treasury.*

Closely approximating the Mount Vernon Banquet Room in size, being twenty by thirty feet, the drawing room has a ceiling height uniform with the rest of the house, instead of a high cove. This difference, and the full paneling of the walls, prevents a close resemblance between the two rooms. The use of paneling here is not surprising, though to some extent it is an anachronism. In this group the only variation in style is in "Gibbs's ancient or modern," that is, Palladian or Baroque. Except in the ornament of the Mount Vernon Banquet Room, probably applied by Washington without the advice of the designer, Adamesque decorations were as carefully eschewed as in Sir William Chamber's own work, and without it the ornament falls into the "Gibbs's modern" school. However, the Elmwood drawing room is generally mid-Georgian with the addition of a Baroque overmantel. The walls are covered with paneling above a pedestal dado and capped by a fine modillioned cornice. It is interesting to note the great breadth of the panels in contrast to the narrow ones of contemporary Brandon and Chatham. Although the original window trim is gone, the drawing room doors, in the east and west walls, have their old tabernacled frames. Though less successful than the West Parlor doorways at Mount Vernon, they have the same elements, Ionic pilasters supporting pedimented overdoors. The detail is much less ably executed and shows the contrast between the product of a joiner trained to the fine work of Alexandria or Philadelphia, and a less accomplished country workman. However, it was more in the general forms that the shortcomings of the designs are apparent. In the doorways, it is in the poor entiasis of the pilasters (which rarely should have an entiasis at all) and the crude shaping of the broken serpentine pediment of the overdoor. With the fine pilasters of the Mount Vernon doorways and the beautiful pediment of the mantel, these would have been excellent architectural features. There is, however, some conflict in scale between them and the sumptuous overmantel, which like that in the library, is now suspended over an ineffectual Victorian mantel. Before this change the effect must have been much enhanced. The overmantel, derived from Plate LXXV of the *Builder's Treasury,* has a broad raised panel with crossettes as in the other rooms. This is crowned by a delicate entablature which is supported by two diminutive Ionic pilasters. The entablature, as in the music room, is advanced in the center bay and capped by a broken serpentine pediment. In the detail of the overmantel excellent craftsmanship may be seen, especially in the carved mouldings and pierced strapwork of the center panel. Of the upper rooms, only those over the library and music room have their original trim, but this consists only of a dado and simply-paneled overmantel in each.

Little known outside its immediate vicinity, Elmwood is one of the outstanding mansions of its period. Few who know it have realized that under the drab dress of the Victorian alterations the house has excellent architectural qualities which, properly taken advantage of, would recreate a house of unusual beauty. Even though its prototype is less surely from *Vitruvius Scoticus,* Elmwood is certainly related to two great houses that were, Blandfield and Mount Vernon, at least one of which was associated with Ariss' name. The variations in plan and elevation between it and Mount Vernon are the kind familiar in other houses of the group embodying improvements and refinements which show the ingenuity and resourcefulness of an unusually competent designer.

HAMILTON HALL HOUSE, Edinburgh, Scotland.

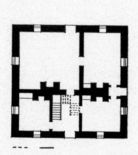

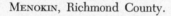

MENOKIN, Richmond County.

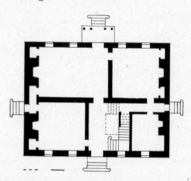

KENMORE, Fredericksburg.

These six mansions, the Carlyle house, Mount Airy, Blandfield, Mannsfield, Mount Vernon and Elmwood, with the possible addition of Camden, seem to have constituted the monumental dwellings inspired by *Vitruvius Scoticus* and attributed here to John Ariss. One other, Fairfield, in Berkeley County, possesses attributes of this first group, but actually all indications point to its inclusion in the traditional type of which Kenmore is the key example. Although deeply influenced by Adam's book, the second group has much of the character of traditional Virginia house building. This group includes Kenmore, Fairfield, Harewood, Menokin, Locust Hill, and perhaps Sara's Creek House (sometimes called Little England), all in Virginia, and Pleasant Valley and Ratcliffe Manor in Maryland.[60]

This group has a stylized plan, but the treatment of the elevations is so simple that only the proportions, fenestration. and roof design betray architectural qualities. Menokin is no larger than the rest, but it possesses highly architectural elevations. This may be explained by its close proximity to Mount Airy and by the fact that it was built by John Tayloe for his daughter Rebecca and her husband Francis Lightfoot Lee. Though there is apparently no documentary evidence as to the date, it was probably complete in 1769, the year of Lee's marriage.

The plan varies from the other houses of the group in having the stair ascend at the left of the hall, in a straight run, with winders at the top. This arrangement tends to equalize the two front rooms while maintaining the large drawing room in the left rear corner of the building, as in all of the Scotch, Virginia, and Maryland examples.

The exterior of Menokin is unusual in possessing the qualities of a mansion, although the building is modest in its actual dimensions. Based in design on both Hamilton Hall House and Lord Milton's house, it shows an interesting blending of the two façades. It is constructed of local stone which is plastered over, except for elaborate stone trim, in the form of quoins, belt courses, and window and door trim. The water table has a bold moulded offset of scotia and torus, as at Mount Airy. The belt courses occur at the floor line and at the sill level of the upper windows. This belt course arrangement is derived from Milton House, as is the window trim, but the latter design is in reverse of the Scotch example. The trim of the lower windows at Menokin is a broad plain band, but above the openings are framed by fully moulded architraves, interrupted by rusticated blocks. At the doorway there is curious and poorly designed trim which is totally unrelated to any other such feature in the group. The single door is surmounted by an arched fanlight, and the whole is framed by broad pilaster-piers and an unmoulded archivolt. At the head is a large keystone carved with a crude spray of leafage. The whole is so crudely detailed as to suggest that the design was misinterpreted by the masons. If Ariss were, indeed, the architect, Menokin was probably built without his supervision, or at least by rare visits of superintendence.

The mansion quality must have been considerably heightened before the destruction of the kitchen building, which stood at the right of the house, and in advance of it, balancing the office still standing to the left. In design, the extant office building is an interesting combination of tradition and style. It is two stories high, with a low gable roof and diminutive inside end chimneys. The end walls have no openings and are unornamented except for a belt course at the second floor. The long side toward the forecourt has a central arched doorway flanked by a single window on either side. This little façade obtains excellent quality through the small-scale detail of the doorway and the well considered fenestration. The interior of the building, which is divided into two rooms on each floor, has some good woodwork, including a Chinese trellis stair rail of unusually open design, and a mantel composed of an architrave with crossettes, supporting a paneled frieze and cornice shelf.

The trim of the main house is less successful and much less academic than that of the office building. The main rooms have paneled dados, and the large drawing room a paneled overmantel. This also has an architrave fireplace frame with crossettes, a wide frieze carved with guilloche ornament in low relief, and a cornice shelf. Above the shelf, three vertical panels occur below a large framed panel. The cornice of the room is enriched with dentils. The stair is entirely traditional, being open string with square balusters set at an angle, and simply-scrolled stair-end brackets. There are no ramps or easings.

A house having both the historical associations of Menokin and its architectural individuality deserves better than its present fate. It is to be hoped that it may be rescued from its semi-ruinous condition and reinstated in its rightful position as an historical monument.

The Virginia and Maryland structures, except for Locust Hill, Harewood, and Sara's Creek House, are related in plan to one in *Vitruvius Scoticus*.[61] This is Hamilton Hall House in Midlothian, Scotland. Although there are considerable variations in the Colonial use of this plan, the scheme is preserved in all. In the original it consists of an off-center stair hall, with the stair ascending from the right-hand side of the doorway. At the left is a large room, and at the right, beyond the stair, two small ones. The rear of the house is divided into two rooms, that at the left being a great drawing room the length of the front room and hall together. From this opens the master's bedroom. This plan has one great defect in that the two small rooms beyond the stair are accessible only by a door under the stair, and could not have full head room. Therefore, in all the American houses this area of the plan was modified. The variations otherwise were merely the location of the chimneys and the modification of room sizes. At Kenmore and Fairfield the front right-hand room is entered by a cross hall running from the stair hall to the side entrance of the house. The chimneys at Kenmore were placed in the end instead of in the cross wall, but at Fairfield they were retained in their original position. Menokin maintained the two right-hand rooms at equal size and moved the stair to the left-hand side of a center hall. The rear rooms, however, were unchanged, as were the chimney locations. Ratcliffe Manor employed the Fairfield modifications with the exception that the chimneys were placed in the end walls. This is true of Pleasant Valley as well, although the stair hall was enlarged by the omission of the right front room.

Hamilton Hall House (left) and Lord Milton's House, Edinburgh, from *Vitruvius Scoticus,* which show features of the Menokin façade, especially the belt courses and window facings.

Menokin, Richmond County. A small house with highly architectural qualities. *Met. Eng.*

MENOKIN, Richmond County, Drawing Room. *Johnston.*

MENOKIN, Richmond County. The hall and staircase. *Johnston.*

Ratcliffe, Pleasant Valley, and Kenmore have an extraordinary affinity in exterior appearance. They are all of brick, two full stories high, and have gable roofs hipped above the tie beams. Each, too, has a pair of chimneys at either end, a stack occurring at the intersection of the hip and gable. The major difference is in the window treatment. Narrow staff beads were used around the windows in the Maryland houses, with twelve over twelve light sash and louvered shutters. At Kenmore, however, wide box frames were used with nine over nine light sash, and shutters are lacking. Except for the shutters, the window treatments seem original, so the difference is real; but in considering it the point must be remembered that narrow staff beads were used at Mount Airy and Carlyle House and wide ones at Sara's Creek and Harewood, so the usage may have been based on caprice or style alone. To a casual observer an even more important difference between Kenmore, Ratcliffe, and Pleasant Valley is in the use of dormer windows on the latter two, but it may be pointed out these are additions of a later period. In both houses the trim is largely original, but it is very simple and does not possess the unique qualities of Kenmore.

Built for Fielding Lewis and his wife Betty Washington (1733-97), Kenmore was erected on land acquired in 1752, two years after their marriage. While no documents attest the exact year of its construction, all evidence points to its being built shortly after the purchase of the land. The simplicity of the exterior is in contrast to the elaborate decoration of the interior. It seems more than possible, due to the fact that it alone of all Virginia mansions lacks rubbed and gauged-brick trim, that it was intended to be stuccoed like Mount Airy and Menokin. If this had been done, perhaps with relief features such as quoins, the effect of the house, with its dwarf portico of two pairs of stone Doric columns, on the architectural or north front, would have been nearly as stately as that of Menokin. The impression of richness of the interior is largely due to the superb plaster relief ceilings and overmantels that probably date from shortly after 1770. The earlier trim may comprise all the present woodwork, except perhaps the fine carved mantels. The stair is remarkably like those of Ratcliffe and Pleasant Valley and is practically a replica of that at Fairfield. In all these examples the stair ascends against the right-hand wall of the hall in three flights, a short initial and top run at right angles to the long run. The balustrade forms a volute or swirl at the first step, then with ramps and easings continues to the end of the second-floor gallery.

The handrail at Kenmore is moulded and is supported on turned balusters, all posts being omitted. In form the balusters are unusual, having almost a spool turning at the bottom instead of the usual vase;

KENMORE, Fredericksburg. South front of house. The dependencies have been recently reconstructed on old foundations. *Author, HABS.*

KENMORE, Fredericksburg. View from southeast. *Author, HABS.*

KENMORE, Fredericksburg. Detail of north porch. *Author, HABS.*

KENMORE, Fredericksburg. Stair hall from drawing room. *Smith.*

KENMORE, Fredericksburg. Dining room, view looking west. *Bagby.*

KENMORE, Fredericksburg. Dining room mantel. *Author, HABS.*

KENMORE, Fredericksburg. Library chimney piece. *Author, HABS.*

above is the typical tapered colonette. This baluster turning agrees in detail with that at Harewood. Being an open string type, the step ends are bracketed with a simple scroll terminating in a thistle and leaf.

The only ceiling-height paneling in the house is that of the dining room. Here the condition is unusual in that only the fireplace end is fully paneled, the other walls having a low dado. Normally, in important houses in Virginia, the "paneled end" so familiar in New England was avoided, and the whole room paneled. However, in the Kenmore group this treatment is found in each house which retains its original trim, only Harewood having a fully paneled room.

The dining room paneling at Kenmore is simple in treatment though somewhat confusing in effect. The wall paneling is divided into two tiers, one of broad, tall panels which carry across the top of the doors which flank the mantel, and a series of small panels framing the latter. The mantel now in place is one of a set of three. It would seem, however, that they dated from the elaborate scheme of decoration that was embarked upon about 1770. They closely parallel the west mantels in Mount Vernon, one of which was completed in 1775.

The probable lapse of ten or more years between the date of completion of Kenmore and the execution of the plaster decorations brings up the question as to whether they are part of the original design. In spite of the curiously countryfied paneling of the dining room, it would seem that they were, for throughout the house the woodwork is apparently contemporary. If this is the case, it is extremely significant, for it is the first time a Virginia mansion appears with its major rooms plastered and with even the dados unpaneled. This plastering was evidently no measure of economy but a deliberate expedient to keep in step with English style. As has been observed, in the first half of the eighteenth century in Virginia architecture the style Wren had created was universal in the design of the great plantation houses. This involved the lining of the interior walls with wood paneling, the areas above and below the chair rail usually being worked with moulded panels. This type of finish was thoroughly satisfactory to the owners, for it was stylish, warm, and permanent.

In early mansions, plaster was used only to lessen the expense of finishing unimportant rooms. It was the antithesis of paneling, for it was not stylish, was cold, and being applied directly to the masonry of the exterior walls, subject to condensation and spalling. To deliberately use plaster as a finish for major rooms was an innovation that must have taken some courage, but its growing popularity in Georgian England must have inclined both the architect and the owner to its use.

As has been observed, Inigo Jones eliminated paneling from his buildings as a decorative feature, employing, as in Italy, plastered areas with judicious ornament. This was in the tradition of Palladio and at variance with the practice of other Italian architects who used the walls and their openings as a field to be strewn with baroque ornament. It was not until the end of Wren's period that this type of baroque plaster-work came into use in England. Under the Georgians walls and ceilings were often encrusted with high relief plaster-work. At its worst it had little relation to the space or surface to which it was applied, and at its best was well modeled and applied with reserve.[62] During his time in Great Britain Ariss must have seen examples, many of which were executed by Italian craftsmen such as Artari and Bagutti, both of whom worked for Gibbs and other fashionable architects. Indeed, even if he had not, *Vitruvius Scoticus* contains drawings of many examples such as the temple at Castle Kennedy with its pilasters, festoons, and shell-topped panels. These features reoccurred in the hall at Yester House, which also contained a superb salon decorated in the same material.

Perhaps the Lewises were unwilling, like George Mason at Gunston, to abandon entirely the old style, and compromised on having their southwest room, which caught the winter sun and summer breeze, finished in the familiar way. Even here the use of plaster above the dado on three walls was perhaps a concession to the architect. To appreciate the change that Kenmore initiated, it is only necessary to consider the interior of Carter's Grove and Wilton, both exact contemporaries with it, which in the first case is fully paneled on the first floor, and on the second, fully paneled throughout.

The limitation of Colonial means and the scarcity of competent crafts-men preserved American examples of decorative plaster-work from the extravagance of the English. The difference can be understood by com-paring Kenmore and the hall of Honington Hall, Warwickshire. In the first the walls are completely unornamented except for the rich mantels and bas-relief overmantel panels. Above are fine elaborate cornices and superb stucco ceilings. The decorations give richness to the rooms, but the plain wall surfaces give them balance and repose. At Honington Hall the walls are covered with baroque ornament echoing the over-mantel, all with bas-reliefs, scrolled ornament, and busts as finials in broken pediments. There are as well rococo brackets, masks, and festoon wall ornaments. Also the cornice is fully enriched and the ceiling covered with strap and scroll decorations. The elaboration of the ornament im-parts to the room restlessness and a feeling of pretentious display.

That it was not merely the limitations under which the designer worked that gave the Kenmore rooms their superiority is evidenced by the excellence of the form and distribution of the ornament in the various features. The great room of the house, and one of the finest of its style in the country, is the drawing room, which occupies over one half of the north range of the building. It opens into a companion but smaller room in the northeast corner, now called the library. These both have richly carved wood mantels formed by brackets resting on eared architraves and supporting full cornices, which are utilized as mantel shelves. All the members are superbly carved, and the friezes between the consoles are filled with carved and applied rinceau ornament which, in the matching mantel in the dining room, has the Washington crest displayed in the center. These are adapted from examples in Abraham Swan's *British Architect,* but whether they were executed in this country or in England is a moot point. In either case, they were undoubtedly intended to frame rectangular fireplace openings with marble facings, as in the Dining Room at Mount Vernon. The arched and plastered facings give them a Colonial quality often found in even the most ambitious work of the period.

The decoration of the mantels is of carved wood, but the overmantels in the two north rooms are of "stucco duro," or decorative plaster work. Though such a usage is extremely rare in this country, they compare favorably with English examples. That in the drawing room is the more elaborate, but the repetition of the ornaments and the tightness of the modeling make it inferior in artistic effect to that in the library, with its charmingly free and crisply-executed floral forms and leafage.

The drawing room overmantel is famous as containing the bas-relief of the fable of the Fox, the Crow, and the Cheese, said to have been used at Washington's suggestion as a moral to his nieces and nephews. The scene, with quaint early-American background, is more interesting historically than artistically, and hardly compares with the beautiful classic scenes in English examples such as those in Hagley, Stoneleigh, and Honington.[63] The Aesop scene is framed by an oval band of fruit and flowers within an architrave richly decorated with crossettes and drops. The library overmantel has only the upper crossettes and lacks the enrichment of the other, but the side pendants and the large festoon and basket of flowers in the center are unusually beautiful.

Kenmore's magnificent series of stucco-duro ceilings are unparalled by any other American house and occur in all the lower rooms except the office. They are all in the same geometric and floral style of the Conservative school, as opposed to the Baroque. Although they are apparently to some extent from English style books, the ornament itself seems to bear out the evidence that they were executed by Frenchmen. Both in the distribution of the ornament and its modeling, the character is much more the style of Louis XV than of English contemporary examples.

KENMORE, Fredericksburg. The drawing room, finest American room of its type. *Bagby*.

KENMORE, Fredericksburg. Library, with other rooms, in James Gibbs's "modern" style. *Bagby*.

Two of the KENMORE ceiling designs were derived, in general, from Plates CLXX and CLXXV of Langley's *City and Country Builder's Treasury*. The central part of the drawing room ceiling comes from the latter, and with the others is the work of French craftsmen. *Smith*.

KENMORE, Fredericksburg. Library ceiling from Langley's Plate CLXX, with season's symbols. One of the finest examples of American plaster work. *Smith.* (Below) Dining Room ceiling, perhaps a design of itinerant French craftsmen dating from between 1770 and 1775. *Smith.*

The entrance hall ceiling has a series of large oval motives, containing medallions of leafage in the center, and bordered by richly-modeled festoons of fruit and flowers. Outside of the moulded frames are festoon spandrels, and, filling the spaces between, circles of leaves framing rosettes.

The scheme of the ovals is used again in the drawing room (with substantial changes in detail) in four-corner motives which, with two matching circular features, border the superb centerpiece of the ceiling. This, in beauty of design and execution, may perhaps be the finest piece of American plaster-work. Only in its relation to the bands of the ovals and circles is it disappointing. It employs again a strong geometrical pattern, this time a large circle within two overlying half-circles at the ends and intersecting rectangles at the sides. In plan, this forms a rectangular bay with apses at either end. In the corners outside the frame are four spandrel panels.

All of this center is covered with ornament, and there is frame within frame. The leaf medallion reoccurs in the center and is bordered by a series of circles formed of rosettes and enclosing baskets of fruit and flowers. These circles are tied to the design by concentric festoons of husks and pendants. The field of the figure outside the circle is filled with convolutions of vines in low relief, and the spandrels beyond with cornucopias, leaves, and ribbons. Certainly the design of this motive was derived from Plates CLXX and CLXXV of Batty Langley's *Builder's and Workman's Treasury of Designs*, both in form and design of the leafage.

Closely related to the drawing room center piece is the library ceiling, which is based on Plate CLXX, showing a circle within a quatrefoil. Varying from the drawing room design, the festoons inside the circle fall toward the center instead of away from it, and the small circles are lacking. The background of the quatrefoil is filled with interlacing festoons and pendants, and the spandrels with symbols of the seasons, crossed palm branches, grape vines, oak leaves, and mistletoe. Excellent as the others are, in spite of some overcrowding, the ceiling of the dining room is perhaps the most successful and most individual of them all. This is a veritable net of strands formed of leafage and circles of daisies, framing a numbus radiating from a sculptured face. There is a concentric series of circles enclosing rosettes, forming a band, then a field of interlacing festoons beyond which the circles and rosettes reappear as a border. Here the cornice is of wood, of conventional form with dentils; in the hall one of the same profile is of plaster containing small leaves in the cymatium and egg-and-dart ornament in the bed mould. In the drawing room and library, however, the classic cornice form disappears and an enriched frieze is employed between two decorative mouldings.

Another unusual feature of the house is an arched doorway between the entrance hall and the drawing room. Although quite ambitious in scheme, it has an air of being incomplete. It may be noted that the same design was used for the entrance, in stone, of the Tebbs house in Dumfries. At Kenmore there is a narrow double door framed by Doric pilasters which support a moulded arch with key. On the room side this is elaborated by spandrel panels enriched with palm branches. This addition is not entirely successful, for there is a gap between the top of the spandrels and the cornice.

Architecturally, Kenmore as it stands is contradictory in style, for within a plain traditional exterior lies an interior of unusual richness with high-Georgian attributes. The only explanations readily at hand are that when the house was built competent craftsmen were not available for the work or that economy was necessary and the plaster decorations were not completed. In the later sixties the present elaborate interior scheme was embarked upon, but a possible scheme of exterior stucco decoration was never carried out. The form of the house, with its hipped-end gable roof, does not seem to predicate an elaborate decorative treatment, but the same roof type was used on the Pinckney house on Colleton Square, Charleston, South Carolina (1745-46), where full-height Ionic pilasters were used for a pseudo pavilion on the façade.[64] Also in South Carolina, Crowfield,[65] Berkeley County, and Brick House on Edisto Island[66] were simple brick structures formalized by stucco quoins at the corners of the buildings and at the door and window openings. In the case of the latter there are scrolled bibs under the windows and on the side elevations, and arched panels with keystones modeled with masks. In view of these examples and the extensive use of stucco planned at Mount Airy (attested by the scored stone work), Menokin, and the Carlyle house, such a finish for Kenmore is not unlikely.

What Ariss meant by Gibbs's modern and antique styles is exemplified in the contrast of the interior of Kenmore with that of Harewood, in Berkeley County (now Jefferson County), West Virginia, built by Betty Lewis' brother, Samuel Washington, about 1756.[67] The house is large-scale and unpretentious but possesses a very fine paneled room of quiet Palladian style. This house exhibits no baroque forms, all the architectural features being based on Gibbs's early style, and no wood carving or plaster enrichment is utilized. The room occurs in one end of the house, which is only a single room deep. It is lighted, therefore, on either side by two windows, and opposite the entrance door is the fireplace wall. The treatment of the walls, which are paneled to the ceiling, is highly architectural, with all the window-openings, entrance door, and mantel flanked by Doric pilasters on pedestals. A full entablature that carries around the room breaks out over the pilasters, creating verticals from floor to ceiling. This accentuates the twelve-foot ceiling height and gives the room an unusually monumental quality for domestic work.

In detail, the order is excellent, with full academic quality. The entablature is elaborated with a pulvinated frieze and dentil course in the cornice. It is interesting to observe that the architect here has preserved the classic proportions of his pilasters by placing them on low pedestals which do not line with the chair rail. At Carter's Grove, where the pedestals are continuous with the dado, the truncated proportion of the pilasters is obvious. At Harewood any sense of unrest which might be caused by the staggered horizontals is minimized by the use of a bold pedestal cap and an unusually delicate chair rail. It is unfortunate, perhaps, that the latter does not return at the line of the panel styles instead of almost butting the pilasters.

The areas between the pilasters are treated with broad, simply-moulded panels, and the overmantel is a large, single panel over six feet wide and four feet high. This unusually simple overmantel contributes to the excellent scale of the composition and allows the attention to center on the superb fireplace facing. This is of dark green marble, perhaps Anglesea, or Purbeck, in the form of a broad architrave. The backband is richly carved with egg-and-dart ornament, beautifully mitred with acanthus leaves at the corners. This frame is mounted on bold plinths and the opening is bordered by a crisply-moulded, beaded fillet. Extraordinarily simple in form, this mantel is certainly one of the outstanding marble mantelpieces in Virginia, and the room is one of the best of its period in the country. The house has, as well, a fine stair.

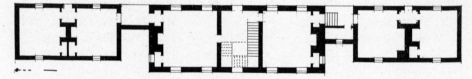

HAREWOOD, Jefferson County, West Virginia.

Harewood itself embodies the virtues of the room. Its simplicity and excellent scale endows it with great distinction. Unlike any of the houses of this group so far discussed, it exemplifies the full traditional Virginia plan of a central hall with a single room on either side and end chimneys. Supporting the main block, dependencies with connections were planned, and perhaps built, though only the kitchen wing now stands. In eleva-

SARA's CREEK HOUSE, Gloucester County. Traditional stair, resembling Harewood. *Johnston*.

HAREWOOD, Jefferson County, West Virginia. Example of James Gibbs' "ancient" style. *Johnston*.

HAREWOOD. Balustrade of stair, with fluted newel. *Johnston.*

HAREWOOD. The drawing room paneling, on the side wall. *HABS.*

BELVOIR, Fairfax County. Probably developed to final form c. 1757. Destroyed in 1783. *Perspective, author; rendering, R. E. Collins.*

tion, the main house, two full stories high, is covered by a low hipped roof. The one-story wing possesses a jerkin-head roof (like that at Kenmore) from which rises a huge central chimney.

The nearest parallel to Harewood in form and decoration is Sara's Creek House (Little England) in Gloucester County. This has the same elementary plan, but the side wings are lacking. What may be an earlier house was used as a rear wing until recently when it was moved to an end. The house is of brick, two stories high, and evidently originally covered by a hipped roof. Unfortunately, this was changed to a gable and dormers added, so the original effect has been impaired. One of the rooms has a pilastered over-mantel in a paneled end, but there is no full-paneled room as at Harewood, though the stairs in the two houses are so alike as to be almost indistinguishable. In each, fluted newels are used, the scheme of three unequal flights employed, and the wall treated with a paneled dado. The balusters, however, have minor variations, those of Harewood being turned like those of Kenmore and Fairfield, and those of Sara's Creek House with the traditional vase and shaft.

The location of Sara's Creek House, so far distant from the other related houses, is puzzling, but if Ariss had any hand in it, the reason was probably his connection with the Washingtons and the Lewises, which latter family were apparently the builders of the house. Not far away, on the Severn River, was Warner Hall, the home of Washington's great grandfather, Augustine Warner II, and the birthplace of Betty Washington's husband, Fielding Lewis. Warner Hall, which may have resembled Rosewell, was burned in 1849, and a relatively new mansion stands on the site.[68]

A project that seems to have been carried out contemporaneously with the building of Harewood and Sara's Creek House was the modernizing of Belvoir, (built 1741)[69] the mansion of the Fairfax family adjacent to Mount Vernon, and the laying out of a new architectural setting. This work was probably done by Ariss about 1757, subsequent to the accession of George William Fairfax to the estate. In 1774, Belvoir was described in a rental notice, which said: "The mansion is of brick, two stories high, with four convenient rooms and a large passage on the lower floor; five rooms and a large passage on the second."[70] This is all that is known of it, since the house, abandoned by the family on their return to England in 1774, was burned in 1783 and the walls destroyed. The recent excavation of the site has shown not only the plan of the house itself but also of the dependencies and garden walls. The house is of the general plan of Marmion with variations. From the length of the front it could be assumed that it was divided into five bays, but if it was, the three center openings would have been grouped like those at the Palace in Williamsburg. There is no indication of the fenestration on the land front, but on the river front can be seen remains of three windows. The window toward the north is about ten feet from its center line to the corner of the building; that toward the south is about thirteen. Some three feet from the south jamb of the north window is another jamb, splayed like the rest, but this comes against the cross-wall, and there is no sign of another jamb. Centered on the house are the foundations of the entrance steps, apparently a square pyramid on the river front and a platform and flight of curved steps on the land front. At best the original fenestration of the river front is questionable, but from what remains it seems likely that an asymmetrical façade may have been regularised at some time after the date of the building. This may have been in 1757, when William Fairfax died and bequeathed to George William Fairfax "... my Plantation ... with all the Houses and Edifices thereon call'd and known by the name of Belvoir." [71]

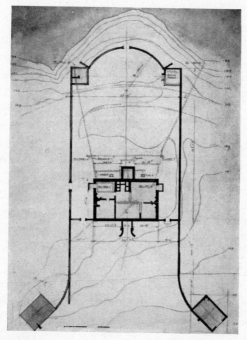

Belvoir, Fairfax County, General plan. *HABS.*

Except for the indications of changes in the basement walls, there is nothing to show the period or authorship of the alterations, but a valuable clue is offered by the garden walls, which extend in an area of about three hundred feet square around the house. There are two parallel walls, ninety-seven feet apart, that parallel the main axis. These are one hundred

and eighty feet long, and enclose an area toward the river about one
hundred feet square. At the line where the high river bank drops sharply
away there are foundations of two garden houses about twenty feet
square. Between them is a segmental projection, on a promontory in the
river bank, of about a thirty-eight foot ten inch radius with a gate on
the center. This curved part of the wall was probably a clairvoyée. On the
land front there was a forecourt, with parallel walls nearly fifty feet long,
which curved out with forty-eight feet five inch radii to a broad approach.
On the lines of the diagonals thus formed, which are forty-five degrees
from the front step, were at least three minor buildings. The two nearest
the mansion, probably the office and kitchen, were roughly twenty by
twenty-five feet and of indeterminate height. One hundred feet (center
to center) further away, on the same line to the north, was another building, probably a stable or a coach house. This was about thirty by thirty-
three feet and seemed to have a lean-to on the back. Although excavations
have not revealed it, this was probably balanced by a similar building.

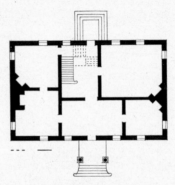

BELVOIR, Fairfax County.

There are, in Virginia, few architectural settings as commanding as that
of Belvoir. The house is set high on the precipitous banks of the Potomac, and around it is a superb view of the river and of the Maryland
shore. In Belvoir it is fortunate that the precedent for the garden layout,
derived from Palladio, can be identified as from Blair Drummond in the
county of Stirling, Scotland, engraved as Plate LXXXIII of *Vitruvius
Scoticus*. However, the scheme was inverted, and the river court of Belvoir was the outer approach court. It was one hundred and sixty feet wide
and two hundred and fifteen feet deep, with a half-round projection instead of the segmental one which was used at Belvoir in deference to the
precipitous grades of the river bank. The gates in both examples were
located and arranged similarly, though the house sites were different. The
broadening approach of Belvoir seems to be paralleled only by that

LOCUST HILL, Jefferson County, c. 1785. Home of John Ariss, the architect. *Author, HABS.*

HAREWOOD, Jefferson County, West Virginia. A traditional house, academic detail. *Johnston.*

of Mount Vernon, where the scale is vastly larger, and the advanced walls were in the form of a double ogee.

It can hardly be doubted that Ariss was the author of the Belvoir alterations, the source of the garden layout being from his much-used source of precedent and recalling the close proximity of his latter-day residence to Greenway, that of old Lord Fairfax, uncle of George William of Belvoir.

Harewood has two neighboring houses which were closely associated with John Ariss, in both of which, in fact, Ariss probably lived. These are Fairfield and Locust Hill, the former now in Clarke County, Virginia, and the latter just over the state border in Jefferson County, West Virginia. Fairfield stands on a hill overlooking the Shenandoah River, near Rippon, and faces the Blue Ridge. It was built probably about 1770, but there is no definite evidence which will establish a date. It was purchased by Warner Washington, a cousin of the President, about 1784, but he does not seem to have built the house. There is a suggestion in Ariss' papers that he may have built it for himself and later found that it was larger than he needed or more expensive than he could maintain. In a letter dated Berkeley County, August 5, 1784, to George Washington, he said: "I am under the Necessity of Giving Up the place I now live at, at the end of this year ... Your Excellency may possibly assist me with a place to live at." [72] And in his will probated in 1800 Ariss wrote, "I desire to be buried with the permission of Mrs. Washington of Fairfield, in the grave yard of that place." [73] It may be, therefore that it was Fairfield he had to give up, but wished to lie there after his death. However, it is obviously one of his designs as can easily be appreciated by comparing it with Kenmore, Harewood, and Locust Hill. It has the plan of the first, however, with the chimneys placed in the center wall.

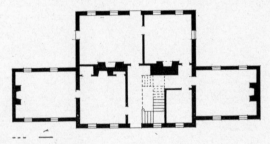

Fairfield, Clarke County.

The drawing room is at the rear and two square rooms in the other corners of the house. The hall is the most striking parallel to Kenmore, for it is precisely the same in arrangement, with the stair ascending in

FAIRFIELD, Clarke County, Virginia. Stone house resembling Harewood. Dependencies, porch, and dormers new. *Courtesy John W. Wayland.*

the same way, and with even the same detail to the balustrade. The house lacks the superb decorative plaster work of Kenmore, but the fine paneled mantel of the drawing room is a distinguished feature. This mantel has Doric pilasters on pedestals framing a paneled overmantel. The order follows the detail of that at Harewood, but is not as large in scale as that of the latter house.

In elevation the house, which is of stone, is two full stories in height with a hipped roof pierced at the ridge by two chimneys. The façade is five bays long with a center door, and at either end are one-story wings with end chimneys. The house as it now stands is considerably augmented, having had terminal buildings added to the wings and dormers to the main roof. The modern additions change the aspect of the house, but it retains much original work of interest.

Just what land Washington leased to Ariss is uncertain, but it may have been the tract requested in the letter of August, 1784. A later letter makes it clear that in 1786 Ariss was living on a farm leased from Washington.[74] The evidence points to Locust Hill, not far from Summit Point, as the house. Appropriately, locust trees surround the house, and many seem to be of considerable antiquity. The building is located on Bullskin Creek, set high on a rocky hillside overlooking the valley of the stream.

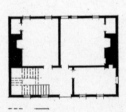

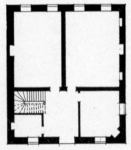

LOCUST HILL, Jefferson County, West Virginia.

MILTON HOUSE, Edinburgh, Scotland.

Locust Hill has definite affinity to Harewood and Fairfield in its interior finish, and to Lord Milton's house in Edinburgh in plan, the latter being shown in *Vitruvius Scoticus*.[75] The prototype is almost square in plan, with a slightly off-center hall leading to a pair of large, almost equal rooms in the rear. At the left, a stair ascends between the rear room and a small room, hardly more than a closet, at the left of the front door. At the right is a larger square room. The chimneys are built in the thickness of the end walls. At Locust Hill this plan is followed except that the stair occupies the whole left-hand corner of the house and the plan itself is longer and narrower. On examination it can be seen that the stair is of the period of 1800, and it is probable that the Milton house arrangement was observed more fully here, too, during Ariss' lifetime, but was altered after his death. The main variation is that the chimneys project into the rooms, allowing closets on either side. Subsequent to the construction of the original building a corner fireplace was installed in the front room.

The house is of wood, stuccoed, and is five bays long on the south front and four on the rear. It is two full stories high, with a hipped roof. There is no exterior architectural trim, but the building is in agreeable scale and design, and, situated on a high rocky site, is unusually picturesque. Unfortunately, it has become a tenant house and lacks well-tended grounds.

The interior has considerable finish remaining from the original period. The northeast room is almost exactly a parallel to that of Fairfield, with Doric pilasters flanking the mantel motive; but here the reveals on either side of the breast are paneled in as closets; so the whole wall is covered with paneling. The other rooms have simple mantels, chair rails, and cornices.

This house may easily have been Ariss' last design, and as such it is interesting in showing how static was his style.[76] From the Carlyle house, in 1752, to Locust Hill, in 1785, the basis for his design was *Vitruvius Scoticus*, and his detail was mainly from Gibbs's plates. There is no suggestion of Robert Adam's influence in form or decoration, though it seems impossible that Ariss should not have been aware of Adam's style. More probably he, like Sir William Chambers, resisted to the end any attempt to modify the classic mid-Georgian of Gibbs and his compeers.

REFERENCES

1. Westmoreland County Deed Book 81, p. 279.

2. *William and Mary Quarterly*, 1st Series, p. 57.

3. Westmoreland County Will Book #8 (1730), p. 396.

4. Westmoreland County Order Book (1743-46-47), p. 6.

5. A Nicholas Spencer was buried at Cople, England, on December 16, 1707.

6. Letter from the Reverend R. C. J. B. Colthurst of Cople, Bedford-shire, England, March 30, 1940.

7. Westmoreland County Deed Book 12, p. 266.

8. Richmond County Deed Book 12, p. 352.

9. Hening, *The Statutes at Large*, VIII, 624. Also in Washington's diary for March 23, 1769, "Breakfast at Mr. Ariss's dined under the Ridge."

10. *William and Mary Quarterly*. 1st Series, XVII, 56-57.

11. Westmoreland County Order Book (1753), p. 104.

12. Hening, *The Statutes at Large*, VIII, 624.

13. Slaughter, *The History of Truro Parish in Virginia*, p. 53.

14. Chambers, *Old Chapel and the Parish in Clarke County, Virginia...*, p. 59.

15. Historic American Buildings Survey.

16. Henry Chandlee Forman, *Early Manor and Plantation Houses of Maryland*, p. 195.

17. Berkeley County, West Virginia, Will Book #3, p. 475.

18. John Swarbrick, *Robert Adam & His Brothers*, pp. 34-43.

19. *Ibid.*, p. 47.

20. Fitzpatrick, *The Diaries of George Washington*, I, 317. (Washington's diary for March 23, 1769.)

21. William Adam, *Vitruvius Scoticus*, Plates LXXXVI and LXXXVII.

22. *Ibid.*, Plate LXXXIII.

23. C. C. Coffin, "Old Times in the Colonies," *Harper's New Monthly Magazine*, 1881, p. 378.

24. Historic American Buildings Survey, plan.

25. Russell Hawes Kettell, editor, *Early American Rooms...*, pp. 127-30. (Article by author.)

26. (Winslow Marston Watson, compiler), *In Memoriam: Benjamin Ogle Tayloe*, p. 2.

27. Waterman and Barrows, *Domestic Colonial Architecture*, pp. 125 *et seq.*

28. Adam, *Vitruvius Scoticus*, Plate LVI.

29. Gibbs, Plate LVIII.

30. Historic American Buildings Survey (Pendleton's lithograph).

31. Historic American Buildings Survey.

32. *Ibid.*

33. Beverley's Letter Books. Manuscript Division, Library of Congress.

34. Brady Collection. Fine Arts Division, Library of Congress.

35. Adam, *Vitruvius Scoticus*, Plate XCI.

36. Transcript of Diary at Mount Vernon.

37. Virginia State Library.

38. These particulars are from a National Park Service report by C. F. Northington (1936) at Fredericksburg, Virginia.

39. *Ibid.*

40. Transcript of Diary at Mount Vernon.

41. Miss Anne Washington.

42. For a full discussion of the development of Mount Vernon see Paul Wilstach, *Mount Vernon, Washington's Home and the Nation's Shrine.*

43. Letter from Worth Bailey, from Mount Vernon, dated December 6, 1944, to the author.

44. Wilstach, *Mount Vernon, Washington's Home*, p. 7.

45. *Ibid.*, p. 23.

46. Historic American Buildings Survey.

47. Architects' Emergency Committee, *Great Georgian Houses*, I, 14.

48. John Clement Fitzpatrick, editor, *The Writings of George Washington from the Original Manuscript Sources, 1745-1799*, I, 142-43.

49. Giacomo Leoni, *The Architecture of A. Palladio; in Four Books*, Vol. I, Plate LX.

50. Architects' Emergency Committee, *Great Georgian Houses*, I, 14.

51. *Godey's Lady's Book*, 1852.

52. Fitzpatrick, *The Writings of George Washington*, II, 334.

53. *Ibid.*, 157.

54. Ordered at the same time as the painting.

55. Philip B. Wallace, *Colonial Houses, Philadelphia, Pre-Revolutionary Period*, pp. 178-87; 196-97.

56. Wilstach, *Mount Vernon, Washington's Home*, p. 140.

57. Kimball, *Domestic Architecture,* Figure 80.

58. Stoney, *Plantations of the Carolina Low Country,* p. 138.

59. William Rotch Ware, *Georgian Period,* pp. 213-18. (Part IV, 1923).

60. For the Maryland houses see Foreman and Historic American Buildings Survey.

61. Adam, *Vitruvius Scoticus,* Plate CXXI.

62. See George P. Bankart, *The Art of the Plasterer,* pp. 279-303.

63. Tipping, *English Homes, Period V,* I, 191, 264-65, 326-27.

64. Kimball, *Domestic Architecture,* Figure 66.

65. Historic American Buildings Survey.

66. *Ibid.*

67. (Edwin Fairfax Naulty), *Historic Harewood,* p. 3.

68. Lancaster, *Historic Virginia Homes and Churches,* p. 247.

69. *Virginia Magazine of History and Biography,* XXXIV, 37.

70. Moncure Daniel Conway, *Barons of the Potomack and the Rappahannock,* p. 216.

71. *Virginia Magazine of History and Biography,* IV, 102-4.

72. Photostat at Mount Vernon.

73. Berkeley County, West Virginia, Will Book #3, p. 315.

74. Photostat at Mount Vernon.

75. Adam, *Vitruvius Scoticus,* Plate XLV.

76. In 1781 he altered Traveller's Rest for General Horatio Gates. (Letter dated June 21, 1783, from Ariss to Gates, requests payment of balance due. The manuscript is in the New York Public Library).

THE RANDOLPH-SEMPLE HOUSE, Williamsburg. Jeffersonian Palladian. *Brostrup.*

5. THE LATE GEORGIAN PERIOD 1765-1776

Palladio's Roman Country House Style; Mansions with Attached Wings

T HE FIRST two periods of Virginia mansion building were characterized by large rectangular structures in Andrea Palladio's monumental style, increased in importance by minor buildings. An architectural composition such as this Inigo Jones first formed in England at Stoke-Bruerne in 1647.[1] To the classically-minded Georgians this was very acceptable, and in England, because of the immense wealth of the ruling class, even the largest of the Palladian villas was none too large for the palaces of the nobles. The Virginians, though wealthy by Colonial standards, could hardly hope to copy the Villa Rotonda or its English equivalents; so they scaled down examples in style books and produced such houses as Mount Airy and Menokin. However, this was still the monumental style, and Palladio's charming lesser villas in what he called the Roman Country House style remained unused for inspiration in designing plantation houses.

At the time the English nobility began to look to Robert Adam[2] for a new style, which he gave to them in a late Roman adaptation of his own, the Virginians turned to Palladio's smaller houses for novelty. Thomas Jefferson, with Monticello in 1770, initiated the purely Palladian phase of this period, but there were several houses, probably complete by this time, that were in the same manner but were based on plates of Palladian adaptations from Robert Morris' *Select Architecture*, published in London in 1757. These marked the breaking away from the large-scale rectangular block universally used in the design of Virginia mansions since the building of the Governor's Palace. In the new style a small-scale central block with a series of connected, decreasing units was evolved, sometimes with terminal buildings. This plan had manifest practical advantages, as rooms more often had cross ventilation and great central stair halls were no longer required, for stairs were minimized and few rooms were on the second floor. Also, the kitchen wing was removed from the family's living quarters, the old semi-enclosed court scheme being abandoned and the units arranged in one long line. This plan was not entirely new, Harewood being an example of an earlier period, but for the first time the whole was formalized and the central block brought down in scale by subdivision.

Morris did not put forward his designs as the basis for a new style in large houses, for he illustrated monumental designs as well, but rather for farmhouses and subsidiary buildings such as garden pavilions. In England the designs were, however, sometimes used by people of limited means for their dwellings,[3] but in Virginia, by adept alterations they were fitted to become mansion-scale buildings. Not content with merely a change in mass and arrangement, Virginians also evolved a new type of architectural treatment for the façades. This too was derived from Palladio's precedent, the main feature being his superimposed porticos, adapted to living porches. These were especially useful in a southern climate, and had already been employed at Drayton Hall in South Carolina.[4]

Virginia houses of this last of the pre-Revolutionary styles were (including Shirley, a transitional example), Brandon, Battersea, Chatham, the Randolph-Semple house in Williamsburg, and Monticello. Two governmental buildings, the Capitol and the Governor's Palace, also exhibited features of the style in their employment of additions to the original buildings. The authorship of this group probably lies with one man, for the kinship is too close to allow them to seem the work of several men. To Jefferson the ascription seems most reasonable. There is the possibility to consider that Richard Taliaferro might have become interested in the style ideas of Morris, but with a practice that extended over thirty or more years and with no radical change of style in the buildings attributed to him, this does not seem probable. In John Ariss' work, where the authorship is more certain, it is obvious that his style never changed appreciably, and the same is probably true of Taliaferro. There is remarkable similarity in detail between Battersea, the Randolph-Semple house, and Carter's Grove, but this is just the similarity to expect in the case of an inexperienced designer working from a style book but having to rely for detail on that which he saw about him.

It is problematical how much Taliaferro would have influenced Jefferson as far as style is concerned. However, the early drawings of the latter and his works show the profound influence of the three books of architectural design he is known to have used before 1770.[5] These included, in addition to Gibbs's and Morris' books, Leoni's *The Architecture of A. Palladio*. Leoni's book came to his attention when he was twenty-seven, in 1770.[6] This date is important in the study of his manuscript drawing, for it places his early studies for Monticello before this time, inasmuch as there is no suggestion of its influence in them. The two later studies, however, and the actual working drawings are permeated by its influence. The two earliest drawings are frankly based on Morris, Plate XXXVII, and form the basis for attributing the Randolph-Semple house, Brandon, and Battersea to Jefferson. Although the first is evidently a study for Monticello, it parallels the design of the Randolph-Semple house to such a degree that there can be no doubt that they are by the same author.

This type of planning entailed a complete break with Virginia tradition, a break that did not occur at Shirley and the Capitol. Here the Palladian feature of the two-tiered portico was merely applied to traditional buildings. If Jefferson designed Shirley it probably would have been before he had access to Morris' book. It could have been designed with the Palace as precedent together with Gibbs's *Rules for Drawing*. The Randolph-Semple house, Brandon, and Battersea all show the influence of this, plus Morris; and Monticello, in its final phase, the influence of these two plus Palladio and Gibbs's later *Book of Architecture*. It is curious that in Morris' work Jefferson found the theme, at the beginning of his architectural life, that was to form the basis of his architecture up to his death fifty-five years later. It may be that Morris' references to Palladio's work caused Jefferson to seek out Leoni's translation of Palladio, and it was undoubtedly due to the text of the latter that his idea of reviving the style of the minor Roman country houses was formulated. Morris himself had long been an admirer of Palladio, and as early as 1728, in "An Essay in Defense of Ancient Architecture," illustrated a plate from an "Example of Composition of that great Genius Palladio."

Even without Leoni's *Palladio* Jefferson had been able to design excellent essays in his future style, as the early drawings for Monticello indicate. The Morris plates gave him the design ideas and Gibbs's *Rules for Drawing* the formulae for proportioning the classic features including two-tiered porticos. The knowledge that Jefferson owned these various books, and the information his drawings give that he freely used them, makes plausible his identity as the architect of the houses under consideration. Furthermore, there is the family tradition[7] to consider that he was the architect of Brandon, and also to be considered are his known close friendships with Nathaniel Harrison of Brandon and Mr. and Mrs. John Banister of Battersea. There is no evidence of another authorship of the designs of these buildings and they relate to no other major houses except Chatham, built for William Fitzhugh, husband of Jefferson's cousin Mary Randolph of Chatsworth.

For many years Jefferson was considered a gifted amateur who had designed his own home, Monticello, and to some extent was responsible for the design of the Virginia State Capitol and of the University of Virginia. He was, in fact, an amateur, for he never seems to have received a commission for his designs. But he was a professional in his aesthetic standards and technical qualifications. Moreover, he was an enthusiast to whom architecture was a source of never-ending delight. In a letter addressed to Madison, from France in 1785, he wrote: "It is an enthusiasm of which I am not ashamed, as its object is to improve the taste of my countrymen, to increase their reputation, to reconcile them to the respect of the world and procure them its praise." [8]

An event occurred on February 1, 1770, that has obliterated the record of Jefferson's early years in architecture. This was the burning of his birthplace, Shadwell, in Albermarle County, and the consequent destruction of practically all of his papers and books of the preceding years.[9] Much of his early life has been reconstructed from letters and papers from the hands of his friends and relatives, but there is hardly a mention of architecture among them. The source of his interest in architecture has been surmised, but has remained unconfirmed. There is no suggestion of an interest in architecture earlier than studies for the building of Monticello, which hardly antedate the fire at Shadwell.

It might be well to recapitulate the scene of his early life to show how devoid it seems of architectural inspiration before his coming to Williamsburg in 1760.[10] The years of his early childhood were spent at Tuckahoe, the home of his mother's family, above the head of navigation on the James River. This was west of the area of fine mansion building at this period. Tuckahoe itself was the most architectural of the region, and it was hardly more than a fine and large frame farmhouse. The years 1752 to 1760 he spent either at Shadwell or at school, first near Tuckahoe and then nearer Shadwell. All of this country had simple frame or log dwellings, courthouses, and churches unlike the sometimes pretentious masonry structures of the lower Tidewater country.

When he arrived in Williamsburg in 1760, he had probably only recently seen buildings such as Westover (which he may have passed on the way) that had academic architectural quality. Williamsburg, the first of planned American cities, must have impressed Jefferson deeply. It had formal avenues and vistas and not only a number of excellent masonry houses but William and Mary College, Bruton Church, the Governor's Palace, and the then recently rebuilt Capitol. He could hardly have realized that these were provincial renderings of a style already out of date in England, but only that they had an unfamiliar formality and seemliness which represented an entirely new architectural medium to him. If, twenty years later, when his taste had been fully formed, Jefferson chose to be hypercritical of Virginia architecture in general and Williamsburg architecture in particular, it does not mean that during his first years there he did not find it artistically satisfying. Even in 1782, when he wrote the indictment in his *Notes on Virginia*,[11] he still called the Capitol "a light and airy structure ... the most pleasing piece of architecture we have," and the Governor's Palace "not handsome without ... spacious and commodious within, and with the grounds annexed to it is capable of being made an elegant seat."

In his new environment he was fortunate in coming under the influence of William Small, who introduced Jefferson to George Wythe, the great Virginia jurist and first professor of law in America, under whom he later studied, and to Francis Fauquier, one of the most competent and admired of the Royal Governors of Virginia.[12] In spite of the great disparity in their ages, Jefferson was welcomed into this famous group, which he described as inseparable friends. To their dinners at the Palace or Wythe House Jefferson was always admitted and at them he said he heard "more good sense, more rational and philosophical conversation, than in all my life beside."

This atmosphere was certainly one to inspire a revaluation of everything he had known on Jefferson's part, but intensive research has failed to show that any of these three older friends had any architectural inclinations at all, though in keeping with the time all must have been conversant with the changing styles in England. It has been said that Jefferson first saw Palladio's book in the Palace library,[13] but the source for this statement was verbal, and it cannot be confirmed.

Though this identification of Jefferson's architectural mentor has not been made before, and there is as yet no confirmation from documentary sources, it seems not only possible but almost certain that he was Richard Taliaferro. The conclusion becomes even more sure when it is realized that Taliaferro was the father-in-law of Wythe, who, Jefferson said, "continued to be my faithful and beloved Mentor in my youth, and my most affectionate friend through life."[14] Many of the meetings of the four friends were held at the Wythe house itself. If Jefferson first knew *Palladio* in 1770, it is unlikely that Taliaferro had it in his library from 1760 to 1770, though details from it appear in earlier buildings which he probably designed. However, he certainly owned other English works on the Palladian orders, and to these Jefferson undoubtedly had access. It may be that Taliaferro owned Robert Morris' *Select Architecture*, which next to Leoni's *Palladio* influenced Jefferson's style more than any other publication. However, as has been observed, Jefferson himself owned it before the burning of Shadwell[15] and used it in his earliest extant designs for Monticello.

To assign any building to Jefferson, as its architect, before the building of Monticello, is to rely on circumstantial evidence alone, but the available evidence seems strong enough to do so. The houses attributed to him here, between the years 1765 and 1770, are largely derived from Robert Morris' plates, renderings of some of which occur in Jefferson's manuscript drawings with modifications that occur in the buildings themselves.

Nothing is known of Jefferson's architectural interests or activities before he started the building of Monticello in 1770. Apparently, the first of his great volume of personal and state papers to deal with architecture are the two plans, considered to be studies for Monticello and dated, after intensive study, by a distinguished authority as before February, 1770. These are well and carefully drawn and do not suggest the work of a novice, though there seems no question that they are Jefferson's own. This being the case, it seems probable that he had already become proficient through instruction and practice, which could have covered the whole period of his life in Williamsburg, after his arrival in 1760.

Even though the absence of positive evidence of his authorship of the Morris group of mansions is, for good reason, lacking, the circumstances cited above certainly tend to confirm a conclusion that Jefferson was practiced in architecture when they were built. His drawings positively associate his early work with Morris' book, and this publication, in turn, is undeniably the basis of the houses under consideration.

In point of style, Shirley is the earliest of the group, and it alone is of the old monumental style. The architectural evidence indicates a date of about 1765, but in the ascription to this period a great many traditions must be overcome. These are that the present house incorporates the seventeenth-century dwelling of the Hill family, through whom the place came to the Carters, that it was created from alterations and additions to the old building about 1740, and that the mansard roof and porticos are additions of about 1830. It is the opinion of the writer that all three traditions are undependable. A careful examination of the structure from cellar to roof makes it clear that it was built as a whole, that it does not incorporate an older house, and that the porticos and roof are original. In denying the first and second, it can be seen, in a sketch preserved at Shirley, that the old Hill house stood to the east, in advance of the line of the front of the mansion and entirely independent of it. In denying the third, the architectural evidence is clear that the pediment and lower pilaster caps are original and that the columns, entablatures, and steps are nineteenth-century work. This conclusion is borne out by Mrs. Oliver, the present owner of Shirley, and the account book of her grandfather, Hill Carter, who came into the property in 1816. At that time the house was in poor condition and he found it necessary to repair the porticos. For this purpose he spent $22.25 in 1817; but in 1831, listed under expenses on the Shirley Estate, is an entry, "Porticos 1440, Painting them 60." [16] This, however, was not a rebuilding, according to Mrs. Oliver, but a replacing of all of the columns and providing new steps. These replacements can be ascertained because of the use of granite in the steps, a material unknown in eighteenth-

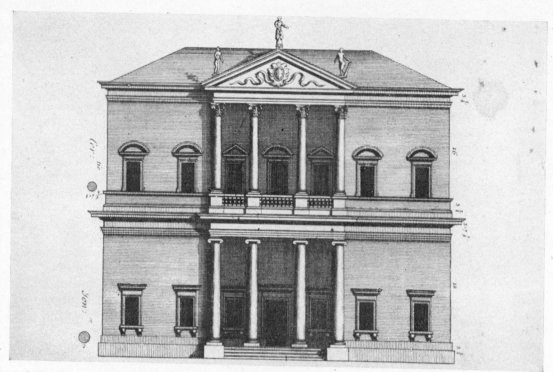

A design by Andrea Palladio showing the two-tiered porticos so suitable to southern houses.

SHIRLEY, Charles City County. Transitional in the two phases of Palladian design. *Met. Eng.*

SHIRLEY, Charles City County. From the southeast showing the Hill house site. *HABS, Burns.*

SHIRLEY, Charles City County. Mansion from the northwest, the present approach. *Johnston.*

century Virginia, in the Greek-style profiles of the wood columns, and in the incorrect entablatures. The lower "drums" of the lower columns are fluted in the Greek manner, but according to Mrs. Oliver, the original ones were fluted their entire height. The fact that the pilaster shafts were cut out and replaced would confirm this. In contrast to the column caps of the lower order, the pilaster caps have Roman Doric profiles, even if they are rather free and unacademic. The upper order may have been Ionic, formerly, as the proportion would indicate, and as shown in Gibbs's *Rules for Drawing* in the example of a two-tiered portico. Each portico is four bays wide and is surmounted by a pediment. Before the vista toward the forecourt was closed by planting, the north elevation must have made an effective terminal to the long approach with its subsidiary buildings. The porticos are emphasized by the wall of the house, which is plastered and whitened behind them. Mrs. Oliver points out that the old portico steps were like those still in place in front of a dwarf portico on the west side. These are of Portland stone with moulded nosings. The columns of this portico are old and are unfluted, with Doric caps and no bases, the cornice and pediment rake are fully moulded with modillions and dentils. This cornice relates well to the order, but in the great porticos the upper cornice, being a continuation of the main cornice, is overheavy for the orders, especially enriched as it is with modillions and Wall of Troy dentils.

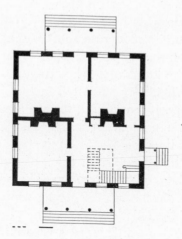

SHIRLEY, Charles City County.

In the plan, no literary source is apparent, but rather that of the Governor's Palace as suggested. To appreciate this fact it must be remembered that the plan of the Palace as it has been reconstructed was that of its latest phase in 1781, when it burned. The foundations of the Palace, Jefferson's plan of about 1773-76, and literary references to-gether demonstrate that originally the plan was much like that of Shirley. Across the north front at Shirley there is a broad entrance salon, extending from the right exterior side wall to the left of the entrance door. Beyond this to the left is a square parlor. To the south the order was reversed, the great drawing room occupying a space corresponding to the salon. Except for the Palace stair and its immediately adjacent closets the plans of the two buildings form a remarkable parallel. The Palace was specified to be forty-eight by fifty-four feet, while Shirley is forty-eight feet, six inches square.

In a sense, the affinity of Shirley to the Palace is borne out in the arrangement of the advance buildings, standing as they do at right angles to the façade rather than parallel to it, as is usual in Virginia architecture. When they were built they may indeed have been inspired by the Palace, or Kingsmill, where the arrangement is the same. The Shirley advance buildings, as has been observed, date from an earlier period than the mansion, probably from the traditional 1740.

As at the Governor's Palace, the two fronts of Shirley are five bays wide and the side elevations four bays, but the spacing of the side windows is free from the asymmetries of the Palace. Unfortunately, the fine roof design of the latter building was not repeated at Shirley and the deck on hip was evolved into a mansard. This, of course, gives more useful rooms but the exterior effect is heavy. A comparison with Drayton Hall [17] and the Miles Brewton house [18] in South Carolina shows the great artistic advantage of more moderate roof pitches on somewhat similar designs. At Shirley, the roof is pierced by over-large dormers with high pediment roofs, and the low hip which surmounts the mansard is termi-nated by a pineapple finial. The two tall medial chimneys occur at the break of the roof slopes. If it were not for the great porticos, the weight of the roof would be more apparent, but these, placed on the axis of the two façades, dominate the design.

The wall areas of the house are of brick of even size and color, laid in Flemish bond without glazed headers. The water table is a single course quarter-round offset, but the string course at the second-floor line is four courses high. This has a broad band coved out to a filet at the top, and the lowest course is a cyma reversa. The brickwork of the chimneys is interesting for the moulded caps, which are formed by large coves below beveled washes.

An individuality of the house appears in the unusual width of the windows, which are four lights wide instead of the usual three. The broad white frames are set almost flush with the brickwork and emphasize the many-light sashes, some of which retain crown glass

SHIRLEY, Charles City County. The west wall and entrance porch. *Johnston.*

SHIRLEY, Charles City County. Great stair, finest of the period. *Johnston*.

panes. Another unusual feature is the use of muntins forming geometric patterns in the transoms of all three exterior doors. No other example of the period seems to remain, those at Kenmore being later replacements.

The interior is notable for many reasons, but especially for the great expanse of paneling it presents. All of the lower rooms, and the hall up to the soffit of the second-floor stair, are fully paneled. The paneling itself is unusual in that the bead of the panel mould is set out on a filet, as is customary in post-Revolutionary building (and in Ariss' work), also in the great width of the panel styles. Whereas these are normally about four inches wide, here they range up to eight inches. The treatment of the paneling is substantially the same in each of the rooms, but diversity is obtained by varying the design of the door frames, cornices, and the mouldings of the panels and dados.

The hall, perhaps the simplest of all, lacks the rich door trim of the other rooms. The range of broad wall panels is set on an unpaneled dado with pedestal-type chair rail and base. At the ceiling line is a small-scale cove cornice, crowned by a simply moulded cymatium, and resting on a band of pierced and applied strapwork. This latter is formed of quatrefoils set in a diagonal fret. The mantel, substantially typical of the house in form, has a marble facing framed by a moulded backband with crossettes and surmounted by a cushion frieze and cornice shelf. The overmantel is a single large panel uniform with the typical wall panels.

The cynosure of the house is the superb stair, certainly one of the finest of its period in the Colonies. This ascends after an initial run of three risers in two long flights, the first of which is against the front wall, and the second at right angles, suspended over the center of the hall.[19] This flight is similar in form to the stair at Sabine Hall, but there the scrolled-soffit steps are apparently corbelled out from the wall. Here they are suspended free from the wall, except for the paneling closing the spandrel on the side away from the stair well. The construction is difficult to determine, but the soffits of the steps are so boldly scrolled across the entire width of the stair that there is scarcely room for even a metal stringer. It seems that a series of wrought-iron straps must have supported blocking for the treads and risers. This scrolled soffit is a type of free-hanging stair construction employed in fine work in England, but the Shirley stair seems to be unique in this country.

Although the first long flight here is supported by a spandrel partition, three of the four flights from the second landing to the attic floor are flyers. In their sweeping movement they make a spectacular ensemble. The feeling of motion which they impart is accentuated by the rich walnut balusters, the turnings of which parallel the rake of the stair,

Shirley. Detail of newel and balusters. *Author, HABS.*

Shirley. A view of the flying staircase. *Author, HABS.*

SHIRLEY. Window trim of the drawing room. *Met. Eng.*

SHIRLEY. Northeast room; doorway and trim. *Met. Eng.*

SHIRLEY, Charles City County. The drawing room chimneypiece showing carved mantel and its marble facing. The fretwork of the overmantel frame is an unusual feature, and the entablature is complete and especially rich. *Johnston*.

instead of each tread, as is usual. A continuous diagonal pattern is thus formed by the balusters, and this pattern is uninterrupted even by minor posts from newel to the third floor. Not content with the tour-de-force of this great flowing design, the designer then enriched it with a baluster also unique in form. In general design it is more like those in the Page (Brush) house in Williamsburg than any other, having double vase turnings below the typical colonette. The upper vase, however, is much broader than the square shanks of the balusters. This was accomplished by glueing on blocks of wood to each of the four faces of the baluster at this point and turning the broad vase with the rest of the profile. In the intervening years since the balusters were made, most of the extra pieces of the broad vase have come off, so the effect of this curious expedient is lost in the design as a whole. The short first run of the stair is notable for its fine terminal swirl and fluted Doric newel. From this start the handrail runs in ramps and easings without a break to the top floor. It is repeated against the wall with a half rail applied to the paneling, and at the point where the stair crosses the windows, half balusters fill the void.

The walnut stair brackets are not enriched beyond the moulding of the soffits, which in design consists of a broad cyma recta, then a beak mould, and a small cyma. Between this latter and the next step the nosing returns across the whole breadth of the soffit, where the latter is open. The resulting effect is one of broad undulating shadows between tight, sharp lines of light and shade. The open soffit of the stair is also of walnut, though now bleached to a grey-brown color. At the head of the stair, leading to a passage that runs between the portico doors, is a fine elliptical arch supported by grouped Doric pilasters with fluted shafts. This terminates the paneling of the stair.

In scheme, the wall covering of the parlor, communicating at the left to the hall, is similar. Here, however, a full cornice is employed above an applied frieze in the form of double, interlacing, Wall of Troy ornament. This same motive, but single, is used also on the chair rail. The six-panel walnut door is framed by an architrave with crossettes at the head. Above this there is an ogee frieze supporting a broken pediment. The cornice repeats the mouldings and details of the main cornice, and framed in the pediment is a pineapple finial.

The drawing room follows the same pattern, but the wall panels are broader and at the ceiling line is a full entablature. This consists of a three-plane moulded architrave, a cushion frieze, and fully moulded cornice with both modillions and dentils. Also elaborated is the chair rail with richer mouldings and an applied fret of strapwork. The mantel, which corresponds in design to that of the hall, has the backband of the facing carved with egg-and-dart ornament, mitred with acanthus leaves, and the frieze enriched with oak leaves banded with ribbons. In the cornice shelf the minor mould of the cymatium is carved with water-leaf and the ovolo of the bed mould with egg-and-dart ornament. Originally there was a band of dentils, now missing like those of the main cornice. The overmantel is treated with a broad panel, framed by a backband, having double crossettes at the head and single at the base. The moulding itself is carved with rosettes on a ribbon between cross bands of reeding, and edged with bead-and-billet ornament. Within the backband is a fascia with curiously applied curvilinear tracery, set off from the panel by a half-round mould, diagonally banded with a ribbon. This fine mantel motive is placed against a broad, plain chimney breast with subsidiary breaks.

The windows of the drawing room are in deep reveals, around which the dado continues, and are protected by inside paneled shutters. Above the dado the window opening is framed by an architrave, with single crossettes at the head, which scrolls out at the bottom. To the dining room, communicating at the north, is a fine doorway with a modillioned cornice and a scrolled pediment, broken in the center for another pine-apple finial. Against this on the dining room side is a matching feature, but with a broken pediment containing a carved vase.

Not only is Shirley notable for its architectural qualities but also for its long, unbroken tenure in the same family.[20] The estate has descended by inheritance from Edward Hill, who patented the land in 1660, through Elizabeth, the heiress of his son, to John Carter of Corotoman and to his descendants. It was the possession of Shirley that undoubtedly dissuaded John Carter from rebuilding his father's house.

This remarkable house, unique in many ways, was built for Charles Carter, father of Anne Carter Lee, and grandfather of Robert Edward Lee. Carter knew Williamsburg well, for he had been a student at William and Mary during the mid-fifties and may have turned to Jefferson for a design when he determined upon rebuilding Shirley on his mother's death in 1769. The features that associate it unmistakably with Williamsburg are the two-tiered portico of the Capitol and the plan of the Governor's Palace. As far as is known, these two prototypes were not paralleled in plan or elevation in Virginia. Shirley is an example of extraordinary individuality. Nothing about the house is of the familiar vernacular; and as a building of that period it must have been an astonishing novelty with its heroic porticos and definite, if amateurish, Palladian aspect.

Except for Monticello, it has not been possible to date any of the houses of this group by documentary means. Of the buildings arranged

SHIRLEY. Drawing room transom. *Met. Eng.*   SHIRLEY. West entrance transom. *Met. Eng.*

SHIRLEY, Charles City County. North wall and chimneypiece of the dining room. *Johnson.*

here by the development of their plans and elevations, Chatham is perhaps the earliest, then Brandon, Battersea, the Randolph-Semple house, and last, Monticello. The architectural evidence indicates that all could have been built between 1765 and 1775.

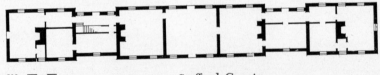

CHATHAM, Stafford County.

Chatham is really a traditional plan adapted to the new ideas. It has a broad central hall (without a stair), a single large square room on either side, and wings connected by passageways. The east passage contains the stairs. The significant feature is the omission of the stair in the entrance hall and the creation thereby of a salon. No other Virginia houses of the period seem to have such a treatment except Mount Airy, the Randolph-Semple house, and Monticello. However, approached from the river, Brandon and Battersea had it, too, though from the land front a narrow cross-hall was entered. At Battersea this is still true, but at Brandon the hall and salon have been thrown together to form a great stair hall.

The central block of Chatham is perfectly rectangular and is divided into three almost equal parts. The central hall has a door in each wall, with windows flanking the doors in the outside walls. This arrangement makes a livable room which is both light and airy in the center of the house. It is interesting to note that most Virginia families living in large, old-fashioned houses use the hall almost exclusively as a sitting room during the hot summer months. The Chatham hall is paneled to the ceiling on all four walls, with tall narrow panels above a paneled dado. This latter has a pedestal-type chair rail and base. For trim the openings have moulded architraves, and at the ceiling line is a full cornice.

The adjoining rooms have a pair of windows on either side, with a chimney breast against the end wall, on axis with the connections. Unfortunately, the west room lost its paneling and that now in place is a replacement, but the east room still retains its original finish. This follows that of the hall, and the chimney-breast is enriched with fluted Doric pilasters. It almost seems, however, as if the mantel motive has been altered in some way, for the pilasters have no entablature and do not relate well to the paneling, though they are of fine design and craftsmanship. The pedestals on which they stand also have been changed, and the chair rail around the room has been replaced. In

CHATHAM, Stafford County. Like Shirley a transition between monumental and pavilion types, but long rather than square. *Johnston.*

CHATHAM, Stafford County. Paneling of the entrance salon. Stair is in a wing. *Johnston.*

CHATHAM, Stafford County. Dining room, showing the paneling and mantel motive. *Johnston.*

the rest of the house there are simple paneled overmantels and other good trim of the period. There is also some nineteenth-century work of c.1840 and modern restorations. The stair ascends against the north wall of the east connection, with winders at the bottom. It has square balusters of the later period with moulded handrail and turned posts, and the spandrel is paneled. On the second floor there is a passage across the south front with three equal rooms to the north.

The wings, one story high, are almost square in plan with central chimneys, and have the rooms grouped around the stack. The exterior of Chatham is notable for the great length of the façade and for its large scale. At present the center doors are trimmed with cut stone architectural frames, but these were installed in 1920 and the old openings were probably untrimmed. The doors are flanked by three windows on either side. Brick, laid in Flemish bond, forms the entire exterior walls, and there are simple flat arches over the windows. Some years ago the house was painted white, so any use of rubbed-brick dressings at the jambs and corners is not apparent.

This mansion alone, of all the great houses of the period, has the main block covered by a gable roof, but there is reason to believe that this is an alteration from the original hipped roof. The gable ends and chimneys bear signs of having been rebuilt. An old photograph [21] shows the gable roof as well as a nineteenth-century, two-tiered porch, which may have been an original one retrimmed. The wings possess broad low-hipped roofs against which the roofs of the passageways are received. At the east end was a dwarf portico porch, which shows in a Brady photograph. There are further detached brick dependencies at either end. The broad terraces, which fall away from the south front of Chatham, are cut into the high banks that here enclose the Rappahannock River. The site is unusually fine and has been enhanced by the present and former owners with magnificent plantings of mature boxwood.

A mansion that has much of the appearance of Chatham, except for the feature of a heroic portico, is White Hall [22] in Anne Arundel County, Maryland. It is a remarkable parallel to Chatham in plan, having the same arrangement of rooms and dependencies. It has one significant departure: it was planned to be all on one floor, with a high, central salon. This meant that no stairs were required, so the passageways could be considerably narrower. However, the flanking rooms later had second floors built over them, and flat stair-pavilions were constructed against the end wall. Thus, while the present two-story house has much the general appearance of Chatham, it did not have originally, though the plan itself did coincide to a remarkable degree.

Although it is not intended to suggest here Jefferson's authorship of

White Hall or to include it in this group, the relationships may be commented on. These include not only the plan parallel to Chatham, and in a lesser degree to Brandon and Battersea, but the definite parallel of its elevation to these latter two houses. They all mark the breaking down of the large-scale block of the mansion house into a group of smaller units, forming a pavilion-type house, as also in the Randolph-Semple house and Monticello. In each case the central unit, one room in width and depth (except where this embraced a hall as well) was carried up two full stories, and in the latter two, covered with a pediment roof. Against the central unit at either side were placed low wings containing one room only. In this way a large structure like Chatham was reduced in scale, and instead of a broad, uninterrupted façade, one containing a central motive, with flanking units, was accomplished. Except for the Randolph-Semple house, this process was continued, with the addition of connections and wings to increase the accommodations of the house without increasing its scale. This design-type was based on Robert Morris' plates, but the final development was far in advance, artistically, of his designs.

No two of the façades of the central pavilion of mansions in this group are the same. At Brandon the central motive was covered by a hipped roof, as were the wings; at Battersea the hipped roof received a two-tiered portico for the focal feature; at the Randolph-Semple house the roof became pedimented, as did the wings; but at Monticello the pediment roof was drawn forward to cover a double-tiered portico, which at White Hall, for the first time in the Colonies, became a full-height portico with heroic columns. As will be seen, Jefferson himself proposed a temple-form portico of this type, but larger in scale, for the alterations to the Governor's Palace, probably between 1773 and 1776. Thus while the authorship of White Hall, or the provenance of the design, is undetermined, both the plan and elevation are identified with this group. It should not be overlooked that a Maryland designer might have produced White Hall, and therefore might be at least the author of Chatham.

White Hall is indeed the culmination of the type, for none of the Virginia examples has the sophisticated development of the façade and of the entrance salon. Both exterior and interior are enriched with architectural carved detail of great refinement and beauty. The columns of the portico have caps of the composite order superbly executed, and the shafts show the proper diminution and fluting. The windows within the portico, like those at Monticello, have wood architrave frames supporting entablatures, but here carved with oak leaves with ribbon banding. In shape and detail the salon also eclipses the other houses,

BRANDON, Prince George County. First of pavilion-type mansions, in which structure is subdivided into small-scale units. *Brostrup.*

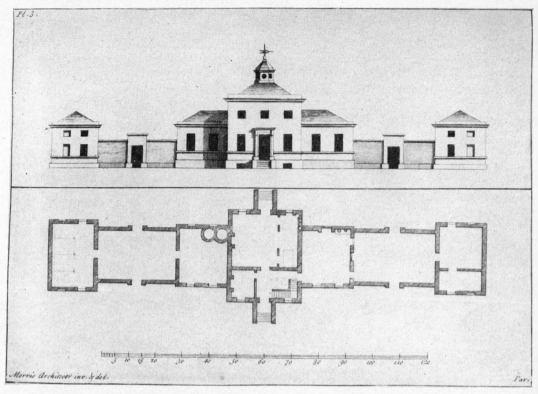

The plate from Robert Morris' *Select Architecture* (1757) from which BRANDON was designed.

BRANDON, Prince George County. Palladio's Roman country-house style. *Metropolitan Eng.*

for it is the full height of the building with a heroic coved ceiling extending into the roof space. This is enriched at each corner with a large baroque relief covering the intersections of the cove. There is a fine enriched cornice and elaborate door and window trim. The former displays Corinthian pilasters supporting an open pediment which encloses a traceried fan light, like that Jefferson proposed for Monticello in his drawing of c.1770.[23] The windows, which rest on a pedestal dado, have architrave frames which at the side have large carved and scrolled consoles. This trim has been ascribed to William Buckland, who in all probability was the carver, but it is doubtful if he produced the design itself, as is sometimes claimed, though the architect is still unidentified.

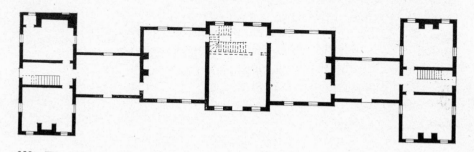

BRANDON, Prince George County.

The source of the design of Brandon is to be found in Plate III of Morris' *Select Architecture*. There are, of course, variations, but the general fidelity to the original is very marked. In plan there is little change except that necessary to changing the house from an English farmstead to a Colonial mansion. The courtyards, shown on the plate, are roofed over and the wings adapted to existing buildings and to the requirement of bedroom wings. The plan is a five-part scheme with central block, wings, connections, and terminal buildings. Originally, the central block seems to have been comprised of a cross-hall with a stair ascending on one side, as at Battersea, and a salon beyond facing the river, but now it is all one large stair hall. At either side are large single rooms in the wings. In Morris, one is used as a kitchen, but at Brandon the kitchen was removed to one of the terminal buildings and is now in the basement. In elevation Brandon also duplicated the Morris plate. The façade in the latter is divided into five units corresponding to the plan. The central block is two stories high with a hipped roof rising behind a parapet, on the peak of which is a curious finial. The wings are one story in height with hipped roofs, the connections are one story and roofless, and the terminal buildings are two story, also with hipped roofs. This scheme is exactly followed at Brandon except that the connections are roofed and the parapets and the turret-like finial are omitted. In the nineteenth century, Brandon suffered several alterations including the addition of Classic Revival dwarf-porticos, the removal of the original pedimented porches, and the substitution of all original sash for others with larger lights and narrower muntins. The house before these changes is shown in a sketch by J. P. Farley, preserved at Brandon, executed before the changes were made.

There has been the family tradition that Brandon was designed for Nathaniel Harrison by Thomas Jefferson, who was groomsman at Harrison's wedding in 1765. It has sometimes been stated that Brandon was built after Jefferson's return from the mission to France in 1789, but the paneled interiors, indicating a pre-Revolutionary period, would deny this. The history of the plantation points to shortly after 1765 as the probable date of building. It was in this year that the Assembly passed an act allowing the breaking of the entail on the Coggin's Point estate and the transfer of the slaves to Brandon.[24] This was undoubtedly the time of the development of the estate and the building of the mansion, coinciding as it did with the marriage of the estate's heir. Up to this time Benjamin Harrison, father of Nathaniel and owner of the plantation, had lived on the estates of his two successive wives in Warwick and Stafford Counties. For this reason there had been no need for other than a pied-à-terre. This purpose had been fulfilled by two four-room story-and-a-half brick houses which were symmetrically placed and evidently were intended as wings for a later house, and which were finally incorporated in the Morris scheme. The buildings were raised to two full stories, the roofs were hipped, and the interior of the west wing was paneled. The exterior of Brandon is characterised by excellent uniform brickwork and an interesting massing of elements. The detail is sparse and includes in the central block a fine modillioned cornice with scrolled and carved modillions and an elaborate pineapple finial on the apex of the roof. The minor cornices have typical uncarved modillions.

The interior has a fine group of paneled rooms which were injured during the Civil War. The east paneled wall of the drawing room, which was removed, has been replaced. As at Chatham the panels at Brandon are unusually narrow and occur above paneled dados with pedestal-type chair rails and bases. The cornices in both rooms are fully moulded, but in the parlor a Wall of Troy dentil course is introduced. There are interesting minor variations such as this in the trim of the two rooms. Both have frontispiece mantels with large overmantel panels framed by architraves, broken out in crossettes. In the parlor, these project only at

BRANDON, Prince George County. The parlor (above) and dining room (below), finished in traditional paneling, with Palladian trim. The design of these two rooms is nearly identical, variations occurring only in the type of pediment employed, in the frieze profiles, framing of the overmantels, and use of dentils in the cornices. *Johnston, Met. Eng.*

BRANDON. Dining Room, with window trim like Shirley. *Johnston.*

BRANDON. Drawing Room, with paneling like Chatham. *Johnston.*

Brandon. Chinese trellis stair, west wing, Post later. *Brostrup.*

Brandon. Main stair, dating from the alterations. *Johnston.*

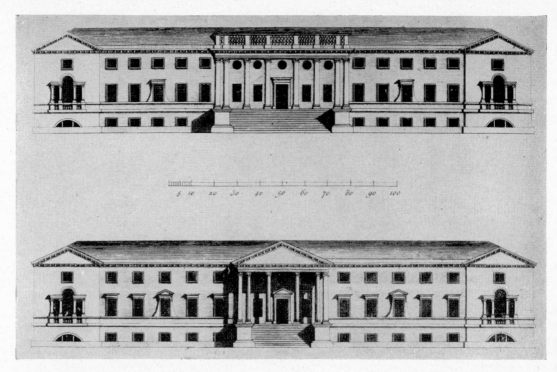

A plate from Morris, suggestive of Battersea composition, with pedimented terminal wings.

BATTERSEA (Petersburg), Dinwiddie County. Façade (south). Altered c. 1800. *Peter, HABS.*

the sides, but in the dining room they project at top and bottom as well. The latter room has a full pediment resting on a plain frieze, but in the former room a broken pediment was used, the cornice and rake enriched with Wall of Troy dentils, and the frieze is pulvinated. These same variations occur in the doorways, except that the pediments are lacking, entablatures taking their place. In both rooms the window architraves curve out in consoles at the chair rail, as at Shirley, and there are crossettes at the head and a projected frieze around which the cornice breaks.

The paucity of trim of the period is to be observed in the entrance hall. It is clear that most of the trim here dates from an alteration of the early nineteenth century. The whole central area of the house is devoted to a huge stair hall which is divided midway of its depth by a triple arcade of Corinthian columns and elliptical arches. Ascending to the second floor is the broad stair, with slender square balusters characteristic of the later period, simple handrail, and brackets carved with Empire-type ornament. The Morris plan gives a clue to the original arrangement of the hall. This apparently consisted of a large salon facing the river, with an entrance hall across the front as in Morris' plate and stair ascending at one end. Old pictures of the hall showing a paneled dado only at the south end would confirm this arrangement. The same plan exists at Battersea, and the confined result there indicates the reason for the change at Brandon. The present great stair is illogical, for it leads only to the small area of the central block. The quality of the stair design and detail is good and the effect individual, so much so, in fact, that its common authorship with the interiors of Hampstead, New Kent County, and Horn Quarter, King William County, is evident. The architectural provenance of these mansions, dating from after 1800, is at present unknown.

In the west wing of Brandon is a fine eighteenth-century Chippendale trellis stair rail with elaborate grilles such as probably once existed in the main hall. The stair is of the open-string type with moulded brackets and is original except for the newel. In spite of the small size of the hall, a full Doric entablature is used, with triglyphs, metopes, and mutules. The adjoining rooms, both upstairs and down, are paneled. The east wing is simply trimmed but has a fine example of a large kitchen fireplace. The general aspect of Brandon, set in superb gardens on the banks of the James River, is of exceptional beauty and it must be regarded as one of Virginia's finest Georgian survivals.

An extraordinary parallel to Brandon is Battersea, near Petersburg. This was built for John Banister, who by marriage to Martha Bland was a connection of Jefferson's through the Blands and Randolphs.[25]

Banister studied in England at the Middle Temple, and after his return in the sixties built this house. His associations with Jefferson were many, and included sitting in the Assembly with him in Williamsburg from 1769 to 1771, in the Virginia Convention in 1776, and in the Continental Congress. To his close friendship with Mrs. Banister Jefferson referred in a letter to her husband from Paris dated August 14, 1786, in which he said: "Mr. Jefferson will be very happy...to renew an acquaintance which he has always held among the most precious of those he has ever made." [26] Young John Banister was placed in Jefferson's care while he was in Paris.

Battersea is a remarkable example of a distinguished house altered some fifty years after its building without much detriment to the original design. The elements are the same as at Brandon, though the subsidiary units between the main block and the connections are omitted. The plan is exactly as it was originally, the central block comprising an entrance hall with stair, and a salon beyond. At either side are connections and wings, both having large rooms nearly square in plan.

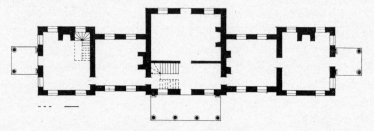

BATTERSEA, Petersburg.

Battersea is really superior in design to Brandon, being more compact, and the elevation counting more as a façade than a number of units, as at Brandon. Originally, it apparently had a two-tiered portico, which would have given the design more of a center of interest than it has now with a low porch. There are dwarf porticos on the end elevation, and these count as well in the façade. That the porticos are original and not a later addition is made clear by a description of the Marquis de Chastellux, who observed them in 1781. He said: "Mr. Banister's handsome country-house...is really worth seeing. It is decorated rather in the Italian, than the English or American style, having three porticos at the three principal entries...."[27] The effect is now more Italianate than it was originally, for the original Flemish bond brickwork has been stuccoed over, the windows altered to triple and Palladian windows, and a broad arched door has been inserted in the middle.

The central block, two stories high, is about as wide as it is deep and

BATTERSEA. Dwarf portico, end of the east wing. *Author, HABS.*

RANDOLPH-SEMPLE House. West wing. *Brostrup. HABS.*

has three openings across the façade on each floor. The center, in each case, is a door, the lower the main entrance, and the upper, as at Shirley, to the porch gallery. Connected to the house by one-story units, the wings are a story and a mezzanine high, having low second-story windows under the cornice. The fenestration of the connections and the wings has been changed on the façade, but the arrangement of the paneling within shows that in both cases the triple windows superseded pairs of single windows. On the side of the wings can be seen the original mezzanine windows, one of which in the east elevation retains the original wide barred sash.

On the side elevations of the wings are the fine original dwarf porticos shielding the minor entrances. These employ a Roman Doric order, with unfluted columns, and an entablature showing triglyphs and mutules, and metopes enriched with disk ornaments. The third, or main, portico has been altered to the form of a low columnar porch. Three of its four columns are original, of Roman Doric style, fluted, and one is a later replacement. The porch entablature is a plain, unarchitectural eaves casing. An examination of the main cornice of the house reveals mitered splices near either corner of the main block. This indicates that the third portico reached the full height of the building, in which case here it must have been double tiered. Three of the old lower columns were reused in a new porch of c.1840-50, but the upper columns were discarded.

On the interior some of the old woodwork has been removed, but the original classic arch between the entrance hall and the salon remains, as does the fine trellis stair. The stringer and wall paneling of the stair display the use of the Greek fret for which Jefferson showed a marked predilection. Its source is Gibbs's *Rules for Drawing,* the design having been copied even to the inadvertent use of the alternative repeats of the fret in single and double forms. Frets are seen as an enrichment in the stair landing and as a filler in the paneling. Two alternating forms of trellis designs were used on the stair ascents, another on the landing, and a Gothic arched motive at the turn of the stair to supplement the lattice grille above. The newel and posts carved with strap-ornament are unusual if not unique in Virginia. Unfortunately, the great part of the original trim in the rest of the house was replaced in the early nineteenth century, but the paneled dados in the west wing and connection remain.

In its original state Battersea must have been a charming American essay in the Roman country-house style, beloved of Jefferson and Palladio. Its red brick walls and white wood trim, however, must have given it the same indigenous quality that they later gave to the University

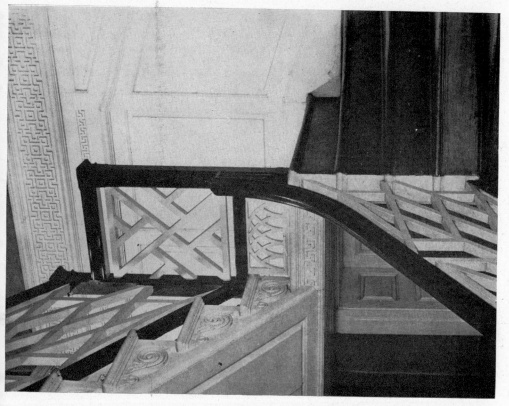

BATTERSEA. A detail of stair at first landing. *Brostrup, HABS.*

BATTERSEA. The great Chinese trellis stairway. *Brostrup, HABS.*

A plate from Morris, the prototype for design of MONTICELLO and RANDOLPH-SEMPLE HOUSE.

RANDOLPH-SEMPLE HOUSE, Williamsburg. Perfection of Colonial Palladian design. *Johnston.*

of Virginia. Of the Virginia mansions, Battersea is perhaps the least well known, but it richly deserves proper recognition. Unfortunately, it stands between three railway lines in the outskirts of Petersburg, so its situation is far from pleasant. This is in great contrast to the beautiful situation, to the south of the Capitol in Williamsburg, of the newly-restored Randolph-Semple house, which is probably next in chronological sequence.

Through the burning of the James City County records during the Civil War all documents relating to the Randolph-Semple house seem to have been destroyed. Research authorities can find no references to it before about 1781, when it was shown on a map of Williamsburg made by a French army officer.[28] The fire insurance records,[29] however, place its value in 1801 at $2,000, or half the appraiser's estimated cost of its building. This indicates it was not new when Judge Semple bought it shortly before, and confirms the architectural evidence that the date of erection was about 1770. The ownership at this date is obscure, but it may have rested with Peyton Randolph, cousin of the signer, son-in-law of Elizabeth Bassett Harrison.

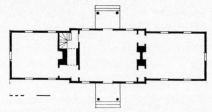

RANDOLPH-SEMPLE HOUSE, Williamsburg. Diagrammatic.

The house was inspired by Morris' book, the basis of the designs being Plate XXXVII. This plate is described as "A little Building intended for Retirement, or for a Study, to be placed in some agreable Part of a Park or Garden...", and in plan the central block, thirty-four by forty, shows a single large room across the front, a smaller room behind, and a stair hall in the right rear corner. There are two wing rooms, each sixteen feet wide, whose long axes are parallel to the depth of the house. In elevation there is a central block three bays wide and two full stories high below a pediment roof. The wings are only one story high and are covered by hipped roofs that are received against the side walls of the main house. The elevation of the central block is satisfying, but the design of the wings is most unfortunate, creating a stumpiness which is accentuated by the roof lines. These latter give the whole façade a broad angular effect which is poor. The actual aspect of a literal use of the plate can be seen in an old house in St. Margaret's, Middlesex, England.[30]

The central area of the Randolph-Semple house contains only a salon, above which are two small bedrooms reached in a typically Jeffersonian way by a stair concealed behind a chimney. In one wing is a dining room and in the other a large drawing room. The trim throughout the house, though simple, is of large scale. The only ornament is the familiar Jeffersonian fret in the frieze of the drawing room mantel. Perhaps by a coincidence, a mantel strikingly like this is shown in a drawing of thirty years ago by Frank Wallis, now identified as having come from the Randolph-Peachy house.[31] This dwelling Peyton Randolph at one time owned and occupied, but the two houses were in the common ownership of the Hansfords later.

The exterior of the Randolph-Semple house is famous for the beauty of its façade. Of frame covered by white painted weatherboards, the central pavilion is two full stories, the lower of considerable height with tall windows, and the upper correspondingly low with almost square windows. The centered door is richly paneled and protected by a fine pedimented porch supported by Doric columns on pedestals. This middle block is covered by a pediment roof, the tympanum containing a circular window. The cornice, as at Battersea, is delicate in scale with both modillions and dentils. The wings, only one story high, continue the fenestration of the main block and are covered by pediment roofs at right angles to the main roof. The end of the west wing is one of the finest details in Williamsburg and reflects perfectly the taste and philosophy of the days just preceding the Revolution. In it, as well as in the rest of this exceptional house, the innate English Georgian quality of the architectural design is apparent but strongly tinged with the classic flavor that colored all phases of thought at the period.

Attributed to Jefferson, this building forms an important link in his architectural development. In it is achieved the complete symmetry that he desired; the rusticity of a gable roof is effectually concealed as a pediment, and the central salon contains no implication of the mechanics of the house or of the upper story, and privacy is assured by the subordination of the stair hall.

Morris' book was the source of the design of countless Virginia and North Carolina houses.[32] At best they were fairly close copies of the plates or of other buildings derived from them. At worst they were naïve or illiterate interpretations of them. One of the most faithful renderings is Belnemus, in Powhatan County, built by the Mayo family about 1765. It is based on the same plate as Brandon but is a three-part scheme instead of a seven, comprising only a central block with wings. Actually the composition has seven elements, as there are detached terminal buildings in the form of square, high-hipped roof smokehouses. The central block is three bays wide and two stories high. Piercing the

A plate from Morris, basis for the design of BELLE ISLE, but adapted to different needs.

BELLE ISLE, Lancaster County. A small house with wings and dependencies. *Green, HABS.*

NANZATICO, King George County. A traditional house with an architectural exterior. *Smith.*

BELLE ISLE, Lancaster County. East room. Original chimney piece, as rebuilt. *Brostrup.*

BELLE ISLE, Lancaster County. The finish of the great room dating from c. 1800. *Brostrup.*

apex of the hipped roof is a curious pyramidal finial after the style of the upper stage of the cupola of the Morris plate. The whole design has an appealing rural quality, heightened by its frame construction, which is apparent also in the interior woodwork. The plan is a central salon and wing rooms with staircases in the thickness of the partitions between. At present there is a large addition in the rear. The woodwork of the interior is remarkable for its usage and elaboration. The salon has a richly worked frontispiece mantel, and, balancing it on the opposite side, a wall cupboard of corresponding design.

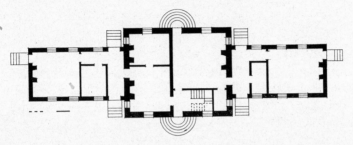

BELLE ISLE, Lancaster County.

Less attributable to Morris and more academic than Belnemus is Nanzatico, in King George County, a beautiful frame house with heroic pilasters against a pedimented pavilion.

Another house certainly based on Morris is Belle Isle in Lancaster County. It is from Plate XXXIII with few variations. The main house, built of brick, is divided into three elements, the center unit of which is two full stories high beneath a hipped roof. Its long rectangular shape results in a ridge rather than in a sharp apex as at Brandon and Battersea. The fenestration achieves interest in the use of low second-floor windows, in contrast to the tall lower ones. The center is three bays long with a central door, but the one-story wings are both four bays. A doorway is next to the main unit with three windows beyond. The original interiors from Belle Isle were removed about 1930, and those now in place are simple Georgian designs by the author. The house had a curious and impractical plan with an off-center hall on the north side, to the right, with a large room behind, and two square rooms on the left. The wings had cross halls next the main house, with two poorly-arranged rooms beyond. This plan has now been somewhat modified.

The interior had an unacademic air due partly to a country builder's interpretation of the designs and partly to the fact that different parts of the interior were of different dates. Especially unacademic, the stair had crudely-turned balusters and posts, and the handrail ascended in mitered ramps over the posts. This was of the first phase of the building (about 1760), but the delicate wall paneling of the great room was of the period of about 1790. In common with other rooms, this was in two tiers of rectangles above the chair rail, with flat panels and delicately moulded styles and rails. This contrasted with the heavy dentilled cornices, which remained in several rooms of the early period. The finish inserted in the great room in the refurbishing at the turn of the century is of particular interest. It is perhaps unique in the country as exhibiting full paneling at a time when such, as a wall finish, had been superceded for at least twenty-five years. No attempt was made to simulate early work, but the mouldings and forms of the period of 1800 were freely used. The chimney breast was flanked by arches, but here they were half-round instead of segmental, as elsewhere in the house. The other arches lacked moulded trim, but in this room they were framed by delicately paneled Doric pilasters supporting moulded archivolts with keystones. The walls of the room were paneled above and below a dado, which had a simple pedestal-type base and cap. The panels themselves were sunk with a delicate panel mould and raised field mould, and had the indented corners also seen in the mantel. These panels, of considerable width, had narrow horizontal panels placed above them, in the style of those of Tuckahoe about half a century earlier. This curious panel mould treatment was carried into the arched recesses, occurring in reveals and back walls. The room has no mannerisms familiar in the region and may be the work of a man brought here for the purpose. Now, re-erected elsewhere, the woodwork is a notable example of a vagary of style, but cleaned down to its original creamy pink paint and furnished with beautiful late eighteenth-century furniture, it has great significance. The upper rooms at Belle Isle, with their paneled chimney breasts, retain their old trim, which is of the later period.

Resembling Belle Isle and perhaps also inspired by Plate XXXIII in Morris was one of the largest mansions of the period, Laneville, in King William County. This was built by Richard Corbin in 1758. On March 15[33] of that year the old house burned, and on August 21 he wrote to his son Gawin, in England, that he was "repairing with all expedition the loss of my house." [34] The work was evidently underway by that time, for he ordered on June 13 the following:

"6 pair of best Dove tail Hinges   3 —
8 pair of smaller do   4 —
6 best 8 Inch brass locks   3 —
6 best 6 Inch brass do   3 —
2 Ironbound Stock locks   3 10"

The second Laneville was burned probably after 1843,[35] and in 1854 James

BELLE ISLE. The fine southeast room mantel, dating about 1760.

BELLE ISLE. Great Room; late paneling, early cornice. *Brostrup*.

Monticello, Albemarle County. Perspective showing original design of c. 1771, before the alterations of c. 1776-1808. *Perspective, author; rendering, Collins.*

Parke Corbin, who had inherited it from his father, built his great house, Moss Neck, in Caroline County. The only contemporary description of Laneville seems to be a reminiscence of a one-time visitor, who wrote in 1908: "I spent a night at this old place some sixty-five years ago. It was then still owned by James Park Corbin, but occupied by Mr. Benjamin Robins. I was impressed with the length of the building. The middle portion was of two stories, square built, with four large rooms...and spacious hall passing through it, and flanked by two wings in which were pantries, storerooms, servants quarters, bed rooms, etc..."[36] Fortunately, the insurance policy remains to verify this description. It is dated March 10, 1802,[37] and gives the dimension of the main block as twenty-seven feet by fifty-two feet and of each wing as twenty by seventy-one feet, giving a total length of 194 feet, indeed an enormous size. The material is given as brick, the roof of each section is shown gabled (though this is not necessary dependable), and six chimneys are shown in the length of the house.

Belnemus and Belle Isle show the popular use of Morris' plates and the interpretation country builders and craftsmen could make of them. The wide gulf between these two houses and Battersea, Brandon, the Randolph-Semple house, and Monticello is apparent not only in the exteriors but in the scholarly designs of the interior trim of the latter group. With these vernacular renderings from the same plates in mind, one can turn to the last house of the academic group, Monticello, and see Virginia mansion design at the full development of the pre-Revolutionary period.

As early as May 18, 1768,[38] Jefferson had begun grading on a mountain top near Shadwell a site two hundred by six hundred feet, for his new house. The land that encompassed it had been acquired by his father Peter Jefferson in 1735,[39] and Jefferson had long dreamed of building on the summit he later called Monticello. The work, up to 1770, was probably desultory, owing to his residence at Shadwell and to his frequent absences pursuing his law practice. However, the fire of February, 1770, that destroyed Shadwell gave an urgency to the project it had never had before. From this time until the relative completion of the first house, in 1778, work was prosecuted diligently. By January, 1772, the house must have been well along, but not enough to receive Jefferson's bride, Martha Wayles, of The Forest, Charles City County; so their honeymoon was spent in the little office he had completed for his own use in 1771.[40] It was of this that he wrote on February 20, 1771, saying, "I have lately removed to the mountain from whence this is dated...I have but one room, which like the cobblers serves me for parlor, for kitchen and hall. I may add for bedchamber and study too... I have hope, however, of getting more elbow room this summer."[41] This building, Honeymoon Cottage as it has come to be known, is in the form of a tiny pedimented pavilion, and is the south terminal building of the great forecourt.

Apparently, the complicated architectural history of Monticello begins with the simple plan Jefferson restudied from the Morris design, which also formed the basis for the Randolph-Semple house. As has been observed, the redesigning of the wings of the prototype, which Jefferson allowed himself, immeasurably improved the resulting plan and elevation. However, in his first study for Monticello [42] he left the central block almost exactly as Morris arranged it, with a salon entrance hall, behind which was a stair hall and a smaller room. In this he used the same circulation as Morris did, the wings being entered from the rear room and hall. This was unfortunate in that it did not allow the three important rooms to be used together. In the second study [43] he overcame this difficulty by moving the doors from behind the chimney wall to in front of it, so that the wing rooms opened directly into the salon. This also allowed him to rearrange the stair into two equal flights, with an initial run long enough to give good headroom under the landing at the back door.

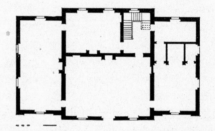

Plate from Robert Morris' *Select Architecture*.

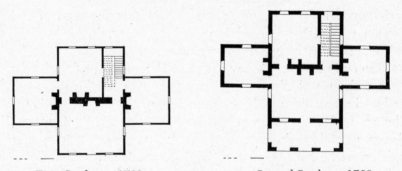

First Study, c. 1768.   Second Study, c. 1768.

Monticello, Albemarle County.

Another improvement over the first scheme, which the indications of wall thickness show, was the substitution of brick wall construction from frame. This not only made the house less inflammable and more

permanent but also gave it a more monumental character. In keeping
with the latter quality Jefferson added to the façade "a Piazza below.
Portico above." The former was probably arcaded, with a portico of
four columns above, perhaps inspired by Plate LV in Gibbs's *Book of
Architecture*, which work he apparently owned before 1771. No example
of this motive seems to have existed in Virginia at this time; so the
literary source seems likely. It is interesting to note that in his last
scheme, the fourth, he replaced the lower arcade with another colonnade.
Thus he achieved a two-tiered portico in the style of those of the Capitol
and Shirley, the style which is so familiar in Palladio. There are no
elevations of the two early plans, though the schemes for them are
indicated by notes. These show that in both first and second studies the
main block and wings were to be pedimented and the latter treated with
the arcaded portico.

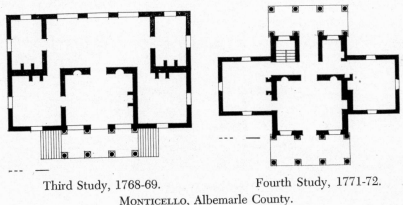

Third Study, 1768-69.   Fourth Study, 1771-72.

Monticello, Albemarle County.

The third scheme [44] shows revolutionary changes that were certainly
caused by ideas obtained from Leoni's *The Architecture of A. Palladio*,
to which he first had access in 1770. In plan the building became two
rooms deep, in one long rectangular block, with an entrance hall of
exactly the same size as the old one. There were a pair of square rooms
flanking it and a long salon or loggia in the rear, this also flanked by
a pair of rooms which were considerably smaller than the front ones.
Entrance to the building was by means of a portico of three bays with
broad steps at either end. The absence of any interior stair indicates that
Palladio's single-story villas were the inspiration for this scheme, and
the highly articulated plan betrays the new source. However zealous
Jefferson became in adapting classic schemes to his architectural needs,
he was confronted by the fact that even the smallest of Palladio's villas
were hopelessly too large for the needs of a Virginia planter. Therefore,
like Ariss he adapted the elements of the monumental plans to use at

smaller scale. The plan, resulting in scheme number three, was not unlike that of Carter's Grove and Cleve, but its source was undoubtedly in Palladio. It has been identified as Plate XLI, and this with its arcaded loggia, two pairs of flanking rooms and entrance salon, is more like that of Monticello than any of the others shown. However, the salon and loggia are the same width, but Plate XXXIV shows the variations in widths that Jefferson's drawing also shows, though with a triple depth of rooms. An arrangement even closer to this plan is an element in a much larger building shown on Plate XLV. In this the areas flanking a central rotunda have broad arcaded loggias with small flanking rooms and a narrower stair hall with larger flanking rooms. From studying Palladio's plans it can be seen that Jefferson's was an essay in the style adapted from various prototypes but altogether more like Plate XLI than any of the others, especially as will be seen later in the disposition of the outbuildings.

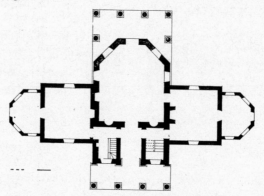

MONTICELLO, Albemarle County, final plan (before alterations).

Apparently, he was not able to forget the attractive qualities of Morris' plan, which his fourth study [45] adapted to Palladian ideas. He maintained the wings as they were in scheme number two but rearranged the main block to obtain symmetry and to create a vista toward the Blue Ridge mountains. The salon, no longer an entrance hall, remained much as it was, but the central chimney in the cross wall was done away with and two flanking the main block were substituted. This allowed an entrance hall, on axis, to the north with arched openings to the salon and the north portico, now added. To the left was the stair hall and to the right a room with a small stair, which he called the antechamber, and which was probably a servants' lobby. Although accomplishing a vista and obtaining symmetry the new arangement was cramped and awkward, but this was the plan on which the building was erected. The north portico was apparently an addition of this time, although the

MONTICELLO, Albemarle County. Jefferson's own drawing for the façade. *Mass. Hist. Soc.*

MONTICELLO, Albemarle County. Façade toward Blue Ridge, from northwest. *Author, HABS.*

Plate from Gibbs's *Book of Architecture*, which influenced MONTICELLO before and after 1796.

MONTICELLO, Albemarle County. South front. Wall below balustrade is original. *Johnston.*

paper on which the plan [46] was drawn was too narrow to allow other than the wall respond of engaged columns to show. The basement plan,[47] nearly contemporaneous, shows a foundation for it. The wing rooms remained the same as in the Morris scheme, except for minor adjustments. Above was a fine library following the plan of the salon.

Of all of these schemes, only the elevations for the last survives, but notes on the plans suggest them all. The first was to be a parallel to the Randolph-Semple house with a two-story pedimented central block and low wings, with pediment ends shown to the side elevations. It was noted, on the plan, that the cornice of the wings was to carry around the main block creating a sort of an attic story above the main story. This was following the Palladian idea as seen, for instance at the Villa Foscari at Malcontenta. Such a division may have existed at one time at the Randolph-Semple house, but it seems unlikely. On the second plan the same scheme was to be followed, but the pediment was advanced to cover a Tuscan portico resting on an arcaded porch. This was in the style of Pavilion VII [48] at the University of Virginia, later designed by Jefferson from a sketch by William Thornton, but here probably inspired by Plate LV in Gibbs's *Book of Architecture*. For the one-story Palladian villa at Monticello no elevation was suggested, but it was probably meant to have an arcaded loggia to the north and a portico to the south.

The elevation survives for the semi-final scheme in a drawing by Jefferson. This shows a high first story, surmounted by a low attic above the wings, and a high second story in the main block. The wings were covered by low-hipped roofs and the central part by a pediment which was supported by superimposed Doric and Ionic orders. As at Battersea there was a central door on each floor and a pair of flanking windows. In each wing was a tall window on the first floor and a short window in the attic.

Jefferson partly restudied this elevation, using Palladio's proportions instead of Gibbs's, but he never carried his drawing above the second-floor line.[49] (This restudy is the one the order was executed from and produced a much more classic effect than the first elevation could have had.) After this drawing was finished, a final change was made to the plan. This entailed a great polygonal bay at the end of the salon, projecting into the portico, and two smaller similar bays at the end of the wings. These bays created two new small rooms entered from the wing rooms.

The great central bay still exists as built, projecting into the portico, but it is not clear what the condition was on the second floor. If the two tiers of the portico were complete, the upper bay would have repeated the condition of the lower. Some authorities feel, however, that the upper tier was never built, in which case the bay would have had a curious effect and would have presented a difficult roofing problem.

An axial bay, of polygonal form, was an innovation of the late Georgian period. It became a familiar feature in English architecture of the time, but except for one other (unexecuted) design it had no other parallel in pre-Revolutionary architecture in Virginia. This was a project for altering the Governor's Palace in Williamsburg to provide more space and create a new façade for a building nearly seventy years old.

Among Jefferson's manuscript drawings in the Coolidge Collection in the Massachusetts Historical Society are a number for alterations to the Palace. The date of these cannot be conclusively determined and there are neither watermarks nor other means of dating them. They have been called as late as 1779, but as the act for moving the Capitol to Richmond was drawn by Jefferson in 1776 (it was finally passed in 1779 and the move made in 1780), it seems reasonable he should have made them before the change of site was seriously contemplated. It seems plausible that he might have made them for Lord Dunmore, for whom he made plans for the extension of the College of William and Mary in 1773. In this case they would be between that date and 1775 when Dunmore fled from the Palace. It is also possible that the alterations were made in 1776 for Patrick Henry, first Governor under the Republic, for whom the Palace was repaired and redecorated.

It is impossible to be sure of the sequence of the drawings. Probably the simplest scheme was not the first since it was the one executed. This scheme merely was a replanning of the house within the old walls. Another, of which there are various studies, contemplated building to the north a new structure the same size as the old Palace,[50] the two being connected by the ball room wing of 1751 and new loggias. This produced a very extensive H-shaped building, which must have been obviously too large for the requirements. The intermediate scheme comprised not only replanning within the old walls but covering them with a new pediment-form roof.[51] This extended over an octastyle portico on the front, within which was a polygonal bay, as at Monticello, added to the entrance hall to increase its size and to obtain interior symmetry. This solution of the problem was epochal, for it created the first temple-form mansion proposed for this country. Two mansions in the form of cellas of temples were built. These were Berkeley, Charles City County, and Nelson House, Yorktown, but both lacked porticos, perhaps on account of the technical difficulties of providing columns.

The Capitol at Richmond, by Jefferson and Clérisseau, was the first monumental temple-form building erected in the United States. That Jefferson contemplated such a structure when he wrote the act of

MONTICELLO, Albemarle County. The salon. This was a feature of the early house but was redecorated after Jefferson's return from Europe. One of Virginia's noblest rooms, it is a monument to the skill of the designer. *Tebbs*.

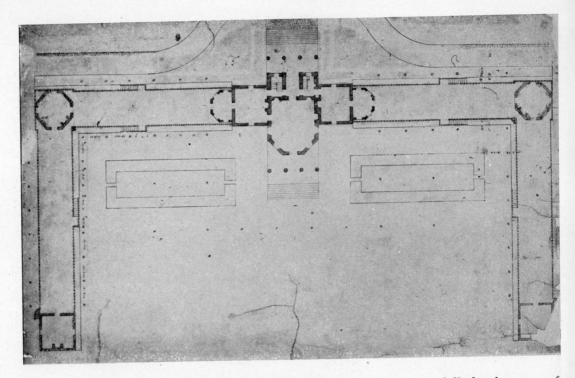

The plan of MONTICELLO, after 1772, drawn by Jefferson, showing the full development of the great forecourt in Palladio's Roman country-house style. Since the building of Stratford the plantation offices had been designed in formal relation to the Virginia mansion, according to Palladio's precepts, but until Jefferson's design for Monticello had never been fully integrated with it. (Below) Jefferson's plan for alterations of 1770-76 to the Governor's Palace, Williamsburg (left) and an unexecuted study, which would have created the first temple-form mansion in America (right.) *Coolidge Collection, Courtesy Mass. Hist. Soc.*

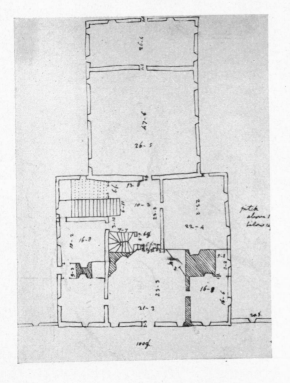

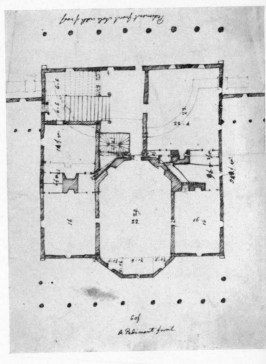

October 14, 1776, is proved by the act itself, which provided that "The said houses shall be built in a handsome manner with walls of brick, or stone, & Porticos where the same may be convenient or ornamental, and with pillars and pavements of stone."[52]

Perhaps Jefferson had dreams of transforming colonial Williamsburg into a rural Vicenza. The idea of terminating the noble vista of the Palace Green with a classic portico was demonstrably his. The addition of the two-tiered portico to the Capitol as the feature of the Duke of Gloucester Street vista was possibly, or probably, his. Perhaps too, the accenting of the Court House Green cross axis with the Court House portico was his contrivance as well. The designs of the latter building were advertised as being ready for bids in 1769,[53] and it may be surmised that Jefferson or Taliaferro drew them. It is a T-shaped building with a full-height portico on the front. The pediment is cantilevered out and columns are lacking, but in keeping with Jefferson's act, quoted above, the columns were probably to be of English stone. The pediment was perhaps cantilevered out to await their arrival and insertion, but on account of the Revolution they never arrived. That the Capitol columns were stone was indicated by the finding of a derelict three-fourths engaged Portland stone column base in the excavations at the site. In support of Jefferson's authorship of the Capitol portico, which might date from any time after 1750, it should be observed that this base was the same type as those shown on Jefferson's Monticello portico. It has been authoritatively asserted that those at Monticello were the first three-fourths engaged bases used in Virginia,[54] and that they were directly inspired by Leoni's *Palladio*.

When Jefferson commenced his studies for the replanning of the Palace he was probably confronted with the asymmetric plan of 1705, shown in the excavation of 1930.

His own sketch indicates that he had three definite objects in mind for the alteration scheme, symmetry, practicability, and privacy. To obtain the first he introduced a wall to the right of the entrance door, as far distant from the axis as that existing at the left. To heat the hall he added a corner fireplace (as no other location was possible) and balanced it with a corner closet, thus producing the familiar demi-octagon of his style. For privacy, he apparently readjusted the old stair and introduced a new stair, enclosed by paneling. This is remarkably like the Monticello stair in size and arrangement. Lastly, he probably rebuilt the chimneys, worn from long use, either in the old form or a new one. By these adroit changes the interior of the Palace was given a new style and a new livability. It is unfortunate that so few years of usefulness were left to the building. It stood for Jefferson to use during his governorship, and it was utilized as a military hospital during the final stages of the Revolution, after which it fell a victim of fire in 1781.[55]

Aside from Monticello, the only architectural project of Jefferson's of the pre-Revolutionary period, which is proved by documents, was the proposed enlargement of the College of William and Mary. The original building, constructed in 1695, had been planned as a quadrangle and was so shown on Theodrick Bland's map, drawn in 1699, of the site of Williamsburg.[56] However, only two sides were completed, the front and north, or great hall wing, forming an L-shaped structure. This was burned in 1705, and when rebuilt, the north wing was shortened and was balanced by a chapel wing to the south; the court was left permanently open.[57] Apparently, the proposal to enlarge the building was made during Dunmore's term of office, and he requested a plan from Jefferson. The original drawing for the structure which shows a doubling in size of the building,[58] remains. This was to be achieved by closing the court by another U-shaped building of the same size to the west, but the work was not carried out.

The College drawing, and those of Monticello of this early period, show that Jefferson was already a competent draftsman and designer. That some of the drawings are poorly executed is no criterion, for many are obviously sketches made with no effort at careful draftsmanship. Many, on the other hand, are beautifully and accurately drawn, showing an ability not excelled by other architects of the epoch. It is fortunate that it has been possible to identify the books he used, for they show clearly that Jefferson was no copyist. As architects have always done, he adapted and attempted to improve published plans; that he did notably improve them is shown in the Monticello study of the Morris plan. In this case, he took a clumsy rendering of an interesting scheme and produced a plan of extraordinary excellence. The elevations, resulting from it, as at the Randolph-Semple house, are individual and beautiful and testify to the unusual ability of the architect. The rearrangement of the Palace plan shows the ingenuity Jefferson possessed as a planner, an ability later to be so freely offered to Virginia and Virginians for public buildings and dwellings.

Progressive cataloguing of early papers, or analysis of those now known, will perhaps provide substantial knowledge of Jefferson's architectural works during his early years. In the meantime, the clues at hand make it clear that to his first major design, that of the Virginia Capitol (1784), he brought the abilities of a trained designer and the skill of a native architect.

REFERENCES

1. Blomfield, A History of Renaissance Architecture, pp. 120, 285.

2. Dictionary of National Biography, I, 88.

3. Stanley C. Ramsey, Small Houses of the Late Georgian Period 1750-1800, Plate XC. (House at St. Margaret's, Middlesex.)

4. Stoney, Plantations of the Carolina Low Country, pp. 142-61.

5. Kimball, Thomas Jefferson, Architect, p. 22.

6. C. J. Heatwole, "Thomas Jefferson as an Architect," Virginia Journal of Education, XIX (May, 1926), See Bibliography, pp. 360-63.

7. Sale, Interiors of Virginia Houses of Colonial Times, p. 345.

8. David Chambers Mearns, and Verner W. Clapp, compilers, Thomas Jefferson, the Architect (1936), p. 1.

9. Andrew Adgate Lipscomb, editor, The Writings of Thomas Jefferson, IV, 18.

10. Mrs. Marie Goebel Kimball, Jefferson, The Road to Glory, 1743 to 1776, pp. 3-38.

11. Thomas Jefferson, Notes on the State of Virginia, p. 222.

12. Marie Goebel Kimball, Jefferson, The Road to Glory, p. 48.

13. Thomas Jefferson Wertenbaker, The Old South; the Founding of American Civilization, p. 34.

14. Marie Goebel Kimball, Jefferson, The Road to Glory, p. 73.

15. Fiske Kimball, Thomas Jefferson, Architect, p. 34.

16. Manuscript at Shirley.

17. Architects' Emergency Committee, Great Georgian Houses, I, 24-29.

18. Ibid., pp. 34-38.

19. Fiennes, Through England on a Side Saddle, p. 43.

20. For Carter Genealogy see C. G. Lee, Jr., William and Mary Quarterly, 2nd Series, XVI, 417.

21. Lancaster, Historic Virginia Homes and Churches, p. 349.

22. Architects' Emergency Committee, Great Georgian Houses, I, 146-53.

23. Fiske Kimball, Thomas Jefferson, Architect, Plate XX.

24. Virginia Magazine of History and Biography, XXII, 200.

25. For Banister genealogy see Horner, The History of Blair, Banister and Braxton Families.

26. Manuscript in Library of Congress.

27. Chastellux, Travels in North America, p. 272.

28. Architectural Record for December, 1935, LXXVIII, 372.

29. Mutual Assurance Society of Virginia (microfilm). Virginia State Library.

30. Ramsey, Small Houses of the Late Georgian Period, Plate XC.

31. Frank Edwin Wallis, Old Colonial Architecture and Furniture, p. 16.

32. Johnston and Waterman, The Early Architecture of North Carolina, pp. 90-95.

33. Virginia Magazine of History and Biography, XXIX, 523.

34. Corbin Letter Book (1758-68). Virginia State Library.

35. Alfred Bagby, King and Queen County, Virginia, p. 14.

36. Ibid., p. 78.

37. Mutual Assurance Society of Virginia (microfilm). Virginia State Library.

38. Marie Goebel Kimball, Jeffer-

son, *The Road to Glory*, p. 150.

39. *Ibid.*, p. 17.

40. *Ibid.*, p. 176.

41. *Ibid.*, p. 156.

42. Fiske Kimball, *Thomas Jefferson, Architect*, Plate V.

43. *Ibid.*, Plate VI.

44. *Ibid.*, Plate XI.

45. *Ibid.*, Plate XVIII.

46. *Ibid.*, Plate XVIII.

47. *Ibid.*, Plate XXII.

48. *Ibid.*, Plate CCXII.

49. *Ibid.*, Plate XXIII.

50. *Ibid.*, Plate XCVI.

51. *Ibid.*, Plate XCVIII.

52. Fiske Kimball, *First Monument of the Classic Revival*, p. 7.

53. *William and Mary Quarterly*, 1st Series, XVI, 32-37.

54. Fiske Kimball, *Thomas Jefferson, Architect*, p. 24.

55. *Tyler's Quarterly, Historical and Genealogical Magazine*, IV, 422.

56. Lyon Gardiner Tyler, *Williamsburg, the Old Colonial Capital*, p. 20.

57. *William and Mary Quarterly*, 2nd Series, VIII, 217-307.

58. *Ibid.*, pp. 218, 240.

CHARACTERISTIC MOULDING PROFILES (OPPOSITE) OF VIRGINIA GEORGIAN HOUSES.

1. Chair Rail, Morattico.

2. Chair Rail, Wilton.

3. Chair Rail, Westover.

4. Chair Rail, balustrade type.

5. Chair Rail, variation.

6. Chair Rail, pedestal type with base.

7. Muntin, Morattico.

8. Muntin, typical.

9. Muntin, Carter's Grove.

10. Muntin, Shirley.

11. Window Trim, Randolph-Peachy House.

12. Architrave, minimum.

13. Architrave, three plane type.

14. Architrave, Nelson House.

15. Archtrave, typical.

16. Architrave, alternative backband.

17. Architrave, variation.

18. Panel Mould, typical.

19. Panel Mould, field beaded.

20. Panel Mould, bisection type.

21. Panel Mould, bisection and beaded.

22. Panel Mould, maximum elaboration.

23. Panel Mould, bevel coved.

24. Panel Mould, ogee (Ariss type).

25. Panel Mould, Ariss type, variation.

26. Panel Mould, eccentric bisection, Shirley.

27. Panel Mould, eccentric type, Wilton.

POSTSCRIPT

THIS POSTSCRIPT was undertaken at the suggestion of Fiske Kimball, dean of historians of American Architecture, who reviewed with me the manuscript and illustrations for this work at Lemon Hill in Philadelphia in February of 1943. It was his opinion that the manner in which the material was accumulated was as interesting in its way as the material itself and would make a valuable supplement. He suggested that in addition to the information in the text an outline of the fields covered would assist other investigators working on the same subject to carry the study farther. Mr. Kimball also advised that a consistently chronological sequence be observed in the account of the buildings. The necessary revisions were accordingly made and resulted in many improvements in the text, especially in the chapter on the Early Georgian Period.

In retrospect it seems curious that circumstances dictated that my study of early Virginia architecture be nearly chronological. It began with the College of William and Mary (1693), which I first saw on a visit from Boston in 1927, together with Rosewell (1726). After 1928, while I was living in Williamsburg, I had an exceptional opportunity to study the early brick mansions of lower Tidewater. After 1933, in travelling between Washington and Williamsburg, I was able to make a careful investigation of the mid-Georgian houses on the Rappahannock River, near my present home, Port Royal. In 1942 an invitation to make an address at the National Gallery on Jefferson's architecture, and another to write an article for the *Gazette des Beaux Arts* on his early works, crystallized certain theories that had been growing in my mind concerning some late Georgian mansions. These, treated individually, failed to relate to the familiar groups, but when related to each other produced an entirely new group, especially significant in the changing style.

During the first two of my five years in Williamsburg the late John A. Barrows and I undertook a survey of fifteen important early houses, which was published in 1932 as *Domestic Colonial Architecture of Tidewater Virginia*. The measuring of these and many other houses stimulated my interest and curiosity in their design; and, on my return from a trip to England in 1933, after I became Architectural Director of the Historic American Buildings Survey in Washington, I began work on an analysis of the early mansions with a view toward a history of Virginia's major domestic architecture. It is singular that a study of this nature had not already been undertaken, considering the deep general interest in these great houses. However, only two comprehensive works have been published up to this time; and these are Robert A. Lancaster, Jr.'s *Historic Virginia Homes and Churches* (1915), and Edith Tunis Sale's *Interiors of Virginia Houses of Colonial Times* (1927). These together with the Virginia Garden Club books are invaluable as catalogues of the early houses, and all of them contain much historical and genealogical material. Both of the former two, however, were written by laymen without architectural training, and the authors made no attempt to group other than geographically the buildings discussed or to analyse their designs. Various books of photographs and drawings, intended for use of architectural precedent rather than for architectural history, have been published from about 1900 to the present. This, therefore, seems to be the first attempt to present a full architectural study of the houses, and thus is necessarily incomplete and subject to revision.

To those familiar with the condition of the early records it is not surprising that a study of the mansions cannot be made from documentary sources. Although there are, in some quantity, extant records regarding public buildings or churches, those concerning the building of the great houses are almost nonexistent. In addition to this lack of written information there is also the problem to consider that hardly any Virginia mansion has survived the passing of the years without substantial alteration or mutilation, and great numbers have been destroyed by fire. The examples still remaining therefore tell only part of the story. Photographs or drawings of a few of the houses that have been destroyed have come to light and are discussed in this work. These include houses of major importance such as Nomini Hall, Peckatone, and Mannsfield Hall, all destroyed in the last century.

This work, besides arranging and classifying the plans and designs, attempts to attribute them to certain designers, perhaps with some success. Up to this time only one has been so attributed, Gunston Hall, which the late R. T. H. Halsey was able to assign in part to William Buckland through the fortunate discovery of the latter's papers of indenture. These are now in the Annapolis, Maryland, archives. Few records of any of the other architects are seemingly in existence, and the conclusions reached here are largely from stylistic or structural evidence. Although mistakes have undoubtedly been made, the conclusions reached have appeared conservative and the evidence pro and con has been cited.

It was my observance, in England in 1933, of the identity of the

Palace plan with that of Ashburnham House in London that led to the long study and final conclusions elaborated in the text. Such a hypothesis is almost hopeless of proof, however, for the Wren papers and the Palace records have been thoroughly studied for years, and there is no new information concerning the relationship or authorship of the two buildings. However, the attribution to Wren is new in both cases.

The year or more spent on the design of the restoration of the Palace provided me with an insight into the methods and ideas of the early architects and builders of Virginia. The method which I employed in my work for Messrs. Perry, Shaw, and Hepburn, the architects of the Restoration, on the design of the Palace, as well as of the Capitol and the College of William and Mary, was evidently much like that of my Colonial confreres; for within the limitations of the building English architectural precedent was used and was always modified and adapted to the necessities and individuality of the building. Except for extracts from William Paine's book, republished in the Monograph Series, there were no early style books at hand in Williamsburg, and H. Avray Tipping's superb *English Homes,* a gift from the lady to whom this book is dedicated, provided me with the inspiration for the design of the great suites of rooms in these buildings.

The number of important architects practicing in Virginia from the beginning of the great Colonial building period, about 1700, to its end in 1776, seems to have been small. In fact, there were apparently only three in addition to the architect of the Governor's Palace and William Buckland. It is possible that the mannerisms and the decorative characteristics of two or more designers may have been so alike that their work could be confused, or that the influence of English style books reduced the level of several to a formula, but at present this does not seem likely. The early architects continually modified and adapted plans, elevations, and details from the style books with the result that their buildings were never slavish copies of English prototypes. This practice has made it difficult always to determine the precedent, but it has also made the search for and the analysis of the designs the more interesting. In architecture as in other arts, individuality can best be discerned in details. In both the early and mid-Georgian houses here discussed, the relationship of the balusters in each group is striking, and the turnings are individual to each. It is interesting to note, also, that after my segregation of the two groups of houses I observed that they each have a characteristic panel mould.

The work of these three early architects covered somewhat different periods and localities. The first of these men, Richard Taliaferro, of Williamsburg, practiced mainly between the years 1725 to 1755. He seems to have worked in the lower Tidewater region from Leoni's *Designs for Buildings,* William Salmon's *Palladio Londinensis,* Gibbs's *Book of Architecture,* and Batty Langley's design books. Most of his buildings lie on the James and Rappahannock Rivers. The second, John Ariss, of Westmoreland County, who was already at work in 1751, probably practiced until about 1785. His work was profoundly influenced by William Adam's *Vitruvius Scoticus* and to a lesser degree by Gibbs's and Langley's books. His buildings range from Richmond County to Berkeley County, now in West Virginia. The third, the great amateur, Thomas Jefferson, seems to have been working in the vicinity of Williamsburg and the James River from about 1769, creating at least three distinguished mansions on the basis of Robert Morris' *Select Architecture* and Gibbs's *Rules for Drawing,* both of which he apparently possessed before 1769.

The still woefully incomplete story of Richard Taliaferro, probably the architect of that great group of early houses built for the Carter and allied families, began with my observation of the similarities in plan between Rosewell and Cound in England, and developed with a brief visit which I paid to Shrewsbury in England in 1933. This visit was particularly helpful as showing the extraordinary likeness of the architectural detail of Shropshire and Virginia and the unusual similarity of the Judges' Lodging in Shrewsbury to Sabine Hall. Study of this subject prompted a paper read, in 1938, to the American Philosophical Society on the "English Antecedents of Virginia Architecture." This paper related Rosewell and Christ Church in Lancaster County and traced them to Shropshire antecedents. Further study had deepened my conviction that their designer must at least have known Shrewsbury buildings. In 1939 my attention was drawn to a letter from Thomas Lee of Stratford, the acting Governor, to the Lords of Trade and Plantations which apparently referred to Taliaferro as "our most skillful architect." From the relationship of his own house to the others of the group it has been inferred that he was their architect. It was the chance observation of the relationship of *Palladio Londinensis* to the whole Carter group and Leoni's Queensferry House plan to Westover and its related houses that allowed a more reliable tracing of the development of the group of buildings and the inclusion of other houses until now never associated with them. From this analysis it seems that Rosewell, Christ Church, and Sabine Hall belong to the first phase; Nomini Hall, Westover, Berkeley, Nelson House, Wilton, Wythe House, and Elsing Green to the second; and Cleve and Carter's Grove to the third and final. The plans of each phase (which slightly overlap) show a close affinity and each an improvement over the former. Rosewell and Sabine Hall were spacious but wasteful; Nomini Hall, Westover, Wilton, Elsing Green, Berkeley, and

Nelson House were compact but rather awkward; but Cleve and Carter's Grove were spacious, with a perfection of plan never equalled in a Virginia mansion of any period.

The story of John Ariss and his buildings stems from the first pertinent observation which I made toward a grouping of early houses. This observance was the similarity of the balusters of Kenmore and Harewood, and of the stair of the latter and that of Sara's Creek House in Gloucester. The relationship of Mount Airy, Mount Vernon, Blandfield, and Mannsfield Hall is obvious, but it was not until I chanced upon the source of these designs in *Vitruvius Scoticus* that I realized that Kenmore and Menokin, also derived from the book, were related to them. In spite of their dissimilarities of appearance I became convinced that they, as well as the Carlyle house in Alexandria, were actually of the same group.

About this time, Mr. Halsey brought to my attention John Ariss' advertisement, dated from Westmoreland County in 1751, advising that he would undertake buildings in the style of Gibbs. This was an open sesame, for as Mr. Halsey had pointed out, the garden front of Mount Airy was designed from a plate in Gibbs's *Book of Architecture*. Mr. Halsey's inability to find further information on Ariss was due to the misspelling of his name as Oriss in the advertisement.

An inquiry to Miss Lucy Brown Beale of Montross revealed the fact that John Ariss, a builder, had lived in Westmoreland from his birth about 1725 to about 1750, but his will was not on file. Fortunately, Swem's index listed a letter from Ariss to Councillor Carter, a former neighbor, headed "Berkeley." On the chance that this might refer to the county of that name, I addressed a letter to the county clerk at Martinsburg, Berkeley County, now West Virginia. A reply to this inquiry revealed that Ariss' will was filed there in 1800. A copy of the will produced little information except that he was a person of means whose manumission of his slaves and devotion to the church showed him to have been of high principles. The will requested that he be buried at Fairfield, in Berkeley County, "with permission of Mrs. Washington."

On my visit to this latter house, which was unknown to me, I was struck by its extraordinary resemblance to Kenmore in plan and detail. That Ariss may have built Fairfield for his own occupancy, but had to give it up in 1784 is purely a surmise. Fairfield is now in Clarke County, Virginia, only a mile or so from the Jefferson County, West Virginia line, beyond which stands Harewood. With the knowledge that Fairfield had been in the family of Warner Washington, that Harewood was still in that of Samuel Washington, and that George Washington had held great tracts of land in this area, I addressed an inquiry concerning Ariss to Mount Vernon. The reply stated that Ariss had applied for a lease of land on Bullskin Creek in 1784, but there was no confirmation of the lease or location of the property.

In the spring of 1940 I therefore explored the creek, which flows between Harewood and Fairfield, and found only one house of architectural quality. This was Locust Hill, which later comparison with *Vitruvius Scoticus* showed to have been based on Plate 11 of that work. After a lecture on Ariss at Charles Town, a home of my mother's family, I received a letter from Mrs. Walter Washington, who advised me to consult with Miss Anne Washington whose father Lawrence was the last male member of the family born at Mount Vernon. I followed Mrs. Washington's suggestion without revealing the suspicion I had formed that Ariss had designed the alterations to Mount Vernon. To my inquiries Miss Washington replied that all she knew of Ariss was what she had recently read in a book in her library that he had made the drawings for the enlargement of Mount Vernon for the General. Unfortunately, she has not been able to give me the reference to the title of the book.

Miss Washington, however, referred me to a descendent of Ariss who told me that the old family home was called Locust Hill and was near the Shenandoah River, but just where she did not know. This information seems to confirm this as the house which Ariss built on Bullskin Creek about 1786, and in which he died in 1799. However, both search and inquiry have failed to locate either his papers or any of his direct descendants. The story of John Ariss thus patched together is that of certainly the most distinguished American architect of his period, a gentleman and a man of high artistic and technical achievements.

The theory that before the building of Monticello Jefferson designed several large houses in the James River region has not as yet been proven by documents. However, in the years since I first publicly broached it in a lecture to the architectural fraternity of the University of Virginia about 1939, nothing has come to my attention to disprove or discourage my supposition. Jefferson's own drawings seem to confirm it. It was these, published in Fiske Kimball's superb *Thomas Jefferson, Architect*, that led me to the conviction that he was responsible for the design of the Randolph-Semple house in Williamsburg, which is certainly closely akin to his study for Monticello in figure 5. This study shows a house comprising one large salon with one-room wings, all three gable ends of which are marked as pedimented. This is significant since at the date at which Mr. Kimball places the manuscript there seem to have been no other Virginia pediment-roof houses except Nelson House and Berkeley, plans of which are utterly unakin to Jefferson's designs. However, subsequent to the building of the Randolph-Semple house a large number of nearly identical houses were built, though none was as fine.

The design of Brandon had the half-hearted tradition of Jefferson authorship, though the differences from his usual manner of planning and designing the elevations had long made me disbelieve this tradition. With the Randolph-Semple house in mind, however, I have come to believe that it is reliable. At about the time of my change of conviction I came to know Battersea, in Petersburg, and this, following as it does the villa style of the other two houses, seemed a logical addition to the group. It was only then that I first saw Robert Morris' *Select Architecture*, on which all three houses are based. This book was owned by Jefferson before 1769, as was Gibbs's *Rules for Drawing*, both of which seem to be the source of much of the detail of these houses. Morris' book not only related to these houses but also to the study for Monticello, which is drawn almost exactly from Plate XXXVII except that it shows the modification of pedimented wings, also shown in the Randolph-Semple house. Monticello remains the only actually known example of Jefferson's architecture before 1770, but this example is definitely related to all three other houses.

Although this work was undertaken purely as an historical study, the text and photographs will undoubtedly be used as precedent in the restoration of early buildings. It should be pointed out that in undertaking such restoration work the restorer assumes a certain responsibility to preserve the individuality and integrity of the building. If this is accomplished the building remains a significant monument of early architecture. If, however, the character of the building is willfully changed it loses its value as an exemplar of its period. To preserve the character of a building, as little work should be done as is consistent with the utility, stability of the structure, and completeness of the finish. Weakened walls should not be rebuilt unless they cannot be underpinned and stabilized. Old plaster should not be knocked down unless it is insecure, and plaster work should be carefully patched and the old work retained. Doors, sashes, and all old wood trim in bad condition should be carefully repaired and superceded by new only when repair is impossible. Disused pieces may have significance at a future time, and so, where possible, they should be stored away rather than discarded. A case in point concerns the Morattico room, perhaps the most important example of the Colonial Queen Anne style, which was demolished with the house about 1928. The trim, much cut up, was installed in a new house near the site, and the fragments were thrown into an attic and sealed up. Fortunately, these came to light when the trim was taken out for the rebuilding of the old room elsewhere, and they alone provided the information necessary for reassembling this important room.

In restorations where new work is necessary such work should blend with the old but should not be "faked" to appear old. In brickwork and stonework, the new can be differentiated from the old by the use of a mix of yellow sand and white cement rather than oyster-shell lime. New woodwork in important restorations can be dated with a small metal die for the benefit of future students. In restorations the integrity of the building should not be confused by using trim or features from one old house in another. This hopelessly distorts the history of the building. If there is trim of various periods which is authentic with the house it should be left, for such trim is part of the history of the structure. It should be removed only when it destroys or mars the significance or beauty of the original work. Many of the most interesting early buildings have features of various periods.

Two fates that often overcome early houses are the removal of interior finish for re-erection elsewhere, and the moving of the structure either as a whole or piece by piece from one site to another. The first is only fully justified when a building is actually being demolished, as in the case of the Belvin house in Richmond, from which during demolition was removed a superb room, with mahogany trim and Pennsylvania marble base, signed by the maker "Theo. Nash." The second destroys the building's integrity and its relationship to its environment. When buildings are skillfully rebuilt after moving the result is less unfortunate, but more frequently they are poorly reconstructed and important features or conditions are lost. In many cases houses have been demolished with the intention of rebuilding them elsewhere, but the rebuilding has never been carried out. Some examples of this sad fate are Belle Farm, Gloucester County; Liberty Hall, Nelson County; the Tabb house, York County; and Bathhurst, Essex County.

Unfortunately, many old buildings, of which not even photographic or measured records remain, have been destroyed for their materials, which are then used for "restoration" work. Important remains of early structures also have been thus destroyed. Some examples are Peckatone, Westmoreland County; Kingsmill Mill, James City County; the Douglas house and the office of Eltham, both in New Kent; and Hayfield in Fairfax County.

So much valuable information has been lost that it is imperative to preserve records of existing buildings and to recover those of destroyed buildings and deposit them in suitable repositories such as the Historic American Buildings Survey of the Library of Congress in Washington. The plans and many of the photographs here used, and transcripts of the Ariss papers, have been deposited in this collection and are available for study there. There are also in the Survey measured drawings and photographs of Virginia buildings, many referred to in the text and many not mentioned. Most of them are listed in the Survey's catalogue.

So many people have extended their assistance to me in preparing this volume that it would be impossible to list them here. However, I take this opportunity to thank them sincerely for their assistance and their courtesy.

I am particularly grateful to the Library of Congress for access to its collections and for innumerable services freely rendered, and to the American Council of Learned Societies for a grant made in 1943. This latter enabled me to complete the photographic material and to have the manuscript transcribed. I deeply appreciate the assistance given in criticism of the manuscript by Fiske Kimball and Cazenove G. Lee, Jr., and in its transcription by Elizabeth Sherier.

I wish to accept full responsibility for the statements in this work, some of which may be at variance with the findings of other writers, or with the ideas of the owners of the buildings. The research, the interpretation of the evidence, and the conclusions reached are all my own.

This can hardly be more than a beginning in the study of Virginia's early architecture, for many gaps in the story here told will have to be filled and corrections made. The history of the churches, public buildings, and minor domestic architecture remains to be written. The sequence of styles, the derivation of the architectural designs, and the authorships here covered may contribute to a comprehensive study of the whole subject. With the excavation of sites of early building, accumulation of pertinent documents, and a thorough analysis of all buildings now standing, such a study should do justice to the great subject of Virginia's early architecture.

T. T. W.

Caithness, Port Royal,
Caroline County, Virginia,
September, 1944

SUMMARY SKETCHES OF MANSIONS

AMPTHILL, formerly Chesterfield County. Pages 212-14.

Built before 1732 by Henry Cary II with his father, builder of the Governor's Palace, and later of the President's House at the College of William and Mary in Williamsburg. On his death in 1750 it passed to his son Archibald, who altered and refinished the house. Ampthill was sold on Cary's death and passed through many hands. In 1929 it was taken down and rebuilt in Richmond by a descendant of a brother of the builder. It is now the home of the Hon. Hunsdon Cary and Mrs. Cary.

BATTERSEA, Petersburg, Dinwiddie County. Pp. 373-79.

Built about 1765-70 by John Banister, third of the name in Virginia. He studied law in England, where he was a member of the Inns of Court, but returned to Virginia about 1765. It is said that the old house burned while he was away, and the new one was built shortly after his return. The architectural evidence indicates that Thomas Jefferson was the designer. Banister was a member of the Revolutionary Conventions and of the Continental Congress. Battersea descended to his son John Monro Banister, who later sold it.

BELLE ISLE, near Farnham, Lancaster County. Pp. 383-84.

Built about 1760 by Rawleigh Downman, son-in-law of Joseph Ball. It remained in the Downman family for over a hundred years, but was later sold, and about 1930 the interiors were removed. Belle Isle was acquired in 1940 by the present owners, Mr. and Mrs. H. Lee Boatwright, who repaired the house and made it their home.

BERKELEY, Charles City County. Pp. 165-68.

The initials of the builder, Benjamin Harrison (d.1745) and of his wife Anne Carter, and the date, 1726, are carved in a panel in the wall. Berkeley descended to Benjamin Harrison V (1726-91), Burgess, member of the Continental Congress, signer of the Declaration of Independence, and Governor of Virginia. His son William Henry Harrison, President of the United States, was born at Berkeley. The place was sold about 1882, and, now restored, is the home of Mr. and Mrs. Malcolm Jamieson.

BLANDFIELD, near Caret, Essex County. Pp. 261-65.

Blandfield, like Mount Airy, is an example of long land tenure by one family. Robert Beverley patented the land before 1686, and his great-grandson William Beverley built the house. It was probably designed by John Ariss, and Beverley's letter book shows it was under construction in 1771. Just before the Civil War the house was modernized by the re-finishing of the interior, and during the War it was sacked by Northern troops. It has passed in the male line to the present owner. Mr. and Mrs. Bland Beverley now reside at Blandfield.

BRANDON, Prince George County. Pp. 367-73.

Built between 1765-70 by Nathaniel Harrison (1743-1807) whose son George Evelyn (1797-1839) inherited Brandon, and whose widow Mrs. Isabelle Ritchie Harrison lived there until her death in 1898. It was purchased by the late Robert Daniel, whose family still reside there. Architectural evidence as well as tradition indicate that it was designed by Thomas Jefferson.

CAMDEN, near Port Royal, Caroline County. P. 261.

Built about 1770 by John Pratt, a connection of Lord Camden, the original house seems to have been one of John Ariss' designs. However, in 1857 the old house was either rebuilt or remodeled by N. G. Stark-weather, the architect, of Baltimore. His drawings for the alterations, in the Italian Villa Style, remain in the house. In the basement can be seen the original walls and finish. Camden has remained in the family and is now the residence of Mr. and Mrs. Richard Pratt and Miss Margaret Pratt.

CARLYLE HOUSE, Alexandria. Pp. 248-53.

Built in 1752 by John Carlyle, one of the founders of Alexandria. Carlyle figured prominently in American affairs preceding the Revolution. In this house the first inter-Colonial council of governors was held, and here General Braddock had his headquarters before the disastrous expedition to Ft. Duquesne. About 1830 the house was radically altered and during the Civil War was sacked by Union troops. It remained with Carlyle's descendants, the Herbert family, until 1910. It is now open for exhibition purposes, but its site between a large apartment house and factory entirely destroys its original setting.

CARTER'S GROVE, James City County. Pp. 183-92.

Built between 1751-53 by Carter Burwell, grandson of Robert Carter of Corotoman and son of Nathaniel Burwell of Fairfield, Gloucester

County. It descended to his son Carter Burwell II, who sold the plantation about 1790 and moved to Clarke County, where he built Carter Hall. Carter's Grove was enlarged and rehabilitated in 1928 and is now the residence of Mrs. Archibald McCrea.

CHATHAM, near Falmouth, Stafford County. Pp. 360-63.

Built about 1770 by William Fitzhugh (1741-c.87), who married Anne Randolph of Chatsworth. Fitzhugh was a member of the House of Burgesses (1772-75) and of the Revolutionary Conventions of 1775 and 1776, also of the Continental Congress. Churchill Jones purchased Chatham from Fitzhugh, and it passed through various hands until its acquisition by the present owners, Mr. and Mrs. John Pratt. The house was used as a hospital during the Fredericksburg campaigns, and Lincoln visited Burnside while the latter was quartered there.

CHISWELL HOUSE, Williamsburg, James City County. Pp. 65-69.

Built by Charles Chiswell, who came from Scotland to Virginia in the late seventeenth century and patented lands on the South Anna River. The house, notable for its curious plan and early finish, was demolished about 1941.

CLEVE, near Dogue, King George County. Pp. 178-82.

Built about 1750 by Charles Carter, son of King Carter, Cleve descended to the latter's son Landon and grandson St. Leger Landon Carter, who sold it to the Lewis family in 1852. The house was destroyed on January 17, 1917. A new house, incorporating fragments of the old, is now the home of Mr. and Mrs. John Armistead Lewis.

ELMWOOD, near Loretto, Essex County. Pp. 298-308.

Built by Muscoe Garnett probably about 1774-76 on land acquired about 1768. He was succeeded by his son James Mercer Garnett (1770-1843), politician, educator, and agriculturalist, and grandson Muscoe Russell Hunter Garnett (1821-64), anti-abolitionist, lawyer and Confederate statesman. The latter's daughter, Mrs. J. Clayton Mitchell, has deeded it to M. R. H. Garnett, the present owner of Elmwood. The plan of the house seems to be modeled on that of Mount Vernon, and the interior details possess many features in common with the latter. The brickwork is in the style of Blandfield, ten miles to the southeast. From the architectural evidence, John Ariss may have been the architect. The extensive alterations in 1852 changed the appearance both of the exterior and interior, but much fine work of the original period remains. Except for two brief intervals, the house has been uninhabited since the 1870's, but will soon again become the residence of the owner.

ELSING GREEN, King William County. Pp. 200-203.

The date 1758 and initials of the builder, Carter Braxton (1736-97), are in a brick in the walls. It is said to have been built by his brother George during Braxton's absence abroad (1757-60). He was born nearby at Newington, the son of George (d. 1757) and Mary (Carter) Braxton, and grandson of King Carter. Carter Braxton was a Burgess (1761), sat in the Revolutionary Conventions of 1774-75 and 1776, and was a signer of the Declaration of Independence. The house passed by purchase to the Browne and Gregory families and is now the home of Mr. and Mrs. Beverley Causey. It is said to have been burned before completion and again about 1800, but was rebuilt within the old walls, and recently has been rehabilitated.

FAIRFIELD, near Berryville, Clarke County. Pp. 334-36.

The date of this house is undetermined, but it may have been built by John Ariss for his own occupancy about 1770 and sold to Warner Washington about 1783. Both were buried here, but their graves are unidentified. When it was purchased by the present owner, Mrs. John B. Richardson, the house was considerably enlarged. The interior contains a good stair and other finish of the original period.

GOVERNOR'S PALACE, Williamsburg, James City County. Pp. 31-61.

Built, 1706-c.20; altered, 1749-51 and 1770-76; burned, 1781. Probably designed by Sir Christopher Wren. Here resided, during the Colonial period, the Deputies of the Royal Governors, Alexander Spotswood, Hugh Drysdale, William Gooch, Robert Dinwiddie, Francis Fauquier; and the Royal Governors, Norborne Berkeley, Baron de Botetourt, and John Murray, the Earl of Dunmore; and two Governors of Virginia during the Revolution, Patrick Henry and Thomas Jefferson. The building was burned while in use as a military hospital on December 23, 1781, but the advance buildings remained until demolished during the Civil War. The Palace was rebuilt in 1932-33 and is now an exhibition building of the Williamsburg Restoration.

GREENSPRING, near Williamsburg, James City County. Pp. 19-21.

Built after 1642 by Sir William Berkeley (1609-1677); demolished about 1806. Berkeley, son of Maurice Berkeley of Bruton, Somerset, and member of the Privy Chamber, was Royal Governor of Virginia from 1642 until 1676, except for the period of the English Civil War. Lady Berkeley who inherited Greenspring took it to her third husband Phillip Ludwell, whose great-great-grandson William Ludwell Lee sold the property in 1816. Near the site of the old dwelling he had built, about 1806, a new mansion, designed by Benjamin H. Latrobe (1764-1820), the distinguished architect. This was destroyed in the Civil War. Many details of interest remain at the site.

GUNSTON HALL, near Accotink, Fairfax County. Pp. 223-30.

Built between 1755-58 by George Mason (1725-92), author of the Virginia Declaration of Rights, distinguished jurist, and a leader of the Revolutionary movement. The elaborate interiors are the work of William Buckland, an English artisan who came to Virginia, under an indenture, for the purpose. The house was restored in 1915 and is now the property of Mr. Louis Hertle, who has deeded it to the Commonwealth of Virginia.

HAREWOOD, near Charles Town, Jefferson County, West Virginia (originally Berkeley County, Virginia). Pp. 325-30.

Home of Samuel Washington, brother of General Washington. The house must have been in the course of construction in 1756, when stone was drawn to the site. The builder's son George Steptoe Washington married Lucy, sister of Dolly Payne Todd, who was married to James Madison here in 1794. During his exile, Louis Philippe of France and his brothers, the Duc de Menpensier and the Compte de Beaujolais, were entertained here. This house was probably designed by John Ariss, who later lived nearby. It has remained in the Washington family and is now owned by John Augustine and S. Walter Washington. Harewood has been little changed since it was built and it contains one of the finest Virginia rooms of the period.

KENMORE, Fredericksburg, Spotsylvania County. Pp. 313-25.

Originally known as Millbrook, this house was erected by Fielding Lewis for his bride Betty Washington after he acquired the land in 1752. It seems to be a design of John Ariss, with interiors in his "Gibbs's modern" style. Lewis was a prominent mover in the Revolution, and at his own expense manufactured large quantities of arms and ammunition for the American army. His estate, impoverished by this expense, was sold, and the house changed hands many times before it was purchased by the Kenmore Association in 1928. It is now open as an exhibition house, and its rooms, famous for their fine decorative plasterwork, are furnished with objects of the period. Its interiors are superb examples of Virginia Georgian at its best.

LOCUST HILL, near Rippon, Jefferson County, West Virginia (originally Berkeley County, Virginia). Pp. 336-37.

The home of John Ariss (c.1725-99), built on land leased from

Washington before 1786. After Ariss' death the stair hall was altered, but there is good paneling of the original period remaining. It is now owned by Mr. Caleb Burns, but is used as a tenant house.

MANNSFIELD, near Fredericksburg, Spotsylvania County. Pp. 265-68.

The date of the building of Mannsfield is unknown, but it was probably designed and built by John Ariss for Mann Page II of Rosewell about 1760-70. Page was the husband of Anne Corbin Tayloe of Mount Airy. Their son Mann Page III inherited the Spotsylvania property and in 1776 married his cousin Mary Tayloe of Mount Airy. By 1796 Page was involved in financial difficulties. He sold the place to William Bernard, whose family resided there until its destruction in the Fredericksburg campaigns of 1862-63. In 1934 the site was excavated by the National Park Service, and from the foundation and other evidence a pictorial restoration has been made.

MARMION, near Comorn, King George County. Pp. 77-81.

Early eighteenth century. Probably built by John Fitzhugh (d.1735), son of the immigrant, William, whose house may be incorporated in the existing structure. Purchased about 1785 by George Lewis, son of Fielding and Betty (Washington) Lewis, his descendant, Mrs. Carter Grymes, now resides in the house.

MENOKIN, near Warsaw, Richmond County. Pp. 309-10.

Built about 1769 for Francis Lightfoot Lee (1734-97) on his marriage in that year to Rebecca, daughter of John Tayloe. Lee was a brother of Richard Henry, William, and Arthur Lee of Stratford, where he was born. He was a Burgess, first from Loudoun and later from Richmond County, a member of the Continental Congress and signer of the Declaration of Independence. He died at Menokin in 1797, and from his wife the property descended to his nephew Ludwell Lee. It passed from the family many years ago and now stands in great dilapidation.

MONTICELLO, near Charlottesville, Albemarle County. Pp. 387-94.

In 1768 Jefferson started preparations for the construction of the house. Building was commenced in 1770 after the burning of his birthplace, Shadwell, in February of that year, and the house in its first form was complete in 1778. On his return from Europe in 1789 Jefferson restudied the design, and between 1796 and 1808 the mansion was reconstructed in its present form. After Jefferson's death Monticello was sold and in recent years has been purchased and restored by the Thomas Jefferson Memorial Association. It is open to the public and is a superlative document of the taste and skill of the first architect of the Republic.

MOUNT AIRY, near Warsaw, Richmond County. Pp. 253-61.

The Mount Airy estate has been in the Tayloe family since the middle of the seventeenth century. On it in 1758 John Tayloe erected the present mansion, probably from plans by John Ariss. Mount Airy was perhaps the finest Palladian mansion built in the British Colonies, and except for the loss of the interiors in the fire of 1844 is the finest American house in the style. From Colonel John Tayloe, son of the builder, the estate descended to his son Benjamin Ogle Tayloe, whose town house was The Octagon, in Washington. It is now the residence of the Misses Tayloe.

MOUNT VERNON, Fairfax County. Pp. 268-98.

The estate of 5,000 acres was patented by John Washington and Nicholas Spencer, both of Westmoreland County, in 1674. A house to validate the patent must have been built within three years, but there is no record of the actual date of its construction. The dwelling owned by Augustine Washington, grandson of John, is generally thought to have burned in 1739, but there is reason to believe it did not and was enlarged and deeded to Lawrence Washington in 1740. This was the house which George Washington inherited on his brother's death in 1752 and which he enlarged in 1757-59 on his marriage to Martha Dandridge Custis. The house was again enlarged in 1773 and was completed in its present form by 1787. There is reason to believe that John Ariss designed both the alterations of 1757 and 1773, but no documentary proof is at hand. Washington left the property to Martha Washington, and on her death to his nephew Bushrod, a Justice of the Supreme Court. From him it descended to John Augustine Washington and later to his wife Jane. It was their son John Augustine Washington, Jr. who sold the property to the Mount Vernon Ladies' Association, formed by Ann Pamela Cunningham of South Carolina, for the purpose of preserving the almost ruinous home of the first President. Mount Vernon stands in carefully tended grounds. The interiors are furnished with a superb collection of Washington's own furniture and pieces of the period to fill in where original pieces are not available. Mount Vernon is the perfection of Virginia Colonial architecture. It has an incomparable setting on the banks of the Potomac and is an amazingly personal document of Washington the planter.

NELSON HOUSE, Yorktown, York County. Pp. 168-75.

Built about 1725-40 either by Thomas Nelson (d.1745) or his son William Nelson, who was Burgess (1742), member (1744-72), and President of the Council (1770-71). William Nelson married Elizabeth Burwell, granddaughter of Robert Carter. Their son Thomas Nelson

(1738-89) was a leader in the Revolutionary movement, member of the Continental Congress, signer of the Declaration of Independence, and Governor of Virginia. The house remained in the family until 1914. It is now the residence of Mr. and Mrs. George Blow.

NOMINI HALL, near Montross, Westmoreland County. Pp. 136-45.

Built by Robert Carter II (c.1703-32), son of King Carter, about 1730. His son Robert (Councillor) Carter (1728-1804) made considerable alterations about 1770. It came to the Arnest family through the marriage of Councillor Carter's granddaughter, Frances Carter Maund, with J. Arnest. The house was destroyed by fire in 1850 and a frame dwelling stands near the site. The superb, though incomplete, avenue of tulip poplars, to which Fithian, the diarist, referred in 1772-73, remains. The plantation, owned by Mr. Thomas Arnest, continues in the possession of the builder's descendants.

PECKATONE, near Hague, Westmoreland County. Pp. 192-95.

Built about 1750 by Gawin Corbin, husband of Hannah Lee of Stratford, on land patented by Henry Corbin in 1664. It was transmitted in the female line to Martha Corbin (Mrs. George Turbeville), Mary Willis (Mrs. William Taliaferro), and Mary Fenton (Mrs. George F. Brown), and passed from the family after 1865. It was burned on October 21, 1886. Part of the foundations and one dependency remain.

POWHATAN, near Five Forks, James City County. P. 222.

Built about 1730-50 for himself by the architect Richard Taliaferro (1705-79), grandson of Richard Taliaferro, the immigrant, who was patentee of lands in Gloucester and York Counties. Taliaferro was Sheriff of James City County in 1740 and a member of the Committee of Peace in 1737. In 1749 the acting Governor, Thomas Lee, apparently called him Virginia's most "skillful architect." At this time he had charge of the extensions to the Governor's Palace. His political activities in Revolutionary affairs was terminated by his death. Powhatan was burned in the Civil War and later rebuilt within the old walls. It is now the home of Mr. and Mrs. E. M. Slausson.

PRESTWOULD, near Clarksville, Mecklenburg County. Pp. 195-96.

Built between 1760-70 by Sir Peyton Skipwith (1740-1805), and descended to his son Humberston, and grandson Fulwar. In 1914 it was sold by Austin Skipwith and in 1918 became the property of the present owner, Colonel W. T. Hughes.

RANDOLPH-PEACHY HOUSE, Nicholson Street, Williamsburg, James
City County. Pp. 69-74.

Probably built before 1725 by Sir John Randolph (c. 1693-1737;
knighted, 1732), son of William and Mary Isham Randolph, of Turkey
Island. He was called to the bar at Grey's Inn in 1717 and on his return
was elected Clerk of the House of Burgesses (1718-34). He was also
Speaker of the House, Attorney General, and Representative of the
Virginia Assembly in London in 1728 and 1732. It was later the home
of his son Peyton Randolph, and in 1781 was the headquarters of the
Compte de Rochambeau. For many years the residence of the Peachy and
Ball families, it is now owned by the Williamsburg Restoration. The
house is distinguished for its early date, fine finish, and interesting plan.

RANDOLPH-SEMPLE HOUSE, Williamsburg. Pp. 379-80.

Though always known as the Peyton Randolph house it was apparently not built by the Signer but perhaps by his cousin, Peyton Randolph
of Wilton. The house belongs to the period of 1765-70, and was probably designed by Randolph's kinsman, Thomas Jefferson, whose early
drawings for Monticello closely parallel it. The first existing records,
those of 1801, show that it was then owned by Judge Semple. The
house, now restored, is the property of the Williamsburg Restoration.

RANDOLPH-TAZEWELL HOUSE, Williamsburg. (Popularly called
Tazewell Hall.) Pp. 81-85.

Probably built and occupied by Sir John Randolph about 1730. It was
also the home of Edmund Randolph (1753-1813), Attorney General,
Governor of Virginia, and Secretary of State of the United States. It was
substantially altered by Senator Tazewell before the Civil War and was
later moved. It is now the property of the Williamsburg Restoration. The
exterior is much changed, but the interior retains the fine paneling of the
early period.

ROCKY MILLS, Hanover County, Virginia. Pp. 196-200.

Built about 1750 in Hanover County by John Syme II, half brother of
Patrick Henry. The house was taken down in 1928 and rebuilt in Richmond. It is the residence of Dr. and Mrs. Robert F. Preston.

ROSEWELL, near Whitemarsh, Gloucester County. Pp. 110-123.

Built in 1726; burned March 24, 1916. Built by Mann Page I (1691-
1730) on land that his father Matthew Page (1639-1703), the son of
immigrant John, inherited from his mother Mary Mann, of Timberneck
Hall, Gloucester County. It was left, incomplete, to Mann Page II

(grandson of Robert Carter of Corotoman) and descended to John Page (1743-1808), churchman, Burgess, Councillor, Revolutionist, member of Congress, and Governor of Virginia. Rosewell remained in the Page family until the death of Governor Page's widow in 1838, when it was sold. It was the largest and finest of American houses of the Colonial period. At the site the ruined walls remain, and nearby is a superb group of Page tombs.

SABINE HALL, near Warsaw, Richmond County. Pp. 130-36.

Built about 1730. The builder, Landon Carter (1710-78), was a son of Robert Carter of Corotoman by his second wife Elizabeth Landon. Sabine Hall has never passed by purchase, but on failure of the male line in 1851 it was inherited by Carter Wellford, son of Elizabeth Carter and Dr. Armistead Nelson Wellford, with whose grandsons it remains.

SCOTCHTOWN, near Negrofoot, Hanover County. Pp. 74.

This was the country home of Charles Chiswell of Williamsburg and probably dates from before 1725. Chiswell's son John married Elizabeth Randolph of Turkey Island. Patrick Henry purchased Scotchtown in 1771, but after the death of his wife sold the place in 1778. The house was sold again in 1781 to John Payne, father of Dolly (Payne) Madison, who spent her youth here. In the nineteenth century the house was somewhat altered and now is untenanted.

SHIRLEY, Charles City County. Pp. 173-78; 346-58.

Built about 1769 by Charles Carter (1732-1806) on land inherited from his mother Elizabeth Hill Carter, Shirley had been patented in 1660 by her grandfather Edward Hill I, and descended to his son Edward Hill II (1637-1700), and his grandson Edward Hill III (d. about 1739). From Edward Hill III Shirley seems to have descended to his sister Elizabeth, wife of John Carter of Corotoman. After the latter's death about 1742, she married Bowler Cocke, and they resided at Shirley until their deaths in 1769 and 1771, respectively. Charles, son of John and Elizabeth Carter, lived at Corotoman until his mother's death, immediately after which he probably began building the new mansion. Hill Carter, son of Charles, inherited Shirley in 1816. It is now the home of his granddaughter, Mrs. Marion Carter Oliver. A seventeenth-century house stood just east of the present mansion, which was altered in the early eighteenth century, probably by Edward Hill III. This stood until about 1870, when it was demolished and the materials used to build Upper Shirley. John Carter, on his accession, perhaps planned an entirely new layout and completed the four buildings of the forecourt before his death three years later. The new mansion, projected for this time, probably was not built until his son Charles Carter came into possession in 1769.

STRATFORD, near Montross, Westmoreland County. Pp. 92-102.

Built about 1725 by Thomas Lee (1690-1750), Burgess, Councillor, and acting Governor in 1749. It passed to his son Phillip Ludwell Lee (1727-75), whose daughter and co-heiress Matilda married her cousin Henry Lee. His son Robert Edward Lee, by his second wife Anne Hill Carter of Shirley, was born at Stratford on January 19, 1807. Here also were born Richard Henry and Francis Lightfoot Lee, signers of the Declaration of Independence. On the death of the son of the latter, Major Henry Lee, in 1822, Stratford passed from the family. It has been restored by the Robert E. Lee Memorial Foundation and is open to the public.

TUCKAHOE, near Richmond, Goochland County. Pp. 85-92.

Probably built about 1712 and enlarged after 1730. The builder, Thomas Randolph (1689-1730), son of William of Turkey Island, left the house to his son William, husband of Maria Judith Page of Rosewell. During the minority of their son Thomas Mann Randolph, Thomas Jefferson and his parents lived at Tuckahoe. It was sold by the Randolphs in 1830 and is now the residence of Mrs. N. Addison Baker.

WESTOVER, Charles City County. Pp. 146-63.

Built by William Byrd II (1674-1744) about 1730 on land his father William Byrd I (1652-1704) inherited from his uncle Thomas Stegge. William Byrd II was Burgess and a member of the Council, and was twice the representative of the Virginia Assembly in London. It remained in the Byrd family until 1814, when on the death of Mary Willing, widow of William Byrd III, it was sold. The east wing, burned during the Civil War, was rebuilt and the house rehabilitated about 1900 for Mrs. Sears Ramsey. It is now the home of Mrs. Richard Crane.

WILTON, formerly Henrico County. Rebuilt in Richmond. Pp. 203-12.

Built in 1753 by William Randolph III (d.1761), son of William Randolph II of Turkey Island and husband of Anne Carter Harrison, daughter of Benjamin Harrison of Berkeley. Wilton remained in the Randolph family until the middle of the nineteenth century, when it was sold. It was purchased in 1933 by the National Society of the Colonial Dames of America in the State of Virginia, was taken down and rebuilt in Richmond, where it is open to the public and now the headquarters of that society.

WYTHE HOUSE, Williamsburg. Pp. 214-20.

Built about 1755 by the architect Richard Taliaferro (1705-79), who placed it at the disposal of his daughter Elizabeth and her husband George Wythe (1726-1806). At his death Taliaferro bequeathed them a life right in it, with remainder to his son Richard. Wythe, born in Elizabeth City County, was one of Virginia's most distinguished legal personages and was the first American professor of law. He was a Burgess, Attorney General of the Colony of Virginia, signer of the Declaration of Independence, member of the Continental Congress, Chancellor of the Commonwealth of Virginia, and Speaker of the House of Delegates. In 1781 Wythe House was Washington's headquarters before the Siege of Yorktown. In 1791, after Wythe's removal to Richmond, the house was advertised for sale in the *Virginia Gazette*. It passed to several purchasers during the nineteenth century and in 1939 was restored as an exhibition building as part of the Williamsburg Restoration.

BIBLIOGRAPHY

[Acton, Mrs. Frances Stackhouse]. *The Castles and Old Mansions of Shropshire.* Shrewsbury, Leake and Evans, 1868.

Adam, William. *Vitruvius Scoticus....* Edinburgh, A. Black and J. & J. Robertson, 1750.

Addy, Sidney Oldall. *The Evolution of the English House.* Revised and enlarged. London, G. Allen & Unwin, Ltd., (1933).

Andrew, Charles McLean. *The Colonial Period of American History.* New Haven, Yale University Press, 1934-38. 4 vols.

Architects' Emergency Committee. *Great Georgian Houses of America.* New York, Kalkhoff Press, 1933-37. 2 vols.

The Architectural Record. "The Restoration of Colonial Williamsburg in Virginia." New York, F. W. Dodge Corp., (c. 1935). (Reprinted from *The Architectural Record*, December, 1935).

Armes, Ethel Marie. *Stratford Hall, the Great House of the Lees.* Richmond, Garrett and Massie, 1936.

Bagby, Alfred. *King and Queen County, Virginia.* Washington & New York, Neale Publishing Company, 1908.

Baldwin, Frank Conger. "Early Architecture of the Rappahannock Valley." (*In Journal of the A. I. A.,* 1915 and 1916).
Kenmore: March, pp. 113-18.
Cleve: June, pp. 234-40.
Gaymont and Belle Grove: August, pp. 329-36.
Marmion: March, 1916, pp. 87-95.
Mount Airy: November, 1916, pp. 448-54.

Ball, Joseph. Letter book, dated January 12, 1743 to December 3, 1759; followed (in same volume) by Letter book of Rawleigh Downman, of Westham, England, later of Virginia, dated March 12, 1760 to April 1, 1780. *In* Joseph Ball Collection, Manuscript Division, Library of Congress, Washington, D. C.

Bankart, George P. *The Art of the Plasterer...* London, B. T. Batsford; New York, Charles Scribner's Sons, 1909.

Beverley, Robert. *The History and Present State of Virginia,* London, Printed for T. R. Parker, 1705.

Bishop, John Leander. *A History of American Manufactures from 1608 to 1860...* 3rd ed. rev. and enl. Philadelphia, E. Young & Co., 1868. 3 vols.

Blome, Richard. *The Gentleman's Recreations, in three parts,* 2nd edition, corrected, with near one half of additions. London, Printed for R. Bonwicke, 1709-1710. 3 vols in 1.

Blomfield, Sir Reginald Theodore. *A History of Renaissance Architecture in England, 1500-1800.* London, G. Bell and Sons, 1897. 2 vols.

Bolton, Arthur Thomas. *The Architecture of Robert & James Adam (1758-1794).* London, Country Life; New York, Charles Scribner's Sons, 1922. 2 vols.

Briggs, Martin Shaw. *The Homes of the Pilgrim Fathers in England and America (1620-1685).* London and New York, Oxford University Press, 1932.

Brock, Henry Irving. *Colonial Churches in Virginia.* Richmond, The Dale Press, (1930).

Bruce, Philip Alexander. *Economic History of Virginia in the Seven-*

teenth Century...New York, P. Smith, 1935. 2 vols.

———. Social Life of Virginia in the Seventeenth Century. Richmond, Printed for the author by Whittet and Shepperson, 1907.

Bullock, Albert Edward, ed. Grinling Gibbons and his Compeers...London, J. Tiranti & Co., 1914.

Burwell, Carter. Account books. In Collection of George Burwell, Millwood, Virginia.

Byrd, William. The Secret Diary of William Byrd of Westover, 1709-1712. Richmond, The Dietz Press, 1941.

———. William Byrd's Histories of the Dividing Line Betwixt Virginia and North Carolina. Raleigh, The North Carolina Historical Commission, 1929.

Campbell, Colin. Vitruvius Britannicus...London, The Author, 1717-71. 5 vols.

Carter, Hill. Shirley Estate Book, 1816-73. Manuscript at Shirley, Charles City County, Virginia.

Carter, Robert. Memo and Account Books, 1774-1795. In Robert Carter Collection, Manuscript Division, Library of Congress, Washington, D. C. 5 vols.

Chamberlayne, Churchill Gibson, ed. The Vestry Book of Christ Church Parish, Middlesex County, Virginia, 1663-1767...Richmond, Old Dominion Press, 1927.

Chambers, Benjamin Duvall. Old Chapel and the Parish in Clarke County, Virginia...Washington, D. C. (Press of W. F. Roberts Co.,) 1932.

Chancellor, Edwin Beresford. The Lives of the British Architects from William of Wykeham to Sir William Chambers. New York, Charles Scribner's Sons, 1909.

Chandler, Joseph Everett, ed. The Colonial Architecture of Maryland,

Pennsylvania, and Virginia. Boston, Bates, Kimball & Guild, 1892.

Chastellux, (Francois Jean) Marquis de. Travels in North America in the years 1780-81-82...New York, 1828.

Clark, Kenneth. Architectural Inspiration from Northern Virginia. New York, R. F. Whitehead, (c. 1931). (On cover: The Monograph Series Recording the Architecture of the American Colonies and the Early Republic. Vol. XVII, no. 3.)

Coffin, Charles Carleton. Old Times in the Colonies. New York, Harper & Bros., 1881.

Coffin, Lewis Augustus, Jr., and Holden, Arthur C. Brick Architecture of the Colonial Period in Maryland & Virginia. New York, Architectural Book Publishing Co., 1919.

Connor, Harry R. Gunston Hall, Fairfax County, Virginia. New York, R. F. Whitehead, (c. 1930). (On cover: The Monograph Series Recording the Architecture of the American Colonies and the Early Republic. Vol. XVI, no. 3.)

Corbin Letter Book. Virginia State Library, Richmond, Virginia.

Corner, James M. and Soderholtz, E. E. Examples of Domestic Colonial Architecture in Maryland and Virginia. Boston, Boston Architectural Club, 1892.

Conway, Moncure Daniel. Barons of the Potomack and the Rappahannock. New York, Grolier Club, 1892.

Country Life. London, 1924-25. Vol. 74, (Dec. 2 and 9, 1933).

Dictionary of American Biography. New York, Charles Scribner's Sons, 1928-1937. 20 vols.

The Dictionary of National Biography ...London, Oxford University Press, 1937-39. 24 vols.

Dimmick, Jesse. "Green Spring." William and Mary Quarterly, 2nd series. IX (April, 1929), 129-30.

Earle, Swepson. *The Chesapeake Bay Country.* 3d ed. rev. Baltimore, Thomsen-Ellis Co., 1929.

Elwell, Newton W. *The Architecture, Furniture and Interiors of Maryland and Virginia During the Eighteenth Century.* Boston, G. H. Polley & Co., (c. 1897).

Eubank, Henry Ragland. *Touring Historyland; the Authentic Guide Book of Historic Northern Neck of Virginia* ... Colonial Beach, Virginia, Issued by the Northern Neck Association (c. 1934).

Evelyn, John. *Diary and Correspondence of John Evelyn* ... New edition, cor., rev., and enl. London, H. Colburn, 1854. 4 vols.

Fenning, Daniel and Collyer, Joseph. *A New System of Geography* ... London, Printed for S. Crowder. ..., 1764-65. 2 vols.

Fiennes, Celia. *Through England on a Side Saddle in the Time of William and Mary* ... London, 1888.

Fiske, John. *Old Virginia and Her Neighbours.* Boston and New York, Houghton Mifflin Company, 1897. 2 vols.

Fithian, Philip Vickers. *Philip Vickers Fithian, Journal and Letters, 1767-74* ... Princeton, N. J., The University Library, 1900.

Fitzpatrick, John Clement, ed. *The Diaries of George Washington, 1748-1799* ... Boston and New York, Houghton Mifflin Co., 1925. 4 vols.

———. *Some Historic Houses.* New York, The Macmillan Co., 1939.

———. *The Writings of George Washington From the Original Manuscript Sources, 1745-1799* ... Washington, U. S. Government Printing Office, 1931.

Fletcher, Banister. *A History of Architecture on the Comparative Method* ... 11th edition, rev. and enl. London, B. T. Batsford, 1943.

Ford, Worthington Chauncey. "Some Jefferson Correspondence." *New England Historical and Genealogical Register,* LV, 272.

Forman, Henry Chandlee. *Early Manor and Plantation Houses of Maryland* ... Easton, Md., Privately printed for the author, 1934.

Forrest, Herbert Edward. *Some Old Shropshire Houses and Their Owners* ... Shrewsbury, the author, (1924).

Frary, Ihna Thayer. *Thomas Jefferson, Architect and Builder.* Richmond, Garrett and Massie, 1939.

Gardner, John Starkie. *English Ironwork of the XVIIth and XVIIIth Centuries* ... London, B. T. Batsford, 1911.

Georgian Society, Dublin. ... *Records of Eighteenth Century Domestic Architecture and Decoration in Dublin* ... (Dublin), Ponsonby & Gibbs, 1909-13. 5 vols.

Gibbs, James. *A Book of Architecture, Containing Designs of Buildings and Ornaments.* London, 1728.

———. *Rules for Drawing.* 3rd edition, London, 1753.

Gillespie, James. *Details of Scottish Domestic Architecture* ... Edinburgh, G. Waterston and Sons Ltd., 1922.

Glenn, Thomas Allen. *Some Colonial Mansions and Those Who Lived in Them* ..., Philadelphia, H. T. Coates & Co., 1898, 2 vols, 2nd series, 1900.

Godey's Magazine. Philadelphia and New York, L. A. Godey, 1830-1898.

Goolrick, John Taquette. *Old Homes and History Around Fredericksburg; the Northern Neck and the Southside, Stafford and Spotsylvania Counties and Battle Sketches* ... Richmond, Garrett & Massie, Inc., (c. 1929).

Gotch, John Alfred. *The Growth of the English House from Early*

Feudal Times to the Close of the Eighteenth Century. 2nd ed. rev. and enl. New York, Charles Scribner's Sons, 1928.

Gurlitt, Cornelius. *Andrea Palladio.* Berlin, Der Zirkel, 1914.

Harper's New Monthly Magazine. 1881. Vols. 41 and 42.

Heatwole, C. J. "Thomas Jefferson as an Architect." *Virginia Journal of Education,* XIX (May, 1926), 360-63.

Hening William Waller. Comp. *The Statutes At Large; Being a Collection of All the Laws of Virginia From the First Session of the Legislature in the Year 1619.* Richmond, 1810-23. 13 vols.

Historic American Buildings Survey. National Parks Service. Comp. *Historic American Buildings.* Catalog of the measured Drawings and Photographs of the survey in the Library of Congress, March 1, 1941. 2nd edition. (Washington, U. S. Government Printing Office, 1941.)

Horner, Frederick. *The History of the Blair, Banister and Braxton Families.* . . . Philadelphia. J. B. Lippincott Co., 1898.

Howe, Henry. *Historical Collections of Virginia* . . . Charleston, S. C., Babcock & Co., 1845.

Howells, John Mead. *Lost Examples of Colonial Architecture* . . . New York, W. Helburn, 1931.

Innocent, Charles Frederick. *The Development of English Building Construction.* Cambridge, Eng., University Press, 1916.

Jefferson, Thomas. *Notes on the State of Virginia* (2nd American edition). Philadelphia, 1794.

Johnson, Robert Underwood, and Buel, Clarence Clough, eds. *Battles and Leaders of the Civil War.* New York, Century Co., (1887-1888). 4 vols. *See* Vol. III, p. 136.

Johnston, Frances Benjamin, and

Waterman, Thomas Tileston. *The Early Architecture of North Carolina* . . . Chapel Hill, The University of North Carolina Press, 1941.

Jones, Hugh. *The Present State of Virginia.* London, Printed for J. Clarke, 1724.

Jourdain, Margaret. *English Interiors in Smaller Houses, From the Restoration to the Regency, 1660-1830.* New York, Charles Scribner's Sons, (1923).

Journals of the House of Burgesses of Virginia. Richmond, 1912.

Keith, William. *The History of the British Plantations in America (1710).* London, Printed at the expense of the Society for the Encouragement of Learning, by S. Richardson, 1738. 4 vols.

Kettell, Russell Hawes, editor. *Early American Rooms* . . . Portland, Me., The Southworth-Anthoensen Press, 1936.

Kibler, James Luther. *The Cradle of the Nation, a Dictionary of Jamestown, Williamsburg and Yorktown, Virginia's Historic Triangle.* Richmond, Garrett & Massie, [1931].

Kimball, Mrs. Marie Goebel. *Jefferson, The Road to Glory, 1743 to 1776.* New York, Coward-McCann, 1943.

Kimball, Fiske. *Domestic Architecture of the American Colonies and of the Early Republic.* New York, Charles Scribner's Sons, 1922.

———. *Thomas Jefferson, Architect; Original Designs in the Collection of Thomas Jefferson Coolidge, Junior, With an Essay and Notes by Fiske Kimball.* Boston, Printed for Private Distribution at the Riverside Press, 1916.

———. *Thomas Jefferson and the First Monument of the Classical Revival in America.* (Harrisburg, Pa., and Washington, D. C., 1915.)

Lambeth, William Alexander, and Manning, Warren H. *Thomas Jef-*

ferson As An Architect and a Designer of Landscapes. Boston, Houghton Mifflin Co., 1913.

Lancaster, Robert Alexander. *Historic Virginia Homes and Churches.* Philadelphia, J. B. Lippincott Co., 1915.

Langley, Batty. *Ancient Masonry...* London, the author, 1736.

————. *The City and Country Builder's and Workman's Treasury of Designs...* London, Printed for S. Harding, 1756.

Latrobe, Benjamin Henry. *The Journal of Latrobe...* New York, D. Appleton and Co., 1905.

Leighton, Stanley. *Shropshire Houses, Past & Present...* London, G. Bell and Sons, 1901.

Leoni, Giacomo. *The Architecture of A. Palladio; in Four Books,* 3rd edition, corrected. London, A. Ward, 1742. 2 vols.

————. *Designs for Buildings.* London, 1726.

Lipscomb, Andrew Adgate, ed., *The Writings of Thomas Jefferson.* Washington, D. C., Issued under the auspices of the Thomas Jefferson Memorial Association, 1903-04. 20 vols.

Lloyd, Nathaniel. *Building Craftsmanship in Brick and Tile and in Stone Slates.* Cambridge (Eng.), The University Press, 1929.

————. *A History of English Brickwork...* London, H. G. Montgomery (1925).

————. *A History of the English House from Primitive Times to the Victorian Period.* London, The Architectural Press, 1931.

Macartney, Mervyn Edmund. *English Houses & Gardens in the 17th and 18th Centuries...* New York, Charles Scribner's Sons, 1908.

Massie, Susanne Williams, and Christian, Frances Archer, eds. *Homes and Gardens in Old Virginia.* Rich-

mond, Garrett & Massie, Inc., 1931.

Meade, William. *Old Churches, Ministers and Families of Virginia.* Philadelphia, J. B. Lippincott Co., 1861. 2 vols.

Mearns, David Chambers, and Clapp, Verner W., comps. *Thomas Jefferson, the Architect.* Typewritten. Washington, Library of Congress, 1936.

Millar, Donald. *Measured Drawings of Some Colonial and Georgian Houses.* New York, Architectural Book Publishing Co., 1916-30. 3 vols.

Miller, Francis Trevelyan, ed. *The Photographic History of the Civil War...* New York, Review of Reviews Co., 1912. 10 vols.

Milman, Lena. *Sir Christopher Wren.* New York, Charles Scribner's Sons, 1908.

Moorehead, Singleton Peabody. "Christ's Cross." *Virginia Magazine of History and Biography.* XLIII (January, 1935), 1-7.

Morris, Robert. *Select Architecture: Being Regular Designs...* London, sold by R. Wayer, 1757.

————. *An Essay in the Defense of Ancient Architecture.* London, 1728.

Morton, Louis. *Robert Carter of Nomini Hall...* Williamsburg, Va., Colonial Williamsburg, Inc., 1941.

Moxon, Joseph. *Mechanick Exercises: or, the Doctrine of Handy-Works.* 3rd ed. London, Printed for D. Midwinter and T. Leigh, 1703.

Mutual Assurance Society of Virginia. Records (microfilm). Virginia State Library, Richmond, Virginia.

(Naulty, Edwin Fairfax). *Historic Harewood.* (Special edition. Philadelphia, The Washington Manor Association for the Purchase and Preservation of Historic Harewood, c. 1901.)

Neve, Richard. *The City and Country Purchasers and Builders Dictionary*

... 3rd ed., corrected and improved throughout. London, B. Sprint, 1736.

Nicholson, Peter. *Encyclopedia of Architecture.* New York, Johnson Fry & Co., c.1850. 2 vols.

Pepys, Samuel. *The Diary of Samuel Pepys* ... London, G. Bell and Sons, 1928. 10 vols.

Powys, Albert Reginald. *Repair of Ancient Buildings.* London and Toronto, J. M. Dent and Sons; New York, E. P. Dutton, (1929).

Price, Francis. *The British Carpenter* ... 3rd ed enl. London, Printed by C. and J. Ackers for C. Hitch and L. Hawes, 1753.

————. *Builder's Dictionary.* London, Bettsworth and Hitch, 1734. 2 vols.

Primatt, Stephen. *The City and Country Purchaser and Builder* ... London, [1667?].

Prime, Alfred Coxe, comp. *The Arts & Crafts in Philadelphia, Maryland and South Carolina* ... (Topsfield, Mass.), The Walpole Society, 1929-32. 2 vols.

Ramsey, Stanley C. *Small Houses of the Late Georgian Period 1750-1800.* London, Technical Journals Limited, 1919.

Richardson, Albert Edward, and Gill, C. Lovett. *London Houses from 1660 to 1820* ... London, B. T. Batsford, (1911).

Richardson, Albert Edward, and Eberlein, H. Donaldson. *The Smaller English House of the Later Renaissance, 1660-1830* ... New York, W. Helburn, (1925).

Riley, Edward M. *The History of the Founding and Development of Yorktown, Virginia, 1691-1781.* Mss. with U. S. National Park Service.

Sale, Mrs. Edith Dabney (Tunis). *Interiors of Virginia Houses of Colonial Times.* Richmond, Byrd Press, 1927.

Salmon, William. *Palladio Londinen-*

sis: or the London Art of Building. 3rd edition, London, S. Birt, 1748.

Saunders, Anne Page. *Leonora and the Ghost.* Baltimore, Charles Harvey & Co., printers ... 1876.

Scott-Moncrieff, George, ed. *The Stones of Scotland.* New York, Charles Scribner's Sons, 1938.

Shute, John. *The First & Chief Groundes of Architecture* ... *First Printed in 1563* ... London, Country Life, Ltd., 1912.

Slaughter, Philip. *The History of Truro Parish in Virginia.* Philadelphia, G. W. Jacobs & Co., (1908).

Small, Tunstall, and Woodbridge, Christopher. *Houses of the Wren and Early Georgian Periods.* London, Architectural Press, (1928).

Stannard, Mrs. Mary Mann Page (Newton). *Colonial Virginia, Its People and Customs.* Philadelphia and London, J. B. Lippincott Co., 1917.

Stoney, Samuel Gaillard. *Plantations of the Carolina Low Country.* Charleston, S. C., The Carolina Art Association, (1938).

Swan, Abraham. *Designs in Carpentry* ... London, The author, 1759.

————. *British Architect* ... 1st ed. London, Meighan, 1745.

Swarbrick, John. *Robert Adam & His Brothers.* London, Batsford, 1915.

Swem, Earl Gregg, comp. *Virginia Historical Index.* Roanoke, Va., Stone Printing and Manufacturing Co., 1934-36. 2 vols.

Tanner, Lawrence Edward. *Westminster School, a History.* London, Country Life, Ltd., (1934).

————, *Westminster School; Its Buildings and Their Associations.* London, Phillip Allan, 1923.

Tipping, Henry Avray. *English Homes, Period IV.* New York, Charles Scribner's Sons, 1920-28. 2 vols. Part I, *Late Stuart, 1649-1714.* Part

II, *The Work of Sir John Vanburgh and his School,* 1699-1736.

———. *Ibid.,* 1921. Vol. I, Early Georgian, 1714-1760.

The Tuileries Brochures, a Series of Monographs on European Architecture. (New York), Ludowici-Celadon Co., 1929-31. 16 nos. in 2 vols. and 4 nos.

Tyler, Lyon Gardiner. *Williamsburg, the Old Colonial Capital* ... Richmond, Whittet and Shepperson (1907).

Vardy, John. *Some Designs of Mr. Inigo Jones and Mr. William Kent.* (London), J. Vardy, 1744.

Virginia (Colony), Council. *Legislative Journals of the Council of Colonial Virginia* ... Richmond, (The Colonial press, Everett Waddey Co.), 1918-19. 3 vols.

Virginia (Colony), General Assembly. House of Burgesses. *The Journal of the House of Burgesses, 1658-1776.* Richmond, Colonial Press, 1905-15. 13 vols.

Virginia Gazette. 200th Anniversary Edition, 1736-1936. Williamsburg, Va., 1936.

Virginia Magazine of History and Biography, Richmond, Va.

Wallace, Philip B. *Colonial Houses, Philadelphia, Pre-Revolutionary Period.* New York, Architectural Book Co., (c. 1931).

Wallis, Frank Edwin. *An Architectural Monograph on Houses of the Southern Colonies.* (St. Paul, White Pine Bureau) 1916. (On cover: *The White Pine Series of Architectural Monographs,* Vol. II, no. 1).

———. *Old Colonial Architecture and Furniture.* Boston, Polley, 1887.

Ware, Isaac. *A Complete Body of Architecture* ... London, T. Osborne and J. Shipton, 1756.

Ware, William Rotch. *Georgian Period.* Boston, New York, U. P. C. Book Company, 1923.

Waterman, Thomas Tileston. "The Bay System in Colonial Virginia Building." *William and Mary Quarterly,* 2nd series, XV (April, 1935), 117-22.

Waterman, Thomas Tileston, and Barrows, John A. *Domestic Colonial Architecture of Tidewater Virginia.* New York, Charles Scribner's Sons, 1932.

Waterman, Thomas Tileston. *English Antecedents of Virginia Architecture* ... (Lancaster, Pa., Lancaster Press, Inc., 1939). Reprinted from *Proceedings of the American Philosophical Society,* Vol. 80, no. 1, 1939.

Waterman, Thomas Tileston, and Johnston, Frances Benjamin. *The Early Architecture of North Carolina* ... Chapel Hill, The University of North Carolina Press, 1941.

Waterman, Thomas Tileston. "Thomas Jefferson, his Early Works in Architecture." *Gazette des Beaux Arts.* No. 918, XXIV (June, 1943), 89-106.

(Watson, Winslow Marston), comp. *In Memoriam: Benjamin Ogle Tayloe.* (Philadelphia, Sherman & Co., Printers) 1872.

Wayland, John Walter. *Historic Homes of Northern Virginia and the Eastern Panhandle of West Virginia.* Staunton, Va., The McClure Co., 1937.

Weaver, Lawrence. *Memorials & Monuments Old and New* ... New York, Charles Scribner's Sons, 1915.

Wertenbaker, Thomas Jefferson. *The Old South; the Founding of American Civilization.* New York, Charles Scribner's Sons, 1942.

William and Mary College Quarterly and Historical Magazine. 1st and 2nd series. Williamsburg, Va., William and Mary College, 1892-1943.

Wilstach, Paul, *Mount Vernon, Wash-*

ington's Home and the Nation's Shrine. Indianapolis, The Bobbs-Merrill Co., (c. 1930).

———. Tidewater Virginia. Indianapolis, The Bobbs-Merrill Co., (c. 1929).

Wormeley, Katherine Prescott. Recollections of Rear Admiral Ralph Randolph Wormeley, R. N. New York, The National Press, 1879.

Worthington, Addison Foard. Twelve Old Houses West of Chesapeake Bay...Boston, Rogers and Manson Co., 1918.

Wotton, Sir Henry. The Elements of Architecture...London, 1624.

Writer's Program. Virginia. Virginia, a Guide to the Old Dominion... New York, Oxford University Press, (1940).

KEY TO THE MANSIONS INDICATED ON THE MAP, p. 433

1. AMPTHILL (Richmond)
2. BATTERSEA (Petersburg)
3. BELLE ISLE
   (Lancaster County, near Farnham)
4. BERKELEY (Charles City County)
5. BLANDFIELD
   (Essex County, near Caret)
6. BRANDON (Prince George County)
7. CAMDEN
   (Caroline County, near Port Royal)
8. CARLYLE HOUSE (Alexandria)
9. CARTER'S GROVE (James City County, near Williamsburg)
10. CHATHAM
    (Stafford County, near Falmouth)
11. CHISWELL HOUSE (Williamsburg)
12. CLEVE
    (King George County, near Dogue)
13. ELMWOOD
    (Essex County, near Loretto)
14. ELSING GREEN (King William County, near Lester Manor)
15. FAIRFIELD
    (Clarke County, near Berryville)
16. GOVERNOR'S PALACE (Williamsburg)
17. GREENSPRING (James City County, near Williamsburg)
18. GUNSTON HALL
    (Fairfax County, near Accotink)
19. HAREWOOD (Jefferson County, near Charles Town, West Virginia)
20. KENMORE (Fredericksburg)
21. LOCUST HILL (Jefferson County, near Rippon, West Virginia)
22. MANNSFIELD (Spottsylvania County, near Fredericksburg)
23. MARMION
    (King George County, near Comorn)
24. MENOKIN
    (Richmond County, near Warsaw)
25. MONTICELLO (Albemarle County, near Charlottesville)
26. MOUNT AIRY
    (Richmond County, near Warsaw)
27. MOUNT VERNON
    (Fairfax County, near Alexandria)
28. NELSON HOUSE (Yorktown)
29. NOMINI HALL (Westmoreland County, near Montross)
30. PECKATONE
    (Westmoreland County, near Hague)
31. POWHATAN (James City County, near Five Forks)
32. PRESTWOULD (Mecklenburg County, near Clarksville)
33. RANDOLPH-PEACHY HOUSE
    (Williamsburg)
34. RANDOLPH-SEMPLE HOUSE
    (Williamsburg)
35. RANDOLPH-TAZEWELL HOUSE
    (Williamsburg)
36. ROCKY MILLS (Richmond)
37. ROSEWELL (Gloucester County, near Whitemarsh)
38. SABINE HALL
    (Richmond County, near Warsaw)
39. SCOTCHTOWN
    (Hanover County, near Negrofoot)
40. SHIRLEY (Charles City County)
41. STRATFORD (Westmoreland County, near Montross)
42. TUCKAHOE
    (Goochland County, near Richmond)
43. WESTOVER (Charles City County)
44. WILTON (Richmond)
45. WYTHE HOUSE (Williamsburg)

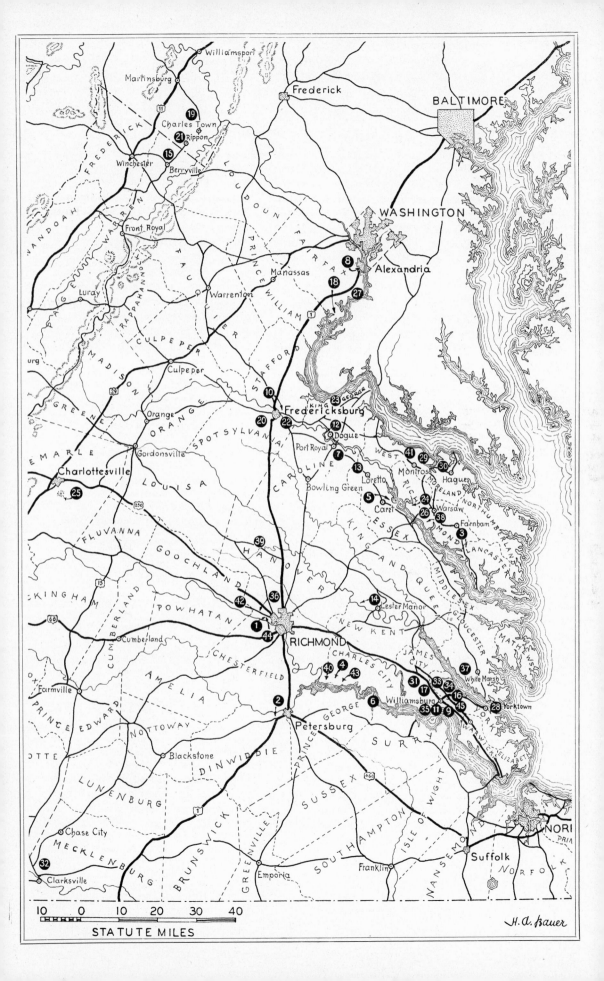

GLOSSARY OF ARCHITECTURAL TERMS

Anthemion: An ornament consisting of floral or foliated forms in a cluster.

Apron: An area of projecting brickwork or stonework below a window.

Apsidal: Apse-like, in the shape of a half round or polygonal projecting bay.

Architrave: The finish surrounding a door or window, or the lowest member of an entablature.

Archivolt: A moulded frame running over the faces of the voussoirs in an arch, or the inner contour of an arch.

Artifacts: A product of human workmanship found in archaeological projects.

Ashlar: A facing of squared stones.

Backband: The outside member of an architrave used for door, window, or other trim.

Barge board: See verge board.

Bay: A subdivision of a building; units of a façade or plan.

Bed-mould: The lower mouldings of a cornice.

Belt course: A projecting course or courses on the exterior of a building, usually at the floor or window-sill line.

Bolection: In joinery, a moulding following the outside edge of a panel and projecting beyond the face of the frame in which the panel is set.

Cartouche: A scroll-shaped ornament used as a feature in a design.

Chair rail: A moulding on a wall around a room at the height of a chair back.

Chamfer: To cut away the edge of a projecting corner.

Clairvoyée: A screen of ironwork in a high wall.

Clipped gable: A gable of which the apex is cut back in hipped-roof form.

Colonette: A small or slender column.

Console: A bracket of scroll form.

Corbel: A projection from the face of a wall designed to support structural or decorative elements.

Corbel table: A projecting course supported on a range of brackets.

Cornice: The uppermost part of an entablature usually used to crown the wall of a building.

Course: In masonry construction, continuous horizontal ranges of brick or stone.

Cove: A concave moulding approaching a quadrant in section.

Crossette: A lateral projection of the head of the moulded frame of a door or window.

Crown mould: See Cymatium.

Curvilinear gable: A gable of fantastic form laid out in geometric curves.

Cushion frieze: A convex band below the cornice in the entablature.

Cyma: A moulding, in section concave at one termination, and convex at the other.

Cyma-recta: An ogee moulding concave at the top and convex at the bottom.

Cyma-reversa: An ogee moulding concave at the bottom and convex at the top.

Cymatium: The upper moulding of a cornice.

Dado: A plain or paneled field, defined at top and bottom by mouldings, that traverses the lower part of a wall surface.

Deck-on-hip: A flat roof surmounting a hip. See Hip.

Dentils: Oblong blocks spaced in a band to decorate a cornice.

Dependencies: The minor or flanking buildings of a composition.

Dog-bars: Vertical spikes in the lower part of a gate.

Dowel: A peg used to fix a tenon into a mortise.

Dressing: A finish used as a facing at wall openings and corners.

Eared architrave (or Crossette): A lateral projection of the architrave mouldings of Classic doors and windows at the extremities of the lintel or head.

Echinus: The rounded moulding between the abacus and necking of the capital in the Doric order.

English bond: A method of laying brick wherein one course is laid with stretchers and the next with headers, thus bonding the double thickness of brick together.

Entablature: An assembly of three parts of a Classic order, cornice, frieze, and architrave, forming the member carried on the column.

Entiasis: The curved diminution of the shaft of a column or pilaster.

Façade: The front of a building.

Fascia: A flat broad member used in a cornice or other moulded part.

Fenestration: The arrangement and proportioning of windows.

Filet: A narrow flat band that separates and defines mouldings.

Finial: A terminating ornament used on the apex of gables, pediments, roofs, etc.

Flat arch: A series of wedge-shaped stones or bricks over an opening which, though simulating the appearance of a lintel, performs the arch function.

Flemish bond: A method of laying brick wherein headers and stretchers alternate in each course, and vertically headers are placed over stretchers to form a bond and give a cross pattern.

Fluting: The surface of a pilaster or column which is enriched with vertical channelling.

Forecourt: The area before a building, in a formal composition, which is enclosed by flanking buildings or walls.

Fret: Ornamental work in relief.

Frieze: The portion of the entablature between the architrave and cornice.

Gable: Often called an "A" roof; a roof section triangular in form.

Gambrel: A roof having its slope broken by an obtuse angle.

Gauging: Brick selected for color and rubbed to a smooth surface on all faces. Used for decorative purposes.

Glazed brick: Header brick bearing a gray or green transparent glaze on its surface.

Grille (window): A grating or screen, usually of wood in this district, though occasionally of iron.

Grisaille: Decorative painting in gray monochrome.

Guilloche: A type of ornament in which two or more wavy bands are interwoven, producing a series of circles, often filled with rosettes.

Haunch: Either of the parts of an arch at the sides of the crown.

Head (window): Top of window; similarly of arch and of door.

Header: End of brick; a brick laid across the thickness of a wall.

Hip: The external angle in which adjacent roofs meet each other; a roof that slopes back equally from each side of a building.

Husk: Flower-like pendant ornaments arranged in a series.

Impost: A horizontal member from the top of which springs an arch.

Jamb: The reveal or lining of a doorway or other aperture.

Jerkin-head: A roof which is hipped only for a part of its height, leaving a truncated gable (see clipped gable).

Key-stone: The wedge-shaped stone at the crown of an arch, binding the whole.

Leading: The method employed previous to the use of wood muntins in sash to secure the glass in casements by the means of narrow lead strips.

Lights: Window panes.

Lintel: The horizontal top piece of a window or door opening.

Lock rail: Rail of a door in or to which the lock is fixed.

Loggia: A covered gallery or portico.

Lozenge lights: Diamond-shaped quarries used in leaded glazing.

Lugs: That part of a window sill or door sill which is carried beyond the opening into the masonry wall.

Lunette: A half-round area in an arch or in the penetration of a vault.

Mansard roof: One having two slopes on all sides, the lower one being steeper than the upper.

Metope: The space between two triglyphs of a Doric frieze.

Mitre: To bevel ends for the purpose of matching together at an angle.

Modillion: An ornamental block, applied to the underside of the projecting members of a cornice.

Mortise: A recess cut into a piece of timber to receive a tenon.

Mullion: A narrow wood or stone division between window openings.

Muntin: The horizontal or vertical members in sash, used to divide the glass. The horizontals are sometimes called bars.

Mutule: A flat block projecting under the corona of a Doric cornice.

Necking: The horizontal moulding which separates the capital of a column or pilaster from the shaft.

Neo-Classic: The revived use of Classic forms in the eighteenth and nineteenth centuries; the name of a style of architecture pertaining to the Classic Revival.

Newel: The principal post at the foot of a staircase.

Nosing: That part of the tread of a stair which projects over the riser.

Ogee: A moulding, in section concave in one termination and convex at the other. See Cyma.

Open string: In stairs, the end carriage which has its uper edge cut out to fit underneath the steps.

Overthrow: Ornamental ironwork spanning a gateway.

Ovolo: A convex moulding, approaching a quadrant in section.

Palladian motive: The arrangement of an arch flanked by lower square-headed openings and separated from them by columns or piers, which was much used by the architect Palladio.

Parapet: A low wall along a roof or terrace, used as a protection or decoration.

Parterre: A flower garden having the beds disposed in some formal form or pattern.

Paterae: Circular ornaments in low relief; also a carved boss.

Pavilion: A projecting motive on a façade to give architectural emphasis.

Pediment: A crowning motive of porticos, pavilions, doorways or other architectural features, usually of low triangular form, sometimes broken in the center to receive an ornament and sometimes of segmental, elliptical, or serpentine form.

Pier: A square supporting member; also the wall space between windows or other apertures.

Pilaster: A flat form of a column applied to a wall.

Plate: The timber in a roof which rests on the walls of a building and receives the roof rafters.

Plinth: A square unmoulded block placed on the floor to receive the mouldings of an architrave.

Portico: A covered colonnade at the entrance of a building.

Portland stone: A limestone from the Isle of Portland in England.

Pulvinated frieze: A cushion-shaped or semicircular frieze.

Purbeck stone: A highly fossilized buff limestone from the Isle of Purbeck in England.

Purbeck marble: A dark blue-green stone with grey fossils.

Quarry: A light of glass in leaded glazing.

Quatrefoil: An ornamental foliation having four lobes.

Quoin: A squared stone at the corner of a building or of architectural features.

Racking: The face of masonry which is alternately indented in the coursing to receive a future masonry wall.

Rail: Horizontal members of panel frames; guard on the outer edge of a stair or gallery.

Rake: The slope or pitch of a roof.

Reeding: A small convex moulding, the reverse of fluting.

Reredos: An ornamental screen or partition wall behind the altar in a church.

Return: The continuation in a different direction of a surface or moulding.

Reveal: The depth of an opening in a wall or other structure.

Rinceau: An ornamental motive consisting essentially of a branching scroll with leaves and other forms.

Riser: Upright piece of a step from tread to tread.

Rubbed brick: Brick, usually selected for an even light color, and rubbed to a smooth surface on two vertical faces.

Rustication: Horizontal and vertical channels cut in the joints of stonework.

Scored: Surface of masonry which is scratched to make a bond for plaster.

Scotia: Concave moulding.

Soffit: The lower horizontal face of any projecting feature.

Spandrel: A triangular space, especially between the shoulder of an arch and a vertical member; also the space between the shoulders of two adjoining arches.

Strapwork: Ornament of interlacing bands.

Stretcher: The long face of a brick when laid horizontally.

String course: See Belt course.

Stringer: The oblique structural member of a stair; also the finish piece.

Stucco-duro: A hard and durable plaster used in modelling relief ornament.

Surround: The stone or brick facing around a fireplace opening.

Swirl: A curve or twist at the termination of a rail or balustrade.

Topiary: The clipping of shrubs in ornamental form.

Torus: A convex moulding, nearly semicircular in cross-section.

Triglyph: A vertical ornament of three sections in a Doric frieze resembling beam ends.

Tympanum: The triangular recessed space enclosed by the cornice which bounds a pediment.

Verge board: The board following the rake or slope of a gable underneath the overhanging shingle or slate.

Volute: A scroll form as in an Ionic capital or scrolled terminal of a stair rail.

Voussoir: One of the wedge-like stones which form an arch; the middle one is called a key-stone.

Wall of Troy dentil: A dentil band in the form of a fret resembling battlements.

Wash: Sloping portion of a chimney cap employed to carry the outer projection of the cap back to the line of the shaft. A sloping surface to shed rain from projections.

Water leaf: A type of leaf ornament covering a moulding.

Water table: A projection of the lower masonry or brickwork on the out-side of a wall, usually at the first-floor line.

Weathering: The sloping portion of a chimney stack which carries the larger dimension of the base to the smaller dimension above. This surface is usually covered with brick laid horizontally flatwise, though in instances it is covered with clay, tile, or stone.

Winder: A wedge-shaped step.

INDEX